School's In

HISTORY OF
SCHOOLS &
SCHOOLING

Alan R. Sadovnik and Susan F. Semel
General Editors

Vol. 25

PETER LANG
New York • Washington, D.C./Baltimore • Bern
Frankfurt am Main • Berlin • Brussels • Vienna • Oxford

Kenneth M. Gold

School's In

The History of Summer Education in American Public Schools

PETER LANG
New York • Washington, D.C./Baltimore • Bern
Frankfurt am Main • Berlin • Brussels • Vienna • Oxford

Library of Congress Cataloging-in-Publication Data

Gold, Kenneth M. (Kenneth Mark).
School's in: the history of summer education
in American public schools / Kenneth M. Gold.
p. cm. — (History of schools and schooling; 25)
Includes bibliographical references and index.
1. Summer schools—United States—History.
I. Title. II. History of schools and schooling; v. 25.
LC5751 .G65   371.2'32'0973—dc21   2001038607
ISBN 0-8204-5657-8
ISSN 1089-0678

Die Deutsche Bibliothek-CIP-Einheitsaufnahme

Gold, Kenneth M.:
School's in: the history of summer education
in American public schools / Kenneth M. Gold.
–New York; Washington, D.C./Baltimore; Bern;
Frankfurt am Main; Berlin; Brussels; Vienna; Oxford: Lang.
(History of schools and schooling; Vol. 25)
ISBN 0-8204-5657-8

Cover design by Dutton & Sherman Design

The paper in this book meets the guidelines for permanence and durability
of the Committee on Production Guidelines for Book Longevity
of the Council of Library Resources.

Printed in the United States of America

In memory of Robert Gold

TABLE OF CONTENTS

TABLES AND FIGURES

Tables

ACKNOWLEDGMENTS

One of my earliest and most ingrained musical memories is of Alice Cooper's rock anthem "School's Out" being played repeatedly on the radio on the last day of school in June. I had an inkling that for some, school was "in" through the summer, but I would never have thought that there might be a history to summer education worthy of investigation had Maris Vinovskis not suggested that it was a ripe topic for study. This book began as a dissertation under his mentorship at the University of Michigan, and Maris has continued to offer expert guidance and frank advice on it since I left Ann Arbor.

While a graduate student at Michigan, Phillip Kearney, Robin Kelley, Michael McDonald, and Terry McDonald all played formative roles in my development as a scholar and in this project. I remember fondly my arguments with the late David Angus; his persistence on issues of demography has made this a stronger book. Marty Pernick's expertise in medical history proved invaluable in directing my research. I was also quite privileged to have Dan Albert, Mollie Cavender, Mary Coomes, Peter Laipson, Rich Sosis, and Caroline Winterer as friends and colleagues in Ann Arbor.

Transforming a dissertation into a book is no small task. My job was made far easier by the institutional support of the City University of New York and the contributions of the Education Department faculty at the College of Staten Island. Much of the work on this project occurred, rather fittingly, during summers, when I was fortunate enough to receive three Professional Staff Congress-CUNY grants, one to conduct additional research and the other two to complete my writing and editing. The office of the Dean of Humanities and Social Sciences at CSI also supported these activities with a summer research grant.

During the academic year, Phil Alsworth, Jed Luchow, Teddy Polito, and Susan Sullivan shielded me from overloading on departmental responsibilities so that I might complete this project. Deborah DeSimone, David Kritt, Greg Seals, David Seeley, Sally Smith and Nelly Tournaki gave close and critical readings of my writing and ideas at our departmental research seminars. Jim Sanders first brought me to the College of Staten Island and has given me sage counsel ever since. Away from CSI, Nancy Beadie, Christine Woyshner, and Lois Weiner read portions of the manuscript and made excellent suggestions for its improvement. Bill Reese was quite helpful in suggesting general principles that distinguish writing a book from a dissertation. Where I have fallen short in addressing the concerns of these fine colleagues, the fault lies with me alone.

The staff at a few key libraries provided assistance in my research for which I am most grateful. Betty Weneck at Teachers College was particularly helpful with the archives of the New York City public schools, as were librarians at the University of Michigan, the New York Public Library, the U.S. Department of Education, and the archives of the Detroit public schools.

Everyone at Peter Lang who was responsible for the manuscript provided expert and expedient work under the direction of Chris Myers and Jackie Pavlovic. As editors of the series in which this book appears, Alan Sadovnik and Susan Semel offered useful commentary on my work but allowed my voice to remain the dominant one.

Finally I applaud the unwavering support of my family. My brother Evan and sister-in-law Sharon, my sister Laura, and my mother Marion have aided me in countless ways. Between them, their generosity with homes, cars, money and time was unstinting and invaluable, and always came at the most opportune time. Their optimism and love for me were constants.

My wife Marcy Felsenfeld has been steadfast in her encouragement of this book. She served as a sounding board as I revised the manuscript and spent hours formatting it just days before our wedding. Most important, she has been the best of all possible diversions from this work.

In my office hangs a photograph from the 1950s. In it, my father the electrical engineer is looking up as he works at his lab. His presence, in so many different ways, has seen me through this project even though he passed away before it started. It is to the memory of Robert Gold that I dedicate this book.

INTRODUCTION

It may at first glance appear quite counterintuitive to consider that summer education has a history. After all, this is a nation where summer vacation has carved out a powerful cultural and professional niche through the closing of schools, the slowdown in economic activity, and the hastening of leisure pursuits. Summer vacation rests comfortably on a mythology that naturalizes it as the vestige of an earlier era. Schools, the thinking goes, have always offered a summer vacation because they mirror the cycles of traditional agrarian life. Today only about 10% of American students actually attend public school during the summer, and expenditures constitute less than 2% of total school costs.[1] Even as these figures rise in cities like New York, which has recently required summer school attendance for students who fail new annual standardized tests, the non-compliance by thousands of families speaks in part to the entrenchment of summer vacation.[2] Thus the central question asked in this study is why universal public education during the summer does not exist in the United States. Looking to the past to answer this question reveals a rich and varied history for summer education that dates back more than 200 years.

In the past, formal education did not merely occur during the summer; it mattered. Summer's role was crucial to public schooling in the nineteenth century, when most young students attended and most female teachers taught during the summer. Urban and rural schools alike included summer terms, and most district schools were closed during the spring and autumn. Only after 1840 in a process that took decades did school calendars largely begin to exclude August and then July from the school year. In the twentieth century, summer programs exerted a significant influence on the regular public schools that far outweighed their levels of enrollment and expenditure. Summer classes served as testing grounds for innovative pedagogics and curricula that eventually worked their way into the regular school year. Summer school became a means for students to gain academic credits in order to catch up, keep up, or get ahead of their age-group. Summer enrichment classes allowed students to pursue interests ancillary to the mainstream coursework. Professional growth opportunities for teachers and compensatory educational efforts for at-risk students often transpired in summer programs.

The reasons for summer's influential but limited place in American public education are not easily reduced to a single sentence. To unfold the complex developments in summer education, this study relied on a research agenda basic to the social historian. The book uncovers the roles that summer has played in American education, considers to what extent those roles have been constant or in flux during the nineteenth and twentieth centuries, and analyzes the factors and conditions that account for those roles and changes in them. To achieve cohesiveness, summer education is defined narrowly to include only those activities run by or affiliated with public schools at the K-12 level. Thus university summer classes, the camping movement, and other worthy topics are not explored here. Instead, case studies from urban and rural communities in several states are informed by the examination of the writings of education professionals, medical practitioners, and social reformers. In so doing, the book suggests the existence of larger national patterns, specifically the demise in the nineteenth-century and resilience in the twentieth-century of formal public schooling during the summer.

Simply put, summer education is not widespread because of past ethnic and class fissions, conflicting beliefs about human physical and mental frailty, and processes of state growth and bureaucratic expansion. Political, ideological, and social forces pulled at summer from multiple directions, and historical actors brought a variety of agendas to bear on it. That the summer's place in schooling and society was a pluralist construction should not necessarily cause surprise—the same could be said of public schooling in general. Summer and regular schools alike took their shape from demographic trends, social-class anxieties, economic conditions, and national events. Summer school, like its September to June counterpart, also served as a battleground for progressivism in education at the turn of the nineteenth century and academic standards today. What stands out about summer education is that even more than its content and structure, its very public existence has been periodically contested.

The overarching theme of this book is the tension between presence and absence that pervades the history of summer education. In any given era, what distinguishes summer schooling is its appearance or non-appearance as a format for school. Since 1800, four historical moments of public summer education are discernible: first, the early and mid-nineteenth century, when summer terms were a vital part of both urban and rural school years albeit through vastly different calendars; second, the middle and latter part of the nineteenth century, when summer was removed from the school year as school schedules were regularized; third, the turn of the century and the first two decades of the new century, when summer returned to the school year in the form of vacation schools and quickly transformed into summer schools; and finally, the mid-twentieth century, when summer school was reestablished after interruptions during the Depression and World War II, and the federal government began sponsoring new forms of summer programs to serve national interests. The scope of this work encompasses all four periods, but its focus is on the middle two—when the most formative shifts took place. For most of the twentieth century, including recent efforts to draft summer school into the war against social promotion, summer learning has conformed to the parameters established through earlier developments.

Throughout this semi-chronological narrative, a number of subthemes arise. One is the impact of summer schooling on the health of children. Many citizens—citing fears of mental and physical fragility—argued that students (and their teachers) needed a substantial break from learning. Alternatively, a focus on the cognitive development of children led to concerns about knowledge forgotten during the long vacation. Another persistent theme is how the summer would fit the needs of school systems, which ranged from the standardization of localities to the improvement of school plants to the reduction of over-age students. Financial considerations always emerged as well, with conflicting depictions of summer schooling as a cost-effective term or a costly frill. Finally, patterns of summer education reflected ethnic and class perceptions of the social and built environment. Urban perils and rural remedies loom large in the making of summer education in the United States.

These themes and perspectives inform each of the six chapters and epilogue that constitute this work. Chapters One, Two, and Three trace the standardization of the school calendar in the nineteenth century. The first chapter asks how reformers removed summer education from the rural school year. It presents case studies from Michigan, New York, and Virginia first to establish the substantial extent of summer education in 1840 and then to measure its subsequent reduction (even as the aggregate length of the school year increased nationwide). It shows how educators altered agrarian school schedules by using existing state apparatus or inventing new ones to impel local areas to amend their traditional practices. Following a state-centered paradigm, it argues that this process enhanced the state's capacity to act while still yielding to economic and demographic factors beyond its control.

Chapter Two asks the same questions, but of urban areas. Using New York City as a case study, it outlines both the extent of summer sessions during the first third of the nineteenth century and the process of decline that followed. The chapter identifies a number of factors that led to the elimination of the well-attended summer terms in New York: tensions first between the Public School Society and the nascent board of education and then between the latter and its local wards, the August vacations increasingly taken by more than just the upper-class reformers who ran the schools, and periodic budgetary crises and disease epidemics.

The third chapter looks more broadly into why educators removed summer education from the school year. Its interpretive framework considers both socioeconomic and ideological developments but focuses on the latter. It relates the strictly pedagogical concerns of educators, such as beliefs that hot summers were detrimental to learning and that summer terms had historically provided inferior education, but argues that underlying them were two larger belief systems. The first and foremost was educators' adaptation of a medical literature that warned against the mental overtaxation of students and recommended set vacation times and specific summer recreational activities. Second, educators steeped in industrial capitalist ideology embedded new thoughts about time usage into their treatment of the summer. For example, superintendents wanted to isolate the summer as a period of professional development for teachers.

As the summer approached its large-scale exclusion from the school year, new ideologies and movements arose to spur its reconnection. Chapters Four, Five, and Six address two interrelated efforts to bring back the summer: the vacation school and the summer school. Chapter Four uncovers the origins of the vacation school movement in late nineteenth-century social conditions, in expanded views of the school's role in society, and in new ideas about how summer might help schools fulfill these functions. Discounting earlier fears for children's health, philanthropists and educators now advocated "vacation schools" to decongest and decriminalize crowded neighborhoods, assimilate immigrant children, and provide practical skills and a natural environment to urban children that lacked them. In addition, vacation school advocates aimed to establish ideal classroom settings for experimentation in pedagogy and curricula.

Chapter Five is an analysis of the vacation and summer school movements. It opens with a brief examination of the first two cities to experiment with vacation schools: Providence and Newark. It then presents a quantitative analysis of the spread of vacation and later summer schools to American cities from 1894 to 1929. The data from it suggest that these programs were popular yet fragile innovations. Most large towns and cities tried vacation schools at some point during this thirty-five year period, but far fewer were able to permanently maintain them. Overall, the data discussed in this chapter demonstrate that vacation schools were an urban institution that moved down through the hierarchy of cities. The chapter then details the origins of vacation schools in late nineteenth-century Chicago and outlines their transformation in the early twentieth century. Vacation schools with nonacademic programs, nonpublic administrators, and unregimented systems became summer schools—publicly funded, bureaucratically administered, and academically oriented. In explanation of this transition, the chapter highlights bureaucratic imperatives tempered by particular and immediate contingencies faced and met by educators and philanthropists.

The remaking of vacation programs into summer schools involved huge changes. By examining the experiences of summer programs in Detroit, Chapter Six depicts and interprets how summer schools reached a seemingly permanent bureaucratic form that is recognizable today. As summer schools now taught mainstream subjects in order to provide academic credit, the experience for students and teachers differed greatly from vacation schools. As educators promoted summer school as a cost-effective use of school time and plant, they offered summer coursework in middle-class neighborhoods that now demanded it. By the 1920s, larger numbers and more diverse groups of students began attending summer programs. Now far less marginalized, summer education became a much more common occurrence for students and teachers. It began to play an increasingly important role in public schooling until it became interwoven into school bureaucracies.

Still, summer school developed a subordinate place in urban school systems and remained easily susceptible to a shift in fortune.

The book's epilogue traces how the summer rose from the ashes of depression and war in order to service national educational aims. With the advent of the Great Depression, summer programs—seen as a frill rather than an essential—were eliminated from the school budget in most towns and cities. From 1945 onwards, summer education became tied to federal efforts in defense education in the late 1950s, compensatory education in the 1960s and 1970s, and educational excellence in the 1980s and 1990s. Nevertheless, localities renewed their summer school programs, and some even initiated forms of summer education that harked back to the spirit of vacation schools. The monograph concludes by looking at policy implications for summer education today—when the advent of academic standards and the concomitant drive to end social promotion have augmented the remediation function of summer school and rekindled debates about its purpose, function, and desirability. Without treating history as a fable, past experience and current research support not only a larger presence of summer education but the special contributions it can make to American schools and society.

CHAPTER ONE

"A Time to Reap and a Time to Sow?": *Rethinking Rural School Calendars in the Nineteenth Century*

In 1869, George Wheeler, a recently appointed school superintendent of Washtenaw County, Michigan, embarked on a tour of the schools in his district. He visited a total of eighty sites, inspecting the number of students, the quality of the teaching, the condition of the buildings, the nature of the schoolwork, and more. Wheeler then submitted his findings to State Superintendent Oramel Hosford, who, in turn, distilled them in his annual report.[1] Often a very mundane task, school inspections made up a large portion of Wheeler's job activity and a part of Hosford's duties as well. What makes Wheeler's survey notable, though not exceptional, is that he traveled to these schools in the summer. Incipient local and state superintendents made regular summer visits because most nineteenth-century district schools were in session and served significant numbers of students by teaching literacy, numeracy, and more.[2]

In 1899 a county superintendent would not be likely to observe as many district schools in the summer because by then, most rural school calendars had shifted in two notable ways. First, the number of days that a country district ran public school sessions increased dramatically, and second, many communities no longer opened schools during the summer. In order to trace and explain the expansion of the school year and the removal of summer from it, this chapter highlights rural school calendar developments in three regionally diverse states: New York, Michigan, and Virginia.[3] In outlining antebellum school year length and term configurations, it suggests that schooling in the summer played a crucial role in the education of thousands of rural children. In demonstrating how patterns evolved over the century, it examines the public policies that spurred change at the state, county (Westchester, NY; Washtenaw, MI; Henrico, VA), town, and district level (Bedford, NY). In short, this chapter delineates the once-prevalent summer term and then accounts for its absence.

The widespread presence of school sessions in the nineteenth century sharply contradicts popular and even some scholarly notions of summer's history.[4] Assumptions about summer vacation tend to congregate around one simple presentist belief—that it has always existed due to long-standing agricultural labor patterns. This explanation is incorrect, but only in its overlooking the summer term and not in its rationale. Agrarian conditions did not necessitate summer vacation, but they did play an important role in the shaping of school calendars. Rural communties closed schools when farm life was most intense, but those closures occurred during spring plantings and fall harvests. As a result, country schools typically opened just during the summer and winter months.

Agrarian labor needs helped determine the student population associated with each term. Many country children over the age of ten only attended school during the winter term because farm activity compelled them to work through the summer.[5] Likewise, many younger children stayed home during the winter when impassable roads made travel to school nearly impossible. Some areas ran schools only during the hot months due to transportation difficulties during the winter.[6] Thus the holding of country school sessions was subservient to weather conditions as well as to seasonal agricultural practices. A school year comprised of brief winter and summer sessions was a mainstay of rural America in the nineteenth century.

The duration of school terms also reflected the economic base of a community. Like the winter terms, summer sessions typically lasted only two or three months.[7] Nevertheless, tremendous variation in length existed within rural areas, especially before consolidation into town or county school systems took place. For example, in the early 1840s in the village of Lima, a small farming community in Washtenaw County, Michigan, the duration of schooling in six distinct school districts ranged from three to seven months.[8] Carl Kaestle and Maris Vinovskis uncovered similar disparities in Massachusetts towns of the same decade. In a multiple regression analysis, they tested several socioeconomic indicators of school year length and found that in 1840 a community's level of agriculture was the best determinant of duration.[9] John Rury's quantitative research confirms that this relationship persisted at least until 1900.[10] Together, these statistical studies suggest the primacy of agricultural factors. In predicting the likelihood of diminutive school years, the best single question to ask was how much acreage a community devoted to farming (Kaestle/Vinovskis) or whether the child's father was a farmer (Rury). Thus farm life did not require a summer break in schooling, but rather a relatively brief and haphazard school year in general.

In fact, extending and standardizing the school year was a key element of the common school reform movement.[11] The incipient professional educators at local, state, and national levels exhorted country school districts to expand their school year.[12] Of course school leaders operated in the context of changing social and economic conditions that facilitated calendar modification, but their efforts went beyond a mere rhetoric of justification. They successfully used several measures—including more stringent requirements for access to state school funds and the consolidation of smaller districts—to prod communities into action. New York's school year, averaging an uncommonly lengthy 167 days in 1835, still expanded to 187 days in 1890. In Michigan, the statewide average rose from 4.6 months in 1842 to 7.8 months in 1890. In Virginia, where statewide public schools first began after the Civil War, the average length of public schools increased from 4.7 months in 1871 to 5.9 months in 1890.[13] Over the same period, many rural communities abandoned the summer session by adopting a three-term school schedule. While it is all too easy today to underestimate the extent of the transformation in the duration and seasons of schooling, nineteenth-century educators were quite aware of and in large part engineered the transition.

The School Year in New York

New York presents a sound alternative to Massachusetts as an example of an eastern state leading the movement towards a lengthy and systemic school year. Its earliest pursuits of public education predated the common school movement. The state's first constitution of 1777 did not address schooling, but constitutional revisions in 1822 and 1846 mandated a school fund created by land proceeds to support common schools.[14] By the latter date, the state legislature had already created a rudimentary system of common schools. Laws passed in 1784, 1795, and 1805 instituted the state's Board of Regents (to run colleges and

Table 1.1. *Average length of New York and Westchester County public school sessions, 1835–90*

Year	New York	Westchester County
1835	32.7 weeks	38.3 weeks
1840[a]	34.4 weeks	39.1 weeks
1845[a]	34.4 weeks	43.0 weeks
1850	33.1 weeks	34.4 weeks
1855	34.0 weeks	36.1 weeks
1860	33.1 weeks	39.6 weeks
1865[b]	31.2 weeks	36.6 weeks
1870	35.2 weeks	41.5 weeks
1875	35.1 weeks	39.7 weeks
1880	35.7 weeks	40.3 weeks
1885	35.8 weeks	39.1 weeks
1890	37.3 weeks	39.8 weeks

Sources: New York Superintendent of the Common Schools. *Annual Reports*, 1835–50; New York Superintendent of Public Instruction. *Annual Report*, 1855–90.

[a] 1840 data for state and county are from 1839. 1845 data for state and county are from 1844.

[b] In 1865, the superintendents switched their school year length tabulations from months to weeks. The pre-1865 figures were converted at a rate of 4.3 weeks per month.

academies) and its public school fund (to spur school formation and attendance).[15] Legislation in 1812 created New York's common education system, regulated the distribution of the state public school fund, and designated a state superintendent position (though not as a "distinct and permanent officer"—the secretary of state soon assumed its duties).[16] Coupled with colonial educational traditions, these laws produced extensive state-wide educational attainments in school attendance prior to the start of the common school era.[17] Likewise, New York's superintendents reported an average school year length of eight months for the whole state and nearly nine months for Westchester County well before 1840.[18]

Despite New York's precocious position in the spread of common schooling, the state presents several advantages as a case study of school calendar transformation. First, even with its relatively lengthy school terms, there was still room for gradual growth in the 1840–90 period. This slow increase is evident in Table 1.1, which provides the average

Figure 1.1. *Average length of public school terms in rural and urban districts in New York, 1860–90*

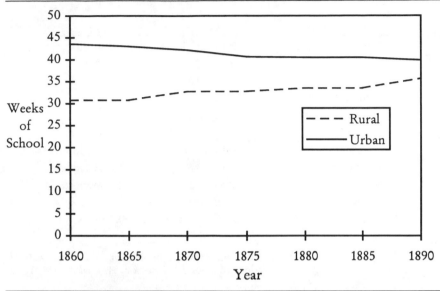

Source: New York Superintendent of Public Instruction, *Annual Reports.*

lengths for the state and for Westchester County. Prior to the Civil War, New York's mean fluctuated somewhat but reached no greater than eight months.[19] In 1865, the state began calculating school session lengths in weeks and reported an average term—most likely depleted by the war—of 31.2 weeks. In the next 25 years several growth spurts occurred, and by 1890 that figure reached 37.3 weeks. School terms in Westchester County, although always longer than the state average, followed a similar growth pattern to the state as a whole. However, the county's average school term fluctuated more widely in the 1840–1865 period, and after a significant increase during the next five years, Westchester's average length actually declined slightly between 1870 and 1890. Overall, Table 1.1 highlights the 1860s as important decade for dips and rises in the length of school terms.

Of course, aggregate figures from New York and Westchester mask significant rural and urban differences in school year length that were muted but not eliminated over the nineteenth century. New York's state superintendents only began distinguishing between city and country school terms in 1857 yet still found the substantial contrasts. In that year, rural school districts averaged 7.5 months, and the state's cities and large towns averaged 11.1 months. The lines graphed

Table 1.2. *School year lengths of District Two, Westchester County, 1836 and 1876*

Town	1836	1876
Greenborough	9 months	42.0 weeks
Harrison	9 months	40.0 weeks
Mamaroneck	8 months	42.5 weeks
Mount Pleasant	9 months	40.0 weeks
New Rochelle	12 months	41.0 weeks
North Castle	8 months	39.0 weeks
Pelham	0 months	41.5 weeks
Poundtree	7 months	33.0 weeks
Rye	9 months	42.0 weeks
Scarsdale	12 months	42.0 weeks
White Plains	12 months	40.0 weeks

Sources: New York Superintendent of the Common Schools. *Annual Report,* 1836–37, pp. 4–9; New York Superintendent of Public Instruction. *Annual Report,* 1876–77, p. 9.

on Figure 1.1, however, suggest that over the rest of the century, this gap closed as rural terms lengthened and urban terms decreased. By 1890, cities still had longer terms than country districts, but the difference was reduced to four weeks and one day. Since 1860, rural terms had grown by nearly five weeks and city terms had dropped by almost four. Leaving aside the question of how and why urban school years declined until Chapter Two, these data identify a more pronounced expansion of schooling in rural New York than suggested by the aggregate statewide figures.

Finally, considerable disparities existed between counties in New York, townships in Westchester, and even districts in Bedford. In 1843, the average length of school by county ranged from five to twelve months.[20] Even a highly schooled county like Westchester exhibited variation in school term length, though no doubt less than counties upstate. For supervisory purposes, the state divided the county into three sections, and Table 1.2 displays the average lengths for townships in one section of Westchester. In 1836, school terms ranged from seven to twelve months while Pelham opened no public schools. Over the next forty years, the range greatly narrowed. In 1876, most towns held between thirty-nine and forty-two weeks of school, although Poundtree opened schools for just thirty-three weeks per year. Districts in

Bedford averaged nine and one-half months of school in 1842, but ranged from five to twelve months. These districts also fluctuated widely over time: no. 4 opened schools for six months in 1841 and eleven in 1842, while at the same time no. 11 dropped from eleven to seven months.[21]

Thus while school year lengths in New York, Westchester, and Bedford were high throughout the nineteenth century, there were always communities far below the average that incurred the attention of state and county school officials. County superintendents statewide regularly complained about "the long and protracted vacations" in towns like Pelham and Poundtree and certain districts in Bedford, indicating that substantial differences were quite common in school year lengths within townships and counties. As one of them noted in 1843, "Although there are many schools which are kept only the time required by law, to draw the public money, there are others continued, with only short vacations, the whole year."[22] New York superintendents had district terms to lengthen, just fewer of them than in Michigan and Virginia. In addition, the summer term itself—no matter how long or short—became a target for school reformers desirous of achieving consistency in school availability and student attendance.

The summer term: deficient or sufficient?

From the dawn of the common school movement, educators derisively caricatured the summer term. With mostly young children in attendance, a low overall turnout, mostly inexpensive and often young female teachers in employment, and the early or sudden abeyance of schools, summer session learning conditions contributed to the altogether meager amount of schooling in many country districts.[23] "It is evident that the summer terms will not compare favorably with those kept in the winter," wrote one county superintendent from Seneca.[24] Nevertheless, such a blanket condemnation of summer sessions appears overdrawn. Despite what New York superintendents wrote, the statistics they collected indicate that summer was an integral part of the school year. If by reputation the summer term fared less well than its winter counterpart, it held its own in at least three areas: the total number of students in attendance, the types of subjects taught, and the number of teachers hired.

With relatively high enrollment rates and so many districts running schools for lengthy periods, summer attendance in New York was substantial. In the early 1840s, a New York teacher's journal estimated that 7,000 teachers opened schools for over 200,000 students in the summers, while State Superintendent Samuel Young reported figures slightly under that mark. In 1843, rural counties in New York reported summer attendance figures that reached nearly 90% of winter attendance. Unfortunately, New York superintendents stopped providing attendance data by term after 1844.[25] Instead, they typically tabulated how long New York students attended school for each year. For example, in 1843 the state superintendent reported that of the 640,354 students in attendance at schools statewide, 25.3% attended for less than two months, 32.3% for two to four months, 19.8% for four to six months, 11.6% for six to eight months, 5.5% for eight to ten months, 1.8% for ten to twelve months, and 3.7% for twelve months.[26] The most obvious conclusion to be drawn from these data is that most students attended school for far fewer days than the schools were open. For a state with an average school year of eight months in 1843, the vast majority of its students attended for six months or less. While these figures do not indicate when students attended schools, they do not preclude summer attendance. Many students enrolling for just a few months undoubtedly came in the summer. Moreover, there was a substantial minority (11%) of students who attended school for eight months or more who most likely attended school in the summer as well.

Examining the course of study during the summer session also lends to its legitimacy as a major component of nineteenth-century education. In 1843 and 1844, the New York state superintendent tabulated the subjects studied by each student in attendance during school inspections. Table 1.3 displays the data from 1843 and highlights two important findings.[27] First, it corroborates the high attendance levels of the summer term. While the totals in Table 1.3 do not represent individual students, who typically studied more than one subject, they do offer a rough correspondence to them. With summer subjects totaling nealy 380,000 in 1843 (consisting of 43.2% of the total recorded), Table 1.3 does show a high level of summer study.[28] Second, the table demonstrates that summer work was not a supplementary curriculum but instead heavily emphasized the academic basics. By far the most common course of work in the summer was in reading, but arithmetic, geography, and spelling also received substantial attention. These subjects were among the most common in the winter as well. Both sessions taught higher-order skills and subjects such as chemistry, geometry, philosophy, and physiology to similarly low percentages of stu-

Table 1.3. *Fields of study in New York winter and summer sessions, 1843*

Course of study	Winter Attendance N = 481,204 (%)	Summer Attendance N = 378,928 (%)
Alphabet	2.0	4.6
Spelling	5.8	10.2
Reading	41.0	39.1
Arithmetic	20.6	13.5
Geography	11.5	13.3
History	2.3	1.9
English Grammar	8.8	6.0
Use of globes or scientific apparatus	0.5	0.9
Algebra	0.5	0.3
Geometry, surveying, higher mathematics	0.1	0.1
Natural philosophy	1.0	0.7
Philosophy of the mind	0.1	0.1
Physiology	0.0	0.0
Bookkeeping	0.2	0.2
Composition	1.2	1.2
Vocal music	2.1	4.7
Chemistry	0.0	0.0
Definition of words	1.9	2.6
Astronomy	0.0	0.1
Other branches not specified	0.2	0.5
Totals	99.8	100.0

Source: New York Superintendent of the Common Schools. *Annual Report,* 1842–43, pp. 7–9.

dents. In both seasons, most students spent time in areas of English and mathematics. Still, some differences are noticeable. Summer students studied more early language skills such as the alphabet and spelling, while winter students learned some slightly more advanced subjects like mathematics and English grammar. Summer students also enjoyed slightly more recreative instruction in vocal music than during the winter. In general, the prevalent summer subjects most likely reflected the younger student population that attended school during the hot months.[29]

A comparison of the teacher cohorts from each school term further emphasizes the importance of the summer in nineteenth-century
education. In antebellum New York, the opportunity for formal instruction in the summer was at essentially the same level as in the winter, even though student attendance tailed off somewhat in the summer. In 1843, rural districts hired only fifty-five more teachers for the
winter terms than for the summer sessions, 6,149 to 6,094, and the following year there were over 400 more teachers reported for summer
terms than winter terms.[30] However, the composition of these two
groups displays sharp contrasts between them that lay at the heart of
contemporary disparagement of the summer session. Incipient educators saw the "clever young misses" predominantly hired to teach summer sessions as their principal weakness, a rather ironic criticism to
make at the dawn of the feminization of teaching.[31]

The New York data support the abundant anecdotal evidence that
female teachers predominated in the rural summer terms. In 1843,
women constituted 84.9% of the summer teachers while men accounted for 74.2% of the winter teachers. Moreover, the already acute
salary differentials between men and women in the winter—$14.28 to
$7.00—became even larger during the summer—$15.00 to 6.00.[32] These
differences alone did not spur censure of the summer term. On the
contrary, women were becoming increasingly valued and hired as
teachers, both for their "maternal" attributes and their cheap salaries.[33]
Summer session critics, however, lambasted their teachers as inexperienced young girls, a label borne out by the data from New York.

Male teachers tended to be older, more experienced, and a more
stable fixture at an individual school than female teachers. These gen-
dered characteristics were particularly accentuated during the summer
term. Tables 1.4, 1.5, and 1.6 present data on the age, experience, and
tenure of New York teachers in 1843. As Table 1.4 indicates, 51% of
the summer teachers were age twenty-one or younger, compared to
31% of the winter school staff. When these figures are broken into
male and female cohorts by season, the youngest group of teachers is
the women in the summer. In the summer term well over half (57%) of
the women were age twenty-one or less versus less than one fifth (18%)
of the male teachers. In the winter term, only 43% of the female teachers were age twenty-one or under compared to 26.5% of the male
teachers. This marked difference in the winter term may stem from
market forces. Communities willing to buck the seasonal labor patterns could hire a somewhat older male summer or female winter
teacher.

Table 1.4. *Composition of public school teachers by sex and age, New York, 1843*

Age group	Winter Term			Summer Term		
	Women (%)	Men (%)	Total (%)	Women (%)	Men (%)	Total (%)
Under 18	10.2	3.3	5.1	18.8	3.3	16.4
18 – 21	32.6	23.2	25.6	38.2	14.4	34.5
21 – 25	35.9	41.5	40.1	29.7	35.5	30.6
25 – 30	13.3	18.9	17.5	9.7	21.3	11.5
30+	8.0	13.1	11.8	3.6	25.5	7.0
N	1,713	5,093	6,806	5,678	1,023	6,701

Source: New York Superintendent of the Common Schools. *Annual Report*, 1842–43, pp. 7–9.

Table 1.5. *Composition of public school teachers by years of experience, New York, 1843*

Years of experience	Winter Term			Summer Term		
	Women (%)	Men (%)	Total (%)	Women (%)	Men (%)	Total (%)
< 1 year	28.7	39.8	37.1	44.4	18.3	40.5
> 1 year	71.3	60.2	62.9	55.6	81.7	59.5
N	1,571	5,040	6,611	5,663	984	6,647

Source: New York Superintendent of the Common Schools. *Annual Report*, 1842–43, pp. 7–9.

The experience level of teachers followed the same patterns of their ages. Winter term teachers had more time in the classroom than their summer counterparts, though not significantly. Table 1.5 breaks the teachers into two cohorts: less and greater than one year of experience. In both summer and winter, around 60% had over one year of teaching experience, and the differential between the two was less than 4%. Looking at men and women separately again suggests the impact of supply and demand in the hiring process. Districts willing to pay for a male teacher in the summer could easily hire an experienced one, as over 80% had over one year of experience. In the winter term, more female teachers (71%) had one year of experience than their male counterparts (61%), but this percentage decreased to 56% in the summer term.

With so little teaching experience, it is not surprising that few teachers had taught at their current positions for very long. As Table 1.6 suggests, summer and winter teachers alike had a tenuous hold on their job. In both seasons, slightly more than 70% of teachers had taught for less than one year at the same school. In contrast, just 6% of the winter term teachers and 5% of the summer term teachers served three years or more at their current school. Moreover, the difference between men and women were less pronounced.[34] Men teaching the winter term essentially enjoyed no more stability than their female counterparts. Only in the summer did men achieve some regularity, as more than half of them had spent more than one year at the same school, while female teachers in the summer had less tenure than in the winter. These figures also suggest a market-based explanation. Since most districts were predisposed to hiring men in the winter and women in the summer, the competitive job markets would exist for male teachers in the summer and female teachers in the winter. As a result, teacher from these two cohorts demonstrated higher age, experience, and continuity levels.[35]

Collectively, the data tabulated by season help delineate the vitality of the summer term in mid-nineteenth-century New York. Yet those same figures illuminate the source of its demise and eventual disappearance. Although summer attendance was high in many districts, it was rarely as great as during the winter. While teachers served in ample

Table 1.6. *Composition of public school teachers by continuity of tenure, New York, 1843*

Years at the same school	Winter Term			Summer Term		
	Women (%)	Men (%)	Total (%)	Women (%)	Men (%)	Total (%)
< 1 year	71.3	70.9	71.0	75.2	43.7	70.4
1 year +	17.5	15.4	15.9	16.0	24.6	17.3
2 years +	7.2	7.5	7.4	6.3	15.5	7.7
3 years +	4.0	6.2	5.6	2.5	16.2	4.6
n	1,735	5,170	6,905	5,699	1,024	6,723

Source: New York Superintendent of the Common Schools. *Annual Report*, 1842–1843, pp. 7–9.

numbers during the summer, they were distinctive by their age and gender and typically disparaged for being young girls. In addition, schools opened but ran haphazardly in the summer due to deficient funds, insufficient attendance, and inclement weather. For example, of Westchester's 156 school districts in 1843, 19 never opened during the summer and another 39 were temporarily closed.[36] Eventually, the summer term became a casualty of efforts to lengthen and standardize school terms throughout the state's rural areas.

School calendar reform: the year is lengthened and the summer is removed

In the nineteenth century, state educational leaders unleashed a barrage of legislative and bureaucratic initiatives at rural localities in order to affect school calendar reform. Most often, New York superintendents used term length mandates, state taxation systems, and new organizational structures to lengthen and simultaneously reshape the public school year. Of these tactics, setting and then raising a minimum school term for eligibility for state funds was often the first and clearly the most direct approach. As one county superintendent opined, "My convictions are, that the evils of long vacations will never be removed until eight months' school, taught by a qualified teacher, is required to entitle districts to receive their proportions of the public money. This will strike at the root of the evil."[37] It would be nearly fifty years, however, before New York would require a thirty-two week school year.

The early superintendents found few statutes and laws with which they could compel changes in school sessions. Few states, including New York, made school year length a criteria when they wrote or revised state constitutions.[38] Similarly, New York's early pieces of school legislation, passed in 1784, 1795, and 1805, did not directly address the question of school session length.[39] The legislature's substantive 1812 school laws, which introduced many elements of the state's common school system, underscored the growing concern by requiring school district trustees to include in their annual reports the number of days the schools were in session. Two years later, revisions of the law further prodded the initial opening of public schools across the state by setting a three-month minimum to gain access to the state school fund.[40] By 1838, when New York's legislature raised the minimum to four months, school terms throughout the state tended to be far higher.[41] If the increase encouraged the rise in average school terms from 1835 to 1840 for both New York State and Westchester County, it did not sustain it through the 1840s (see Table 1.1). At the end of the decade, proponents were unable to augment the minimum in a new school bill passed in 1849, and school term lengths actually decreased the following year due to a financial crisis. Even without a shortage of school funds, the law's effect would have been negligible given that four months was much less than New York and Westchester's averages in 1849 and 1850. Indeed this low requirement targeted the worst offenders and not typical rural school districts.

Subsequent legislation raised the minimum school term to a level that could have an impact. By 1860, the state had pushed the requirement to six months, and in 1864, the Consolidated School Act denied any district that maintained schools for less than 28 weeks a share of the public school funds.[42] Twenty-eight weeks also fell below the length of time most districts opened schools by 1864, but consolidation may have had an immediate impact on the rural school year length averages. State Superintendent Victor Rice clearly attributed the rise in rural school terms and teacher salaries to the 1864 act, and the rural average did increase by one week from 1864 to 1865.[43] But as Figure 1.1 shows, rural averages were no higher in 1865 than in 1860, suggesting that the Consolidated School Act merely helped to negate the Civil War's downward influence on school term lengths. Moreover, some districts still flouted the law. State superintendents often received petitions for a waiver from the requirement, and county officials still reported districts under the 28-week minimum after 1864. Even Westchester County, which had one of the highest averages for school year lengths in the state, reported two districts with fewer than 28 weeks and two more running no schools at all in 1866.[44] Thus even after the Civil War ended, state and county educators remained dissatisfied with local school calendar practices.

The final increase in the state mandated school term occurred in 1889 when the state legislature raised the minimum to 32 weeks.[45] By then, most districts in violation of school year length provisions had been pushed up to the legal level, so this law sought to raise the average term length. State Superintendent Andrew Draper justified the new law through his observation that "four thousand districts out of eleven thousand held school only long enough to share in the public moneys."[46] His reasoning did not sway all relevant parties, however, and this school law revision occurred amid doubts and opposition from within and outside the legislature. Like the earlier changes in school term mandates, legislative debates considered issues of state vs. local authority and financial questions about raising the money to run schools for four more weeks in those 4,000 districts. Surprisingly then, Draper reported an ease in enforcement of the new mandate. He noted "less difficulty during the last year in exacting thirty-two weeks of school in the rural districts, than was experienced in the preceding years in exacting but twenty-eight."[47] What's more, the data on rural school year lengths corroborated Draper's positive evaluation. The bulk of the increase from 1885 to 1890 identified in Figure 1.1 occurred in the final year of that period, when rural terms rose from 33.4 to 35.7 weeks, which pushed the state average to 37.3 weeks. Of course, school term length legislation alone did not produce the desired increases. Raising state minimums in New York typically had only a partial impact on school calendars, which were influenced by a host of social and fiscal indicators.[48] But Draper and his predecessors employed other means to effect change, chief among them the system for raising school money.

The financial mechanisms used by New York to raise school money shaped the length of the rural school year. In their discussion of state and local tax plans, superintendents regularly linked expenditures to school year lengths and other educational outcomes. As Superintendent Abram Weaver observed in 1870, "It matters much with reference to the length of terms, the quality of instruction, and even the ability to comply with the law, in what degree our schools are dependent, in many cases, upon the scanty local resources of poor districts, and in what measure supported by the common fund."[49] Weaver identified a pattern that had existed for nearly sixty years. New York's initial 1812 school legislation met with mostly noncompliance due to a loophole in the tax requirements. In order to obtain state funds, towns had to raise an equivalent amount locally, yet the law did not mandate that communities do so and most did not. In an 1814 revision, the state overrode oppositional forces for local fiscal autonomy by making obligatory a town school tax. As a result, school spending increased and the additional funds were felt in a number of ways. Over the next few years, the state superintendent reported with optimism the system's spread to new towns and the greater participation of students. He also noted that school session lengths increased at a similar rate as enrollment numbers, though he did not include statistical evidence.[50]

By mid-century, educators viewed the lack of a free school system as the greatest impediment to longer terms and other educational improvements. David Nasaw has estimated that local school taxes in New York paid for perhaps 20% of teacher salaries. The state school fund accounted for additional income, but parents paid "rate bills" to cover at least half of the total costs.[51] Therefore the rate bills incurred the ire of a generation of county and state superintendents, who charged that it failed to serve the working poor even when rate exemptions were available. Overturning it, however, proved difficult in the face of local intransigence. A free schools provision was defeated amid constitutional revisions in 1844, and legislation passed in 1849 achieved only a partial victory for common school reformers. The new law eliminated rate bills under the expectation that local districts would raise taxes to maintain educational spending. Instead, legislators were flooded with petitions for amendment or repeal of the law, and many districts kept taxes the same and simply reduced educational services, particularly the length of the school year.[52] Although the bill was amended and passed again in 1850, some districts continued to counter its intent by keeping the school year short. In its next session, the legislature passed a more palatable law. This new piece of legislation replaced local property tax revenue with a new state-levied tax, but it was kept so low, that "districts were allowed to supplement it by reinstating the abolished rates."[53] Thus a decade of efforts to create free schools in New York had failed.

Throughout the 1850s and 1860s, New York's school reformers grew more strident in their attacks on rate bills. They mostly faulted it for failing to provide universally free common schools but also for adversely impacting school term lengths. As one Westchester district trustee argued, "The rate-bill is the true cause of what should be deemed a deficiency in school time."[54] Indeed, superintendents recognized that reliance on rate bills provided no incentives for towns to run schools beyond the legal minimum length because additional school expenditures incurred through extended school sessions were passed directly to the parents.[55] To counter local intransigence, state superintendents reorganized New York's common school system in 1854. The new plan established the Department of Public Instruction and a new state superintendent position with greater organizational, administrative, and supervisory powers. Subsequent superintendents, particularly Rice, provided forceful leadership in the effort to eradicate the rate bills, and in 1867 the Free School Act finally removed them by creating a new state education tax.[56]

The dismantling of the rate bill system stimulated the expansion of the school calendar. It immediately sparked a rise in New York's average rural term, which had held steady at about 30 weeks since the 1850s, to nearly 33 weeks. As a result, the state average experienced its largest period of growth from 1865 to 1870 (see Table 1.1), with most of the expansion occurring during the first two years of the new system. The state mean jumped from 30.5 weeks in 1867 to 32.9 weeks in 1868 to 35.2 weeks in 1869, and Superintendent Weaver openly attributed the rise to the 1867 legislation.[57] After that initial increase, the growth rate in school session lengths abated. By 1880, the state's average length was 35.7 weeks, but it essentially rose no higher until pushed by the 1889 legislation that required thirty-two weeks of schooling.

Financial disincentives for lengthening school years remained despite the elimination of the rate bills. The chief one was New York's method of distribution of its school funds. The state based its allocations on the average daily attendance, and thus penalized districts that ran longer terms without noticeably higher attendance rates. As a result of this practice, districts that continued to run schools for the twenty-eight week state minimum often warranted a larger share of the state school fund than districts with longer sessions. In addition, some local superintendents and trustees blamed the summer term for preventing them from receiving greater shares of the state school fund. One Oswego County superintendent observed that "every week of summer school decreases the average daily attendance, because the attendance is less in summer than in winter, and the shorter the summer terms, the greater the average daily attendance. Therefore, trustees say: 'We draw more money, if we have only twenty-eight weeks of school, than we do if we have more.'"[58] To reverse this outcome, he suggested that school money be distributed based on the whole number of days of attendance. The state, however, did not change its method during the 1860–90 period, and its non-response on this issue affected the dual trends traced in this chapter. It kept local school officials inclined towards reducing the summer session but slowed the effort to lengthen the overall school year.

Consolidation was viewed as an additional spur towards longer terms. Traditionally, New York communities organized schools through numerous local districts within a single town. While early New York superintendents criticized the patchwork of tiny school districts and sought to create a town and county based system, local demands spurred many districts to subdivide during the antebellum period. Small districts allowed parents to send children to nearby schools, making attendance easier, especially during poor weather. These subdivided districts typically were "formed where population is thin; and for the very reason that the number of children is small they are weak also in taxable property."[59] In a district with few children, the tuition per pupil was higher than in more populous districts. Inevitably, many small districts reduced costs by hiring cheap teachers or lessening the school year. Thus in an unconsolidated system, districts with very short school years tended to be very small. In 1836, state superintendent John Dix reported that New York had 800 districts with schools open for less than 3.5 months but greater than the three month legal minimum. Over 475 of these districts contained fewer than thirty children between ages 5–16. Reacting bitterly to this data, Dix argued that the evils of districts too small were far worse than overly large ones. He urged consolidation so larger districts could hire competent teachers for longer periods of time. Then, even if attendance rates were low due to distance, children would experience as much time in school yet have better teachers than in tiny districts.[60]

The 1853 Union Free School Act provided an alternative means for towns to organize schools. The legislation initiated an optional plan for communities to unite small districts and form large graded districts.[61] Its impact on school terms, however, appears negligible.[62] Although cities tended to fulfill the law's provisions, the act only ratified the consolidation, grading, and reduction of school terms already occurring in many urban school districts. Moreover, most rural areas did not adopt the law's plan for school organization. As a result, many rural districts still provided meager educational opportunities and therefore still incurred the attention of state school officials. Sometimes they failed to run schools even for the requisite time period and then petitioned the state superintendent to waive the requirement for obtaining state funds. As Superintendent H. H. Van Dyck denied one such request, he derisively noted that application for relief from the penalty "comes for the most part from districts too feeble in population and wealth to justify their independent existence."[63] After the Civil War, consolidation drives continued well into the twentieth century, always motivated in part by the desire to eliminate short school terms.

School calendar restructuring was a final method used by New York school administrators to increase school term lengths and eliminate summer sessions. Many educators envied university schedules, which by the late nineteenth century had long ago displaced the summer from the school year. In response, they too moved the start of the school year back to September and began to close the schools during July and August.[64] To make this change, they created a three-term schedule, roughly coinciding with the fall, winter, and spring. In absence of data from Westchester County, an examination of upstate

Schenectady County will illustrate this process. Districts in Schenectady traditionally held a twenty-week winter term and a shorter summer session from May to August or September. In the 1870s and 1880s, some added an eight-week term in September and October, retained an eighteen-week winter term from November until March, and started a twelve-week term from April to June.[65] Even with a strong advocate of the three-term calendar in the county superintendent, old practices died hard in Schenectady. In 1888, three-fifths of the county's sixty schools retained a two-term calendar, and of those thirty-six schools, twenty remained open until August. Nevertheless, signs of change appeared in Schenectady as well. Nearly four-fifths of Schenectady's sixty schools opened in September, and only four opened in November.[66] By adding school days in the fall, school districts could reduce classroom meetings in the summer.

The state superintendent's office helped spur these local efforts. In 1883, the state legislature amended the general school law to alter the official school year. It moved the last day of school year from September 30 to August 20, creating a shorter school year for 1883–1884 but a new school year from August 21 to August 20 for 1884–1885 and beyond. Many localities favored this arrangement and claimed it affected practice, as school elections and meetings now took place "in the summer, at a time when the actual work in the school rooms is usually ended, and the schools generally throughout the State are in vacation."[67] It also enabled districts to open a new school session in September more easily. In 1889, the legislature again amended the school year, ending it on July 25 instead of August 20, which further encouraged calendar restructuring.[68] Thus the New York state officials pushed the summer from the school year in part by splitting it in half. The transformation from two to three terms was not complete by 1890, but it was well started.

What was the impact of this top-down reform on local school districts? In Bedford, New York, a prosperous town of independent farmers in the northern part of Westchester County, state legislation on education spurred some reaction. In response to the state's creation of a school fund in 1795, the town elected commisioners of schools at its annual meetings of 1796, 1797, and 1798, although there is no record of any activity by them. Following the school legislation of 1812, the town renewed the annual election of three school commissioners and from three to six school inspectors.[69] At the same time, the township organized itself into eleven (eventually twenty) school districts that subsequently opened up one-room schools through the partial aid of the newly distributed state school fund.[70]

Bedford's incipient school districts structured the school year in the usual rural fashion. Most districts ran distinctive winter and summer terms. The summer session was often the lengthier though not the better attended of the two though. In the 1840s, the Cantatoe School in District 6 opened a six-month summer session in early April and a male-taught, three to five-month winter term in November.[71] Likewise, the early winter terms in District 2 lasted only three months, while its inhabitants quite typically "voted to employ a Lady to teach the summer months."[72] With many districts running schools for nine or ten months a year as early as the 1820s, Bedford's districts outpaced many communities throughout the county and state. Of course, the variation between districts during the same year and within the same district over several years was tremendous, but by 1830 the town's fifteen active districts averaged 8.8 months of school. The town mean surpassed nine months for most of the next twenty years, when the state minimum was being raised from three to four to six months.[73] Thus state and county educators had to be fairly satisfied with the term lengths in most Bedford districts during most years of the antebellum era.

District 2 in particular might have been viewed as a model school district. Located in the center of Bedford village, it opened the "Stone Jug" school house in 1829 and by 1835 had achieved a school session length consistently ten months or longer.[74] Although at first glance not a target of school reformers, Bedford's District Two merits further examination in large part because of extant minutes of annual school meetings from 1826 to 1913—the only district in Bedford with such surviving records.[75] A careful reading of the minutes revealed considerable tension over the location of the "Stone Jug" schoolhouse, but subsequent school issues generated some heated discussions as well. In 1850, nearly two-thirds of the citizens from District 2 voted in opposition to free schooling in the midst of the statewide controversy over recently passed legislation.[76] This resistance, however, appears to have had nothing to do with the specific question of school year lengths. Likewise, when "an unusually large meeting" convened in 1871 to consider consolidation with District 1, the question concerned the shortcomings of District 1 (small size, short terms) not of District 2.[77] Nor did the minutes reveal any internal disputes over school year lengths when they noted the opening and closing dates of school.[78] Thus District 2 reached a substantial school year prior to the state's efforts at establishing minimum length requirements, free schooling, or consolidated districts.

District 2 did not, however, restructure its school calendar in an equally rapid manner, and so proved susceptible to the state's machinations against the summer term. The school minutes indicate that District 2 retained a separate summer and winter term as late as 1860, and this practice most likely continued beyond the Civil War.[79] No doubt, the state's changes in the official school year during the 1880s had an impact. For more than fifty years, citizens in District 2 had met annually in October. Since these meetings set school dates and teacher salaries, it is highly unlikely that a three term (fall, winter, spring) calendar was yet in effect. When the state made the official school year begin on August 21st in 1883 and then on July 25th in 1889, the district pushed its annual meeting first to late August and then to the beginning of the month in 1889.[80] This change was probably more than cosmetic, as September was now available to start the school year, and August became untenable as a school month. Further change followed after the turn of the century: the "Stone Jug" school house was closed in 1912, and District 2 merged with other districts the following year.

In short, New York superintendents fostered the alteration of school calendars in several ways during the nineteenth century. They pushed through legislative changes in school organization and finance that spurred the development of longer school years. Innovations like consolidated districts, free schools, graded classes, and an official school year were all designed in part to increase the length of the school year and to decrease the use of summer for schooling. The state could also be direct in its approach, as it gradually upped the legal minimum term from four months to thirty-two weeks over a fifty-year period. Through this combination of actions, state school officials achieved their desired results. By 1890 the average 187-day, public-school year in New York had reached a size and shape essentially recognizable today. With many summer sessions eliminated, July and August became a time for student vacations and teacher institutes.

Still, New York's current superintendent, Andrew Draper, remained somewhat dissatisfied. Draper hoped eventually to raise rural districts to a 38- or 40-week school term without summer session so that they would match the school results of the cities. In 1890 he sounded much like his predecessors from the common school movement when he wrote "nothing is of more consequence to the school interest of the rural districts of the State than that the old idea, that there should be a winter school for one class of pupils and a summer school for another class of pupils, shall be abandoned, and that all pupils up to the age of 13 or 14 shall have the advantage of the schools for the entire year, deducting only reasonable vacations."[81] Thus while the standards in New York for school year lengths and school terms had grown over fifty years, they did not yet meet the expectations of state school leaders, which had intensified as well.

The School Year in Michigan

Unduly understudied by historians of education, the state of Michigan was a leading reformer in the common school era. In 1835, John D. Pierce became the nation's first state superintendent of public instruction, preceding by two years Horace Mann's appointment as secretary of the Massachusetts Board of Education.[82] Unlike New York's first and revised state constitutions, Michigan's initial one of 1835 contained what Lawrence Cremin labeled as "one of the most inclusive articles on education to appear in any of the early state constitutions."[83] In addition to creating a state superintendency, it charged the legislature to provide a system of common schools and libraries and arranged for income from public land to support the state schools and university. But Michigan had already taken steps for public education. Spurred by the Northwest Ordinance's promotion of free public education, the territorial legislature provided land, buildings, and money for schools starting in 1809.[84] Michigan also had strong New England advocates for schools such as Augustus Woodward, Isaac Crary, and Pierce. Woodward's 1817 plan for a school system crowned by the University of Michigan failed to gain enough support, but it provided Pierce with a precedent for an inclusive public education system. By mid-century, the state had developed an educational ladder from district schools to state university. As Cremin observed of Michigan, "the systemization inherent in a centralized comprehensive scheme was present from the beginning."[85]

Calendar reform at the state level

Michigan's earliest data indicate that inconsistent and short school terms permeated the state during the antebellum period. In 1842, only a small number of districts maintained schools throughout all four seasons, most fell between three and six months, and the average district length was four and one-half months. A rural district in Michigan generally maintained a school for six to twelve weeks in the summer and winter, but it is unclear how these seasonal terms compared to each other at the state level. Unfortunately, Michigan superintendents supplied only anecdotal and not quantitative evidence on when the schools were open and how well they were utilized by season, but one common complaint was that attendance declined drastically in the summer. Another was that tremendous variation in the length of schooling permeated each body politic. The state's 1,656 districts that reported figures ranged from supporting none to twelve months of public schooling in 1842.[86] Michigan's counties averaged from 3.5 to 6 months of schooling, with a state mean of 5.0 months in 1845.[87]

Even more telling than these gulfs were the huge disparities between communities within a county and between districts within one town. Table 1.7 presents the changes in school year lengths for Washtenaw County and its townships from 1840 to 1890. In 1840, the county's communities ranged from 3.5 months in Lindon to 6.5 months in Sharon. These figures still understate the variety because Washtenaw County townships, like most of Michigan and the United States in 1840, ran their schools at tiny district levels. Townships in Washtenaw County consisted of anywhere from five districts (in Dexter) to sixteen districts (in Ann Arbor and Salem), and the districts within a single township displayed tremendous contrasts in the length of schooling. Dexter's five districts, for example, opened their schools for 3.5, 5, 5, 6.5, and 10 months, respectively. Freedom's six districts reported school years that lasted 3, 3, 4, 7, 7, and 7 months. In Salem districts ranged from three to nine months, and one district in Ypsilanti maintained its schools for 12 months.[88] Even within a single district there was great irregularity. School openings, closings, and lengths fluctuated each year, as seen in the experience of some Washtenaw County towns. For example, school District Two in Bridgewater reported a seven-month term in 1837 and a three-month term in 1838. Likewise, District Two in Webster ran schools for six months in 1837 and four months in 1841.[89]

What accounted for the variation in the length of the school year? Historians have identified population size and economic activity as the basis of a community's school term length.[90] In overwhelmingly rural Michigan, urban/rural patterns in school duration persisted but were probably less salient than in New York or Massachusetts.[91] Consider the make-up of the state's seventy-two districts running schools for nine or more months in 1842. The cohort included some districts in the state's largest communities, including Battle Creek, Fenton, Grand

Table 1.7. *Length (in months) of public school sessions in Washtenaw County townships, 1840–90*

Locality	Year			
	1840[a]	1860	1870[b]	1890[b]
Ann Arbor	5.6	8.9	10.0	9.8
Augusta	4.4	6.7	....	8.9
Bridgewater	5.4	6.6	....	....
Dexter	6.0	7.2	10.0	10.0
Freedom	5.2	6.0	....	....
Lima	4.5	7.8	....	....
Lodi	5.2	7.5	....	....
Lindon	3.5	6.3	....	....
Manchester	5.8	7.0	10.0	10.0
Northfield	4.9	7.6	....	....
Pittsfield	5.8	7.6	....	....
Salem	5.7	8.0	....	....
Saline	5.5	6.9	10.0	10.0
Scio	5.9	7.5	....	....
Sharon	6.5	6.1	....	....
Superior	4.2	8.1	....	....
Sylvan	4.1	7.4	10.0[c]	9.8[c]
Webster	4.3	6.9	....	....
York	4.7	8.0	....	....
Ypsilanti	5.9	8.0	10.0	10.0
County Average	5.3	7.6	7.5	8.2
State Average	5.0	6.2	6.9	7.8

Sources: Michigan Superintendent of Public Instruction, *Annual Report* 5 (1841); 24 (1860); 34 (1870); 54 (1890).

[a] The data, actually from 1841, are averages of all the districts within the given township. For most townships, every or nearly every district reported. Only Ann Arbor, Lindon, Sylvan, with less than half of their districts reporting, have averages that might be suspect.

[b] After the Civil War, Michigan state superintendents no longer tabulated data for every township and district. Instead, they only reported statistics for graded districts. It is likely that the ungraded districts in Washtenaw remained below the nine and ten-month school years found in the graded districts. Also, by 1890, Michigan was reporting the length of its school year in days, not weeks. The monthly figure was calculated at the rate of 20 school days per month.

[c] The Sylvan data for 1870 and 1890 are actually from Chelsea, which was a village in Sylvan township.

Rapids, Jackson, Plymouth, and Ypsilanti, but one fourth of the seventy-two districts served fewer than 30 children between ages five and seventeen. Over one third of the districts were mid-sized, containing thirty to sixty children.[92] On the other end of the spectrum of school year lengths, many of the most rural areas of the state had not yet organized school districts at all. In Washtenaw County, the 157 districts reporting data in 1841 did not demonstrate a powerful statistical correlation between the size of the school age population and the length of schooling. Still, the forty-two Washtenaw districts running schools for a mere three months averaged 28 children between ages five and seventeen, while the 117 districts opened school for more than that averaged 39 school-aged students.[93]

The three-month school term was the most common length in Washtenaw and in Michigan as a whole in the early 1840s. Not by coincidence, three months was also the minimum amount of time a district needed to maintain school in order to tap into the state school fund. This correspondence suggests that districts' decisions about the length of school sessions were also mediated by state action, and this relationship is indicated visually on Figure 1.2. It graphs the distribution of the length of schooling among Michigan's 1,656 districts in 1842. Most significantly, the curve in Figure 1.2 does not adhere to a normal, bell-shape but rather has two peaks. Although relatively few districts ran schools for nine months or longer, a large number of districts ran schools for 5–8 months and thus one peak comes at six months. The other acme occurs at three months, which is the single largest group on the graph: 586 districts (35.4% of the total) supported schools for just three months in 1842.

The skewed data in Figure 1.2 indicate the impact of the state legislature in setting parameters for school years in Michigan during the nineteenth century. The school calendar was set at the local level, where district voters determined the length of the school year, the periods of vacation, as well as the hiring of teachers and other matters at annual town meetings.[94] At the same time, Pierce and subsequent state superintendents and legislators strove to get districts to lengthen their terms using similar legislative and administrative methods as their counterparts in New York. The sharpest prod held and earliest wielded by state educators was access to the state school fund. Pierce and Crary wrote the three-months-of-school requirement into Michigan's first state constitution of 1835.[95] The legislature's 1842 school laws retained the three-month minimum school term and denied state school funds for any district that did not comply.[96] These mandates worked to push

Figure 1.2. *Distribution of district school term lengths in Michigan, 1842*

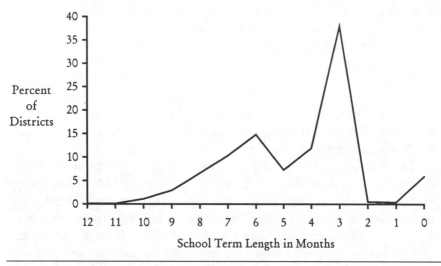

Source: Michigan Superintendent of Public Instruction, *Annual Report* 6 (1842).

districts up to the minimum but provided no incentive for them to move beyond it, resulting in the nearly 600 districts running schools for exactly three months shown on Figure 1.2. Still, the requirement boosted the length of school terms. Many districts had not previously opened schools, and student enrollments increased by six-fold from 1837 to 1839.[97] However, Figure 1.2 also illustrates the fragility of the incipient state system. Some districts were immune to the lure of state funds—15 districts averaged less than three months and 97 maintained no schools at all—and the three-month minimum left a lot of room for variation in the length of the public school year. These patterns did not unnoticed by state schoolmen.

For Michigan educators infused with the spirit of common school reform, the three-month minimum proved unsatisfactory. Pierce observed in his 1841 annual report that most districts maintained schools "just long enough to secure an apportionment of the public money, but too short to affect much in the way of education."[98] While many districts opened schools for three months to obtain funding, Pierce also noted that too often districts ran out of money and closed their schools earlier than intended or legally permissible. In other instances, schools relied on private subscriptions when common school funds ran out, making it even more difficult for students from families struggling economically to continue their school attendance.[99] In pointing out these practices, Pierce derided the localism at the heart of the public school process, but he also highlighted the connection between school finances and education conditions. Pierce criticized earlier legislation for not providing adequate support for schools and advocated higher taxes on property to ensure universal and free public education for every child. In his annual reports, Pierce foreshadowed a central concern for Michigan's antebellum educators of the next twenty years. If the state increased the minimum length requirement or sought to intensify public education in any other manner, it would also have to address its system of generating revenue for schools.

From 1840 to 1860, Michigan educators intertwined the financial and legal approaches to spurring longer rural school terms. In some ways the process was akin to the children's game of leap frog. By pursuing school reform along several avenues, superintendents could use a variety of measurements as targets to reach or surpass, such as enrollments, attendance rates, or school term length. For example, from the state superintendent's perspective, short terms partially stemmed from the growing inability of the state school fund alone to provide enough money to guarantee the three-month minimum. Because this standard was firmly established, legislators were able to raise additional taxes in the 1840s to achieve "the object required by the Constitution" and have schools in all districts open for three months.[100] Over the course of the 1840s, the average term length in Michigan increased by nearly one month, from 4.6 to 5.5 (see Figure 1.3).[101] With more and more districts reaching and surpassing the three-month school year, Pierce and other education advocates attempted to set a new goal. At an 1850 convention to revise Michigan's constitution, they proposed doubling the mandated public school term to six months. This effort failed as most convention delegates focused on "economy in state government and restriction of its authority."[102]

As the current state superintendent, Ira Mayhew, noted, in a sense Pierce had attempted to leap too far. Mayhew accepted the retention of the three-month minimum because he recognized the dependency of the school year length on school funds. He argued that money to guarantee longer sessions could not be raised without further taxes or legislation, which he ascertained, was not forthcoming. The state could raise its minimum requirement, but without additional means of funding, it would be a futile gesture. Mayhew simply refocused his efforts in another area of reform. Since recently imposed taxes ensured free schools for three months, Mayhew concentrated on raising attendance

Figure 1.3. *Length of Michigan and Washtenaw County public school sessions*

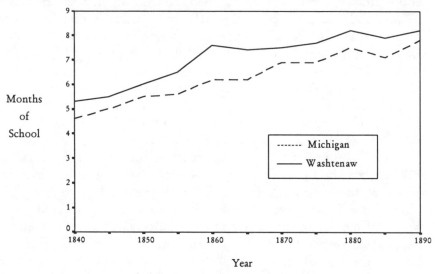

Months
of
School

Year

Source: Michigan Superintendent of Public Instruction, *Annual Report.*

levels.[103] Although the rate of increase of the length of public school years slowed under his leadership in the 1850s, it did not halt and reached a state average of 6.2 months in 1860 (see Figure 1.3).

By 1890, the average length of school sessions in Michigan extended to 7.8 months per year. After the Civil War, Michigan educators succeeded in raising length requirements for the school year by setting up a three-tiered system of mandates. In 1880, the minimum school year length for districts over 800 children jumped to nine months. For districts between 30 and 800 children it was five months and for districts under thirty children it remained three months.[104] While this new system reflected in part the fact that larger communities already instituted longer school terms, compliance with these regulations pushed many areas to increase the number of school days and state averages rose accordingly. In 1887, over 90% of Michigan's districts ran schools six months or more, and 36% supported schools for nine months or longer.[105]

In reading the 1880s reports of state superintendent Joseph Estabrook, one might think that not much had changed. Sounding like his predecessors, Estabrook derided districts that opened schools just three months a year in order "to share in the apportionment of the primary school interest fund and the one mill tax."[106] Accusing these schools of "a false idea of economy," he suggested raising the minimum to six months as in New York, Ohio, Iowa, and California, or at least to four months to be consistent with Michigan's compulsory education laws. He argued that since some districts could afford school for five months yet ran them for three, significant segments of the population still did not accept the value of public education.[107] Certainly many districts' terms remained below the nine plus months desired by Estabrook, but he seemed to lack historical perspective on this matter. Estabrook overlooked the overall irrelevance of the legal minimum for most districts by 1887, when most Michigan towns met and surpassed the five-month minimum term required of them. That year, only 8.2% of Michigan's districts maintained schools for five months or less, a much smaller proportion exhibiting minimal or noncompliance with the requirement than in 1842. The overall distribution of school terms lengths in 1887—as identified on Figure 1.4—demonstrated a far more normal shaped curve than the 1842 distribution graphed on Figure 1.2. Furthermore, the number of students enrolled in a school open for three months or less was only 3,980—less than 1% of the total number of public school students.[108] Compared to the antebellum period, far more communities in 1890 adhered to the spirit of common school reform by surpassing the letter of current Michigan law regarding the length of the public school year, even though the law on school terms was more demanding by then. A good number of these localities lay in Washtenaw County.

Figure 1.4. *Distribution of district school term lengths in Michigan, 1887*

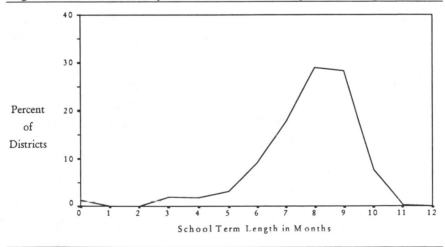

Source: Michigan Superintendent of Public Instruction, *Annual Report* 51 (1887).

Calendar reform at the county level

Washtenaw County led Michigan in the nineteenth-century movement toward public education and school reform. Situated due west of Detroit, located in between the state's largest city and its capital at Lansing, and site of the University of Michigan, Washtenaw consistently placed at or near the top of Michigan counties in many public education indicators used by reformers to measure advancement.[109] Length of schooling was no exception; in 1841, Washtenaw's average school year (5.3 months) was slightly longer than the whole state's (5.0 months). Over the next fifty years, the county experienced significant increases in the average length of its public school year (See Table 1.7). In 1841, no township averaged more than 6.5 months of school. After the Civil War, the county's graded school districts typically opened schools for ten months and the county's average reached 8.2 months by 1890. Compared to the state as a whole, Washtenaw's average school year was longer in 1841 and remained so past 1890. It also increased earlier than in other areas of Michigan. For Washtenaw, the crucial period of growth occurred from 1840 to 1860, when the county average rose from 5.3 to 7.6 months. The state average started at 5.0 months in 1840 but only reached 6.2 months by 1860. In other parts of Michigan, the more substantial growth occurred after the Civil War so that by 1890, the gap between the state and Washtenaw county had narrowed again to one half month (See Figure 1.3).

These differences in the length of sessions and time of growth notwithstanding, the experience of Washtenaw County presents typical trends in school year development. Because it was in the vanguard of school reform, Washtenaw highlights the organizational changes that eventually removed summer terms and produced a longer school year statewide. Much of the data from Washtenaw also resembles patterns found for the state as a whole. For example, a breakdown of the 1842 school term lengths by district roughly paralleled the Michigan figures. Figure 1.5 superimposes the distribution of school year lengths in Washtenaw County over the state distribution presented in Figure 1.2. It too displays a double-peaked curve at three and six months. It also shows that in Washtenaw a larger percentage of the county's districts supported schools for more than the three-month minimum while none ran schools for less than three months. Nevertheless, like the state, the county reported a plurality of districts at three months of school, indicating the effect of the legal minimum even in Washtenaw. These data corroborate the impact of the initial state requirements on the actual duration of the school term in many districts.

Figure 1.5. *Distribution of school term lengths in Washtenaw County and Michigan, 1842*

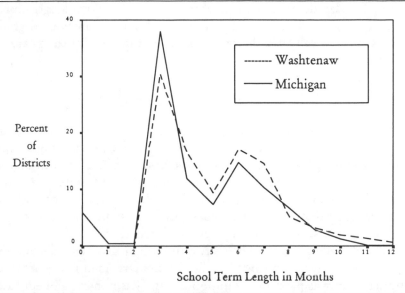

Source: Michigan Superintendent of Public Instruction, *Annual Report* 51 (1887).

The commonalty of the three-month term coupled with the variance between the districts, more than county or statewide diversity, led Michigan educators to consider methods of raising and standardizing school conditions. One solution they chose was the consolidation of tiny districts into town systems so that provisions for education, including the length of the school year, would be less uneven.[110] They spent years promoting this reform, but the first legislative effort to create a township school district system failed in 1861. By then many districts had already consolidated no doubt due in part to the bully pulpit used by the state superintendents. The process was hardly complete, but Washtenaw had reduced its districts from 213 in 1841 to 121 in 1858, so much so that by 1860 the superintendent tabulated data at the township, not district, level.[111] The Washtenaw data from Table 1.7 show a two-month average increase in school terms from 1840 to 1860 and suggest a link between term length and school organization. By then, no consolidated district maintained its schools for less than six months, and one had reached nearly nine.

Introducing a graded system presented another possible means of lengthening the school year. Table 1.7 suggests a correlation between the adoption of age-based grades by Washtenaw's larger towns, such as

Ann Arbor, Dexter, and Saline, and the continued expansion of their school years. The data indicate that graded districts in Washtenaw experienced a decade of substantial growth in school term length during the 1860s. By the decade's end, Washtenaw's larger towns used graded systems and typically ran their schools for ten months of the year with a summer vacation. From 1860 to 1870, Ann Arbor's term rose by 1.1 months, Dexter's by 2.8 months, and Saline's by 3.1 months. Even without data for the nongraded districts, it seems likely that most of them did not grow much during and immediately after the Civil War. In the 1860s, Washtenaw's county average rose by only 0.2 months despite the vast growth of terms in graded districts, suggesting sluggish if not stagnant growth among non-graded districts. Thus the consolidated and graded systems became the model for the state superintendents. Their increasing prominence throughout the county and state only encouraged attacks on the older district system and single schoolhouses for their short terms and other deficiencies.

School leaders also sought to revamp when sessions occurred during the year by restructuring the school calendar. As in many areas, the summer term was particularly unpopular in Washtenaw, and educators there forcefully assaulted it after the Civil War. Long after Pierce left his state position, he served as Washtenaw's first county superintendent, and at an 1867 conference for the new officials he vehemently orated for the abolition of the summer term. His colleagues unanimously adopted Pierce's position and successfully pressed for his paper's publication in the annual report of the state superintendent.[112] The movement to eliminate summer sessions received statewide support, but while the tradition was undermined in many rural districts, the data from Washtenaw also indicate its resiliency. In the early 1870s, summer terms remained nearly as common as winter terms. In 1870, for example, 157 Washtenaw districts supported winter terms and 149 financed summer terms; in 1871 the differential was ten districts.[113] George Wheeler, Pierce's successor in Washtenaw, continued efforts to remove the summer terms. At his urging, districts began replacing the winter and summer, two-term calendar with a three-term system that did not include July and August. Still, progress did not move quickly enough for Wheeler, as he noted in 1873 that over half of the districts clung to the old system.[114] By 1890, however, most districts in Washtenaw used the three-term schedule. Educators dropped summer but incorporated the spring and fall seasons into the school schedule, which encouraged a longer school year.

Were the summer and winter terms really as dissimilar as Pierce, Wheeler, and others claimed? Critics harped mostly on uneven attendance rates between summer and winter terms but offered no systematic data to support this contention.[115] The clearest difference between the two terms was the sex of the winter and summer staffs. As in New York, the winter teacher typically did not teach the summer term, and in most cases a woman replaced a man for the summer session. In 1870, 80 of the 157 Washtenaw County winter term teachers were men; that summer, only three men and a whopping 146 women taught. The 1871 records display a similar contrast, with just four men teaching the summer term.[116] Furthermore, pay rates favored male, winter-term teachers, who averaged $34.18 monthly in 1871. Women earned much less, but those who taught in the winter fared better than in the summer. In 1870, the former averaged $19.20 a month and the latter only $14.99.[117] Wheeler documented an additional pattern, that the "pernicious" practice of boarding around was more prevalent during summer terms. In 1873, he found that 79% of summer teachers were boarded compared to 53% in the winter.[118] While these disparities generated the dissatisfaction of educators, to some extent they also reflect the weakening of the summer term gradually underway since the first generation of common school reformers. Especially in Washtenaw County but certainly statewide, from 1840 to 1890, school leaders lengthened the rural school year and diminished summer's place in it.

The School Year in Virginia

Michigan provided public education from its inception; New York nearly did so, but not Virginia. In colonial times, Virginia's planter elite hired private tutors for their children's education, African-American slaves who became literate did so on the sly, and some communities opened "old field schools" to provide a rudimentary education for the white freeholder or agricultural laborer's children.[119] These schools ran short school sessions where summer education was the norm. As an early school chronicler noted, "it was the custom in the seventeenth century and for much of the eighteenth for the schools to be in session from April to September, instead of during the winter months as at present."[120] One fledgling Virginia institution, the Symms Free School, ran sessions continuously, and by the nineteenth century, field schools were equally as common in the winter as in the summer.

Satisfied with a rudimentary patchwork of schools, Virginians resisted the formation of a common school system. As governor, Thomas Jefferson could not get his 1779 plan for public education enacted. In 1818, free school advocates lost a close vote in the state legislature for the establishment of public education. Nevertheless, some counties started to open schools to educate the children of the poor. Henrico County began these schools in 1818, opened them intermittently until 1836, and ran them regularly until the onset of the Civil War.[121] In 1846, the state legislature provided for a system of voluntary primary schools, but even this optional plan required a two-thirds vote of approval by county electors for any local school initiative. Due to these stipulations and general hostility towards a school system, only nine counties created public schools prior to the Civil War. The legislation was also limited because it did not establish the state supervision and funding found in most states north of the Mason-Dixon Line.[122] Although sentiment for free common schools remained tangible in Virginia throughout the antebellum period, it was never powerful enough to generate a statewide system on par with Michigan's or New York's. Educational options for the ruling plantation class had expanded during these years, with more private schools, colleges, and especially academies available, but the bulk of Virginia's white and black population remained unschooled.[123]

Virginia launched common schools statewide following the Civil War. In order to regain admission to the United States, the state's new constitution mandated a system of free public education. Although the 1870 constitution did not require a minimum length for the schools, it did contain a host of provisions for public education increasingly found in nineteenth-century state constitutions. It established a state board of education, state and county superintendents, and several sources of revenue, including an annual capitation tax on the property of the state, a county or district tax, and interest from a preexisting Literary Fund.[124] The Virginia General Assembly then acted to fulfill the constitutional requirements. It elected William Ruffner as the state's first superintendent and legislated the essential design for a school system he submitted in 1870. Ruffner's plan expected the state to cover about half of the school costs and individual counties the other half, with incidental school expenses paid by the local district. Following the practice long used by northern school superintendents, he proposed that districts open for at least five months and maintain a certain level of average attendance in order to receive state school money.[125] In this endeavor Ruffner was successful but as it turned out, five months was more appropriate as an initial goal rather than as a minimum level of acceptability.

The inaugural year of Virginia's common school system was quite brief. The available figures on the length of schooling indicate that rural districts throughout the state opened schools short of the obligatory five months. Table 1.8 presents data on the average school year length for Virginia, Henrico County, and leading communities in both the state and county. In a turbulent first year, the state itself only averaged 4.7 months in 1871. In rural Henrico County, where some of towns opened schools for less than four months, the mean was even lower. Having worked out some of the initial kinks in the state system, in 1872 Virginia's average school year length rose to 5.7 months. Ruffner noted with pleasure "the addition of more than a month in the average length of the school session, calling it "a most gratifying increase of school privileges over the first year."[126] The towns of Henrico County experienced even larger jumps: Brookland's term went from 4.8 to 6.2 months, and Varina's increased by nearly three months.

Table 1.8. *Length (in months) of Virginia cities and Henrico County public school sessions, 1870–90*

Locality	1871	1872	1876	1881	1886	1891
Alexandria	5.0	10.0	10.0	10.0	10.0	9.8
Fredericksburg	4.1	9.0	10.0	10.0	10.0	9.2
Lynchburg	2.9	5.6	9.6	9.8	9.0	9.7
Manchester	5.6	. . . .	9.0	9.0	7.0	9.0
Norfolk	9.9	10.0	9.6	9.5	10.0	9.6
Petersburg	10.0	10.0	9.3	9.0	9.5	9.2
Richmond	9.0	9.0	9.0	9.0	9.0	9.0
Staunton	5.8	. . . .	10.0	10.0	9.0	9.0
City Average	6.4	8.7	9.6	9.5	9.2	9.3
Brookland	4.8	6.2	. . . .	9.0[a]	6.9	9.0
Fairfield	3.9	5.2	. . . .	6.0[a]	7.5	8.0
Tuckahoe	4.7	5.5	. . . .	. . . .	7.0	8.0
Varina	3.6	6.5	. . . .	. . . .	5.9	6.0
Henrico County Average	4.3	5.8	7.0	6.6	6.8	7.8
Virginia Average	4.7	5.7	5.6	5.9	5.9	5.8

Sources: Virginia Superintendent of Public Instruction, *Annual Report.* 1–21 (1871–91); U.S. Commissioner of Education, *Annual Report.* Washington: Government Printing Office, 1871–91.

[a] Data for graded schools only.

After this year of quick growth, the term lengths in Virginia grew only slightly over the next twenty years. The state's average school year reached over six months in 1883 and 1887, but by 1891 it was still at 5.8 months. Therefore Ruffner remained dissatisfied with the school sessions in Virginia despite most districts' compliance with state law by 1872. He expressed particular outrage at districts which showed "a reprehensible disregard of law" by running schools for less than the five-month legal minimum and saw "the lengthening of the school term to nine or ten months" as an essential task.[127] It was not, however, his immediate goal. Ruffner held a more lenient view of the term lengths in his state than his northern counterparts in Michigan and New York. Ruffner believed that a host of other educational issues took precedence in Virginia's incipient public schools. More than lengthening the typical school term, he struggled to provide schools to all areas of the state and to overcome substantial pockets of hostility.[128] Like many superintendents, Ruffner recognized early on in his tenure that "the financial question lies at the root of all educational prosperity and presents the only remaining difficulty remaining to be overcome."[129]

At the local level, many of Virginia's county superintendents lacked Ruffner's tolerance for short school terms. County superintendents linked a number of shortcomings to the abbreviated school term, such as irregular attendance, unsatisfactory schoolwork, poor teachers, and insufficient schools.[130] When asked to make suggestions on how to improve efficiency in the public schools for the 1890 annual state report, twenty-nine out of Virginia's ninety-seven county superintendents recommended a longer school term.[131] One of these educators came from Henrico County, which made a more concerted effort to lengthen its school terms in the 1870s and 1880s than other areas of the state. A brief examination of Henrico illustrates this local struggle to expand the school year. Henrico County surrounds without including the state capital of Richmond, but in the nineteenth century it remained mostly rural. With no large cities and even few towns, four communities ran their own school districts, and the county superintendent administered the remaining schools. Table 1.8 compares the school year lengths of these four communities with the county and state averages. In examining the data, four distinct patterns warrant notice.

First, school terms lengthened overall among the towns and villages of Henrico and at a faster rate of increase than the state as a whole. Among Henrico's towns, Brookland's school year lengthened from 4.8 months in 1871 to 9.0 months in 1891. Similarly, Fairfield's year rose from 3.9 months in 1871 to 8.0 months in 1891. The other two towns experienced substantial growth as well, partially accounting for a countywide increase from 4.3 months in 1871 to 7.8 months in 1891. Even with a particularly large jump from 1871 to 1872, Henrico's school terms continued to expand over the next twenty years while other areas in Virginia did not. A number of structural factors help explain the rapid development of Henrico's schools: its central location and proximity to Richmond, the number of sizable towns in its midst, its less rural economy relative to more outlying areas.[132] But Henrico also benefited from the leadership of a series of county superintendents—from Daniel Gardner to John Fussell—and the willingness of the county's citizens to tax themselves for schools. By the mid-1880s, Fussell observed that "an increasing interest is manifested [in public schools], checked mainly by want of funds to open more schools and lengthen the terms."[133] Though still not satisfied with the school sessions and other conditions of their district, Henrico superintendents had reached much higher levels of public schooling than their peers elsewhere in Virginia.

Second, Henrico did not start out as a leader in Virginia for school-term lengths. Unlike Westchester and Washtenaw counties, Henrico began with sessions below Virginia's state average. In the initial year of Virginia's public schools, Henrico terms averaged 4.3 months compared to a statewide figure of 4.7 months. Although Table 1.8 indicates that Henrico surpassed Virginia in 1872, the state and county averages actually fluctuated twice during the 1870s. In 1874 and 1879, Henrico's average dipped below Virginia's average to 5.0 and 5.3 months, respectively, suggesting a tenuous existence for nascent pubic schools even in Henrico. By 1880, however, Henrico's average outdistanced the state's for good. In the 1880s, its length of schooling typically exceeded Virginia's by a full month, and the gap widened further after 1890. In 1891, Henrico's 7.8 month average was two full months longer than Virginia's. Thus Henrico moved quickly from a below-average county to a pacesetter for the state with regard to school terms.

Third, the length of public school years in Virginia was substantially lower than in Michigan and New York. In 1890, New York averaged over nine months of school and Michigan nearly eight, compared to Virginia's 5.9 months. Even Henrico's 7.8 average fell far below Westchester's (9.8) in 1891, though closer to Washtenaw's (8.2). These differences are not hard to explain; in fact, they highlight regional variations in schooling long recognizable to scholars and contemporaries. In 1870, Virginia started its public schools practically from the ground up amid much public hostility, whereas both New York and Michigan enjoyed long traditions of statewide educational development. Throughout the 1870s, pro- and anti-school forces battled to take control of Virginia's schools.[134] Opposition to the public school system came to a head after the Reconstruction government was overturned. In 1878, the legislature diverted school funds to other purposes and attempted to abolish the county superintendent position. The impact of its actions was immediate; Ruffner feared with prescience that 100,000 children would be excluded from schools due to closings. From 1878 to 1879, the number of schools opened dropped from 4,545 to 2,491, the number of students enrolled also nearly halved, falling from 202,244 to 108,074, and average daily attendance declined from 116,464 to 65,771. In the midst of this "attempt to destroy our school system," the state's school year length stayed essentially the same, possibly due to a decline the previous year and mostly because these other drops absorbed the loss of funds.[135]

Henrico County was not immune to this statewide dissent. Unlike Virginia as a whole, its school session length average did fall precipitously from 6.7 months in 1878 to 5.3 in 1879. Indeed the county average rose or dropped by a half a month or more several times during the 1870s. When Daniel Gardner took over as county superintendent in 1874, he discovered many schools languishing for a lack of money to pay salaries and buy supplies and found not a single school open in Varina. Much of resistance to public schools stemmed from the larger political struggle against reconstructed Virginia. As Gardner observed, "there is still a deep-seated prejudice with some against the system, and this can never be removed while the abominable 'civil rights' agitation is an open question."[136] Although Virginia gained readmittance to the union later than most Southern states, it experienced an early Democratic overthrow of the Reconstruction government. After 1876, Gardner reported the gradual dissipation of school animosity and increased "demand for longer sessions and more schools."[137] As a result, Henrico's school terms increased rapidly in the 1880s following the uneven growth of the 1870s.

Fourth, school terms in Virginia's towns and villages lagged far behind its more urban areas. In 1871 city terms averaged 6.4 months compared to the 4.7 figure for the entire state. Unlike New York, the difference between the city and state averages widened over time to well over three months, as the mean for urban areas quickly surpassed nine months and stayed at that level through 1891. A number of cities ran ten-month school sessions, and Richmond steadfastly maintained a nine-month school year throughout this period. In Henrico County, only the town of Brookland consistently ran schools for nine months by 1891. The origins of this gap lay in economic and ideological conditions that predisposed urban populaces to establish more substantial forms of education, but this typical American pattern was mitigated in Virginia because it did not have much of a public school tradition prior to the Civil War. As a post-war creation of the state, Virginia's public schools need not have followed the norms for school year lengths found in states like Michigan and New York. The state, however, encouraged the discrepancies between urban and rural schools by enacting finance laws that distinguished between the two types of areas. Virginia school finance law allowed cities and towns to levy up to three mills on the dollar, while most crucially, counties could only levy up to two mills on the dollar for school purposes.[138]

To close the gap, Virginia superintendents sought to raise rural school terms, but they lacked many of the means for rural school reform used by their northern counterparts. Superintendents relied on the five-month term requirement, but the force of the mandate lessened over time because most districts came to open schools for more than five months. State educators did not even attempt to raise the minimum level until after 1890, for an unpopular increase might have only led to greater disregard for the law. Likewise, Virginia's school organization by county made any township consolidation movement inapplicable to the effort to raise school terms. Another option open to school reformers was the generation of revenue, but they rarely expected to receive increased state funding of schools. Even if they persuaded localities to supplement state funds, they recognized that the numerous needs of the schools could overwhelm meager resources.[139] When additional money was found for schools, communities faced a host of ways to spend it other than lengthening the terms in existing schools. Finally, short school terms complemented the agricultural life of Virginia's citizens.[140] In fact, opening schools for longer and different periods of time might not have spurred any greater attendance from students expected to work in the fields in the spring, summer, and fall. Given all these barriers to calendar reform, a seemingly simple but odd plan advocated by Ruffner becomes comprehensible. Ruffner favored the opening of nearby county schoolhouses for alternate five-month periods, enabling students to attend for up to ten months and districts to hire just one teacher who could work for ten months.[141] While his plan was never adopted in any widespread numbers, its very suggestion indicates the difficulties in using means more commonly employed by superintendents in Michigan and New York to achieve longer school terms.

In short, the data from Virginia confirm the most important findings from Michigan and New York. In the early nineteenth century, rural school years were brief and included the summer as a substantial part of an overall inchoate school program. In the middle and latter third of the century school superintendents strove to reform the school calendar by standardizing it. Rural schools were increasingly opened in the spring and fall and closed in the summer. The legislative and organizational procedures that educators used to achieve reform suggest a strong relationship between school term lengths and the structure and financing of public schools. Although conflict over school schedules alone was rare, the issue became politicized when common school reformers battled with local, Democratic, and other oppositional forces over their program for schooling. In this way, the school calendar became caught up in larger educational issues.

Conclusion

As a whole, the data presented here suggest several points worth reiterating. First, this chapter's depiction of the school schedule is more subtle than popular conceptions, which hold that today's academic calendar developed as a logical response to agrarian work requirements and rural lifestyles. What agricultural labor patterns explain is not the current practice of a September to June school year with a summer vacation but the early nineteenth-century rural school year outlined in this chapter. What then accounts for the replacement of the summer and winter term schedule in the latter half of the nineteenth century? While structural factors such as the growth of cities, the improvement of rural roads, and changes in rural labor practices all fostered the transition of the school year, this chapter demonstrates that an activist government induced the transformation as well. Incipient school bureaucracies developed as states monitored and manipulated local compliance on school term durations and other educational features.

Second, this study establishes the summer term as a substantial component of early public education. The historical literature generally treats the summer sessions from the perspective of the common school reformers, who like John Pierce saw them as "untimely and inappropriate."[142] Traditional historiography posits summer terms, like many educational practices of the new republic, as a dated practice ripe for replacement. Thus in the work of Ellwood Cubberley and others, they are only significant for their rudimentary instruction, eventual demise, and symbolism of another victory for Mann and his contemporaries.[143] More recent works submerge the cessation of summer terms under the overall lengthening of school years and attendance even though these were separate, yet clearly related, trends.[144] The eventual elimination of the summer term should not obscure the reality that students attended and teachers taught summer classes in almost the same numbers as in the winter, that they studied and instructed in essentially the same subjects during both seasons, and that many continued to do so well after 1860.

Finally, the data from the nineteenth century suggest the gradual and initially tenuous nature of school calendar reform. County and state educational figures were not steamrollers; local school districts could be resistant to or unaffected by the pressures of consolidation, mandatory minimum terms, or higher school taxes. As a result, the intertwined processes of expanding rural school years and removing summer terms began as early as 1840 yet remained incomplete fifty years later. By 1890, though, the alteration of public school calendars was proceeding steadily towards completion. Aided by the "closing of the frontier" and the countless ways in which rural areas became less socially distant from their urban counterparts, school officials continued their efforts to expand schooling until a standard 180-day, nine-month rural school year was finally reached in the twentieth century. By then, most cities had reached that standard as well, and the vastly different route that they followed is the subject of Chapter Two.

CHAPTER TWO

"No More Rulers, No More Books": *The Elimination of Summer Terms from the Nineteenth-Century Urban School Calendar*

In his 1892 annual report, United States Commissioner of Education William Torrey Harris identified a startling pattern in the public schools of the largest cities in the United States. Over the previous fifty years, all of them had experienced a substantial contraction in the length of their school terms, with most nearing (but not yet reaching) the 180-day school year that became the standard in the twentieth century. New York's school year, for example, fell from approximately 245 days in 1842 to 202.5 days in 1892. Chicago's decreased from 240 days to 192 days over the same span. Other cities witnessed similar declines: from 251.5 to 201 days in Philadelphia, from 259 to 196 days in Detroit, and from 240 to 195 days in Buffalo.[1] The commissioner of education noted this trend with some alarm. Citing a corresponding dwindling of the number of hours per school day, the accrual of new holidays, the elimination of Saturday classes, and the incorporation of many additional, nonacademic subjects into the school curriculum, Harris bemoaned "the steady reduction that our schools have suffered." He denigrated the wisdom of an earlier generation, which had presided over the shrinkage not through oversight but as an avowed policy. Thus he held the "numerous advocates of shorter daily sessions and shorter terms" responsible for the calendar reforms to which he objected.[2]

Commissioner Harris' analysis, however, omitted two important aspects of urban school year shrinkage. First, Harris failed to acknowledge that these great metropolises were exceptional cases. Over the course of the nineteenth century, school terms typically grew in duration. As Chapter One demonstrated, while large urban school systems and smaller cities subtracted days from their school calendars, many towns and most rural districts lengthened their school years substantially. Second, Harris neglected to consider that these cities all chose a similar means of shortening the length of their school year: the creation of a two-month summer vacation. Before the Civil War, city schools were commonly open forty-eight weeks a year, and school boards generally divided the four weeks of vacation, granting one week off after each quarter. Then cities began to apply their four vacation weeks to August and to remove additional school days from the summer months. By century's end, summer terms were all but extinct in cities.

How summer became absent from the shortened urban school year is largely overlooked. Studies of incipient urban school systems are abundant, but they rarely address the topic of school year lengths and almost never isolate the summer quarter for analysis.[3] This omission occurs in part because historians of education often adopt a pluralist framework for explaining the policy outcomes of highly contentious education issues.[4] Admittedly, the duration and timing of school sessions did not generate much interest, let alone conflict, among most individual citizens and social groups. Nevertheless, the exploration of this historical silence reveals much about the meanings of schooling for nineteenth-century participants. In addition, the tranquility surrounding school calendars was never complete, and the periodic outbursts offer insight into the institutional and ideological concerns of schoolmen.

This chapter traces the nineteenth-century evolution of urban school calendars. It identifies the distinct features of the summer term that made it expendable and outlines the process of reducing the terms in two American cities. It begins with a brief treatment of the decline in Detroit in order to convey a basic sense of the pace and timing of urban school calendar reform. The bulk of the discussion focuses on New York City, from which more suitable though never abundant sources exist. Through the case of New York, this chapter will tease out the contours of calendar transformation in greater depth. While not generalizable to the rest of the nation's cities, the patterns identified in New York are suggestive of the changes occurring in cities throughout the Northeast and Midwest. Indeed the stages of school calendar reform are hard to dispute; why such school calendars unfolded is less readily discernible.

Nineteenth-century school calendar reform requires an eclectic interpretation. The transformation of the urban school calendar occurred in a context of old social practices, new economic and demographic conditions, bureaucratic imperatives, and financial parameters. This chapter explores these avenues, and the next one looks at the ideologies that accompanied them. Creating a summer vacation reflected some fundamental beliefs about the fragility of human health and the desirability of time for mental rejuvenation and professional development. Yet Harris' interpretation also yields a significant truth—that many educators did push to shorten city school years. These schoolmen were no doubt driven by summer traditions, funding availability, and medical assumptions, but this chapter emphasizes the power of popular practices regarding time—practices of holiday and celebrations as much as work. Thus the creation and expansion of summer vacation by school officials was not entirely a proactive exercise. In New York, central authorities reacted to student attendance patterns, local school and ward inclinations, teacher needs, and eventually national events. Such concerns may also lay at the heart of the transformation that occurred in Detroit.

School Calendar Change in Detroit

As Michigan's largest town and an urban center even before its automotive industrial growth, Detroit typifies the pattern of urban school calendar transformation. The demise of the summer session in Detroit preceded its elimination in rural areas, and the city arrived at a three-term school year from a four—not two—term calendar. This development emerged concurrently with the piecemeal reduction in Detroit's school year during its first fifty years of public education. Detroit inaugurated its public schools in 1841, and that year a haphazard constellation of schools opened their doors from three to nine months.[5] In 1842, an act by the state legislature created the city's board of education and school system. Required to run schools for only three months like the rest of Michigan, Detroit's first school year contained 259 school days divided into four quarters with one week of vacation after each and a short recess over Christmas and during the summer. While most children enrolled did not attend school all year, a substantial minority did. In 1843 for example, 30% (324 of the 1,093) of the enrolled students came for the entire school year, including the summer.[6]

The initial calendar, however, stirred substantial dissatisfaction. Because the Christmas and summer break did not coincide with the end of the term, the schedule "occasioned great confusion, and almost entirely disorganized the schools." In order to end terms at desired vacation times, Detroit switched in 1849 to a three-term calendar with just forty-four weeks of school, two weeks vacation at Christmas, two in April, and four weeks off in August.[7] Designed partly to free the summer for vacation, this three-term school year nevertheless retained a spring-summer term that ran through most of July and remained a vital part of Detroit's school year. Summer enrollments did not tail off during July, the course of study remained the same, and attendance in that term compared favorably to the autumn and winter. In 1852, for example, the winter term ended on April 10 with 2,644 students, the spring-summer term ended on July 23 with 2,690 students, and the fall term closed on December 18 with 2,783 students.[8]

Once created, the summer vacation accelerated the dwindling of the spring-summer term. In 1850, D. Bethune Duffield, Detroit's secretary to its board of education, observed that the city's nineteen schools ran continuously "excepting the ordinary vacation of four weeks in August," but this summer vacation was to double within ten years.[9] By manipulating the three-term calendar, Detroit school board members further reduced the school year and the summer term in particular. In 1860, switching vacation times resulted in a reduced school year of forty-two weeks. Moreover, the board cut Christmas and April vacations to one week each in order to add four additional vacation weeks to the summer. In the new calendar, students now received eight weeks off in July and August, and schools opened 211 days per year. These changes disrupted the relative balance and equity between the three terms. The spring term, at fifty-five days, was substantially shorter than the fall (eighty-six days) and the winter (seventy days) terms.[10]

By 1867, Detroit's new board of education regulations only required a forty-week school year. Surprisingly, no reasons were given for this or any of the earlier reductions. While it seems likely that economic conditions mattered, the declines did not coincide with any great fiscal crisis faced by the city's schools. To a large extent, board members seemingly sought to meet popular demands and rationalize a chaotic system through calendar reform. Perhaps some equilibrium was reached, as Detroit's forty-week school year remained intact until after 1900. During the latter third of the century, when it set the dates of the three school terms and intervening vacations at its September meeting, the board typically included all of July and August in the summer vacation.[11] In short, twenty-five years of tinkering from 1842 to 1867 decreased the city's school year and removed the summer from it. These two developments were intertwined and mutually reinforcing. As the evidence from Detroit suggests, school leaders shortened the urban school year by removing summer classes from the public school schedule. That they did so with little fanfare proves frustrating for historical scholarship today, but New York City followed similar trends and left a deeper and wider though still not bountiful array of evidence.

School Calendar Change in New York

The origin of public education in New York City is a well-established story.[12] For over two hundred years, a smattering of schools—run by schoolmasters, churches, and eventually charity organizations—served some of the city's population. One of the latter, the Free School Society began to educate an increasing number (as many as 20,000 by one estimate) of poor children after 1805. By 1825 it had become a fierce advocate for free schooling for all, and the following year it renamed itself the Public School Society [PSS] after gaining nearly sole access to public funding.[13] In 1842, it achieved a Pyrrhic victory in the city's first "great school war" over Catholic presence in public education and public funding of Catholic education.[14] The state legislature created a nonsectarian common school system for the city, but it was administered not by the PSS but by a separate board of education and neighborhood school wards. The PSS schools remained in operation but were diminished in importance as the city expanded its ward schools during the 1840s. Dual systems of education coexisted uneasily in New York for over ten years until the two merged in 1853. The PSS became defunct and its schools submerged under the direction of the board of education—submerged but not sunk.[15] Many of the subsequent routines and policies adopted by the board of education stemmed from the initial practices of the PSS, and the structure of the school calendar was no exception to this pattern.[16]

Public education in 1840s New York was a year-round affair, as urban schooling had been for many years. Schools of all types were almost always open: morning and afternoons, weekdays and Saturdays, January and July. The PSS had long divided the school year into quarters of three months each, beginning in the months of August, November, February, and May. Although it had eliminated Saturday classes by 1830, it held sessions twice a day, five days a week, with school holidays on Christmas, New Year's Day, the fourth of July, and Thanksgiving. The PSS schools also offered "the usual vacation of three weeks" in the month of August.[17] Even with such time off, the PSS expected its schools to open for 250 days a year. However, by 1842 the society recognized that numerous factors made it unlikely that any school would be open that many days or that each school would be open for the same number of days. That year, the PSS schools averaged 245 days; in 1845 the schools averaged 240 days but a handful ran for fewer than 200 days. The new ward schools opened sporadically in 1843 and displayed greater variation in length than the PSS schools despite following a similar schedule of school days. In 1844, the newly established public schools ranged from 231 to 245 days per year.[18]

What accounted for this initial pattern of school terms running nearly year round? The few celebratory holidays granted were already firmly established in their religious or nationalistic importance. The August recess reflected the precedent of some colonial schools as well as longstanding vacation practices of the wealthy PSS patrons—who typically escaped to their country estates during the hottest or plague-ridden portions of the summer.[19] Kaestle and Vinovskis have offered other compelling explanations for the length of urban schooling in the early nineteenth century. They concluded that year-round schooling reflected the nature of urban work—it was non-seasonal and increasingly located outside of the household—and the desires of the elites who ran the charity schools to draw in as many poor and immigrant children as possible. Although the records of the PSS include no specific discussion of the rationale for its school calendar, such reasoning is plausible in the case of New York. PSS records do show a large concern for retaining scholars and repeatedly claim that average attendance figures underestimated actual student presence. Of course the intended students and their families rarely complied with the wishes of the philanthropists in the matter of school attendance.[20]

Most children who attended the early public schools in New York City did not do so for the full length of the school year. Antebellum urban students came for as little as one month and as much as twelve months of school. For example, in 1851 most New York City school children spent fewer than eight months in school, and only 1% came for the full year. Across the river, school officials in Brooklyn reported that over 21% of its students attended for twelve months in 1850,

Table 2.1. *Seasonal attendance at Public School Society institutions, 1831–42*

Year	August to Oct.	Nov. to Jan.	Feb. to April	May to July
1831–32	7,386	7,223	7,223	8,148
1832–33	9,151	9,390	9,234	8,550
1833–34	11,390	13,132	13,519	12,108
1834–35	17,329	17,246	16,819	17,980
1835–36	18,433	17,192	16,319	20,101
1836–37	17,543	17,457	17,346	19,382
1837–38	19,950	19,658	19,216	21,205
1838–39	20,481	20,755	19,756	22,831
1839–40	22,096	22,542	23,120	24,064
1840–41	23,949	23,290	22,585	24,793
1841–42	24,530	24,267	24,683	25,186

Source: Public School Society, *Annual Reports* 27–38 (1832–43).

but more than half of its students still came for fewer than six months a year.[21] New York City's surprisingly low year-round total may only indicate different patterns of reporting, as 23.4% of its students attended school for ten to twelve months, compared to 11.6% in Brooklyn.[22] Combined, both cities schooled over one-fourth of their students—around 30,000 children—for at least ten months around 1850. This figure was far higher than for most rural communities, but urban attendance rates were actually lower than rural ones because schools were open year round.[23] Most telling is that by 1860, state superintendents no longer tabulated the number of students who attended school for twelve months because such a category proved meaningless by then—even in New York.

If regularity of urban school attendance remained an elusive goal at mid-century, the timing of attendance was rather evenly dispersed throughout the year. Evidence on the question of when students sat in class comes from the PSS, whose records are distilled in Table 2.1.[24] The table illustrates that while the school quarters did not correspond neatly with the four seasons, students were not deterred from attending school in the summer. In fact, for most years the May-July quarter was the most populous season for school attendance—such as in 1837–38, when its attendance surpassed 21,000 and the other three quarters totaled under 20,000. In the years when it was not, it always attracted a proportionate number of the city's children. Neither the PSS nor its board of education successor ever reported statistics on the quarterly teaching cohorts or curricula, but the absence of seasonal distinctions speaks volumes. There is no reason to believe that either the teachers or the subjects that they taught varied much from one quarter to another.[25] In short, the seasonal variations in schooling that were noticeable in rural areas appear negligible in New York City. Nevertheless, the city eliminated schooling in the summer as it shortened its overall school year during the rest of the nineteenth century.

The first phase of school calendar transformation in New York: 1842-55

William Torrey Harris may have been unhappy with the loss of over forty days from New York's school year between 1842 and 1892, but the decline hardly raised a stir in the city. For one thing, there were few changes abrupt enough to draw notice. Figure 2.1, which plots the average length of school terms annually, indicates that the process was gradual and steady in the long run but inconsistent on a year-to-year basis. Still, Figure 2.1 highlights two intervals of more pronounced decline that merit particular study: 1842 to 1855 and 1864 to 1875. The first was the era of dual management of New York's fledgling public schools. By 1854, after the board of education took over the administration of the PSS schools, the combined average was 224 days, a decrease of twenty-one from 1842. While the Civil War did not correspond with a severe reduction in school days, the ten years following the war marked a second period of steeper decline. In 1865, the city reported a school year of 225 days; in 1875 that number had dropped to 203. The numbers fluctuated in the low 200s through 1882, after which the total fell below 200 days (only to bounce back to 203 in 1885 and again to 202.5 in 1891, the figure used by Harris in his 1892 annual report).

The decrease in the number of annual school days from 1842 to 1855 stemmed from the outright expansion of summer vacation and the addition of official commemorations. Before 1842, the PSS had granted only a handful of holidays and a three-week recess in August. By 1853, the board of education's general regulations allowed three annual vacation days (July 4th, Thanksgiving, commencement), one holiday week (from Christmas to New Year's Day), and an approximately five-week summer vacation (from the last Friday in July to the first Monday in September).[26] It would be a mistake, however, to assume that the lengthened summer vacation came solely as an avowed

Figure 2.1. *Average term length of New York City public school districts,*
1842–90

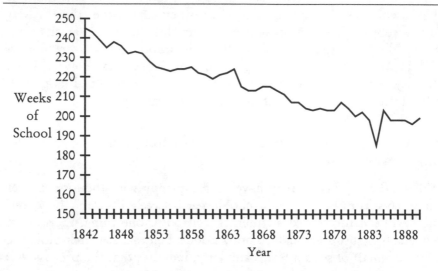

Source: New York Superintendent of Public Instruction, *Annual Reports;* New York
    Board of Education, *Annual Reports.*

policy of the central board. The reticence about and the gradualness of
the change point in a different direction. In fact, the board of education appeared to be responding to two challenges: the standardization
of an unwieldy array of schools and the inclinations of local ward trustees.

The variation between schools under its control proved vexing to a
board of education seeking uniformity. In 1845, its ward schools may
have averaged 235 days a year, but they ranged from 227 to 240. Such
deviation from the norm was typical and is illustrated on Table 2.2,
which shows the 1851 distribution by school of New York City school
year lengths. That year, the median number of days had fallen to 231,
but of the seventy-five departments (boy, girl, and primary) that constituted the city's thirty-one ward schools, only seventeen were actually in session for that number of days. A school year of 235 days was
nearly as common, but many schools opened for fewer days, accounting for the year's average of 229 days. Even within a single school
building, the three departments did not always maintain the same
number of school days. In 1851, the male department of Ward School
8 ran for 234 days while the female and primary departments held only

Table 2.2. *Distribution of New York City school year lengths for 1851*

| Number of School Days[a] | Number of Schools | | |
	Ward	PSS	Total
Less than 200 days	4	0	4
200 to 209 days	5	0	5
210 to 219 days	3	0	3
220 to 224 days	1	0	1
225 days	0	0	0
226 days	2	0	2
227 days	3	0	3
228 days	9	0	9
229 days	3	3	6
230 days	2	2	4
231 days	17	1	18
232 days	3	0	3
233 days	0	2	2
234 days	7	2	9
235 days	13	10	23
236 days	3	31	34
237 days	0	0	0
238 days	0	1	1
239 days	0	3	3
240 days	0	0	0
241 days	0	0	0
242 days	0	3	3
Total number of Schools	75	58	133
Average no. of school days	223	236	228
Adjusted average no. of school days	229	236	232
Plurality/Majority of school days	231	236	236
Median no. of school days	231	236	234

Source: New York Board of Education, *Annual Report* 10 (1851), 9–13.

[a] The board of education reported the number of school sessions not days. Schools generally ran two sessions per day, so the figure listed was merely divided by two. There were mostly an even number of sessions listed, but when not, the number of days was rounded up. The adjusted average removed all schools with fewer than 200 hundred days, since in all likelihood, these schools were newly opened after the start of the school year. Most ward schools listed separate term lengths for male, female, and primary departments. These were treated as separate schools since the number of sessions even within one building sometimes varied.

226 days of school.[27] These haphazard arrangements continued during the 1850s and finally abated by the late 1860s.

The uneasy coexistence of the PSS and the newly formed ward schools added to the confusion. Faced with the prospect of the new state school system of 1842, PSS members expressed "...melancholy foreboding of the future." Their fear that the school legislation would lead to "the blighting influence of party strife and sectarian animosity" never entirely dissipated even as amendments more favorable to the PSS were subsequently passed.[28] They may have been concerned with the shape of the new schools as well. In the case of the school calendar, the ward schools run directly by local trustees and overseen by the central board of education never matched the average length of the PSS school year. As the ward schools began to open in 1843, they fell short of the 245-day standard set by the PSS, and in 1844 they averaged 237 days a year. Table 2.3, which compares the average length of PSS and the board of education school years, indicates that the former declined after 1844 but it usually remained several days longer than the latter. This disparity is also evident in Table 2.2, as the PSS schools ranged from 229 to 242 schools and the board of education ward schools peaked at 236 days and dropped below 200. Still, why did the PSS follow the lead of the ward schools and reduce the length of its traditional school year?

After 1842, the PSS found itself in an increasingly bitter contest with the incipient board of education. Under the new system, the PSS depended on the board of education for its school money, although each institution felt constrained by the likelihood of comparison to the other, particularly with regard to expenditures. As an early historian of New York City public schools noted, it was "highly important to either party that there should be no unfavorable comparative statement

Table 2.3. *Public School Society and New York Board of Education school year lengths, 1842–51*

	1842	1843	1844	1845	1846	1847	1848	1849	1850	1851
Board of education	...	...	237	235	235	235	235	228	228	229
Public School Society	245	...	245	240	235	239	237	234	236	236
Combined average[a]	245	...	243	239	235	238	236	232	233	232

Source: New York Board of Education, *Annual Reports* 1–10 (1842–51).

[a] Averages were weighted by the number of schools run by each organization.

as to cost."[29] Yet financial and other school data of each organization from 1842 to 1851 identify a pattern that boded ill for the PSS and the length of its school year. Table 2.4 presents the numbers of schools, students, and appropriated funds for the PSS and the ward schools. It indicates that each year the PSS received a smaller share of funds, often an outright decrease, and it opened no new schools after 1847. At the same time, the ward schools grew exponentially, typically cost less per student, and by 1851 had overtaken the PSS in the total number of students taught and had therefore received a higher appropriation. Thus Table 2.4 suggests that in many ways the PSS was stagnating while the ward schools were growing. In light of these statistics, its decision to close shop in 1853 is comprehensible, as is the way it kept pace with the ward schools' calendar changes. Shortening the school year and extending the summer vacation attested to "the growing pressure which the new system was steadily exerting upon the old."[30] Restructuring the calendar in ways that were popular with students,

Table 2.4. *Comparison of Public School Society and New York Board of Education institutions, 1842–53*

	Public School Society			Board of Education		
Year[a]	No. Sch.	Monies Apportioned	Number Taught	No. Sch.	Monies Apportioned	Number Taught
1842	97	$119,518	...	7[b]	None	None
1843	...	...	...	...	...	...
1844	104	$122,740	37,985	42	$52,285	20,210
1845	111	$122,185	44,217	44	$55,356	24,233
1846	110	$124,206	48,264	44	$60,275	25,894
1847	115	$115,947	54,732	51	$85,433	32,698
1848	115	$116,189	50,320	58	$103,885	40,938
1849	115	$131,122	53,546	65	$107,681	45,872
1850	114	$104,307	53,239	72	$90,814	50,559
1851	113	$106,818	55,769	81	$104,137	57,106
1852	112	$110,749	54,157	85	$119,142	66,831
1853[c]	112	$125,063	52,748	85	$150,696	65,507

Source: New York Board of Education, *Annual Reports* 1–12 (1842–53).

[a] The year listed is actually year from Feb. 1 to Feb. 1 (e.g., 1847 is from Feb. 1, 1847 to Feb. 1, 1848) and apportionments are rounded to the nearest dollar.

[b] Opened by April 3, 1843, but none in 1842.

[c] 1853 data is from Feb. 1, 1853, to December 31, 1853.

teachers and fiscal conservatives alike made sense in the competitive atmosphere between the two systems.

Finally, the development of new levels of schooling, particularly secondary education, muddled the school calendar even further. When in 1849 the board of education organized a Free Academy for boys, it established three vacations—one month from July 28 to Sept. 1, one week between Christmas and New Years, one week around April 22— and quickly extended the summer recess to six weeks.[31] As a result, the Free Academy opened for 44 weeks and fewer than 220 days in 1851, well below the 236 average of the PSS schools and the 229 average of the ward schools (see Table 2.3). But the Free Academy, which eventually became City College, compared itself to institutions higher, not lower, in the hierarchy of schools. For American colleges at midcentury, 44 weeks of school was actually on the lengthy side. Columbia opened for 42 weeks, Harvard, Yale, Brown, Wisconsin, and North Carolina for 40, Dartmouth, Virginia, and Michigan for 35, and the 55 institutions surveyed averaged 41 weeks of classes.[32] As New York City fleshed out its school system, its school leaders sought to order consistency from bottom to top.

The reduction of New York's school year was not simply about standardization; it was also about control. The school law of 1842 and subsequent legislation created a complex school governance structure that attempted to balance desires for local autonomy and central leadership. It established two commissioners, two inspectors, and five (eventually eight) trustees per ward—all of whom were initially elected but subsequently most of whom were appointed. The commissioners and trustees from each individual ward formed a local board of trustees, and together with the school inspectors they constituted the board of school officers for each ward (the commissioners were ex officio members only). The central board of education was comprised of the commissioners from every ward and concerned itself with budgeting and school building while the local ward trustees hired teachers, set curriculum, and purchased textbooks and supplies. Of course, this structure hardly eliminated clashes between the local and central officials. The central board was "virtually dependent upon the dictum of the local ones" and therefore often powerless to enforce its own regulations or to prevent the rampant nepotism and corruption at the ward level. Disputes arose especially when each body was given a role in a particular aspect of school administration.[33] In the case of the school holidays and vacations, conflict ensued when ward school officials closed schools over the objections of the board of education.

Local ward control over the schools largely accounted for the extensive variation and the gradual reduction in the length of the school year in the 1840s and early 1850s. Although the by-laws of the board of education identified all official school holidays, there were loopholes. The most important one expressly gave the ward school officers the authority for "closing the Schools, upon a particular occasion, for a single day, if they think it necessary."[34] Ward officers and even individual school principals regularly took advantage of this provision, particularly when there was popular support for a celebration such as Washington's birthday, May Day, December 24, or January 2.[35] Likewise, they could close the schools early in the summer if the buildings became too hot. These more or less impromptu school holidays reflected popular desires and were sometimes declared in anticipation of a low turnout of students. Even during the heyday of the PSS, the society struggled to enforce among individual schools its uniform school schedule of 250 days.[36] Under the participatory system created in 1842, school holidays proliferated and school year lengths declined further.

The central school officials were quite dissatisfied with their limited authority. Revisions of the school laws in the decade after 1842 attempted to redress the imbalance in power by strengthening the board of education and the city superintendent of education.[37] The changes did not perceptibly weaken the local ward trustees or diminish their propensity to declare school holidays, but they did help foster the first countermeasures taken by citywide school officials. Ironically, the first phase of decline ended in 1855 (see Figure 2.1), before city school leaders could have had any measurable impact on school year length. Most likely, popular demand for more school holidays had been temporarily sated. Still, through the 1850s, the board of education and its superintendent adopted a multifaceted strategy—part suasion, part disallowance, and part accommodation—for stabilizing a school calendar that remained inconsistent across wards and over time.

With limited powers, school leaders could at first only rail against the disregard for the official school calendar established by the by-laws of the board of education. In 1856, Superintendent Randall took aim at this long-standing problem in his annual report:

> The effect of unusual holidays is bad. They are injurious to the scholar by interfering with the regular course of his studies, aiding whatever natural tendency he may have to waste his time, and exposing him for an additional period to the varied dangers of the street. They are obnoxious to parents, because every hour a child is relieved from the wholesome guardianship at school, is added to the cares and responsibilities of his overseers at home.

And they are detrimental to the school system, in the first place, as will be presently shown, by diminishing its apparent prosperity; and in the second, by exciting jealousies and dissatisfaction in the several schools. If the children in one ward have an extra holiday, those in the adjoining ward are discontented because the boon is not extended to them. The indiscreet action of one Local Board, therefore, affects not only their own schools, but the whole system.[38]

Randall decried the fact that only one ward actually complied with the by-laws and ran schools for 227 days in 1856. Figure 2.2 graphs the distribution that year: the typical wide range (from under 150 to over 234 days) centered below (at 224 days) the legal requirement and displaying no clear cut majority. Merely raising the issue did not halt the deviation from the legal school calendar by local wards. To remedy the inconsistencies, Randall recommended narrowing the authority of ward trustees and eliminating the commencement day of the Free Academy as a holiday for the ward schools.[39] Reform occurred in stages over several years, but by 1860 revisions in the by-laws had tightened the stipulations against any additional holidays by requiring principals who cancelled a session to submit a special report that explained why and by what authority such action was taken.[40]

These changes in board of education policy also served to legitimize longstanding ward practices. Holidays such as Good Friday and

Figure 2.2. *Distribution of New York City school term lengths, 1856*

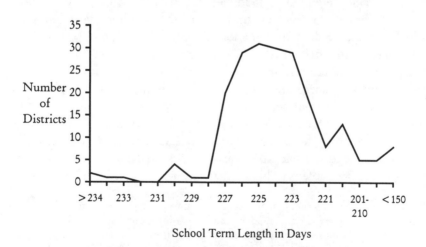

Source: New York Board of Education, *Annual Report* 15 (1856).

May Day were added as official holidays as was the 2nd of January. When a holiday fell on a Sunday or Thursday, the following Friday or Monday was included as a day off from school as well. In addition, the schools were to be closed on "any day appointed by the Governor of the state for a public fast day or thanksgiving."[41] By expanding the number of recognized school holidays, the board of education acquiesced to the holiday traditions of individual wards. The impact of these revisions was immediate. The city-wide average school year decreased by two days in 1861 (see Figure 2.1), but this temporary drop probably stemmed from the upheavals of the oncoming Civil War.[42] More significantly, it was the first year in which the median number of school days represented a majority of individual schools. In other words, the school wards of New York City finally began to show uniformity in their school schedules.

The second phase of school calendar transformation in New York: 1864-75

The advent of relative harmony in the school calendar in the early 1860s did not spell the end in the decrease of school year length. As Figure 2.1 depicts, 1865 marked the beginning of a ten-year reduction of the annual school year from 225 to 203 school days per year. More than the first phase, this decline occurred with some discussion and debate within the board of education. Whereas earlier decisions on new school holidays had been close to unanimous, by 1872 resolutions to add February 23 and Election Day passed only by 6–5 margins. One commissioner's efforts to begin summer vacation with the Fourth of July took over three years to bear fruit. The board itself underwent two shifts in structure and personnel during this era, as the Tweed Ring orchestrated a short-lived reorganization that temporarily vested power in men connected to the political machine.[43] Regardless of its configuration, the board's concern about individual wards and principals strictly adhering to the official school calendar remained persistent. As late as 1877, the central board called the trustees of Ward 19 to task for authorizing the closing of schools for Carnivale Day and a presidential visit.[44] Such episodes, however, became noteworthy for their rarity in the postbellum years. Overall, after 1864 the central board of education faced fewer instances of unilateral ward action on school holidays and acted much more forcefully when local trustees flouted its school schedule.

The second era of decline began with the intrusion of national events into the school schedule of New York. The assassination of President Lincoln in 1865 brought formal learning to a halt as the board of education closed the schools for several days surrounding the funeral. By 1873, it had designated May 30 (Decoration Day, a precursor to Memorial Day) and February 22 (Washington's Birthday) as official school holidays.[45] In taking these steps, the board relied upon powers it had retained for itself in the school by-laws even as it denied such authority to local wards. Such actions on holidays served as another mechanism for shortening New York City's school year, although they affected city schools uniformly not irregularly. Still, at times the board seemed to act almost as arbitrarily as local wards in closing schools for occasions such as the death of a school commissioner or janitor and the extension of the New Year's Day celebration.[46] Likewise, in its own tinkering with the school calendar, the board of education found it easier to add than to rescind school holidays. A case in point was the practice of closing schools on a Friday following a holiday. In 1865, the board voted to end this policy, which had led to several four-day weekends, but a mere two years later decided to close the schools on Friday, July 5th. This decision was no fluke, as the schools were closed for two days in 1872 when Washington's birthday fell on a Thursday.[47] Even more telling, the school year length did not bounce back to its wartime averages after the tumultuous events of 1865.

At most, the addition of individual holidays accounted for a fraction of the more than twenty-day drop in the school year from 1864 to 1875. The bulk of the decrease stemmed from the expansion of summer vacation to include most of July. As late as 1865, summer vacation still began on the last Friday of July; by 1875 it began on July 3, and this contraction occurred in two increments.[48] In 1866, the board voted decisively to increase the length of summer vacation from five to seven weeks by extending it by one week at either end, from "the next to the last Friday in July [to] the second Monday in September."[49] In 1869, the board retained a seven-week summer recess but began it on the Friday following July 15th.[50] These changes seemingly transpired with little debate or fanfare among the board or public.[51] Agitation within the board for an even longer summer vacation began with the Tweed Ring's infiltration of the board of education in 1869. The next three years witnessed a lonely but steady and ultimately successful struggle on the part of school commissioner William Wood to have summer vacation begin on July 3rd.

In July of 1869, an unanticipated debate in the board almost led to an extension of the summer vacation.[52] The board had previously established the length of summer vacation, and indeed school had already let out when a resolution to continue summer vacation into the second week of September produced a heated argument between several commissioners at the July 21st meeting. Although Wood preferred beginning the summer vacation with the July 4th holiday, he still supported the current proposition, asserting that with the warm heat of early September, students "do not get to work with any vim." Commissioner Nathaniel Sands countered with arguments about fiscal prudence and proper procedure. His words offer a glimpse into pervasive mental frameworks about which Chapters Three and Four will elaborate. Acknowledging nineteenth-century perceptions about the human nervous system, he claimed that "while he was inclined to give teachers and pupils proper time to recruit," the multiple days of celebration, weeks of holiday, and two-day weekends were sufficient. Anticipating the rationale vacation school advocates would use at the turn of the century, Sands cautioned against a scenario where children, "were mostly debarred from going into the county, [and were] roaming about the streets while the schools were closed." In the end, his arguments prevailed as the resolution failed in a 4–4 tie vote.[53]

In 1870, Wood embarked upon a similar campaign early and in earnest. At the April 20th board meeting, he resolved to begin summer vacation with the July 4th holiday. In the following preamble in which he outlined his justifications for his resolution, Wood elaborated on some of the concerns raised in the previous year's debate:

> *Whereas*, The national holiday of the Fourth of July, and the extreme heat of the weather at that period of the year, generate a holiday spirit, as well as great lassitude of mind and body, in both teachers and scholars, making the attendance at the school for the remainder of July a weariness of the flesh and spirit to both classes of individuals, therefore...[54]

As in 1869, here Wood grounded the pro-vacation position in assumptions about mental and physical needs of students and faculty alike. After his resolution was referred to the committee for further consideration, Wood gathered statistical support. At the May 18th meeting Wood had the average attendance of schools for the last two weeks of April and July reported to his peers. From his perspective, the data were damning. From April to July 1868, there was a 30% drop in attendance (from 79,079 to 53,901). The following year the April to July decline—at nearly 21% (from 85.096 to 67,404)—was smaller but still substantial. However, the evidence did not sway his colleagues, who instead focused on the outcome feared by Sands in 1869: letting loose thousands of working-class children onto the streets.

In 1871, Wood tried but once again failed to lengthen summer vacation. This time, his opponents on the board cited the extensive increases collectively made over the previous fifteen years as making a further reduction "inexpedient." They also rebuffed the argument that families wanted more vacation time by noting that "parents of such children as desire to give them a longer vacation than allowed by the school laws can do so." Finally, there was a sense that "this agitation had a very bad effect on the pupils, and for the teachers, a longer vacation than the present one was quite unnecessary." In other words, they suggested that the very discussion of increasing summer vacation contributed to the declines in student attendance and effort cited by Wood. On June 14, Wood's resolution was defeated—by an 8–2 margin—even more thoroughly than in 1870.[55]

Given the vehemence with which Wood's position was opposed the previous two years, the board's reversal of its position in 1872 is particularly surprising. Equally unexpected is the lack of attention with which the further extension of summer vacation incurred. The board of education minutes only mentioned the decision while the local press did not cover the event at all. Seemingly, the issue was finally won on the merits of the teachers. In mid-March, the board held several special meetings at which the most divisive question was over teachers' and principals' salaries. At a special board meeting on March 16, 1872, extensive deliberations pitted Board President Bernard Smyth against a majority of board members. Smyth cloaked his opposition to salary increases in pleas for fiscal restraint, reminding his peers of the city controller's recent warning about taking "as great economy as possible" in its expenditures.[56] Ignoring Smyth, the board voted 8–1 to raise pay rates for teachers and principals. Following the tally, board member Nathaniel Jarvis proposed and Wood supported an amendment to begin summer vacation on July 3, and that too passed by an 8–1 majority.[57] Thus in the context of remuneration, the board apparently created a longer vacation as an additional reward for teachers. In 1872, New York City's summer vacation lasted nearly two months, a duration it would gradually surpass over the rest of the nineteenth century.

Material and political factors in the restructuring
of New York's school calendar

The question remains, why did the shrinkage of the school year occur
primarily in the summer? Certainly the cultural and climatic predisposition to grant a vacation in August lay at the foundation of the modern school calendar. As recent work by Cindy Aron demonstrates,
summer vacation was already ensconced in the lifestyle of American
elites by the early nineteenth century and was increasingly becoming a
part of middle-class existence after 1850.[58] Moreover, the colleges that
served the children of these upper-crust families had long provided for
a substantial summer vacation. Yet specific mid-nineteenth century
social and ideological conditions fostered the lengthening of summer
vacation until it included most of July as well. Three material factors
warrant exploration here, while the ideologies cradling the debates
over Wood's resolutions will be considered in Chapter Three.

One possible reason for the shortening of the school year and the
removal of summer from it was the great need for incipient city school
systems to expand their capacity.[59] The period of 1830 to 1860 witnessed the largest urban growth rate in the history of the United
States, and New York's population rose from 202,589 to 813,669 during those years.[60] The struggle to simply house all of the city's school-
aged students could consume a school system with building and repair
projects.[61] These efforts required time and in many cases empty school
buildings during a season when the climate favored construction. They
provided a powerful rationale for having schools empty during July
and August. Did this logic enter into the decisions made by board of
education members in New York?

In New York, concern over the explosive growth of students in
the schools necessitated great attention and devotion of resources to
the expansion of the physical plant of the school system. In 1854 Eras-
tus Benedict, a newly elected board of education president, identified
the needs for alterations and repairs of school buildings and advocated
better advance planning and contracting "in time to accomplish much
of the work during the summer vacation."[62] What's more, school officials acknowledged that school repairs sometimes necessitated additional school closings in specific settings.[63] But such direct linkage between summer vacation and work on school buildings rarely appeared
in archival material. This dearth does not indicate that building concerns were irrelevant to decisions made about school calendars. The
scheduling of repair projects most likely contributed to the tremendous variability in school year length between individual schools in the

1840s and 1850s. In other words, it may help explain why in 1845 Ward School No. 17 was open 227 days and Ward School No. 3 was open 240 days.[64] As to the general expansion of summer vacation, the link is more tenuous, in large part because school construction was not rigidly beholden to the official start of the school year. Each year in the 1840s, there were a handful of new schools that opened during the school year—some early enough in the autumn to hold nearly 200 school days, others so late that they held fewer than fifty.[65]

The prevalence of epidemics in antebellum New York is also a conceivable factor in the lengthening of summer vacation. Again, school officials left no direct documentary evidence connecting the two, but the spread of disease did precipitate a mass closing of schools on at least two occasions. In the summer of 1832, a massive outbreak of cholera first led to slackened attendance and then to the decision of the PSS to close nearly every school "some time previous to the usual [August] vacation."[66] In 1849, another cholera epidemic forced the schools to close earlier in the summer than usual, and schoolhouses were actually used as cholera hospitals.[67] In each case however, the length of school increased the following year. More localized episodes of cholera, smallpox and other diseases sometimes forced individual schools or clusters of schools to close temporarily as well.[68]

A third material concern of school officials, more general than either construction or health, was the overall concern with school spending. As suggested previously, budgetary competition between the PSS and the board of education pushed the length of school sessions downward between 1842–53, but publicly financed schooling remained controversial in subsequent years. Cries of "extravagance" from citizens "in influential quarters" led board of education presidents and superintendents to make regular justifications of public school expenditures. In the schools' defense, they usually spoke of the relative value of New York public schools when compared to the city's private schools and to public schools in other large urban areas.[69] Nevertheless, the opposition of fiscal conservatives periodically crystallized into an acute budget crisis. For example, in 1854, a conflict between the board of education and the city's comptroller arose when the board ran out of money, asked for more, and did not receive it. While one option for the board was to close the schools, as many rural communities did when funding ran short, surprisingly it did not. Instead, the schools stayed open while teachers went unpaid.[70]

From 1869 to 1872 monetary concerns were directly connected to the struggle over the length of schooling. Finances received ample consideration, though less than the issues of student attendance, teacher health, and summer heat. Moreover, Wood came to the board as an avowed fiscal conservative and might have couched his fiscal anxieties in more ideological terms.[71] Yet the actual budgetary impact of ending school earlier in the summer was most likely marginal due to the preponderance of fixed costs, and contemporary arguments on school expenses cut both ways. School board members clearly disagreed as to whether reducing the school year would increase or decrease school expenditures. It is easy to assume, and some participants made the point, that shorter school years would save money. Others, however, spoke of the duty of "trustees to expend the people's money" and debated whether personnel costs, the largest item in the school budget, would decline if the school year were reduced by a week or two.[72] On the whole, extant school records from New York do not reveal much discussion of the relationship between school costs and the length of school terms. This near silence—at a time when fiscal conservatives were publicly seeking to eliminate expenses—suggests the relative unimportance of finances on this particular issue at this moment in time.

What is left then, to explain the reduction and reshaping of the urban school year? Did it stem from powerful common school reformers who created new state mechanisms to further their visions? They certainly fostered many other nineteenth-century school developments including rural school calendar reform discussed in Chapter One, but unlike farming communities, city boards reformulated school terms between 1840 to 1890 without any direct mandates or indirect prods from the state. Even New York City's truncated 1890 school year, for example, remained well above the state's minimum of 32 weeks. Not that state reformers thought urban school terms lasted an appropriate length, but with the rural calendar as a more pressing problem they did not campaign extensively or forcefully for change in the cities. In making the decisions to alter the city's school calendar, school officials were much more likely to look below than above.

In New York, the impetus for reform came from city boards trying to mediate local pressures for school holidays with their own desires for standardized school practice and consolidated power. Its school leaders were successful at calendar reform—when sometimes their state counterparts were not—because they acted on a vision fairly consistent with their constituents. Precisely because the changes fit with popular desires and traditional practice, urban school calendar reform was far easier and more complete than other elements of the common school program that faced substantial opposition.[73] In fact,

New York's post-Civil War dispute over school year vacations—its biggest of the nineteenth century—was an internal one within the board of education that quite frankly did not encapsulate larger societal tensions between Protestants and Catholics or localists and centrists or middle and working classes.

Questions about school schedules simply did not generate much popular concern that became expressed through formal politics. Instead, parents exercised power through their feet, as when they kept their children out of school when the year still ran though July or a school remained open on a day of public festivity. Without meaningful compulsory education legislation or centralized administration of schools in place, parents truly retained the upper hand over school systems.[74] Because they were directly responsive to constituent expectations about when schools should or should not open, local ward leaders sometimes clashed with the city's board of education. Nevertheless, the city's central school authorities, recognizing their own limitations even as they tried to dislodge them, reduced the school year and expanded the summer vacation in part to meet with public expectations. Thus designating public celebrations as official school holidays in New York represented a compromise on the part of schoolmen—with parents, local ward trustees, and even teachers. Was this process of change similar in other American cities?

At the least, patterns established in New York were not atypical. Harris' own data demonstrate that the decline in school year lengths occurred throughout the northeast and midwest regions. The reasons for this reduction appear similar for other cities. In Brooklyn, the school year lasted eleven months and retained a summer term well into the 1850s, but its school officials shared many of the same concerns as their counterparts across the East River. They too bemoaned the decrease in school attendance during July, lack of uniformity in school hours and days, and the willfulness of local ward trustees in closing schools on their own accord. As a result, they took action to reshape Brooklyn's school calendar. In fact, in a possibly coordinated but definitely coincidental move with New York's board of education, Brooklyn schoolmen also all but eliminated July as a school month in 1872. After that year, the number of school days dipped and usually stayed below 205.[75]

Southern cities, like the rest of the region, followed a different path towards systems of common schooling and therefore towards a standard school calendar. Virginia, for example, withstood during the antebellum era the demands for statewide free schooling despite the best efforts of Thomas Jefferson and subsequent governors, including John Tyler. Instead, the state provided money for pauper education and passed a complex plan for voluntary common schools that was ignored by most counties and all but four cities.[76] When schools finally opened across the state in 1871, some but not all urban centers were able to muster an urban school schedule typical in northern and midwestern cities at that time. Instead of adopting a school year of 240 days or more, the school year lasted ten months in Norfolk and Petersburg and nine months in Richmond. Virginia's other cities reached a similar but not higher plateau in another year or two.

As a result of this quick growth, Virginia's state superintendents were satisfied with the status of city school terms. They did not think that city terms were too short, nor did they appear concerned that urban school years became too long or that summer sessions were inefficient. In fact, urban term lengths peaked quickly in Virginia, and after 1880 more cities reduced their sessions than lengthened them. By 1891, the state's eight largest cities averaged 9.3 months of school per year, as all had eliminated the ten-month and most were approaching the nine-month (180-day) school year that became standard in the twentieth century. Here too, there was no overt state effort to reduce city terms, and the small declines most likely reflect a general tendency towards standardization in schooling or financial considerations or holiday demands in the specific cities involved.

Conclusion

As this chapter has shown, school calendar reform occurred in the cities as well as rural areas. The data that William Torrey Harris found so startling in 1892 are equally compelling today, in part because historians have not emphasized the urban experience when approaching the topic of school year length. The developments in the school calendar in Detroit and New York answer some basic questions about the use of summer in nineteenth-century American schools: When were schools open? What were the characteristics of summer terms? How long was the school year? How did these patterns vary by location— both regional and economic? How did these patterns change over time? In answer to these questions, this chapter demonstrated that summer was universally once an integral part of the urban school year with well-attended schools and substantive curricula. By the end of the century, however, several factors brought about the demise of summer terms in these cities: Economic, social, and demographic trends certainly pushed reforms in school calendars; an elite cultural predisposition towards summer vacation grew more commonplace; leaders of urban school systems struggled to make them more uniform; annual budgetary and other crises contributed to the reduction, although superintendents did not dwell on fiscal constraints; and schoolmen attempted to accommodate patterns of school attendance and local ward intransigence even as they tried to overcome them.

Finally, urban and rural school officials alike framed their discussion of the school calendar and the meaning of summer with certain assumptions. They believed that school conditions in the summer were inferior, despite the availability of statistics that contradicted this view. They suggested that teachers would benefit professionally through the proper use of summer vacation. But most important, the removal of the summer from the urban school year stemmed from a powerful belief about the nature and frailty of the human mind and body. How these and other ideologies contributed to the developments described here and in Chapter One is the subject of Chapter Three.

CHAPTER THREE

"School's out for Summer":
Ideology and the Creation of Summer Vacation, 1840-90

> In the heart of Vacation
>   Lies nestling a seed
> To come to fruition
>   For weary ones' need.
>
> Dids't find it, O spirit,
>   Worn out with the strife?
> Thy future will show it
>   In new, stronger life;
>
> The days will be richer,
>   Thy heart more at rest;
> More broad the horizon,
>   More work at its best.
>   —Elizabeth Porter Gould, "Vacation"

The 1896 publication of this vacation verse hardly marked a moment of poetic promise. What Gould's words did articulate were long-standing images of summer vacation that dominated the writings of educators in the 1800s: students and teachers physically and mentally exhausted at the school year's end using summer vacation to recuperate and rejuvenate. "Vacation" encapsulated a powerful ideological context for nineteenth-century school calendar developments—shorter school terms in cities, longer school years in rural areas, and newly formed summer vacations in both—traced in Chapters One and Two. The educators and lawmakers who reformed the school year offered arguments and justifications for their changes that mirrored and expanded on Gould's notions. They—as well as their critics—recognized the pervasiveness of the idea that summer vacation was needed to recharge weary school children and adults. They also understood that summer, as a period of time, was meant to be used to achieve individual and social purposes.

What were the origins of the belief in these and other propositions about absenting summer from schooling? The ideological foundations of the common school movement lay in three layers of bedrock: Protestantism, republicanism, and capitalism.[1] Native Anglo-Americans, convinced of the superiority of their religion, the vulnerability of their nation, and the moral worth of property and hard work, adopted an increasingly activist view of government in order to secure these values. These belief systems led middle-class adherents to a fervent faith in education, but more than that, they encouraged the advocacy of a state system to ensure a common and sufficient schooling experience for all children. The common schools became a crucial institutional bulwark against perceived social threats, and their very structure, their curriculum, pedagogy, textbooks and primers, and rules and regulations were steeped in these ideas. Democratic localists blocking the common school program also rooted their opposition in these same economic, political, and religious values, only they prioritized and interpreted them differently.

Thus beliefs in and fears for piety, virtue, and individualism girded the major developments of the common school movement. They speak to why Horace Mann, Henry Barnard, and their peers advocated free public schools monitored at the state level, and how scattered patchworks of schools were replaced by networks that emphasized centralized control through consolidated township districts and state supervision of a host of activities.[2] What Protestant, republican, and capitalist values do not fully answer is why northern and midwestern states took on certain specific regulatory efforts—most notably the reform of the school calendar—as part of the common school movement. Therefore this chapter presents two additional intellectual constructs—those of medicine and time—to show why common school reformers and their successors altered the school calendar as they did.

Entrenched popular and elite beliefs about health have long influenced the school experience students have received or been denied. For example, after its meteoric rise, the plummet of the infant school movement in the 1830s stemmed in part from public fears that the schools could induce young children to go insane.[3] Likewise, countless numbers of nineteenth-century educators who fretted about the design of schoolhouses were spurred by fears of impure air and stifling heat in overcrowded classrooms.[4] Reformers not only linked building plans to medical concerns, but their conceptions of school time also reflected their ideas about health. Scholarship on the history of homework suggests that beliefs about the frailty of the human mind and body were of paramount importance to how educators used time.[5] Summer vacation, of course, filled a far larger block of time than weekday evenings or weekends.

How educators conceived of time raises another ideological context that influenced the role of summer in education. By the early nineteenth century, Americans in both the North and South developed new constructions of time. From the Puritan ethic and market capitalism, a new commodification of time grew intellectually potent. Educators were not immune to this process, as they treated time as a resource and posited a number of uses for it in addition to its role in preserving health.[6] For schoolchildren, summer's stated function became the restoration of their minds and bodies. For teachers too, it served this purpose but also an additional one: to provide time for the professional betterment of the teaching corps. Thus in discussing the shape of the school calendar, educators more often than not used language that reflected basic assumptions about time and health, though the tenets of Protestantism, republicanism, and capitalism were not entirely left behind.

Common school reformers' efforts to increase the duration of the rural school term fit particularly well with the standard ideological triad. Longer school sessions coupled with raised attendance rates gave schools access to students in order to impart native American values. A three- or four-month session did not allow enough time for the socialization into the Christian, democratic, and market orientation of America; therefore reformers encouraged local districts to raise term lengths on their own and pushed state legislatures to pass minimum term requirements and tax incentives. The incipient state superintendents rarely invoked these social purposes when discussing inadequate school terms, but their general rationales for the intensification of schooling certainly included longer school terms among other items.[7]

The decrease in the length of urban terms poses a larger dilemma, for it exposes the explanatory weakness of the common school ideology as it is currently understood. If expanding the school year gave reformers more opportunity to mold the minds and morals of youth, then why tamper with school terms that already enabled them to do so? With most cities, large towns, and even some village centers running schools for ten months or more, the common school reformers needed only to improve the daily attendance rates and the quality of the education students experienced. Furthermore, these annual or nearly year-round school sessions were primarily located in the communities where immigrant populations, who were favored targets of reformers, tended to congregate.[8] Thus reducing the number of school days per year contradicted the ideology that accompanied the growth of public education through so many other devices. In areas that reduced the length of school terms, medical thinking loomed large behind the process.

Finally, why was the summer selected as the time to be removed from the school year in rural as well as in urban areas? The values underlying Protestantism, republicanism, and capitalism shed some light here if the removal is viewed as reactive. For a variety of reasons suggested in Chapters One and Two, summer sessions were commonly viewed as inferior by educators even if the data collected by superintendents did not always substantiate that assumption. To the extent that reformers believed that they were of poor quality and therefore did not contribute much to their goals for education, summer sessions became targets for removal. But as Gould's verses suggest, summer was also portrayed in a proactive sense. To reformers, summer vacation held an intrinsic worth separate from the elimination of summer terms. These schoolmen attributed benefits to summer that cannot be explained by the pervasiveness of Protestantism, republicanism, and capitalism during the common school era. Once again, a focus on medical and other lines of thought to be presented here can shed light on the creation of summer vacation in rural as well as urban communities.

Supported by these ideological constructs, legislators, school officials and citizens changed the shape of the school year. The components of nineteenth-century school calendar reform, however, were not processes independent of each other. The removal of the summer from the regular school year occurred in conjunction with both the lengthening of the rural and the reduction of the urban school years. Moreover, although educators displayed disparate thoughts about the proper length of schooling and use of summer, they rarely came into conflict, and a broad consensus existed in favor of the school schedule trends that occurred. Unlike other matters of common school reform, there was little ideological debate over the changes made in school year. When discord arose, it was usually over the means used to achieve calendar reform.[9]

Why was there an absence of sustained opposition to the changes in the school calendar? School reformers drew on common beliefs about human physiology as well as Protestantism, republicanism, and capitalism. An examination of the discourse on school sessions reveals the widespread permeation of scientific and popular medical thought and the new formulations of time brought on by the advent of industrial capitalism. Beginning with Horace Mann's writings and expanding to include several leading education journals and state superintendencies, this chapter traces the lines of thought on the school year and the summer vacation during the nineteenth century.

The Nineteenth-Century School Calendar
According to Horace Mann

Given Horace Mann's preeminent position in the common school movement of the mid-nineteenth century, his writings are a good place to begin to tease out the belief systems of the era. Although over the last thirty years the social control and bureaucratizing tendencies of his vision and influence have come under attack, Mann's tremendous impact on the development of American education remains undisputed. Appointed as secretary to the newly formed Massachusetts Board of Education in 1837, Mann encountered haphazard and insufficient public education, and he strove, in the words of one biographer, "to create a well-managed *system* of schooling."[10] During his twelve years of tenure, he exhorted the communities of Massachusetts to embark on comprehensive improvement of their public schools, intertwining qualities of both an idealist and a realist. The goals Mann put forth in his annual reports and other writings articulated the agenda for the first generation of public education professionals. Mann did not necessarily originate them, but no individual in the antebellum decades did more to popularize them. Mann repeatedly stressed increased attendance, improved facilities, and especially centralized control mechanisms including consolidated town districts, state education agencies, and state funds. He also urged the professionalization of teaching through higher wages, education journals, teacher institutes, and normal schools. To pursue both the systemization of schooling and the professionalization of teaching, Mann advocated changes in the typical school year.[11]

In his 1842 school report, Mann urged the standardization of the public school calendar. Although school years in Massachusetts averaged nearly eight months, Mann observed vast disparities in their length, from the year-round classes of its cities to the few months of school in some villages. The latter bore the brunt of his assault. Mann denounced the abbreviated term as a reflection of the lack of value a community placed on education and as an inadequate amount of schooling for students. He discounted any financial explanation for it, noting "it is equally plain that the actual difference in the length of the schools is far greater than is theoretically desirable, and greater than can be justified by any differences in the circumstances of the people."[12] Given his espousal of better educational results through greater standardization, the large discrepancy in school terms irked Mann. However, he did not merely seek to bring the laggards up to the level of the leaders. He also called to task districts with too much schooling and identified two factors which warranted consideration when setting school terms: children's attendance and health.

Mann believed that most districts needed to keep their schools running for longer periods of time. For students of rural communities, he assumed that inferior learning correlated with paltry school terms and therefore remonstrated the educational consequences of two- to three-month winter and summer terms. In promoting extended school terms, Mann opined that "the long vacation almost obliterates the attainments of the short school," thus foreshadowing current scholarly preoccupation with summer setback.[13] Furthermore, he suggested that school term lengths reflected parents' attitudes towards school attendance, and here Mann the crusader hoped to alter popular thinking.[14] In rural areas with irregular attendance, Mann pleaded for citizens to send their children to school. He particularly decried the practice of keeping children home from school to work on the farm. Mann hoped to convince parents that "the season of youth avails but comparatively little for work, but much for education; but in mature age the facts are reversed." Mann the realist, however, refused to fight overwhelming public sentiment for certain vacations, and he acquiesced to attendance patterns. When rural labor practices prevailed over schooling, Mann favored extending vacation rather than opening schools with minimum attendance.[15]

In contradistinction, urban districts erred in maintaining schools for too long. Mann believed that children required some vacation time for their cognitive development, observing that "children return to their studies with greater zest and vigor after a temporary suspension." Likewise, he thought that teachers would benefit from such periods of rest as well. When considering the "capacities, proficiency, and health of the young," [16] Mann grew more convinced that current terms were too long. He accepted the common city practice of dividing the school calendar into four terms, but he wanted the typical one-week vacation after each term lengthened to two weeks (and to three weeks for children under eight years of age). Mann observed with irony that college terms regularly allowed a total of three or four months for vacation while annual public schools allotted that many weeks:

> Students at college, at their mature age, and with their more disciplined minds, must be better able, both physically and mentally, to devote all the year, except three or four weeks, to study, than children can be; and three months of vacation, properly distributed, seem far better adapted to that period of bodily growth and mental immaturity which belongs to the pupils in our schools, than to young men at universities.[17]

Indeed, Mann's fears for children's health dominated his arguments for eliminating the all-year school terms. He suggested that overtaxing the pupil's interest in learning could only lead to "a most pernicious influence upon character and habits." Even worst, he noted that "not infrequently is health itself destroyed by over-stimulating the mind."[18]

Given these concerns, Mann came to reject schooling in the summer. For urban teachers, summer terms denied them needed rest. For city students, summer quarters seemed especially onerous, which to Mann meant that the schools had failed. Mann wanted schools to kindle lifelong "energy and ardor" in students rather than merely impart knowledge on them, and to him the summer term appeared ineffective in that capacity. Within the four-quarter calendar, Mann felt that "probably it would be still better to have a long vacation of three weeks, or an intermediate of one week, during the hottest season of the year, for all Public Schools without exception."[19]

Overall, Mann's sixth annual report defined the parameters of the discourse on the length of schooling for the next fifty years: Rural schools needed to lengthen their terms to provide more and better education. Urban districts had to reduce their school year to avoid the mental and physical fatigue of students and teachers alike. In all locations, the summer should break the school cycle and provide the rest required by the human mind and body. In short, Mann outlined the pedagogic dilemma about the duration of the school year and of sum-

mer vacation: their lengths must allow for rejuvenation but not recidi-
vism. In so doing, he identified the two key ideological foundations for
setting the school calendar: beliefs about health and assumptions about
time. Mann never again directly addressed school calendars in his annual reports, but other educators heard his call, expanded his ideas, and
spread his views.[20]

Summer Education and the Harm to Children's Health through Overstudy

Among city and county superintendents and other contributors to
education journals, the dissatisfaction with the summer term was widespread. A piece in the *American Annals of Education* highlighted the
forms of "neglect of schools in summer," attributing the weakness to
the hiring of unqualified teachers and the disinterest of the parents in
them.[21] Many educators simply associated summer terms with discom-
fort and viewed oppressive summer heat waves as impediments to
learning. Henry Barnard, for example, labeled mid-summer as one of
the worst times for school, because July temperatures deterred school
attendance or sapped classroom energy. Disgusted with summer learning conditions, a Michigan county superintendent intended to replace
the summer and winter term schedule. His proposal for a new three-
term system identified the difficulties with summer classes in the nineteenth century:

> If our school officers would visit their school during the warm summer
> months, and witness the non-attendance of its pupils, the listlessness, indiffer-
> ence, and want of interest in both scholars and teacher, I believe they would
> unceremoniously resolve to adopt the three term system.[22]

Cities also began to readjust their school calendars, allowing for a
recess "in the warmest season in summer" or when a heat wave occurred.[23] Superintendents whose district schedules did not contain a
summer break came to complain about the unpopularity of the unremitting school year. A Providence school superintendent, in evaluating
his city's school calendar, acknowledged that "to carry the fourth term
considerably into July, [was] a step which does not meet the entire approval of those interested."[24] Forty years earlier, a school improvement
group in Connecticut noted that running schools in the hot summer
and the cold winter was an inefficient use of time. It derided the long
vacations during spring and fall, which occupied "those portions of the
year in which it is most pleasant for children to attend school."[25] With

the advent of the common school ideology, summer terms gradually lost the near-universal tolerance if not acceptance that they once possessed in part because the hot school rooms kept students at home or inattentive in class.

Some educators hoped to retain the traditional summer term by counteracting the oppressive heat. They suggested some simple and immediate remedies for the conditions that schools faced in July and August, such as holding only morning classes in the summer. Ira Mayhew, a state superintendent of Michigan, advised sprinkling floors with water during any excessive summer heat waves. The *American Educational Monthly* reminded its readers that "in summer the windows of the school-room should be open all the time."[26] More complex and long-term solutions involved the design and construction of school buildings, which became a regular topic in education journals and superintendent reports.[27]

Nineteenth-century educators offered multifaceted critiques of the typical rural and many urban schoolhouses. They particularly targeted the poor air circulation of most school edifices; for example, deriding the country log schoolhouse for "being badly ventilated at all times" and "uncomfortably cold in the winter and unpleasantly hot in the summer."[28] Educators strove to ensure that new buildings had proper ventilation by promoting buildings "adapted to warm as well as to cold weather."[29] The journals and annual reports grew quite technical in their discussion of school buildings. Mayhew recommended a steam-heating air furnace because it worked well in both the winter and summer.[30] Dr. J. L. Cabell, president of the Virginia State Board of Health, favored an open chimney. Foreseeing summer use of Virginia's incipient public schools, he claimed that the open chimney would remove foul air in the summer while open doors and windows would let in fresh air.[31] Other methods for summer ventilation included open upper apertures to let out hot air, high ceilings, ample windows for light and air, and deep stone foundations.[32] All of the plans devised by builders and advocated by educators offered detailed means of providing ventilation during the summer as well as the winter. Indeed the extent to which educators described and commissioned school buildings suitable for all seasons indicates the presence and resiliency of traditional summer terms despite school reformers' efforts to replace them. However, the urgency and consistency with which schoolmen publicized the need for better ventilation stemmed from concerns about more than mere comfort during the summer heat; in fact, wor-

ries about health substantially contributed to the demise of the summer term.

Most educators criticized schoolhouses as a danger to the health of
students. They based their arguments for adequately ventilated school
buildings on prevailing medical doctrine that held that "foetid vapors,"
or impure air, caused certain diseases.[33] One journal especially vociferous about the jeopardy posed by faulty schoolhouses was the *American
Educational Monthly*. Its articles on school buildings repeatedly identified exposure to contaminated air as the primary health threat to
schoolchildren. It held that "the active and rapidly developing brains of
the occupants are particularly sensitive to the benumbing influence of
close and poisoned air." The consequence of ignoring a noxious atmosphere led to "the paleness and ghostliness of the children at
school."[34] Or as Mann's *Common School Journal* noted in 1840, "the
small size, ill arrangement, and foul air, of our schoolhouses, present
serious obstacles to the health and growth of the bodies and minds of
our children."[35] Journals only echoed what superintendents had long
suggested, that poor ventilation planted "the fruitful seeds of disease,
and premature death."[36] To combat these outcomes, Mann himself had
launched a Massachusetts school construction campaign in 1838 with
his "Report on School-houses," and many other states followed suit.[37]
Some educators even associated summer itself with infectious conditions. In Washtenaw County, John Pierce noted that "it is a well
known fact that all over this western country there are spots in which
bilious diseases prevail almost constantly throughout the warm seasons."[38] Thus educators' discussions of school structures were notably
preoccupied with human physical and mental limitations, particularly
in young children.

This focus on ventilation in school construction need not have
driven the summer from the school year. While widespread public
anxiety stemmed from fears of foul air's impact on children's health,
winter posed its own air flow and heating problems. Furthermore, better schoolhouses were eventually designed and built, making possible a
more physically comfortable classroom. Nevertheless, the gradual improvements in ventilation through new school construction did not
prevent the removal of the summer from the school calendar. For
while stagnant air posed a threat to the health of school children and
teachers, it was not the only prominent medical concern of nineteenth-
century superintendents. To them, another grave danger came from
exerting too much energy towards learning for too long a period of

time. This notion, expressed in many different contexts, will be called here the theory of overstudy.

The belief that overtaxation of the mental facilities debilitated a child pervaded nineteenth-century writings on term lengths and summer sessions. Looking back at the early part of the century, one educator observed that "a few years ago a cry of alarm went sounding through all the land that the nation was in a state of incipient annihilation because of the ruin to the health of the rising generations through over-study."[39] Most educators condemned excessive educational practices, and they identified a variety of negative results that would ensue from too much schooling. Some focused on teachers while most emphasized the cost to students, but in either case the outcome was often mental fatigue. The *Lancaster Examiner*, for example, deplored the practice of some parents who continued lessons during vacations. It asked "do not children, when so closely confined to study, lose their vivacity, and become dull, and stupid scholars?" Hardly a rhetorical question, the newspaper answered that "they become weary, and tired of this constant application. Study loses its interest, its delight. They look upon it as an irksome duty, and long for some cessation, or little relaxation, and they should have it."[40]

Other contemporaries felt the consequences of overstudy were more emotional or physical. The *Pennsylvania School Journal* stressed the former, arguing that "children have a natural and inherent right to enjoyment; and in our anxiety to prepare them for being useful and intelligent members of society, we should be careful lest we overdo the matter and make them dull, unhappy, or morose men and women."[41] Most common was the fear of physical or physiological infirmity caused by mental activity. People worried that children "were growing up puny, lank, pallid, emaciated, round-shouldered, [and] thin-breasted all because they were kept at study too long."[42] One long polemic detailed the physical, mental, and psychological impact of overly long schooling—"to health of the body; to health of the mind; to health of the moral nature; to the happiness of the child."[43] Whatever the specific ailment, most educators believed that an overly taxing education could produce a wide range of negative outcomes in children.

In what ways did schools force children to overstudy? Commentators on this question faulted a variety of educational practices. Homework might prevent pupils from eating and sleeping properly. Lessons of more than three hours without physical exercise might lead to "inefficiency and lack of energy" or to a dislike of study, the teacher, and the school. Other factors cited included the age at which children be-

gan school, the type of work conducted in the classroom, and the tone
set by the teacher.⁴⁴ Finally, the length of the school year in American
cities was criticized. An early contributor to the *Massachusetts Teacher*
effectively summarized the problem:

> Children in towns and cities where annual schools are kept go to school too
> much both for their mental and physical good. They commence at too early
> an age, and are confined too steadily to their tasks. It is not strange that they
> become listless and inanimate; that they too often regard the school room as
> a prison house, and their teacher as a cruel task master. We dwarf and enfee-
> ble the intellect by this constant pressure.⁴⁵

This passage suggests that the causes of debility stem from a variety of
school features, but they can be subsumed into two general categories:
the nature of the learning experience and the length of that experience.
Of course, school factors alone were not the only explanations offered
by educators. They highlighted the impact of "many causes over which
the teacher has little control," such as inadequate exercise, insufficient
sleep, unwholesome food, and limited outdoor activity. Nevertheless,
they recognized that the schools could take specific steps to reduce
their own detrimental effects on students' health.

Of the two general causes of enfeeblement, educators stressed restructuring schedules more than pedagogy.⁴⁶ Quite simply, they strove
for ways to reduce time spent studying, because long periods of respite
could save the mind from injury. Hence the elimination of Saturday
classes, the shortening of the school day, and the lengthening of vacation—all of which occurred over the course of the nineteenth century.
Teachers were cautioned that "when [students] are required to study,
their bodies should not be exhausted by long confinement, nor their
minds bewildered by prolonged application."⁴⁷ Rest also presented particular opportunities for strengthening cognitive and analytical skills.
As one contributor to the *Massachusetts Teacher* suggested, "it is when
thus relieved from the state of tension belonging to actual study that
boys and girls, as well as men and women, acquire the habit of thought
and reflection, and of forming their own conclusions, independently of
what they are taught and the authority of others."⁴⁸ While not all educators would write so gladly of independent thought, many believed
that appropriate breaks would stimulate student development. Overall,
the fears of ill health proved stronger than optimism that better
schoolhouses could improve summer learning. In order to forestall the
pitfalls of overstudy, educators cautioned against overwork and shortened the length of the urban school term by creating a substantial

summer vacation. Thus nineteenth-century school policy powerfully relied on theories of medicine and childhood. But was it consistent with them? What were the theoretical sources of these widely held views within the incipient education establishment?

The Origins of the Theory of Overstudy in Nineteenth-Century Medical Thought

Theories of humoral pathology had long dominated medical thought on sickness, but in the eighteenth century, explorations of the nervous system's importance to health led to their displacement. The work of Scottish physicians William Cullen and John Brown was particularly influential in this development.[49] Cullen identified fever as "'a spasm of the extreme arteries' induced by the state of the brain."[50] He also introduced the notion of debility, which he claimed followed the appearance of fever. Brown, a student of Cullen, believed that debility was a basic state of disease, rather than just the product of a fever. He postulated the existence of two states, direct and indirect debility. Direct was when "remote causes or stimuli (heat, contagion, emotions) were too weak to balance the innate reaction (excitability) of the body." Indirect was when stimuli (heat, contagion, emotions) were too strong and exhausted the body. To relieve these conditions, Brown advocated using stimulants to strengthen or lessen the body's stimuli.[51]

Benjamin Rush proved influential in popularizing these theories in America.[52] Like Brown a student of Cullen's, Rush viewed debility as "neither a consequence of disease nor disease itself." Instead, he defined it as a cause of illness—an exhausted body brought on by too much mental excitement.[53] Cullen, Brown, and Rush's pathology—systematized and centered on "rationalistic explanation"—was challenged in late 1700s. Centered in Paris, the new approach was far more empirical and therefore stressed the specificity of disease identified on a clinical-anatomic basis. While some American physicians turned towards the French ideas after 1820, others adhered to Rush's theoretical foundation even if they followed a more empirical pathway to it. Furthermore, there was a renewed acceptance of Rush's universalistic approach to disease around mid-century with the publication of Rudolf Virchow's work in 1858. Virchow's theories on cellular pathology re-emphasized bodily reactions to outside stimuli, but this resurgence was, as one historian noted, "overwhelmed after 1880 by a new ontology."[54] Nevertheless, these theories of debility entered medical writings as well as school journals and reports and seeped into educators' thinking on how to structure the school experience. That the use of time in schools changed in ways consistent with the tenets of debility theory only corroborates their influence. Thus nineteenth-century medical thought served as an intellectual underpinning for school practice. In particular, it helps explain why many doctors and most educators adhered to the theory of overtaxation for much of the century yet came to reject it by the time William Torrey Harris served as United States commissioner of education in the 1890s.

Nineteenth-century school administrators based their concern for children's well-being on a substantial body of contemporary cross-Atlantic medical literature steeped in assumptions about debility. For example, John C. Warren's short manuscript, *Physical Education and the Preservation of Health,* outlined a number of medical propositions that could and did serve to justify creating a summer vacation.[55] Warren, a Professor of Anatomy and Surgery at Harvard and an occasional correspondent with Horace Mann, contended that "too steady an application to literary pursuits" led to infrequent bodily exercise, that the impact of a "debilitated body" was particularly dangerous to females' health, and that schools were complicit in fostering "the regular repression of the physical powers."[56] His ideas about overstudy retained their resiliency well after the Civil War even as newer medical doctrines challenged their underlying theories.

An examination of medical journal articles from the late-nineteenth century indicates that educators closely borrowed physicians' ideas about the hazards of overtaxation. Medical professionals regularly wrote of the "impairment of mental and physical vigour" due to "mental strain in early life."[57] They claimed that "overtasked it [the brain] falters and its growth is retarded."[58] They described cases of "breaking down under the absurd regimen of many of our schools."[59] In his exhaustive study, *Health at School*, Clement Dukes sounded familiar themes when he discussed the damage too much school pressure could cause: "Owing to excessive work, and insufficient sleep during term-time, growth, again, without the intervening aid of vacations, would be more stunted, the nervous system more jaded, and disease more frequently generated."[60] Medical professionals identified many of the same specific sources of overstudy: "keeping them [scholars] in after school, by long home lessons, or by and injudicious use of emulation."[61] Problems with ventilation in school buildings also earned the attention of the medical profession.[62] Sometimes educators directly cited the work and views of doctors. In 1870, the *American Educational Monthly* published Virchow's findings on school room diseases. Virchow listed the environmental hazards he discovered in schools. Not surprisingly, the air of the school room appeared first, followed by other material shortcomings: insufficient lighting, poorly designed desks and chairs, unsanitary drinking water and privies, even textbooks with print too small. In addition to these poor physical conditions, he also warned against the overstimulation of the mind—caused by "mental exercises, [the] extent, manner in which they follow each other, individual measure, length of free time and vacations."[63]

The nineteenth-century medical literature contained other themes that were less discernible in but still consistent with the writings of educators. For one thing, doctors stressed that young children were more open to the ill effects of overstudy. Warning against "severe work at too early an age" because "early precocity mostly means adult enfeeblement," they feared that overtaxed children would experience nervous disorders and stunted physical growth later in life.[64] On the other hand, older students, though less vulnerable, still faced school pressures such as examinations. As tests for advanced educational opportunities became increasingly institutionalized and competitive, doctors began to caution against the "excessive mental activity" that preceded an important exam and pushed young adults beyond their abilities or endurance.[65]

Adults were not immune to these dangers either. Medical journals decried not just entrance examinations for professional schools, but the lives of the professionals themselves.[66] While even nonmanual labor jobs often entailed physical hardships on the hands and eyes, the emotions and anxieties produced by professional careers were frequently cited as sources of nervous disorders and therefore mental and physical debility.[67] Contributors to medical journals saw teaching as an occupation especially rife with pressures dangerous to good health. They typically noted that the length and nature of the school experience threatened teachers as much as children. However, the special problems associated with teaching also reflected the feminization of the profession that occurred over the nineteenth century and prevalent ideas about differences between the sexes. Thus medical journals highlighted the susceptibility of women to problems of the nervous system.[68]

How complete was the adherence to the overstudy doctrine in the cross-Atlantic medical world? Proponents often wrote of the "confirmation from a consensus of opinion in the medical profession" and contradictory views were rarely published until the late nineteenth century, when the consensus began to crack.[69] For example, a paper published in 1883 by J. Chricton Browne, M.D., titled "Education and the Nervous System," sparked a heated debate among contributors to the English journal *Lancet*.[70] The publication's readers could not agree on the question posed by its editors: "Is it, or is it not, the fact that over-pressure exists, and that it is doing mischief?"[71] Still, most letter writers supported Browne's assertions. Furthermore, the *Lancet* itself accepted the link between debility and overwork, as it concluded that there were undoubtedly students whose bodies could not take the mental strain of school.[72] If there was substantial opposition to the theory of overstudy, it was rarely published in the leading American and British medical journals of the nineteenth century.

The medical journals went into great detail in describing the actual disorders stemming from overwork. Dukes, in *Health at School*, listed symptoms in a wide range of areas: character and disposition, general appearance, the muscular system, the nervous system; the circulatory system, the respiratory system, the digestive system, the urinary system, and the generative system (particularly in girls).[73] Most physicians emphasized the harm done to the nervous system and intellectual capacities. One doctor argued that mental strain, or the "condition of cerebral tension...prematurely exhausts cerebral power."[74] Another wrote that it "tends to produce nervous exhaustion, which may end in brain-softening or some other marked nervous disease." But as he continued that it "may find its outcome in a pneumonia or a fever," he reiterated the clear link between nervous disorders and physical conditions assumed by doctors and educators alike.[75] Mental strain left students and teachers with a varied and lengthy list of physiological and behavioral symptoms. Most commentators highlighted sleeplessness and headaches, but some wrote of weariness, numbness, flushed cheeks, weak circulation, loss of muscle control, unduly dilated pupils, and weight loss.[76]

When did the medical problems occur? Most writers emphasized the immediate symptoms, observing that school terms always ended with pupils and teachers jaded, irritable, and querulous, and left some with physical debility or cachexia.[77] However, Horatio Charles Wood, a Philadelphia physician, focused on the long-term damage produced by too much mental strain at an early age:

> The injury thus wrought in the young brain by excessive study may not be apparent at the moment, though, for this, it is none the less real. There have been numerous cases in which the brain of the studious child has developed rapidly for awhile, and then suddenly ceased to expand. It is perfectly conceivable that a too rapid growth shall give an imperfect result.[78]

The most serious long-term repercussion attributed to immoderate amounts of education was insanity. In 1832, Amoriah Brigham published *Remarks on the Influence and Mental Cultivation and Mental Excitement upon Health*, which made and popularized that claim. His book articulated the changing sentiment on childhood and warned against the drastic consequences from intellectual overstimulation, especially among young children.[79]

The fear of insanity remained among some medical professionals and educators well past the Civil War. In 1871, the United States commissioner of education published Dr. Edward Jarvis' inquiry on the "Relation of Education to Insanity." Jarvis attributed most cases of insanity to business stress and disappointments. He concluded that "education causes directly but little insanity." Still, he found that overstudy caused 205 out of 1,741 cases of insanity. In addition, he claimed, in language consistent with the overtaxation theory, that education played a substantial but indirect role:

> Education lays the foundation of a large portion of the causes of mental disorder. It unlooses the brain from its bondage of torpor, and encourages mental activity in the numberless paths of life. It opens the fields of enterprise; it adds intelligence and reason to the power of the muscles, and makes them more available for every purpose. It stimulates energy and bold adventure. It offers temptations for the assumptions of mental burdens in business. It holds out rewards to ambition, for the strife for knowledge, wealth, honor, political success. These and other motives act in various degrees on civilized communities, and few people completely escape their influence; and among nearly all there is more mental activity, more cerebral labor, in thought, anxiety, more exhilaration from hope and success, and more depression from anxiety and disappointment, than is found among people that are untaught. All these have their dangers, and among those thus engaged some lose their mental balance, and some become insane.[80]

Thus Jarvis argued that the "incompleteness and the perversion of education" caused insanity. When children started school too young or misapplied the mental power they had developed, then insanity might follow. Yet too much education for appropriately aged children remained problematic. Schoolmasters went wrong, Jarvis argued, in teaching as if "there is no danger of overtasking the cerebral powers, of exhausting their energies, or of disturbing the mental balance."[81]

Having theorized and described the medical condition, physicians did not hesitate to make suggestions on how schools could prevent it. Not surprisingly, there were general recommendations such as adequate rest, exercise, and nutrition, all of which held implications for schools.[82] For example, one doctor stressed the need for balance between mental and physical activity: "If the constant bodily exercise, upon which a healthy development so materially depends, be at this age neglected in favour of study, the opportunity, the inclination, and the beneficial results are alike wanting later in life."[83] By reducing the length of the school day, educators created more time for physical activity, and schools eventually added physical education to their programs. Similarly, doctors recommended recreation and play, which also enjoyed increased roles in public education towards the turn of the century.[84]

Most advice doctors gave educators dealt with how and when to run the schools. Some physicians—as well as educators—decried the competitive culture of the school and favored "less studying for prizes and more for knowledge."[85] They particularly cautioned against too difficult work at too early an age. Daniel Clark presented an age-based curriculum with "no teaching beyond object lessons up to six years of age" and "object lessons with reading and writing up to nine years of age."[86] Medical professionals also limited the amount of time to be spent studying. Clark advocated "no studies in the evening until after fifteen years of age" and the following school day lengths: "three hours daily of school time up to nine years of age, four hours to twelve, and six hours until fifteen years of age."[87] Clement Duke's time restrictions were even more stringent for young children, as the figures in Table 3.1 indicate. Sometimes recommendations such as these were published *verbatim* in educational journals. For example, in 1870 the *American Educational Monthly* published the proposals of the Medical College of Middlesex, Massachusetts, on proper school policies to maintain student health. The college noted the need for effective ventilation, but most of its positions pertained to the proper use of time: no school

Table 3.1. *Recommended school hours per week*

Age	Hours	Age	Hours
5–6	6	11–12	25
6–7	9	12–14	30
7–8	12	14–15	35
8–9	15	15–16	40
9–10	18	16–17	45
10–11	21	17–18	50

Source: Dukes, Clement. *Health at School Considered in its Mental, Moral, and Physical Aspects*, 4th ed. London: Rivingtons, 1905.

attendance before age six, no school days more than five and a half hours (and one hour less for primary schools), no more than one hour of homework, and ample outdoor recess time.[88] Medical professionals typically addressed air quality, physical comfort, and mental strain all together, but they usually emphasized the latter. Because they viewed overtaxation as a grave threat to school children's health, the improvement of a school's physical plant could not alone save the summer term from assault.

In fact, the final remedy for overstrain suggested by doctors was a suitably lengthy annual vacation. Dukes recommended "a uniformity of vacations" for schools that included 7–8 weeks in the summer. He was quite adamant that the chief purpose of vacation was "that the pupil and master shall, after hard and prolonged work, obtain a period of rest."[89] Therefore, he criticized those who did not allow students to experience the respite. Dukes enjoined teachers not to assign holiday tasks unless they were of some alternative form such as natural history collections, drawn maps, foreign languages learned while abroad, sketches of nature, or objects of carpentry. He asked parents not to complain about the length of vacation but to understand and accept its purpose and to try to provide a strong home influence.[90] Some doctors even spoke for working men and women as well. Wood felt that the summer vacation must be in better proportion to the winter's strain. He argued that for most adults, two weeks vacation was not enough, that three was better but that even six weeks off would actually increase productivity by allowing for rest of the weary brain and restoration of the body's weary muscles and organs.[91]

Overall, the similarities in the writings of educators and doctors are overwhelming: both were deeply troubled by the medical impact of schooling on children; both acknowledged the damage caused by improper ventilation or lighting; both mostly stressed the risks of overstimulating the mind; both believed that too didactic learning for too lengthy periods of time caused a variety of medical problems of a physiological, physical, or psychological nature; and finally, both suggested reducing the time spent in school each day, week, and year. Educators accepted and incorporated these basic premises of nineteenth-century medical thought and acted on them to reshape the school calendar. A last yet additionally revealing example of how attuned educators were to the prevailing medical literature is their regular use of a particular analogy to explain the danger of overtaxing the mind.

Both medical and education professionals likened the brain to a muscle. In this manner, they held it subject to the laws of muscular activity without actually calling it a muscle. As the *Lancet* argued, "if we look upon the brain, then, as analogous to any other part of the human frame—as a muscle, for example—we shall easily conceive of its being over-excited and over-wrought, and as a consequence exhausted, and even in process of time altered in its structural elements."[92] Similarly, Jarvis observed that "the child's brain, like its muscles, cannot bear the burden of a more advanced age."[93] In these and other examples, comparing the brain to "other portions of the body" allowed educators to convey more emphatically the physical and mental dangers of overexertion.[94] On the one hand, they warned that overwork of the brain, like any muscle, could lead to permanent injury. On the other hand, they also stressed that proper and regular use of the brain allowed for a much longer and healthier mental life. This second line of thought, paradoxically, offered a potential challenge to the theory of overstudy.

The brain as muscle analogy opened an avenue of opposition to the removal of summer from the school year. For if excessive use harmed the brain, physicians argued that it could also atrophy from inactivity. Edward H. Clarke denoted a fine line for the maintenance of any part of the body: "Without exercise, an organ will attain little or no development: excessive or premature exercise will monstrously develop or abort it—in either case to the injury of the rest of the organism."[95] Thus doctors began to describe a mental regimen that neither overtaxed nor underutilized the brain. Clarke wrote at great length about "brain exercise, that is cerebration, [which] strengthens and develops the brain."[96] For him, one purpose of education was "to build a brain" through imitation of "the process by which Nature performs the same task."[97] Jarvis argued as well that the brain needed a gradual and careful development in order to achieve mental strength:

> By training and use the brain becomes not only strong, but flexible and versatile; it is more easily brought into action, more readily turned to new purposes; its powers are more under the command of the will. It becomes more refined, and its functions, both intellectual and emotional, more delicate and intense in their operations. Its sensibility is exalted; it is more susceptible of impressions and influence for good and for evil.[98]

Echoing the cry of physicians, some educators after 1850 also began to claim that insufficient brain work was just as dangerous as too much. Arguing that the brain was "not designed to lie dormant," they recommended "systematic and vigorous exercise, in order to keep their brains in good working order."[99] Others argued that inordinate amounts of mental activity could not permanently damage the brain because rest could replenish it like any sore muscle.[100] Contributors to the *Massachusetts Teacher* appeared especially hostile to the conventional wisdom about overstudy. In 1857, a teacher responded to the question "Does Study Injure the Health" with a resounding "No," retorting that study was "on the contrary, favorable to the health of both mind and body." The journal presented a comprehensive mental workout plan, noting that "the brain, like any other member of the system, requires food, rest, and regular employment of all its powers."[101] After mid-century, then, there evolved a growing recognition that educators needed to carefully meter the pace of learning to avoid extreme use or stagnation. In this way, educators began to question the prevailing theory of overstudy.

In rural districts, the mind as muscle analogy rationalized the lengthening of the school year. As usual, educators cited scientific learning regarding the development of the brain as evidence for the need for longer terms. For example, a mid-nineteenth century superintendent of York County, Pennsylvania, justified the extension of the minimum session from four to six months in the following manner:

> All the teachings of Mental Philosophy point to this one grand fact, that the mind is most rapidly and most thoroughly developed when the intervals elapsing between its periods of action suffice, by rest, to invigorate it, but not by inattention to debilitate it. Wherever and whenever the greater portion of the year is spent in idleness and inattention to mental development, we need not look for that progress, that proficiency, which the young mind is capable of achieving.[102]

In urban areas, this line of thought also began to weaken resolve to reduce school terms. To liken the mind to a muscle enabled both urban advocates of reduced sessions and rural proponents of extended terms to recommend regular mental activity intertwined with periods of dormancy. Thus the analogy gave an intellectual underpinning for the increasing standardization between rural and urban schedules. Rest and activity bounded the prescriptive possibilities for all school terms, with either extreme to be avoided.

How to Pass the Summer Vacation

These two parameters for brain usage also shaped the contours of a new issue that increasingly appeared in the education literature. As the medical beliefs about the school calendar started to be reflected in changing school term lengths, educators began to address how to spend the newly created summer vacation. The journals presented students and teachers with often contradictory messages about the uses of vacation. In keeping with the muscle analogy, the underlying issue was whether to experience rest or exertion during time away from school. On the surface, however, commentators appeared in agreement. For example, one piece of advice was given consistently—educators nearly universally counseled a communion with nature. For urban children especially, they recommended traveling to a pastoral setting and encountering rural life. They viewed cities as devoid of the natural elements crucial to the physical and moral development of youth. "Well, children," the *Massachusetts Teacher* proclaimed as one summer began, "may it be as you wish; visiting, berrying, boating, fishing, or what not, a good time to you, we say. The city boys and girls may all go out into the country and the boys and girls there must entertain them, and show them how to be happy."[103] The *Pennsylvania School Journal* echoed those thoughts as it quoted Shakespeare, "Let him plunge into the running brook and gather the moss which it kisses, and hear the sweet music which it makes with the enameled stones."[104]

How to interact with these natural elements was an equally vital matter. Some believed that mere existence in a rustic environment alone would suffice. More commonly, educators advocated a vigorous and unimpeded interaction with the outdoor life. In 1861, to quell the fears mothers might have for their unsupervised children during the summer vacation, the *Massachusetts Teacher* imparted the following advice to parents:

> Give them pretty loose rein. Let Mary run and be as hoidenist as she pleases; let Tommy roll in the mud and if you cannot keep him clean let him go dirty. They will be all the better for it, more hardy, blooming, and vigorous when vacation is over.[105]

This suggestion was typical of its time, as freedom and action were the appropriate hallmarks of a summer vacation in nature. Educators recommended these attributes precisely because they supplemented rather than equaled the regular school experience, balancing sedentary brainwork with physical exercise. To them, the newly created summer vacation held pedagogical and medical value for children that was missing from the classroom. As the *Pennsylvania School Journal* advised, "Let the vacation free the child from the bondage of the school, but not from the noble aim which it has in view." Instead of learning botany through memorizing and classifying names of plants, the journal opined that children "tramp through the meadows and woods and worship nature in the hill and valley, not knowing what he loves."[106] Considering Mary and Tommy mentioned above, the *Massachusetts Teacher* suggested that the summer fun and activity of these two children would have positive and tangible results at the season's close. Their parents could expect Mary to be "more graceful in your parlor next winter" and "to escape coughs, and colds, and all the list of ailments that beset the weak." Tommy would develop "bright sparkling eyes," a "handsome brown face all glowing with health."[107]

Most commentators on the issue of summer vacation focused on urban children, but educators shared the same fears, only less intensely, for country school children. The rural student also required a "change of occupation [and] physical exercise" to countermand school's effect on "that attenuated form of his, which bends over the book until his face becomes as bloodless as the page he scans." To attain this end, the *American Educational Monthly* advised all students "to go out into God's free air, and all the better for him if the hand that is idle should swing the ax or pull the oar upon the stream."[108] Thus in rejecting summer terms, educators did not indicate that the hot season lacked its own worth and function. Indeed, they viewed summer vacation as a vital time to ensure children's mental and physical well-being through proper activity.

Teachers could also gain from a lengthy and well-spent summer vacation, as the theory of overtaxation clearly dictated time off for them as well as students. "Teachers need a summer vacation more than bad boys need a whipping" proclaimed one ebullient educator who worried about exhausted practitioners.[109] But the most prevalent and powerful argument for school calendar reform made on teachers' behalf was that it would ameliorate teaching conditions. In urban areas, teaching was a fairly viable way to earn a living, and school leaders recognized the annual term's role in fostering relatively positive working lives. As one New York superintendent observed of city schools:

> The schools are kept in session during the entire year, except vacations, which are too few and too brief, rather than too frequent and long; and thus, by holding out the inducement of continued employment and fair compensation, competent teachers are easily secured, and the evils of frequent changes are, to a very large extent, avoided.[110]

Still, this commentator recognized that the drive to make teaching more attractive to talented individuals included adding more vacation time to the school year. This change would ease the physical and mental burden teachers faced and thus fulfill the dictates of the theory of overtaxation. Again, the balance between lengthy terms that professionalized and substantial vacations that rejuvenated was crucial.

Rural areas, however, faced great professional needs in the nineteenth century. Country teaching was a stressful, haphazard, and low-paying job, and superintendents claimed numerous benefits for teaching with a lengthened school year. First, it would allow administrators to visit schools more often to improve the quality of teaching that occurred. Many superintendents expressed dismay with the nepotism involved in hiring summer teachers, railing against the practice of hiring young women "...just out of school, whose friends intercede, with the trustees to allow them an opportunity to 'keep' their district schools, just for the Summer, perhaps."[111] A New Hampshire county commissioner of schools, noting that many rural schools were rarely in session for twenty weeks and some for as few as eight, observed that "many of them are of but little value to the intellectual and moral natures of the young, especially as they are usually kept by *cheap* teachers in very *cheap* school-houses."[112] His solution was to mandate a 30- or 40-week school year. Another proponent of calendar reform similarly argued that "the school terms in most of our rural districts are too short to offer inducements to secure professional teachers, or even those of a lower grade, to follow teaching as their profession."[113] Most nineteenth-century educators contended that a longer school term would pay more and therefore attract better personnel.

Eliminating the summer session would also challenge many of the customs of teaching seen as impediments to higher professional status. One such practice was boarding around, in which members of the community housed the teacher during the school term. "Ancient and honorable as the custom is," one county superintendent noted in 1873, "its effects upon teacher and school are generally pernicious."[114] Reformers targeted the summer term in part because during it teachers boarded around more commonly than during the winter term. School administrators deplored as well the second jobs held by many teachers "as a great barrier against the establishment of our profession."[115] With five to six months of work at paltry salaries, teaching was a precarious economic existence for many country practitioners.

In short, calendar changes in rural education aimed to draw a better cohort into teaching by making employment in schools more regular, prolonged, and rewarding. Reformers linked the abbreviated calendar with the overall low caliber of schooling in many rural areas.

They lengthened school terms and replaced summer sessions in order to alleviate the conditions that superintendents regularly criticized. Enhancing the quality of teaching was a cornerstone of the entire common school program, and by 1870 many school leaders felt that longer summer vacations and school years had helped to raise the level of teaching. The *Massachusetts Teacher* triumphantly noted that "vacations now extend seven, eight, ten, and even twelve weeks, with salaries correspondingly increased."[116] Educators reveled in the rise in teachers' pay and steady employment and the demise of boarding around, all of which they hoped would promote the excellence and status of teaching.

The question of what teachers should do with their vacation time revealed new ideological tensions among superintendents and between them and other officials. The professionalization rationale behind the creation of summer vacation also suggested that teachers use it for their own betterment, yet medical concerns about overtaxation remained powerful. As a result, the professional and medical intellectual paradigms came into conflict with each other. The idea that teachers should actively work to improve their knowledge and skills during the summer grew more prevalent as the nineteenth century progressed, but proscriptions against precisely that type of activity remained common as well. Thus the advice regularly given to teachers for summer vacation roughly fell into two categories based on the perceived needs of the brain for activity and dormancy. On the one hand, journals recommended that teachers "spend the summer in self-improvement," and on the other they labeled summer "the teacher's resting time."[117] These seemingly contradictory pieces of advice most often appeared in what became a standard item in teacher journals, the summer vacation editorial. This particular piece of writing appeared in June and offered teachers "a sober hint or two as to how it [vacation] may be profitably employed, as well as greatly enjoyed."[118]

As the end of school approached each year, many administrators and experienced teachers beseeched journal readers to rest during the summer months. They encouraged teachers to find serenity not excitement and to prepare for the next year through quietude, not travel. The *American Educational Monthly* consistently told teachers to "welcome, then, the summer vacation, in which both the mind and the body may have recreation, relaxation, and more especially, repose, *rest.*" It bemoaned the failure of many teachers to follow its counsel: "But we, poor fools, refuse to drink of the cup of recuperation when the draught is most needed."[119] When it argued that "few persons need recreation more than our teachers," the journal did not suggest a modern pursuit of leisure activities but rather a more literal renewal of body and spirit.[120]

Like students, teachers could best drink from the "cup of recuperation" in a pastoral setting. For urban teachers, an escape from the city for summer vacation allowed them "to enjoy the broad fields and the free pure air of the country." Nature offered the sights and experiences that could regenerate the teacher from a year of "work and worry, toil and care."[121] Treating nature as something to be sensed through immersion rather than experienced through action, the *American Educational Monthly* described to its readers an ideal summer of outdoor rest: "We pluck the wild daisy, recline under the wide-spreading tree, listening to the rippling stream and the music of the birds. We watch the flocks upon the hill-side, and delight our vision in the brood that sails upon the stream."[122] Simply by going to the country and soaking up its elements, teachers could replenish their energy.

Not surprisingly, the education journals relied heavily on medical opinion to justify their call for teacher rest during the summer. Vacation editorials regularly reminded teachers of "the wear and tear of mental machinery" that occurred during the school year.[123] Ignoring directives for rest led to unfortunate health conditions because "excess of oxygen burns up the blood [and] too much excitement paralyzes the brain."[124] Even the *Massachusetts Teacher*, which tended to minimize health concerns, admitted the widespread acceptance of such ideas: "It is a common remark among our brethren, that the business of teaching is burdensome and wearing. Many think it endangers the health."[125] With more and more women serving as teachers, the requirement for rest appeared particularly critical as it played on nineteenth-century ideologies about sex that posited distinct natures and separate spheres for women and men.[126] For one physician, the play, rest, and relaxation he advocated was "doubly true of the women whose more delicate nervous organization can less easily stand the strain."[127] This consideration was especially important in rural areas, where women were much more commonly employed in the summer term than during the winter term.[128]

Some educators continued to cling to the theory of overstudy even after medical thought discarded the causal role of debility and other nervous system disorders at the close of the nineteenth century. In 1896, a contributor to *Education* sounded much the same as his common school era forebears:

Let the mind lie fallow for two months and the increased efficiency will be noticed in his next intellectual harvest. So may he gather up a store of energy that will stand him in good stead and rescue him from nervous prostration during the month of his arduous school-work.[129]

In short, this persistent view held that the summer best served teachers by allowing them to regain their dynamism and hardihood through relaxation. The fears of overwork, which helped create the summer vacation, remained a potent influence on how to use it.

Not all educators unequivocally recommended rest for teachers during the summer. The *Massachusetts Teacher* and other teacher journals challenged the prevailing wisdom on several fronts. First, the *Massachusetts Teacher* presented the fears of overtaxation as an antiquated idea formulated by an earlier generation and unthinkingly transmitted to the present one. As one editorialist observed, "the wise men who went before us, have decided (thanks to their memories) that the weight that gives motion to the machinery of our life, descends too certainly and rapidly to the earth; it must be drawn up again and our frames recruited by long sessions of relaxation from toil."[130] Second, unable to fully dismiss the medical concerns, it argued that a much more physically active summer better restored the health of teachers. Telling them to "avoid cities, use books sparingly, and keep close to nature," the *Massachusetts Teacher* suggested that teachers "divert the mind and develop muscle." Climbing mountains or swimming in lakes was "the best preparation you can have for the labors of the coming Autumn."[131] Physical activity to prevent muscular atrophy and counter mental strain became one alternative to summer rest. Nevertheless, the argument for bodily exertion remained beholden to and consistent with the medical theories of Cullen, Brown, and Rush.

Education journals offered an alternative vision for a useful summer vacation: professional development. In contrast to prescriptions for both mental rest and physical exercise, educators increasingly promoted organized pedagogical events in order to professionalize teaching. Health concerns remained, but activity calculated to better teaching performance became permissible. In fact, the journals increasingly favored mental as well as physical stimulation that was geared towards improvement of the self and the school, and this argument justified a program for the professional development of teachers. For example, when the *Pennsylvania School Journal* raised the question of summer travel, it noted that "summer excursions, both at home and abroad, are excellent only so far as they give enlargement of knowledge, and better furnishing of the mind and body for future needs."[132] The journal only rejected frivolous travel as a harmful use of energy during of vacation time. By the mid-1800s, the vacation editorials offered a number of concrete steps to be taken during the summer that were legitimized by the drive to professionalize teaching.

The journals most often recommended teacher attendance at summer conferences. They promoted budding professional organizations, listed their upcoming meetings, and encouraged teachers to participate. A conference, the *Massachusetts Teacher* told its readers, "will give you many new ideas upon your profession, extend your acquaintance among your fellow teachers, revive your jaded spirits, and give you a new and wonderful zest for your occupation."[133] Therefore, it directed teachers to "Rusticate, recreate, in some way or other, and don't fail to be at some of the above named conventions."[134] The journals also suggested that teachers engage their intellect more directly by enrolling in the growing number of summer normal classes. For example, one editor argued that teachers should be "devouring the contents of our scanty library, or attend some popular institution of learning, to increase our store of knowledge for the next winter's use."[135]

Finally, the journals asked teachers to gear even their daily activities towards their own professionalization. The *Massachusetts Teacher* recommended allocating part of the day to self-improvement, through rising early, reading, attending lectures, performing bodily labor, engaging in regular conversation, and other activities.[136] Even the more cautious *American Educational Monthly* suggested some professional engagement. While acknowledging the need to avoid "school on the brain during vacation," it "confessed that certain matters can better be attended to during vacation than in session time." The journal deemed several proposed activities as appropriate for the summer, including reading, selecting textbooks, and meeting with associates to compare experiences and ideas.[137]

Overall, the vacation sermons on how to spend summer time never fully resolved the tension between the medical and professional requirements of rest and development. Instead, they simultaneously warned teachers not to remain idle and not to overexert themselves. The *Massachusetts Teacher* perfectly embodied these contradictory lines of thought. Even as it reminded its readers, "Do not think that all must be given to repose," the journal acknowledged that "the body and mind must be rested, it is very true."[138] In 1853, it felt compelled to conclude its summer editorial by hedging its earlier recommendations for activities: "In anything we have said, we would not imply that you neglect your health, that is a matter of the first importance, and must be attended to by rest, by exercise, by change of scene, by travel."[139] In the summer of 1861, the *Massachusetts Teacher* could admonish its readers, "by all means keep cool intellectually, if not physically," while two years later encourage them "to do anything that will improve your moral, mental, and physical constitution."[140] Even as late as 1870 the *Massachusetts Teacher* reminded its readers to "ignore the whole subject of schools and school work"—other than when they attended educational meetings.[141]

Educators carried their dilemma of choosing between professional activity and healthful repose to the end of the century. Praise for New York University's summer school for teachers was still followed by an admonition: "It is questionable whether the strain which ten months of incessant school work has made upon the teacher's and the pupil's intellectual powers, should be continued for even six weeks more."[142] Fears regarding health remained in 1900, but leading educators, after removing the summer from the school year, had clearly claimed a portion of it for professional purposes. In so doing, they adopted the language of a larger American, indeed Western, discourse on time that had developed with the spread of capitalism. This chapter now turns to how educators' discussions of summer reflected and partly helped reshape larger cultural meanings and senses of time. Placing the vacation editorials and writings on the school calendar in this broader context is important because it highlights an additional intellectual framework for understanding the changes in school policies over the nineteenth century.

"Spending" Summer Vacation and the Social Construction of Time

Typically the domain of anthropologists rather than historians, the study of time in a culture suggests a great deal about how its members live and think. Time is both a measurement of intervals between occurrences in all beings as well as a cultural construct conceptualized by societies in vastly different manners.[143] While there are subtle cultural variations in time, they are often subsumed under the broader categories of Western and non-Western time. The contrasts between them are stark; the former tends to be far more quantifiable, progressive, and absolute than the latter. In Anthony Aveni's apt description of the Western conception of time, "We have socialized it, circularized it and linearized it, artificialized it and corrupted it."[144] In many ways, Western culture has removed time from the natural world and conferred independent status on it. As an "imposition of order" rather than a non-Western cyclical "following the order of the skies," time in the West is a commodity in which, E. P. Thompson noted, "it is not passed but spent."[145]

A small but impressive historiography traces the development of linear and absolute time. Not surprisingly, Western culture did not always adhere to sequential notions of time. Aveni suggests that in ancient Greece, "time was the ordered cycle of sensible natural events to which human beings were meant to relate the events in everyday life from tilling the soil to worshipping the gods."[146] The invention of the mechanical clock in late thirteenth-century Europe played a tremendous role in shaping Western time.[147] The clock, with its potential for portability, held "the promise of the private knowledge of time."[148] Urban elites, Catholic monks, and regal courtiers began to structure their lives around the hour and proclaim an ideology of time usage. "It was this possibility of widespread private use," argued David Landes, "that laid the basis for *time discipline,* as against *time obedience*" and "made possible, for better or worst, a civilization attentive to the passage of time, hence to productivity and performance."[149] Adherents of time discipline structured their day around the clock and articulated an ideology of labor, thrift, and progress.

The diffusion of this new time sense to the working classes was slower and more contested than its spread to the bourgeoisie. In eighteenth-century England, recorded time remained in the domain of the gentry, but the synchronization of labor in the factory, along with school environments and domestic servitude experiences inculcated a sense of time thrift.[150] In the United States, time discipline always had powerful backing of Puritan ideology; nevertheless, colonial American work habits were not ruled by the clock.[151] These began to change, along with working-class notions of time, with the advent of industrialization in the nineteenth century. David Brody has suggested that "the logic of the factory ran strongly toward coordinated operations— whether because of a common power source, the division of labor, or, in the simplest case, the desire to create a disciplined work force—and this, among other things, called for a common starting and stopping time."[152]

Eventually the laboring classes recognized that time itself had become a commodity and their nascent unions struggled with corporate interests over its control or ownership.[153] Even so, Western notions of time continued to permeate American society as workers fought more about controlling time discipline—through eight-hour days and hourly wages—than about rejecting it in favor of an older time-sense. As Brody stated, "Journeymen observed their calculating master, and became themselves calculating."[154] This newly pervasive understanding of time was reflected and strengthened through discussions of and changes in school calendars and summer activities. A careful look at the nineteenth-century discourse, however, also cautions against underestimating the extent to which older notions of time retained their potency even amid an industrial capital revolution in a Protestant nation.

The commodification of time is abundant in the writings of nineteenth-century educators. Consider the very nature of the medium— the vacation editorial—and much of its message of professional development. Its entire purpose was to dictate to teachers how to pass time during the summer. As one editor put it, teachers were "to be told what to do with the precious hours between the last day of this school-term and the first day of the next term."[155] The themes embodied in the editorials are equally revealing of a sense of time discipline. By suggesting that "the teacher should use his vacation for the benefit of his school," educators treated the summer vacation as time to be spent and formulated a vision of professionalization based in part on time usage.[156] While the editorials were not always in agreement on whether rest or activity was the best way for teachers to develop professionally, all participants in the debate demonstrated the same assumption—that a vacation was not about pure leisure but rather that it was time to be used. Thus they wrote about "the blessings of a well-spent summer," about its value if "profitably employed," about "spending your vacations as you ought," and about how to "spend the summer in self-improvement."[157] Critics of the traditional summer term, like Pierce of Michigan, offered no more damning commentary than to label it "a waste of time."[158] A commodity in the eyes of educators, time was valuable and potentially profitable if not squandered, spent carefully, and used wisely.

The leaders of the common school movement also conceived of students' time in very linear terms. Several diverse examples will illustrate this thinking: Summer vacation provided the opportunity to "slacken our speed on the journey of life" or to make a pit stop during "our yearly race."[159] The graded school, an innovation spurred by swelling urban enrollments, was consistent with the notion of progressing through school over time. The clearest case of linear assumptions is in the reformers' very understanding of knowledge and learning. Horace Mann's writings clearly evoked a desire, often unfulfilled, for school progress over time: "The commencement of each succeeding term finds the pupils but little advanced, except in age and stature, beyond the point they occupied at the commencement of the preceding."[160] Mann and others viewed learning as both the acquisition and accumulation of knowledge. They opposed long rural vacations not because the time away from school halted the receiving of information, since mental rest was deemed necessary, but because it depleted the storehouse of knowledge. Long before modern researchers coined the phrase summer setback and quantified how students' knowledge and skills erode during vacation, common school reformers sensed and attacked the problem. Mann, Barnard, and others particularly regretted the wasted time spent reacquainting students with previously learned material at the beginning of each school year.[161] Thus their campaign for longer terms aimed to improve the linear progression of students through school.

Not all journal contributors comfortably imposed the use of time on teachers. In a revealing moment in *The American Educational Monthly*, its editors begged off the task of writing a summer editorial. Acknowledging the "moralizing strain" of the text, they confessed to being "in the dark in regard to the logical necessity of saying, just at this time, 'something about vacation.'" Why then did they persist with the vacation editorial tradition? "All we know," they answered, "is that a vacation editorial (bother the word!) is demanded: that is, by the worthy publishers of the *Monthly*."[162] Perhaps one reason for the editors' reluctance is that they did not fully conceive of summertime in a utilitarian manner. If so, in this instance they acquiesced to the wishes of their publishers and directed their readers to spend their summer in professional improvement. Or maybe they sensed opposition from their readership. In a rhetorical question ringing with incredulity, they asked "is it possible...that anxious ma'ams and masters are really waiting to be told what to do with the precious hours between the last day of this school-term and the first day of next term?" Both possibilities beg the question of whether pockets of resistance to time discipline persisted in the educational world. In fact, alternative understandings did exist, and older conceptions of time remained essential components of educators' discussion of school time and vacation during the nineteenth century.

Educators regularly associated school term schedules with cycles of the year. Horace Mann observed that school sessions (four in the cities and two in the country) and vacations roughly corresponded to the seasons and occurred at natural points in the calendar.[163] Mann and others recognized that neither they nor their predecessors had self-consciously determined the placement of vacations. While implying that they left the devising of the school calendar up to nature, superintendents and school boards proceeded to change the schedule for vacations over the course of the century. They relied on the same cyclical logic to justify the transition: that the new summer vacation, particularly the month of August, was an ideal moment for closed schools.[164]

Educators might also invoke the dictates of the natural world when discussing the proper length of vacation. Proposing several two- or three-week vacations rather than a single one of substantial length, one journal contributor made an analogy to a nightly sleep: "What if we should change the order of nature? What if we should not take our usual nightly rest, but put it together. Work for two weeks and then sleep one? What would be the result? Can any argument in favor on one long vacation, be found, that would not apply to the taking of fewer and longer sleeps?"[165] In comparing vacations to sleep, this statement left the reader with at least two implicit messages. First, the very familiar one that rest is an important purpose of vacation, and second, that cycles of rest are required by teachers and students, if not all organisms. An *American Educational Monthly* vacation editorial expanded on these themes:

> Nature enjoins periodical rest, and in a thousand ways reminds us of its necessity. The active, exhilarating influences of spring are reversed by the more deliberate processes and calmer enjoyments of autumn; the matured powers of summer are succeeded by winter's torpor and repose. Sunlight stimulates the operations of nature; but the energies thus exercised can be sustained only by the repose which ensues, when the activity of day gives place to the stillness of night, and the countless exhalations from ocean, and lake, and stream, which had arisen as a morning incense, are succeeded by the noiseless gathering of dewdrops on closed flowers and quiet leaves.[166]

The idea of cycles of time reflected through elements of the natural world stands in stark contrast with the arguments made for linear time. Vacations might foster greater academic progress in the long term, but they were also in sync with the natural flow of the seasons and the body.

It is important not to overplay the tension between these two senses of time. That some educators naturalized time and others commodified it is certainly not the case. Most expressed these oppositional but not necessarily contradictory ideas at some point in their writings. Indeed, permutations of both senses of time often coexisted in a single discussion of schooling. Horace Mann, for instance, derided parents who removed their children from schools to work in the fields or elsewhere. On the one hand, he argued that youth was a time for school, manhood for labor because "the productive power of the mind is as much greater in childhood as that of the body is in adult life." But while Mann criticized these parents for defying nature, to him they were also misusing time: "they are taking time from a pursuit where it has the greatest value, and appropriating it to one where it has the least," an act that was "more wasteful than to use gold instead of iron for ploughshares."[167] Likewise, a proponent for a school day schedule change aimed to "save much of the time" by replacing the traditional morning and afternoon sessions with a day-long class. But the author recognized that the resulting efficient use of time threatened pre-existing conditions and norms—in this case hunger for lunch and the traditional family dinner at mid-afternoon.[168]

The distinctions between the cyclical-natural and linear-commodified time were not always clear because even the most seemingly biological acts have a social component to them. In the case above, the author blurred the contrasts because eating is a physical function and mealtime is a cultural construction. In rearranging the school day around lunchtime, this educator seemed concerned with keeping time consistent with both the natural and social processes. William Ruffner, Virginia's first state superintendent of schools, also expected school to defer to labor patterns that he understood through both senses of time. Ruffner hoped to condense the total duration of a student's schooling by lengthening each school year and improving student attendance. He felt that six straight years of school were better for the student than 12 interrupted years and that education should be complete by age 14. "After the school period," he advised, "let labor have the field."[169] By allowing minimal labor during the school period and minimal school during the labor period, he hoped to keep the school session consistent with both the developmental needs of children and the social needs of their community.

Although disagreement among educators over the school schedule was limited, much of it is reflected in their notions of time. Underlying the contradictions in the vacation editorials are the two different senses of time in American culture. Those who wanted to retain older school calendar schedules, particularly the summer and winter terms, did not necessarily reject Mann's concerns for standardization and health. But their conceptions of time remained rooted in older, agrarian sensibilities that treated it as both natural and part of the social fabric of rural life.[170] As Ruffner admitted, short school terms were "by no means an unmitigated evil," because the "five months' school term harmonizes with the necessities of the people, the great body of whom are compelled to use the labor of their children during a large part of the year."[171] A Michigan schoolman similarly wrote that "schools must harmonize with the industries and with the situation of the people."[172] Rural area educators often stressed keeping the school calendar consistent with the labor patterns of the community, which often meant resisting the new trends in school calendars.

In short, this discursive resistance indicates that older notions of time remained potent despite assertions that the invention of the clock removed time from nature and that the routinization of the factory furthered the process. In the nineteenth century, the ways in which schools organized time reflected larger community patterns, both natural and imposed, cyclical and linear. Moreover, participants experienced and understood school time in both manners. Students progressed from kindergarten through grade twelve and beyond, but they also underwent repetitive transitions from school year to summer vacation to school year and so on. Time discipline became embedded in the very organization of incipient school systems, and schools grew to play a larger role in the way time was structured in American society. In their efforts to make school time fit work time and provide vacation time, educators contributed to future reorganizations of work time around a summer of relative leisure. School, like the factory, became an agent of modernizing time for communities. As a result, the closing of schools now signals the start of the summer more than changes in the weather. The school year challenges the calendar year for primacy in people's understanding of the passage of time. School graduation has become a life cycle rite. An issue as seemingly innocuous as redesigning the school calendar, amid much more vociferous debates about other elements of education, has set parameters for American education and culture that hold today.

The newly dominant pattern of the American school year far outlasted the ideologies that helped spawn it. When medical thought moved away from the ideas of Brown, Rush, and Virchow, educators followed suit.[173] As the nineteenth century came to a close, William Torrey Harris and other nationally prominent educators began to reject the fear of overtaxation and so came to regret the decline in urban terms to 200 or fewer school days per year.[174] Moreover, they perceived new social threats to children's welfare—explored in the next chapter—that superseded most remaining health concerns about overly long school years. Nevertheless, in its time the theory of overstudy exerted a powerful influence over the shape of the school calendar and never entirely disappeared. It provided the most significant ideological context for the shortened urban term and helped spur the lengthened rural term and the expanded summer role as a vacation.

Conclusion

Why had the initial generation of professional educators advocated the removal of summer from the school year? The foremost justification for urban areas to reduce their school years was the prevalent belief that too much schooling impaired a child and teacher's health. Educators feared that keeping people confined to a stuffy, dark school room engaged in mind-numbing activity would lead to physical and mental debility. They worried that too much education would stunt growth, produce dumbness, foster fatigue, and even precipitate melancholy. Studying nineteenth-century educators' treatment of school time and summer offers a clear reminder that beliefs about human anatomy are internalized and influence peoples' worldviews and their actions. In the case of the common school movement, educators intellectualized their school program not just through their faith in Protestantism, republicanism, and capitalism but through their understandings of the human mind and body. Thus scholarly and popular scientific beliefs helped shape the school systems adopted in the mid-nineteenth century. While social fears alone primarily accounted for the creation of common schools, concerns about children's health advanced many of the specific calendar policies enacted by the school reformers.

For a variety of reasons, summer seemed the logical term to eliminate in the city school schedule. For one thing, it gave teachers the opportunity to pursue professional development activities. For another, it afforded teachers and students alike the opportunity to interact with the natural world in order to resuscitate themselves. Thus a properly spent summer away from school became infused with properties for children's physical, mental, and emotional well-being. In farming areas, where terms might last weeks instead of months, overstudy was not a concern but intellectual atrophy was. Educators were anxious to lengthen rural terms in order to prevent the academic setbacks that occurred over long breaks from schooling. They also hoped to enhance the profession simply by improving teaching conditions, which would attract better candidates and ameliorate the lives of current practitioners. Finally, new commodifications combined with traditional cycles of time shaped educators' thinking about how to use time for pedagogical purposes. In this new era of time discipline, neither moments of schooling nor vacation could be wasted.[175] Ironically, by the latter part of the century urban reformers began to look for and find waste not in summer school but in summer vacation.

CHAPTER FOUR

"Mitigating Mental and Moral Stagnation": *Reassessments of Summer Education amid Social Transformations, 1865-1915*

> The establishment of schools for the benefit of children who must remain in the city during the long vacation, and for whom some wholesome and improving occupation ought to be provided, must commend itself to every thoughtful mind.
>
> —Ezra S. Carr, California Superintendent
> of Public Instruction, 1877

In the last quarter of the nineteenth century, these words of California's chief school official began to resonate with many philanthropists and educators. Facing a summer vacation increasing in length and perceiving an urban environment deteriorating in quality, they endorsed a new form of education—the vacation school—to ameliorate social conditions. Started by settlement workers, woman's club members, businessmen and superintendents in cities of the Northeast, vacation schools spread across the nation during the first three decades of the twentieth century. Initially intended to occupy street urchins with structured activity during the summer, the schools soon emerged as centers for innovation in pedagogy and curriculum. Eventually, they became a branch of the regular public school system and adopted a more traditional educational format. But Carr's quotation heralds the vacation school at its inception. It suggests the existence of a new articulated need for summer education by 1876—one that would lead to the vacation school movement.

Carr's statement marked a shift in thinking about the summer that poses an interpretive quandary. For the turn his words signify was not subtle; it was a jug handle away from the prevailing nineteenth-century sentiment outlined in Chapter Three, that too much schooling was detrimental to the mental and physical well-being of children and teachers. More than any others, this belief powerfully justified the demise of summer education nationwide after 1840. Carr's position, however, indicates the development of an oppositional rationale that led towards the reincorporation of the summer into the educational process. Unlike earlier educators reluctant to eliminate summer terms completely, Carr did not fear students' mental atrophy over the long summer vacation. Instead of a narrowly pedagogical concern, he desired some "wholesome and improving occupation" for children remaining in the city. The ideological movement represented by Carr's words raises some obvious questions: How exactly did thinking about the summer begin to change at the end of the nineteenth century? What social experiences help account for this transformation? Who needed "improving"? Why wasn't the city an acceptable environment in which to spend summer vacation? Finally, what educative roles and functions did summer take on as a result of this renewed emphasis on it and with what effect on the regular school year?

To formulate answers to these questions, this chapter depicts the social conditions and the ideological constructs that gave rise to the vacation school movement. It begins with a brief and general discussion of city life amid late nineteenth-century urbanization, industrialization, and immigration. The new urban configurations posed dilemmas for diverse groups of inhabitants, many of whom looked toward the public schools for help. The heart of this chapter considers what Carr's contemporaries and subsequent vacation school supporters hoped to achieve through this novel form of summer education. To trace their arguments about vacation schools, it examines the substantial body of writings published in journals and reports around the turn of the century. In so doing, it uncovers nine strands of thought about tenement neighborhoods, industrial needs, natural environments, and efficient practices commonly held by vacation school founders. These topics were constants in the vacation school literature, even though the early schools began and expanded in distinctly local contexts that are explored in subsequent chapters.

No treatment of the vacation school would be complete without analyzing its broader meaning as an institution of the Progressive Era. The vacation school was just one of many school expansions deemed progressive by participants and observers alike. In addition to initiating vacation schools, public systems also adopted kindergartens, built playgrounds, sponsored clubs, hosted athletics, and provided medical services. Furthermore, the same reformers and superintendents often instituted these various activities and offered similar justifications for all of them. Intertwined, these programs and people constituted Progressive movements in education, and they too occurred in a larger social context.[1]

Progressivism in schooling was not isolated from the change occurring in other public institutions in the 1890–1917 period. While historians have regularly linked trends in schooling to other social and political developments of the Progressive Era, the precise nature of this relationship remains in question.[2] A longstanding and highly influential interpretation viewed progressivism as an organizational revolution by a new urban middle class.[3] A number of scholars, however, have forced a reconsideration of this thesis over the last twenty-five years. The Progressive movement has been replaced by Progressive movements in which, in response to corporate capitalism and municipal machines, a wide range of interest groups produced reforms through shifting coalitions and new forms of politics.[4] As the product of such local and national movements, vacation schools began amid an era of tremendous social upheaval.

American Society in the Late Nineteenth Century

The murky origins of vacation schools achieve some clarity when viewed through the lens of the economic and demographic alteration of America's urban landscape. But what Richard McCormick astutely calls "those all-powerful, ubiquitous forces in modern American history: industrialization, urbanization, and immigration" only somewhat illuminate the reform process embodied by the vacation school.[5] Considered alone, these factors lead to an overly deterministic analysis and offer a limited explanation for specific events and trends. As Daniel Rodgers perceptively notes, these three engines of social and political transformation had existed for years without producing progressivism, yet suddenly at the dawn of the twentieth century the movements appeared, including one for vacation schools.[6] Without discounting the importance of social change, recent scholarship has offered a new underlying framework for Progressive movements. McCormick's work in particular has led to the replacement of a fractious but all encompassing partisanship with a politics comprised of muckrakers, interest groups, fragile coalitions, weakened parties, and a diminished electorate.[7] To ignore either the revised political or the more traditional socioeconomic context would therefore omit a crucial element of the vacation school movement. What follows, then, is a brief summary of the excellent historiography that traces the urbanization, industrialization, and immigration of the postbellum era and the new types of politics they yielded at the *fin de siècle.*

The vacation school movement arose from the urbanization of the United States during the last third of the nineteenth century. American cities grew more rapidly before the Civil War, but while the rate of increase in population slowed after 1860, cities reached unprecedented sizes by 1900. In 1860, only New York and Philadelphia had populations over 500,000. Brooklyn and Baltimore ranked next, but both contained under 300,000 inhabitants. Chicago and St. Louis had populations of 109,260 and 160,773, respectively. In 1900, the recently consolidated New York City counted nearly 3.5 million residents. Chicago and Philadelphia also topped the one million mark, Baltimore, Boston, and St. Louis surpassed 500,000, and nine other cities totaled 250,000 or more.[8] Moreover, the number of cities with populations over 100,000 had nearly doubled since 1880, from twenty to thirty-eight.[9]

Industrialization and demographic shifts fueled this population growth and, in turn, were stimulated by it. As many urban dwellers migrated from the rural hinterland, hundreds of thousands of immigrants from Southern and Eastern Europe crossed the Atlantic Ocean and settled in eastern seaboard and midwestern cities. Many found work in the large-scale industries that developed in American municipalities, which served as transportation nodes, supplies of labor, sources of capital, and consumer markets in the new era of corporate capitalism.[10] These changes in city size, make-up, and function altered the entire urban fabric. After the Civil War, the predominant spatial form of America's largest urban centers became what some scholars have labeled the radial center.[11] The specialized and segregated space of the modern city formed, varying from commercial downtowns to industrial parks to ethnic ghettoes to residential suburbs. The end of the walking city, however, did not entirely fragment urban populations. Baseball games, department stores, vaudeville, newspapers, museums, and skyscrapers provided city inhabitants with a shared urban cul-

ture.[12] By the turn of the century, the industrial city had become, as
Jon Teaford has suggested, the site of both the promise and problem of
America.[13]

The blemishes on this urban transformation unsettled many established citizens. Poverty, slums, and corruption accompanied the great
wealth, skyscrapers, and commercialization wrought by corporate
capitalism. Some business elites and the burgeoning professional middle classes, spurred by long-standing humanitarian and hegemonic impulses, strove to counter the ill-effects of urbanization.[14] Efforts to create large recreational parks, public health policies, playgrounds, public
works, police, fire, and other departments began in the mid-nineteenth
century.[15] By the century's end, several types of reform work—the social settlement house, muckraker journalism, and the anti-machine
mayorality among others—constituted Progressive initiatives that responded to the new urban-industrial conditions.[16] While a Jane Addams, a Lincoln Steffens, or a Tom Johnson chose such paths for ame-
lioration, others looked to the schools as instruments of reform. In so
doing, they encountered a revolution in pedagogical thought that
stemmed in large part from the currents of a new psychology.

Thinking about the human mind had undergone its own metamorphosis in the latter half of the nineteenth century. With antece-
dants dating as far back as Johann Pestalozzi but mostly rising from
Darwinism, the new psychology explored the evolution of the mind
through scientific methodology. It rejected the faculty psychology that
had long upheld an academic curriculum taught using memorization
and recitation. In its place, the new psychology offered no single sub-
stitution as the variations between the child-study of G. Stanley Hall,
the voluntaristic functionalism of William James, and the proto-
behaviorism of Edward Thorndyke attest. What united these men, and
educators like Francis Parker and John Dewey who were conversant
with them, was their focus on the emotional, physiological, and social
aspects of thinking and behavior. They also all saw science as "a
method of problem solving" rather than an "organized body of knowledge."[17] Their ideas approaches flourished in the 1890s, a decade that
witnessed the publication of seminal works by Dewey, James, Parker,
and Thorndyke.

The modification of the urban environment and of prevailing
theories of the mind did not pass by the fledgling field of education.
Amateur and professional educators alike shared the late nineteenth-
century impulse to rectify the excesses of the new urban-industrial environment while also acclimating citizens to it.[18] To accomplish these

dual and somewhat contradictory goals, they expanded and extended the role of public schooling in several ways: by adopting student-centered pedagogics, by teaching vocational and other nontraditional curricula, by forming new organizational and governing structures, and by providing wider social services. The vacation school was one such addition, therefore many of the rationalizations offered by its founders were identical to those given for other reforms. For example, vacation school proponents spoke of its value in Americanizing immigrants, in forming human capital, and in offering a natural experience for urban children, but these arguments were also made to justify evening classes, manual training classes, and nature study excursions.

Nevertheless, the vacation school was also a distinctive educational innovation of the Progressive Era. Reformers ascribed to vacation schools some purposes that were uniquely their own, such as providing a locus for child study, a place for experimentation, and a means to avoid summer losses of learning. In total, turn of the century school reformers commonly made nine major propositions to elicit support for vacation schools. All nine explanations were rarely found in one piece of writing and varied in emphasis over the 1885–1915 period, but together they constituted the intellectual underpinnings for vacation schools. Of them, one idea was clearly foremost in the minds of vacation school advocates—a concern for the social environment of the city during the summer. It is with this issue that the next section on the beliefs behind the vacation school movement will begin.

The Ideological Origins of Vacation Schools

Vacation school advocates who traveled around cities in the summertime disliked what they saw in pockets inhabited by the immigrant poor. Henry Curtis, vacation school chronicler and playground advocate, described their plight during "the long summer vacation" as "twelve weeks in which there was no place for the children of the poor but to remain in the narrow tenements or roam the streets."[19] Class and ethnic differences, already accented by the increasing residential and occupational separation of industrial urban life, were augmented further in the summer through leisure patterns. Even as some recreational activities became common to many Americans, travel remained a mark of wealth. Affluent and many middle-class families typically left the city for country homes or vacations during July and August, but the urban poor lacked such options.[20] Philanthropists and educators feared the extent and consequences of this particular social cleav-

age and sought to mute it through vacation schools, which would
mimic the leisure activities available to more wealthy children. They
also believed that vacation schools would serve poor mothers, who
faced summer "with dread rather than pleasure" because of their "can't
get away children."[21] Without vacation schools, they viewed poor
youth as caught between Scylla and Charybdis—the home and the
street.

In some ways, the domestic life of the indigent became especially
unbearable during the summer. Reformers reported little open space
and small crowded living areas in the ethnic enclaves. They found
homes "located on narrow streets which are very seldom shaded by
trees. The hallways are narrow and dark; the rooms are insufficiently
lighted."[22] Inside, "six or eight or even ten human beings, of various
ages and conditions, are crowded into two or three rooms, rendered
neither attractive nor inviting by baby crying and mother washing,
perhaps. Nothing to do but get in the way; nothing to play with, no
books to read or pictures to look at; no one to talk to, but to be
scolded."[23] To another observer's eyes, "the iron fire-escapes, jutting
out from the tenements, were hung with trailing sheets and soggy pil-
lows. Here and there a woman lolled in a window, to catch a moment's respite from the suffocation of her apartment."[24] Inadequate or
nonexistent ventilation was obviously most problematic during the
summer, when "the rooms become unbearable on a hot day and the
children cannot remain in them."[25] Thus vacation schools offered children an opportunity "to escape from their hot stuffy apartments into
the cool, well ventilated school rooms."[26]

Released by schools and driven from their homes during the summer, the children of the urban immigrant poor crowded the streets.
"The streets were so full of people, push-carts and wagons," described
one reformer, "that it was difficult to make one's way."[27] The rallying
cry "to save the child from the streets" was the chief standard of most
every supporter of vacation schools.[28] In fact, the "street" became the
metaphor through which educators expressed the perils of urban life.
Curtis provides a vibrant example of this image:

> The education of the street does not lead to a love of the beautiful or the
> good, and it has little intellectual value. Physically it means overstimulation
> of nerves and dangers from heat and dust. Intellectually it gives a certain
> alertness and cunning, but causes distrust. There is not much in the sight of
> passing trucks and push carts that can have a high intellectual value or exert
> an elevating influence. The manners of the street are derived from its law of
> success—to push yourself forward and grab the thing you want. Its moral

code is, 'They should take who have the power, and they should keep who can.'

> If one of these crowded sections in which there has been no provision made for the children be visited in vacation time, scores of the children will be seen sitting listlessly on the steps of the tenements or playing half-hearted games on the streets. Many will be seen pitching pennies, or at games of cards, or playing craps, despite the law. The sight of boys stealing fruit is not infrequent. There is always a tendency for the boys of a neighborhood to organize into gangs for purposes that are not always good.[29]

As the passage suggests, Curtis and his peers believed that the street posed a multitude of dangers for children.[30] It was unhealthy to the young's physical well-being because it overtaxed their energies and befouled their bodies. Even worst, the associations they made on the street challenged their moral rectitude in several ways. The streets spawned gangs, so vacation schools aimed at "keeping the children out of mischief."[31] In contradistinction, the street also encouraged idleness so vacation schools offered a location for wholesome activities. The lack of leisure and vacation opportunities for many children were compounded by the gradual increases in the length of summer vacation over the 1800s and the proliferation of more effective child labor laws after 1900. The abstract problems of power identified by Curtis also entered the contemporary critique of corporate capitalism, and the confluence was no coincidence. Curtis saw in the street what other Progressives saw in the factory or political machine—a dual threat to the individual and to the commonweal. Through vacation schools, educators aimed to restore both.

Vacation school leaders employed a number of rhetorical devices to popularize their programs. Typically, they reported juvenile crime rates and linked them to summer time. One noted that "in fact, investigation has shown that juvenile crimes greatly increase during summer, for the restless nature of children craves excitement, their native energy employment, their imagination food, and there is no source in the streets to furnish the supply."[32] Sadie American, a founder of Chicago's vacation schools, claimed that gangs and juvenile arrests in a poor Chicago precinct increased by 60% in July and August. In her mind, the street was "a school of crime," and "the enforced idleness and the company in which it is apt to push him" necessitated vacation schools.[33] To these and other reformers, the "street fights, games of chance, saloon brawls, [and even] arrests" they witnessed or read about mandated a response.[34] Moreover, vacation schools seemingly had a positive impact on crime rates among youth. Seth Stewart, a New York schools superintendent attributed a decrease in accidents and a

50% decline in juvenile arrests over the summer months to the presence of vacation schools and playgrounds.[35] In one instance, a vacation school advocate named Joseph Lee argued for the lengthening of an existing program by presenting data from Boston that showed an increase in crime from March through October. Lee suggested that the warm weather, not the start of summer vacation, accounted for the increase in crime but nevertheless wanted to limit vacation as much as possible.[36] In short, the vacation school began as a means "to combat the evils of the gang, the poor home, and the street."[37]

Clogged streets, dirty children, and increased crime were only tangible symptoms of what these educators and reformers truly feared in the modern city. Many believed that these tenement and street conditions threatened the very fabric of American society. Within this urban immigrant context lay anxiety over the breakdown of the family and of parental control over their children. For some, summer only became a problem "when there is little or no home influence and intelligent parental responsibility to guide and restrain the restless young life of our congested business and manufacturing centers."[38] Without denying individual agency and control over one's life experiences, the vacation school advocates also recognized a social context for urban life. Thus they designed vacation schools that physically removed children from the slums but simultaneously taught them moral and practical knowledge that would help prevent slums.[39] In this way, proponents believed that they provided both palliative and curative measures for the urban ghettoes.

Embedded in the fears of urban excess was a yearning for an idyllic pastoral life. Proponents of vacation schools repeatedly bemoaned the disappearance of the "country" influence on urban youth. Where cities were crowded, farms were open. Where cities were synthetic, rural areas were natural. Where urban environments were immoral, country life was virtuous. "Few people," wrote Curtis in 1903, "have fully realized how artificial child life has become in our great cities."[40] Turning to the public schools to address this concern, Evangeline Whitney, a New York City vacation school superintendent, asked rhetorically, "What relation have the educational authorities to those who seldom see the country?"[41] To Whitney and her peers, the connection was strong. They created the vacation school in part to forge a link between the city child and the country air.

Such a naturalistic agenda was not new in American life. Horace Mann and other educators of the antebellum era had championed

Pestalozzian naturalism in the common schools.[42] Nineteenth-century reformers of urban space held similar hopes for urban life in general, but the building of great parks and public areas did not entirely alleviate their concerns. For one thing, many crowded immigrant neighborhoods lacked close proximity to the new city landscapes. New York's Lower East Side, for example, was a good distance, both spatially and socially, from Central Park. Despite intensive municipal efforts to develop green spaces, Curtis still judged that "our cities have failed to make any provision for the play of children, nor have they striven to retain for them an environment of nature."[43] Like parks and other forms of urban recreation, the problem of the street had class dimensions.[44] Children able to travel to the country would encounter the natural environment, so it was "for the children of the poor [that] the close of the school year opens a period fraught with special danger and difficulty."[45] In fact, this apprehension lay behind the creation of a number of outdoor programs, such as playgrounds and Fresh Air Funds, which competed with vacation schools.[46]

Promoters of vacation schools believed that the city left poor immigrant children bereft of crucial experiences encountered by rural youth or vacationing urbanites. Time spent in nature was seen as altogether beneficial to the child's mind and body, especially when youth enjoyed the freedom to frolic unfettered in an outdoor setting. "Viewed as a general preparation for life," noted summer farm school founder Caroline Hill, "the value of childhood and youth spent in the country has long been known."[47] Hill was entirely correct, as Chapter Three argued that throughout the nineteenth century, educators invoked the replenishing power of nature in their polemics for the creation of summer vacation. But as it became apparent by the end of the century that many children could not enjoy such a summer on their own, a new generation of educators used the same justification for the birth of vacation schools. For example, American reminded her followers that "there is an old-fashioned notion that pictures vacation as a period of relaxing all the restraining discipline of the school year—a time when the whole being can stretch itself, as it were, and attain fuller proportions by doing as it liketh, running about in green fields, chasing butterfly, or bird, or bumblebee, climbing trees and wading brooks, or browsing in pure animal enjoyment."[48] Her vacation schools in Chicago aimed to offer a similar experience to city children by making nature study and excursions a large component. Of course, vacation schools filtered nature for students, but their advocates seemed undeterred by this fact. As one observer noted, "that contact with nature which is denied by the child's circumstances is supplied at least partially by the vacation school."⁴⁹ Thus many reformers favored vacation schools for their effort to recapture the natural setting that the city denied its youth.

Vacation school designers found much of value in an outdoors experience. At one level, they praised the learning of biological sciences through contact with the natural world. As Hill argued, "if pupils could do laboratory and museum work in the winter, and in the summer do field work in botany, biology, entomology, and geology in connection with some applied science, the results would be far more satisfactory. Farm architecture, field engineering and machinery, animal husbandry and horticulture, represent the applied side of much that pupils in the elementary and high schools study in the winter." In general, Hill believed that a country education allowed children "to make the most of the magnificent opportunities it offers in science, to come in contact with real things, and to co-operate in productive labor." In the end, her advocacy of a country education led her beyond the vacation school—where nature study was a mere "dilettante affair"—to inaugurate the Prairie View Farm School outside of Chicago. Yet in attributing cooperation in "productive labor" to the nature program, Hill hinted at benefits beyond the mere improvement of science education.⁵⁰ Vacation school advocates believed the ultimate worth of nature was its power to inculcate morals and habits. Rural encounters would Americanize poor immigrant children through the development of industriousness, probity, and other virtues that middle-class reformers feared were lacking in the newcomers.

Nature study, then, became a key element of the vacation school curriculum in most cities. To its advocates, contact with nature, even mediated through a vacation school program, could be transformative:

> The influence of this nature study upon those who seldom or never see green grass and running brooks was strongly brought to my attention one day. In visiting a school, I chanced on a group of five rude, unkempt boys whose actions betrayed their strangeness to this place, and their desire for mischief. Without realizing it, they suddenly found themselves ushered into the nature room where the teacher received them as graciously as though they were honored guests. When I had made the rounds of the building, curiosity impelled me to return and see how my rough specimens fared. The transformation was wonderful; the sneer on their faces had given place to expressions of intense interest; it may be that for the first time in their lives they had come into touch with the world beautiful.⁵¹

Immersion in a country environment, reformers reasoned, would lead these youth to new values and proclivities that would alter their pursuits, especially during unsupervised time. As Helen Putnam of Providence explained, "The object is to cultivate refining enjoyment of outdoor life by intelligent interest in natural objects and pleasure in scenery" in order to counter leisure pursuits deemed less redeeming.[52] Thus nature study connects to a third motivation for and a goal of vacation schools: to redeem the morals and shape the thinking of immigrant children led astray in part by an oppressive and unnatural urban setting.

The moral education of the non-native poor infused the entire vacation school program, not just nature study classes and trips to the country. In Detroit, superintendents deliberately selected "useful occupations as to encourage habits of thrift."[53] In New York, vacation schools aimed to "create the deepest life for morality" and "prevent their [students] moral contamination" through almost any device other than the textbook.[54] Superintendent William Maxwell of New York argued that both components of the early vacation school curriculum—manual and recreative education—contributed to the moral upbringing of summer students. "To this end," he wrote in 1902, "in work as in play, children are taught to respect the rights of others, to be unselfish, courteous, and companionable, and to find a real happiness in prosecuting the industries which appeal to the practical side of their natures."[55] New York was not atypical in this respect. Most of its vacation school activities, from instruction in ironwork to supervised play, stressed proper behaviors and beliefs. In Chicago, Progressive teaching methods were also incorporated into the program in order to "give direction to his [a child's] whole being."[56]
To vacation school leaders, moral education was nearly identical to Americanization. The morals they strove to instill were the cultural habits of the dominant Protestant population of English descent. To one New York state superintendent of public instruction, the main educational problem addressed by the vacation schools was "making good American citizens of the great mass of children who are either foreign born, or the children of foreign born parents, who come to us from many lands, each race having its own ideal of social life and government."[57] As "an assimilating and Americanizing agency" located in "foreign colonies," vacation schools served a wide range of immigrant groups.[58] One chronicler of Los Angeles vacation schools found classes filled with "Indians, Mexicans, Italians, Spaniards, Russians, Servians,

Irish, English, Americans, Hebrews, Swedes, Austrians, Germans, Africans." Rather than discovering a "seething, reeking melting pot," he credited vacations schools with producing a "joyously bubbling" mix of ethnic groups.[59] The ultimate goal, however, was not to foster cultural pluralism. Many cities nationwide rarely achieved this sort of diversity within one vacation school. Educators placed the programs in dense, immigrant neighborhoods, where typically only a handful and often just one nationality dominated each school. Moreover, these groups encountered a staff eager to assimilate their students to American ways. Only some school programs appeared to acknowledge overtly the contributions that immigrant groups could make to the definition of American.

The Americanization efforts of vacation schools also included citizenship education. To vacation school proponents, immigrants not only needed to adopt mainstream values but also to learn the functions of a republican citizen. They aimed to make the "vacation school a powerful factor in civic progress" through elements such as schoolwide assemblies and student government.[60] In Buffalo, for example, the vacation school day began with an opening and closing ceremony in which students sang American songs and recited the following civic creed:

> We are citizens of the United States, whose flag stands for self-sacrifice, for the good of all the people. The city of Buffalo is our home; we pledge ourselves to be true citizens of our great country and our beloved city, and to show our love by our works. Many brave men and women have died for love of home and country, but we can also show our love by living brave and honorable lives. Our country and our city will remain strong and great if we are honest, pure, and ever watchful for their welfare.[61]

Vacation school students in Chicago also sang songs, saluted the flag, and recited an anthem that incorporated similar ideals of patriotism, integrity, sacrifice, and dedication.[62] Sometimes programs promoted a more proactive and oppositional citizenry. For example, one Windy City school formed a Clean City League which taught that "the children and their parents... had a right to go directly to the city hall and demand that their neighborhood be cleaned."[63] All of these creeds and activities sought to embed the virtues deemed essential for participation in civic life even if there was some variation in just what those virtues were thought to be. Whitney from New York summed up the dominant thinking behind the Americanization goal of vacation schools quite well: "We can never unite into one people a 'congeries of races' until we teach them to speak our language, to read our books, to appreciate our institutions, and to find happiness in honest toil and wholesome recreation."[64] In this regard, the vacation school was consistent with the long-standing historic purpose of the public schools in the United States to absorb foreign populations.

If a democratic system required functioning citizens, a capitalist economy necessitated an appropriately educated workforce. Vacation schools were created in part to prepare students for industrial jobs. What economists now call human capital formation—the development of knowledge, skills, and habits of workers to make them more productive—was an integral piece of the vacation school purpose and program. Vacation schools offered all sorts of manual training classes, including basketry, woodwork, sloyd, iron work, leather work, and clay modeling.[65] More importantly, the vacation school literature treated manual training from a human capital perspective. For example, Whitney claimed that "the economic value of manual training to the child is incalculable."[66] By emphasizing crafts and industry, vacation schools attempted "to teach the children and youth in our crowded metropolitan centers useful kinds of handicrafts."[67] Summer students learned these practical skills for no other reason than "to enable the child to discover a line of work which he may successfully prosecute."[68]

New York's vacation schools present a clear demonstration of the human capital formation purpose. The school board's committee on special schools designed the manual and industrial work for vacation schools using occupation data tabulated by the U.S. Commissioner of Labor. Identifying workers in four major classifications—trade, manufacturing, domestic service, and agriculture—it attempted to offer summer work in each area. In the end, only "the exigencies of time and place" limited the committee's options and led it to propose a curriculum with a decidedly industrial bent.[69] Most cities made curricular choices similar to New York's, although the timing of such decisions was rather ironic. Late nineteenth-century industrialization was actually decreasing the need for skilled labor in the factory, a contradiction not acknowledged by vacation school leaders.[70] Nevertheless, the development of industrial values and habits was perhaps more necessary for the formation of human capital than providing knowledge and skills. Most vacation school planners, like New York's William Maxwell, incorporated this inclusive sense of human capital: "It is by upholding the dignity of labor, by encouraging the child to make something useful or ornamental, by awakening inventive genius and by directing energies in the right channels that vacation schools are doing very important work."[71] A rural vacation program in Iowa presented similar aims: "To teach the boys and girls industry, thrift, economy, persistence, and application to things that are worthwhile."[72]

Maxwell's emphasis on individual morals suggests that many areas of the vacation school program, not just manual training, attempted to develop human capital. Recreational programs, for example, made up a large part of the effort. As one observer noted, "the most helpful effects [of vacation schools] have resulted in the homes and characters of the boys and girls."[73] The crucial component in this endeavor was organized play. "What is wanted," wrote one reporter, "is to secure such upbuilding recreation as shall ensure such occupation of leisure hours as shall be indeed, a re-creation of body and spirit."[74] Highlighting the "play instinct of children," New York's vacation schools set up "a system of physical training and character building" through recreation. Superintendent John Jasper of New York believed that the program worked as intended, claiming that "many boys were led from play to an intelligent appreciation of the beginning of some industry, and many girls to an intelligent appreciation of the beginnings of some department of domestic science."[75]

The popularity of play generated a playground movement related to the vacation school. In some cities, the origins of vacation schools and playgrounds were conjoined. Long after public vacation schools became academic institutions that offered little formal recreation, public playground programs and private play schools remained a part of the educational landscape during the summer. Overall, the industrial training, the recreational exercises, and other elements that filled the vacation school day served more than to remove children from the city streets or Americanize them. In the minds of vacation school sponsors, these activities marshaled a productive industrial labor class and harmonized its social relations with American capitalist society.

Despite proffering some compelling reasons for their programs, vacation school leaders encountered earlier patterns of thought with the potential to derail the movement. Chief among them was the belief that too much education could harm a child's mental and physical health. As the previous chapter suggested, the notion of overexertion contributed to a number of reforms in the school schedule: the reduction of the hours in the school day, the days in the school week, and the weeks in the school year, as well as the alteration of the type and schedule of learning in the daily classroom. In terms of seasons for learning, this powerful belief system had led to the removal of schooling from summer over the course of the nineteenth century. Vacation schools reversed this earlier trend by reintroducing formal schooling to the summer; therefore proponents had to challenge and overcome the pre-existing theory of overstudy. Since the latest medical thought had not entirely dissipated nineteenth-century popular ideas about the fragility of children's minds and bodies by the turn of the century, the advent of vacation schools signaled a further renegotiation of the once-dominant assumptions of overtaxation. In the face of urbanization and immigration, conventional wisdom on children's needs adjusted to accommodate vacation and later summer schools. By 1900, the most common view held by educators was that social and bodily danger stemmed not from summer education but from its nonexistence. This ideological tack occurred in several ways and stages.

First, some educators began to doubt and deny that school attendance would drain children of their vitality. In their advocacy of vacation schools, they recognized claims that vacation schools "would make child-life too strenuous" or that "one may do himself permanent injury by not relaxing during these months."[76] Yet they normally raised these concerns only to refute them. Reformers began to draw on the growing body of medical literature that discounted any connection between poor health and schooling. They especially disputed the belief that the mind was a muscle and as such risked overuse. Instead, educators and medical experts began to assert that "the evils affirmed to spring from mal-methods of instruction, are figments of the imagination" and "that no one will claim that the addition of 400 or 500 hours to the number now spent in school would be a burden to any child."[77] As proof, they pointed to the strong health of initial vacation school students. Administrators of Newark's groundbreaking summer program found the view that "schools are necessarily detrimental to the health of pupils" to be "erroneous" and consistently noted that "the health of teachers and pupils was good throughout the term of six weeks."[78] These ideas gradually seeped into a more public discourse. By 1902, letter writers to the *New York Times* consistently absolved schools—of all types and lengths—from any impact on the health of children.[79]

More often, concerns about the urban environment simply outweighed fears of overtaxation. Without denying the danger of fatigue through excessive schooling, some vacation school leaders focused on the risks to health and morals entailed by ignoring the home and street life of immigrant children. To them, the elements of slum life—poor ventilation in apartments, improper dietary habits, hot to cold transitions, exhausting excitements, disregard for the laws of health, poor working conditions, and even reading sensationalist literature—debilitated children far more than too much time in school.[80] In fact, the "bad cooking, irregularity, inadequate sleep, lack of ventilated bedrooms, improper clothing, inadequate exercises and lack of bathing" associated with tenement life replaced the conditions of the school house as the bane of good health.[81] Furthermore, experts and citizens alike increasingly suggested that inactivity, not overexertion, led to the decline of a child's health. Decrying the blind adherence to summer vacation as a time for the "hammock" and "dull idleness," they argued that this "tradition produces pale faces, gummy eyelids, flabby flesh, and lack of appetite" in an urban environment.[82] Thus for many, health concerns remained paramount, and vacation schools served the public welfare by replacing idleness with activity.[83] In short, loafing on the street became as loathed as relaxation in the country was previously idealized.

Vacation schools leaders also accommodated the fears of excessive education through the type of program they advocated. Many still accepted the link between health and schooling but held that the type of schooling, not the amount, posed risks for students. Strenuous mental activity was debilitative, but a well-planned summer program could avoid this potential pitfall. The vacation school did not present any danger, they argued, because of its nonthreatening curriculum and schedule. American used this approach in a piece on vacation schools in *Kindergarten Magazine*:

> 'Open vacation schools' they have said, and this they have done. 'But school again?' ask many doubting. 'Are not heads already overburdened, and back and eyes and lungs weary unto exhaustion from bending over books and desks?' Indeed, yes, and no further strain will be put upon them; on the contrary, an effort will be made to turn the whole being into a new channel.[84]

To American and others, these "new channels" that vacation schools opened—nature study, manual training, play, and excursions—did not burden weary school children. They contended that the voluntary attendance policy, as opposed to a mandatory one, forestalled any threats to children's well-being.[85] Thus vacation school design, with its unregimented organization and nonacademic curriculum, deliberately deterred opposition based on health considerations. Vacation schools were never meant to extend the regular school program, nor were they intended to fill the entire summer. Most ran morning sessions, typically three hours, for six weeks of a ten-week summer vacation. In short, vacation schools both acknowledged and circumvented health concerns by incorporating relaxation into the daily schedule and offering a wide range of nonscholarly activities.[86]

What is most striking about the turn-of-the-century vacation school discourse was its almost complete one-sidedness on the issue of overtaxation. Despite the ideological maneuverings described above, there was little contention among educators over the vacation school's impact on health. Advocates regularly challenged earlier beliefs about debility stemming from excessive education even though few educators denounced vacation schools on that basis. The overstudy theory was not dead by 1900, but it retained few adherents among public educators. Thus in the literature on vacation schools, it functioned as a straw figure—granted recognition but easily blown away by the three methods previously described: through denial, de-emphasis, or accommodation. Residual beliefs that summer education overtaxed childrens' fragile minds and bodies continued, but such proclamations by vacation school leaders appeared more by rote than by conviction. For example, when Newark expanded its vacation school curriculum in 1906, its superintendent still admitted that "nor should the work of the summer schools be so exacting as to affect unfavorably the health and general physical condition of the children who attend."[87] Yet in practice vacation school administrators did not hesitate to expand and extend summer learning even though they remained deferential to the power of the overstudy thesis in their writings and speeches. The fears embedded in this weakened ideology had not prevented vacation schools' birth, nor by 1910 would they prevent the adoption of the "regular school course" that would turn vacation into summer schools.

The addition of academic classes to vacation schools in the early twentieth century tested the malleability of the overstudy theory. Vacation school leadership had long asserted that the schools were not harmful because they were not academic. Now that the schools took on traditional school subjects and characteristics, this earlier defense was undermined. Superintendents, however, were ready with well-honed counterarguments to the theory of overtaxation. They relied on all three rationalizations used by the earliest wave of vacation school advocates, and if anything, these justifications grew more forceful in the service of summer academic programs. First, some suggested that the excessive schooling thesis was unscientific and lacked evidence. "No sound reason," wrote a contributor to the *Journal of Education*, "has been advanced for permitting pupils' minds to lie dormant for two or three months in the year. Science has taught that agreeable mental activity conserves the strength of the body."[88] Another noted the lack of "any data to justify the belief that a healthy, rugged child needs a long vacation."[89]

Other educators reiterated the urban ills that in their minds took precedence over any fears of overeducation. If "continuous school work throughout the summer" was risky, so were twelve weeks of idleness on the urban streets.[90] Finally, many emphasized the varied activity of vacation schools even after they added academic classes: "Hence we seek to make a new and more practical use of the school. We alternate work and play; we change frequently from studies to manual activities and from manual activities to studies. Thereby, exhaustion is avoided."[91] In time, the easy replacement of recreational vacation schools with academic summer schools marked the final downfall of the overtaxing theory among school administrators. Until then, it had remained strong enough to attract considerable attention from early vacation school advocates eager to generate favor for their programs. Its indirect impact continued long after its demise, however, as twentieth-century summer schools typically provided a less rigorous course of study than their regular school counterparts.

The justifications for vacation schools centered on the broad social concerns discussed so far: the inactivity or misbehavior of tenement youth, the artificiality of the urban environment, the seemingly unassimilability of recent immigrants, and the human capital needs of workers and industrialists. But reformers, particularly those attached to the public schools, also added more straightforward educational reasons for launching vacation schools. They identified two ways in which summer programs would benefit students and schools. First, vacation schools would counter the setback in students' cognitive development over summer. Second, vacation schools would serve as sites for experimentation that would eventually lead to innovation in the regular public schools.

As the length of vacations increased over the nineteenth century, some educators began to caution against mental atrophy during the summer. They feared that a lengthy layoff caused students to forget what they had studied and forced teachers to spend an inordinate amount of time each fall reviewing previously learned material—what modern researchers call summer setback.[92] Summer idleness led not just to unfortunate social consequences in morality and health but also to a diminished level of scholarship by September. Since long summer vacations dulled the mind, an appropriate level of activity could sharpen it.

Thus a Providence school superintendent reasoned that "six weeks of [summer] instruction in spelling and reading, and in a knowledge of common things, which does not unduly exercise the brain, keeps up the habit of study, and prepares them to engage with more intelligence in the subsequent lessons of the school year."[93]

Most vacation school proponents discussed summer setback in much more consequential terms. One suggested that vacation schools would end the "mental and moral stagnation" which required "3 or 4 months of most persistent effort during the early part of the regular school term for the teachers to overcome."[94] Sadie American held that "a great number of teachers and principals testify to the demoralizing effect of the long weeks of idleness and the necessity of spending the greater part of the early fall months in over-coming the summer deterioration."[95] Another observer similarly noted that the teacher "dreads the task of undoing the ill-effects of two or three months of idleness or worse."[96] Vacation and later summer schools were favored "to prevent vacation time [from] destroying the good effects of the school term."[97] Through vacation schoolwork, "the children returning in the fall from their excursions are in exceptionally good condition for school work during the winter."[98] In short, vacation schools were believed to counter summer setback.

Even before the advent of vacation schools, administrators began to disapprove of the long summer break. By minimizing the dangers of overexertion in order to justify vacation schools, they further weakened the ideology that accompanied the nineteenth-century reduction of the urban school year and the elimination of the rural summer term. As early as 1875, a Providence superintendent argued that "a vacation of two weeks at the close of the summer term, and of a week previous to the commencement of the fall term, suffices for recreation."[99] William Torrey Harris, the United States Commissioner of Education, argued strenuously in the 1890s that cities should no longer reduce their school sessions.[100] Likewise, the child study movement of the 1890s augmented the reaction against the long vacation.[101] One journal contributor argued against lengthy vacations on the grounds that children's growth did not conform to the school calendar and that students missed enough time already due to illness and other conditions.[102] Overall, educators offered and adopted numerous proposals to achieve greater flexibility in the use of time.[103] Vacation schools became the first of several reforms aimed at restoring a place in public education to the summer. From them sprang year-round schools, summer evening schools, continuation classes, and lengthened school years.[104] More than any of these options, the academic summer school that evolved from the recreational vacation school became the predominant form of fighting summer setback.

Reformers also described the vacation school as the locus of experimentation for public education. In fact, vacation schools did present opportunities for teachers and administrators to try new approaches in schooling. By providing additional and unrestricted school time for educators, the vacation school enabled them to spend it in innovative ways. Vacation school leaders were quite explicit about this goal. Mostly, they expressed it in very general language, for example, writing of "its desirability as a sort of educational proving ground for testing the newer plans for school work" and that "the summer school was regarded as, to some extent at least, a favorable place to try experiments."[105] Sometimes, however, they incorporated specific Progressive language about a "new education" which was "to explore the individuality of the child, to show his natural bent, and give direction to his whole being."[106]

For the more visionary leaders, vacation schools could play a transformative role in an entire school system. While regular schools relied on a predictable and proven program, vacation schools strove for something less routine in the hopes of influencing mainstream education. Superintendent Jasper highlighted this distinct purpose of the vacation school:

> The system of vacation schools may well be used for experimental purposes. The work should not follow any form so set as to prevent experiment. It is not wise to experiment with the course of study in the larger system of schools during the other terms of the year, but new forms of work and methods of work may properly be tried in the vacation schools. The experience thus secured may then be used to advantage in the other schools.[107]

Generally conservative, Jasper showed reluctance to tinker blindly with the regular school curriculum, but he also recognized its inflexibility.[108] To him, the vacation school could be an innovative force of the school system, and he therefore rejected any predetermined form for it. Most advocates, like California's Carr, simply asserted that vacation schools "should differ essentially both in the subjects pursued and the methods employed, from the ordinary school terms."[109] As a result of this approach, there was substantial variety among vacation schools within a city, as well as divergence in emphasis between programs in different cities.[110] Although there was no uniform blueprint, vacation school leaders did envision three specific areas in which the schools would challenge rigidity and chart new ground: in school organization vacation schools adopted novel features and relaxed guidelines; in pedagogy teachers felt free to move away from traditional rote learning; and in curriculum vacation schools offered work in several cutting-edge subjects such as nature study, play, and manual training. By highlighting these elements, proponents presented vacation schools as both a source and site of school reform.

Vacation schools eased many of the standard administrative policies of the regular public school. Most vacation schools dispensed with required attendance, truant officers, grades, and other mechanisms of control. A Denver superintendent described a looseness to his vacation school program that was typical:

> Pupils were allowed the freedom of the halls; they played bean bag, swung Indian clubs, danced, sang, and marched. There were no lines and no regulations as to the doors by which the pupils should enter. No attention was paid to tardiness, and to absence only the rule that three days' absence vacated the pupil's seat in favor of the next on the waiting list.[111]

To some extent, this design bowed to certain limitations. A strict program would most likely have failed to attract students and garner popularity. A compulsory program might have proved less successful in silencing the long-standing beliefs about over-taxation and habits of summer.[112] Vacation school administrators, however, did not view the laxity purely as a concession to the summer heat and conditions. They also saw it as a strength of the vacation schools, consistent with their intentions. As one commentator put it, they were "very inspiring to those who have believed our school system [was] quite too pedantic and formalized, as well as restrictive, for the best development of children."[113] Of course vacation schools did not dispense with all forms of traditional administration, as they maintained hierarchical relations between teachers, principals, and superintendents. Still, they offered a revolutionary form of school organization to the students who attended, and for teachers, they granted significant freedom of action inside the classroom.

A second area of vacation school innovation was in pedagogy. Some advocates saw the schools as ideal for training new teachers and incorporating new teaching methods.[114] While a few cities employed novice teachers, most believed that the move away from traditional pedagogy required especially talented and experienced practitioners, or in the words of one supporter, "women of quick wit, good sense, sound judgment, and ready resources."[115] Likewise, Chicago's first vacation school hired current teachers "chosen because of their special fitness for the work in question."[116] Most commentaries, however, focused on the attributes of innovative classroom practice, not the composition of the faculty. In the vacation school "there was much more freedom of movement and much more latitude given to the teachers."[117] By allowing teachers to depart from the severity of standard practice, the schools encouraged more child-centered classrooms that altered the relationship between teacher and students. The excursions in particular fostered "a companionship between teachers and pupils, not possible upon school premises."[118] In general, vacation school teachers transcended traditional routines of recitation and memorization most often when they taught courses in new subjects—like manual training and nature study—which necessitated innovative and individualized approaches. While these elements of Progressive pedagogy did not originate in the summer activities, the vacation schools often served as the site for experimental practice, as in Chicago where John Dewey designed one school's program.[119]

Vacation school leaders generally made two related boasts about the summer curriculum. First, as with pedagogy, they claimed that their programs offered activities ancillary to the regular schools. As one early chronicler noted, "vacation schools add a very desirable supplement to conventional public education by securing a much greater amount of muscular activity; by encouraging a much greater degree of self-expression, self-reliance and initiative; by presenting the more refining possibilities of environment, to mold tastes in choosing recreation and occupations."[120] Teachers College Professor Samuel Dutton and Massachusetts Commissioner of Education David Snedden agreed, stating in their massive and influential *Administration of Public Education in the United States* that "when one examines the courses of study which have been followed in different cities, one sees to what an extent the vacation schools have been educational experimental stations."[121] Thus vacation schools foreshadowed the expansion of schooling into social and vocational roles.

In the movement's initial years, vacation schools had no direct link to the curriculum taught from September to June. Administrators rejected what was called a "lock-step" connection between classes in vacation and mainstream schools. As one early vacation school leader in Chicago put it, "the curriculum should not cover the same ground as the regular course in the schools, since it is not the function of the vacation school to educate the bright beyond nor bring the backward

child up to his trade." Instead, the schools aimed to provide poor children with summer "opportunities to acquire a kind of instruction
which parents only can supply, by their own preference, through
travel or home environment."[122] With a vision of both liberation and
control, they hoped to spark children's creativity and shape their habits through nature study and manual training classes, recreational activities, and excursions. Only when vacation schools adopted academic
classes geared towards promotion through the regular schools did they
lose this innovative quality.

As a second curricular goal, vacation school leaders intended to
guide public education towards the school subjects of the future. In
New York's first vacation schools, philanthropists spoke "of the ultimate extension of manual training and kindergarten instruction to a
place of greater usefulness in the methods of our Public Schools."[123]
Indeed, in the eyes of their supporters, vacation schools greatly contributed to the extension of public schooling into new functions.
Clarence Arthur Perry argued that New York's vacation schools had
led to the inclusion of play in the city's primary schools and new industrial and domestic science departments in its high schools.[124] Another observer attributed new regular school classes in whittling and
gardening to vacation schools. Whether rhetoric or reality, these results were not unanticipated by the heralds of the movement.

To what extent vacation schools actually led to the broadening of
the regular school curriculum is difficult to pinpoint. Proponents like
Perry were clearly inclined to argue the affirmative. In pedagogy, for
example, one chronicler contended that "the effect of these vacation
schools has been already largely to modify methods of teaching in
school houses."[125] But Larry Cuban has found that Progressive teaching
techniques did not readily permeate public school systems, and it
seems likely that vacation schools only encountered mild success in
that area.[126] However, the vacation school achieved its "ultimate goal of
modifying the regular schools" substantially more through its curriculum than its organization or pedagogy.[127] By promoting vacation
school work in manual training and play, vacation school founders
articulated reasons for adding them to the regular school program. In
some cities, these subjects entered the regular curriculum only after
they appeared in local vacation schools. Even with this mixed record
of influence, the vacation school movement provides insight into the
educational changes of the Progressive Era.

Progressivism in education was nearly as intellectually unwieldy as its counterpart in American society at large. Although it did not exist as a uniform ideology, there were a number of consistencies in the thought of educational reformers. Some of these were evident in the discourse on vacation schools presented above: the expansion of schools' programs and functions into more social roles; the application of psychological and sociological knowledge in the classroom; the adjustment of instructional methods to the individual needs of each student; and, as Lawrence Cremin put it, "the radical faith that culture could be democratized without being vulgarized."[128] To find these features present in the literature is not to say that vacation schools were the source of Progressive educational thought. As argued earlier here and elsewhere, progressivism in education came out of the social and intellectual transformations of the late-nineteenth century.[129]

Vacation schools' importance to educators was as one of the earliest spaces where their innovations in organization, pedagogy, and curriculum were put into practice. Through their experimentation, these summer programs encouraged the adoption of new approaches in the regular public schools, albeit with limited success. Many well-known Progressive teachers and administrators enjoyed formative experiences in the vacation schools, including Edwin Cooley, Ella Flagg Young and John Shoop of Chicago; Frank Cody of Detroit, William Barringer of Newark, Julia Richmond of New York, and Helen Putnam of Providence. This leadership groomed in the vacation schools went on to notable expansion and restructuring of public school systems even though they may not have substantially altered classroom practice. In fact, the larger outcome was the opposite of what these men and women intended. Instead of changing school systems, vacation schools were transformed by them into credit-bearing, academic programs known as summer schools.

The remaking of vacation schools into summer schools was a key moment in the history of summer education. As subsequent chapters uncover the process and impact of change in local settings, this section will only consider how the literature that justified the initial emergence of summer programs treated their transition. In fact, as vacation schools turned into summer schools, new rationalizations achieved prominence among the chroniclers of the movement. Chief among these were two related emphases—that summer schools enhanced system productivity through wider use of the school plant and that they saved students time and schools money by bestowing academic credit to participants. These notions, however, were not a perversion of Progressive ideology even though summer schools fundamentally differed from their vacation school predecessors. Rather, they highlight the contradictory ideological strands of the Progressive Era and reflect an intellectual shift towards an emphasis on social efficiency.[130]

The idea of social efficiency encompassed a vision of rationalization and social engineering and gained prominence around 1910. It stemmed from "the merger of the prestige of science with the prestige of the well-organized business firm and factory" and the term was used by political and school reformers alike.[131] For example, the superintendent of Lynn, Massachusetts, launched several programs, including summer schools, "to increase school efficiency."[132] More often, the desires for efficiency were clear even if the specific word went unmentioned. To some extent, the ideas already described in this chapter partially incorporated language in the social efficiency vein, but two final justifications for vacation schools—the wider use of the school plant and the saving of time and money—evolved directly from it.

The 1910 publication of Clarence Arthur Perry's widely acclaimed book, *Wider Use of the School Plant*, heralded and named the movement for school extension.[133] In it, Perry delineated an important educational trend of the previous thirty years: the expansion of activity conducted in public school facilities. He described the typical school of 1880— open for at most seven hours a day—and decried the waste of such under utilization. Perry then traced the many new roles that now kept its twentieth-century counterpart open during the evening, weekend, or summer. He attributed a broad range of school developments to the wider use of the school plant movement, including vacation schools, evening schools, playgrounds, public lectures and entertainment, evening recreation centers, social centers, organized athletics and games, folk dancing, and organization meetings. Perry applauded these novel school functions, arguing that they prevented the waste of infrequently used million-dollar school facilities and that they achieved "social betterment through wider use."[134] Despite the variety in origin and purpose, the new activities constituted a single development in education. Most school additions responded to similar concerns for the urban social environment, involved similar recreational activities, and served similar immigrant populations. Contemporaries and later scholars alike correctly recognized that vacation schools formed a part of the larger effort to increase the utilization of school facilities.[135] In short, the expansion of the public school's social role through the summer use of its buildings and grounds became an important component of school systems during the Progressive Era.

Long before Perry published his book, educators and reformers used his arguments to justify the existence of vacation schools. When school leaders suggested that "extended vacations entail great waste," they meant not just the summer setback experienced by students but also the disuse of the school facilities themselves.[136] Superintendents in Cleveland, New York, and other cities all discussed the value of vacation schools in terms of preventing the waste of the school plant.[137] For example, an administrator of Chicago's first program asked rhetorically, "Is it not poor economy for the city to spend millions of dollars of public money in the erection of buildings for the use of the children and then to allow these buildings to remain unused for months?"[138] As schools undertook new functions, many administrators began to tabulate the number of uses of school buildings outside of the regular school day. In 1911, Baltimore's superintendent reported 4,457 wider uses of the school plant; Richmond's tabulated 5,551 in 1923.[139] School officials valued the financial efficiency of such activities but believed they led to greater social benefits as well. In counting the number of uses, educators articulated a vision for public schools that were open nearly round the clock, active throughout the year, and that served the social and educational needs of both children and adults.

Vacation schools were not just a part of this school extension movement; they stood at its forefront. Perry's work demonstrated that vacation schools inspired several of the new uses for the school plant. As Dutton and Snedden observed, "the marked success of the vacation school has also called attention anew to the desirability of a further extension of public education, in the line of evening schools, vacation playgrounds, continuous sessions, public lectures, etc."[140] Vacation schools certainly encouraged the wider use of the school, but there was clearly some exaggeration in this statement, as evening schools and playgrounds also had nineteenth-century origins. In fact, vacation schools and playgrounds were often conceptually, developmentally, and organizationally interwoven, and one program usually led to the other.[141] In some cities like Pittsburgh and Detroit, vacation schools developed out of preexisting playground programs. In contradistinction, playgrounds in Baltimore, New York, and other cities grew out of vacation school programs. Pittsburgh's privately run Playground Association ran both the city's vacation schools and its playgrounds for over ten years.[142] In Cincinnati, a schools superintendent advocated "a union of the two [separate] movements" because he noted how vaca-

tion schools and playgrounds complemented each other.[143] In all of
these cities, the origins of both forms of school extension occurred
within five years of each other.

Unlike the school playground, the year-round school undeniably
grew out of the vacation school. The chronology of this type of school
extension is quite clear. The first recorded year-round schools started
in Bluffton, Indiana, in 1904, but school systems in Newark, Nashville,
and Omaha became well known for opening schools with all-year
schedules during the 1910s.[144] These cities experimented with the
twelve-month school year well after they began vacation schools; indeed, year-round schools developed subsequent to the addition of academic classes to vacation schools. "One of the best arguments in favor
of the all-year plan," noted one chronicler, "is the success of summer
sessions."[145] Similarly, another stated that "the logic of these summer
schools with their promotion classes led inevitably to the all-year
school."[146] Part of the logic stemmed from the vacation school's defus-
ing the overtaxation ideology that had detonated the year-round
schools of the mid-nineteenth century. With their partial return after
1900, urban administrators hastened to draw the connection between
all-year and vacation schools:

> The vacation school, which has developed in recent years, has changed our
> conception of summer work for children and the amount of vacation that is
> necessary to healthy development in children. Moreover, it has changed the
> conception of the school and has led to provision in the school program for
> periods of relaxation following periods of study.[147]

The year-round schools never became nearly as widespread as vacation
schools, but they did contribute to the backlash against long vacations
and short schools terms. As part of the wider use of the school plant
movement, they were simply one of several programs to follow the
vacation school's pioneering role in school extension.

The transformation of vacation schools into summer schools provided educators with one final justification for the summer education:
the saving of time for the students and money for the schools. By offering classes in English, math, and other regular school subjects and
by granting academic credit for passing them, these schools served a
number of children. Summer schools allowed overage students additional time to catch up to their ideal grade. They also enabled excellent
students to accelerate their progress through the school grades and
graduate early. Mostly, educators aimed summer schools at students

who had failed classes during the previous year. These children could now remain with their age cohort by retaking and passing the subject during the summer. School administrators were quick to point out the advantages for these students. Perry stressed that "one of the most important benefits of the vacation school lies in the opportunity it affords backward pupils to make up work left unfinished at the close of the school year."[148] In Cleveland, which was the first large city to adopt an academic summer program, the superintendent explained the innovation as a "saving work" that had prevented 1,000 dropouts. Looking back on its first six years of existence, Cleveland's superintendent stressed the economic and educational merit of the summer school.[149] Educators valued these schools for their social efficiency because they saved school systems money as well as students time.

Many communities were persuaded to open summer schools by the supposed financial benefits they would reap. As one state superintendent observed, "more and more towns and cities are offering pupils opportunity for school work in summer, as a result of which many boys and girls are saved from repeating a grade. Demonstrably a saving of time for the pupil means a saving of expense for the town or city."[150] In fact, superintendents often calculated the costs averted by running summer schools. Pittsburgh's superintendent, for example, determined that summer schools saved the city $11,635 in 1912.[151] The linkage of the summer and regular schools, however, was attractive to more than just bean counters. Reformers imbued with a faith in the social efficiency of large-scale public organizations moving age-based cohorts of students through school in a lock-step manner lauded the merging of the two programs. Their commendations represented an ironic switch since they once praised vacation schools for their distinctiveness from public schools. Thus an emphasis on savings emerged to overshadow the initial social and educational functions of vacation schools.

Conclusion

By highlighting the efficiency of summer schools, educators did not entirely supplant the original justifications for vacation schools. Together, nine themes made up the ideological context for the origins of vacation schools and the development of summer schools. Proponents of both institutions continued to draw on fears of urban slums, longings for rural lifestyles, and desires for Americanization and human capital formation of immigrants. In addition, they stressed vacation schools' more narrow contributions to education as a locus of experimentation and a cure for summer setback. They also rearticulated the over-taxation ideology to make it consistent with the vacation school program. Finally, they incorporated notions about the wider use of the school plant and the saving of time and money represented by the summer school.

These nine ideas, isolated in this chapter for the sake of analysis, were nevertheless linked in the minds of vacation school advocates. The connections are not surprising, given that their multifaceted concerns all spawned from similar socioeconomic and school conditions in the cities. For example, an early chronicler of Boston's vacation schools expressed several of the themes as stemming from an overly long urban summer vacation:

> The school year as a rule only comprises about forty weeks. While the remaining period of nine or ten weeks, spent in delightful recreation in the country is a boon to many children, to many others it is a detriment, passed in the profitless glare of the hot city streets; much of the discipline of the winter term being swallowed up in the general lawlessness engendered by an unrestrained, idle summer.[152]

Well after the ascendancy of summer schools, such images remained interwoven with conceptions of efficiency. A journal writer in 1914 linked the social problems on city streets, the moral problem of idleness, and the educational problem of summer setback in one remonstrative sentence: "Much that was learned in school at previous sessions is forgotten; many of the children become criminals, and still more form habits of idleness."[153] Educators continued to draw on this discourse of summer education to justify various sorts of vacation programs during the 1920s and 1930s.[154] Telescoping backwards in time, similar language was also present at the creation of vacation schools. To see how the nine strands of thought intersected with social conditions and shaped the development of vacation schools, Chapter Five outlines the vacation schools in Providence and Newark—the first two cities to launch and sustain them, traces their subsequent spread to much of urban America, and analyzes their transformation to summer schools in Chicago.

In short, vacation school leaders harbored ideas central to progressivism in American education. In their advocacy roles, educators articulated languages of social bonds and social efficiency that underlay much early-twentieth century reform in the political economy of the United States. Progressives as disparate as Jane Addams, Jacob Riis and James Reynolds looked to the schools as a vehicle for change and specifically proposed that they expand the hours, days, and seasons of their usage.[155] Within the realm of public school leaders, the same strands of thought justified the growth of kindergartens, recreation centers, Americanization classes, and other programs. To view vacation schools as the linchpin of a fresh understanding of progressivism, then, overstates their impact and misses their true significance. Vacation schools, like these and other institutional innovations, embodied much of the educational thinking of the Progressive Era.

What separates the vacation school from these other programs and therefore accounts for its central importance is its particular reconstruction of the meaning of summer. With the reduction of the city school calendar essentially complete by 1890, the summer vacation posed a relatively new dilemma for educators. An unprecedented urban landscape wrought by immigration and industrialization precipitated new views of the school's roles in society and how summer might help fulfill them. Discounting earlier fears for children's health, educators now proposed vacation schools to ease congestion and reduce criminality in crowded neighborhoods, assimilate immigrant children, and provide practical skills and an experience in nature to urban children lacking both. Yet the nineteenth-century fears of overtaxation and the summer ideal of relaxation remained strong enough to force an accommodation between the pitfalls of summer education outlined by an earlier generation and the social and educational needs of the present. The shape taken by actual vacation school programs would reflect these ideological negotiations.

Vacation schools opened in Providence and Newark and eventually other cites and towns. In the end, the overstudy theory was overshadowed by anxieties about the physical and social environment for children in industrial cities and vacation schools. As a result of the schools and the discourse surrounding them, the distinctiveness of summer as both a period of learning and leisure grew further entrenched in the United States. Educationally, the summer became the locus for school experimentation, although the form varied from organized play to manual training to nature study to child-centered pedagogy. Even as the subsequent public summer schools abandoned the ideology of innovation; the summer itself would retain this educative purpose throughout the twentieth century.

"Keeping up with Superintendent Jones": *The Origins, Diffusion, and Bureaucratic Transformation of Vacation Schools, 1866-1929*

> It is impossible to predict just how far this work is to spread in this country, but the present indications are that every city in the North of 15,000 to 20,000 inhabitants will soon have vacation schools and that these schools will also exist in many villages from 3,000 inhabitants upward.[1]
>
> —Henry Curtis, *Report of the U.S. Commissioner of Education*

Henry Curtis, an early proponent and chronicler of vacation schools for the United States Bureau of Education, had valid reasons for his optimism in 1903. Starting in 1894, when the Association for Improving the Condition of the Poor [AICP] opened three vacation schools in New York, the idea of summer education jelled with educators and prominent citizens in the great cities of the Northeast and Midwest. Churches, charity organizations, women's groups, and later school systems hastened to launch local vacation schools. Education journals and superintendent reports bristled with encouraging accounts of vacation school development and expansion in numerous cities. Indeed, advocates believed that they heralded a social and educational movement that would sweep the nation. Since 1894, they had seen vacation schools established in many of America's major industrial centers: New York and Providence (for a second time) in 1894, Cleveland in 1895, Chicago in 1896, Brooklyn (for a second time as well) and Indianapolis in 1897, Baltimore, Buffalo, Minneapolis, Philadelphia, and Syracuse in 1898, and so on.[2]

Like several educational innovations of the Progressive Era, vacation schools began as private educational work but swiftly became a part of public school systems. Again, New York lead the way in this trend when its board of education assumed full responsibility for the AICP vacation schools in 1898, but other urban school systems soon followed suit: Buffalo's in 1900, Philadelphia's in 1901, Cincinnati's in 1906, and Baltimore's in 1911. Elsewhere, as in Chicago, Cleveland, Indianapolis, and Minneapolis, the transfer occurred gradually over two or several years but was ultimately no less complete. In none of these cities was the takeover hostile; rather the public financing and administration of vacation schools was welcomed by their founders. Like her contemporaries, Sadie American, a leader of Chicago's vacation schools and Woman's Club activist, was outspoken in her "hope that before long the boards of education in their respective cities will undertake their [vacation school] management."[3] In Chicago and other large cities, her wish was realized during the early part of the twentieth century.

The public takeover of vacation schools held important consequences for the types of educational roles assumed during the summer. Vacation schools began with an improvisational spirit in pedagogy and curriculum, but their transfer to public control thoroughly remade them and even renamed them. As public institutions, summer schools adopted a regular academic focus and a credit-bearing function, and they soon bore little resemblance to the vacation programs that preceded them.[4] Instead, they took on the dominant twentieth-century purpose for summer education: to enable students to catch up or to get ahead in the age-graded sequence of K-12 education. Thus a crucial moment in the history of summer education occurred in the early twentieth century. By 1929, every major American city and many smaller communities had experimented with vacation schools, and most had experienced their transformation into summer schools. This chapter analyzes these intertwined processes of diffusion and change. It begins with a short examination of two early vacation school programs in Providence and Newark. It then briefly outlines the nature and extent of vacation schools' radiation across the United States. Finally, the bulk of this chapter traces the development and evolution of vacation schools in Chicago.

The Origins of Vacation Schools in Providence and Newark

Had Curtis written ten years earlier, he probably would have exuded far less confidence. The previous twenty-five years had witnessed several fleeting trials of vacation schools. Many proposals found in public school reports were disregarded entirely, and most city school systems were unable to find the funding and support needed to implement such institutions.[5] Boston's school committee, for example, created a committee on vacation schools and recommended $2,000 for the establishment of two schools in the summer of 1878, but the city council refused to make any provision for this endeavor.[6] At the private level, vacation schools fared slightly better. The First Church of Boston initiated a short-lived summer program in 1866. Boston teachers maintained vacation schools irregularly after 1878, and the North Bennett Street Industrial School started a vacation school in 1885. Groups in Brooklyn, Cincinnati, and New Haven also started vacation schools in the late 1880s. Until the 1890s, however, most other cities lacked even the intermittent beginnings of Boston. While the precedents for vacation schools remained few and isolated until 1894, two cities stand out as exceptions: Providence and Newark.[7]

In 1868, Providence launched the nation's first system of vacation schools. The city provided a summer learning experience distinct from antebellum summer sessions in several manners. First, its summer program did not continue the regular school year but rather supplemented it. Providence's vacation schools used methods, materials, and curricula designed especially for the summer. The schools offered nonacademic classes in sewing, drawing, and object teaching and emphasized student behavior, manners, and habits. Moreover, they achieved high enrollments partially because they did not require regular attendance.[8] Finally, the schools blurred the distinction between public and private. Housed in public school buildings, taught by mostly public school teachers, and reported on regularly by the city's superintendent, the impetus and direction for the schools still came from outside of Providence's education system. A voluntary private committee ran the schools and relied on donated and city council funds to finance them.[9]

Providence's vacation schools attracted scores of children from the city's primary and intermediate grades. By 1870, summer enrollment reached 10% of the city's fall term registration, a level of participation maintained through 1876. That year, enrollment peaked at 1,238 students, who attended classes in eight public schools that employed twenty-two teachers. In fact, the 1876 vacation school registration totaled nearly 25% of the 5,054 children enrolled in public schools during the regular school year.[10] Pleased with the numbers, school administrators viewed the schools as a success and advocated further expansion and public administration of the summer programs in Providence.[11]

Superintendents highlighted several accomplishments of Providence's vacation schools. One bragged that children "were not only kept from the dangers of the streets, and, in a great measure, from evil associates, but were well cared for and taught many valuable lessons."[12] Another noted the satisfaction of the parents of the vacation school children: "It was a great relief to maternal anxiety to know that, during their necessary absence, their children were not exposed to the perils into which, uncontrolled, they might thoughtlessly have run."[13] Despite the nonacademic focus of vacation school activity, he believed that through the vacation schools "the discipline and scholarship of the regular school in this way materially advanced."[14] Among the very first practitioners, citizens and school officials in Providence helped formulate the subsequent vacation school dogma. In general, they emphasized the elements presented in Chapter Four: the negative influence of the street, the inability of many children to leave the city, the usefulness of play and object learning, the different (though not explicitly experimental) curriculum, and the prevention of summer setback.[15] Not surprisingly, only the social efficiency rationalizations were missing from this incipient vacation school literature.

Despite the fast accomplishments, the city's vacation schools faced some difficulties. School reports expressed frustration with the average daily attendance, which typically was far lower than the number of students registered. Attendance also varied tremendously each year due to climatic and economic conditions. In 1876, inclement weather pushed the average attendance down to 56% from more typical figures around 80%. Although superintendents had not reported previous financial difficulties, the economic downturn of 1877 doomed Providence's summer program. In 1878, the vacation schools were discontinued as suddenly as they were started ten years earlier. Offering little explanation, the current superintendent of schools hinted that no appropriation had been made for that summer due to tighter budgets. In a fiscal crisis, Providence's vacation schools were not preserved because they were seen as supplemental. Although the city's first vacation schools lasted only one decade, a similarly philanthropic Committee on Public Play and Vacation Schools renewed them in 1894 and turned them over to the administration of Providence's public schools in 1900.[16]

When vacation schools opened in Newark, New Jersey, in 1886, they were an instantaneous popular success. First promoted by Superintendent William Barringer in 1884, the city's board of education approved them over mild resistance in 1885. In the inaugural session, they immediately encountered three times as many applicants as anticipated. Newark ran three schools in 1886, and the 1,400 enrolled students between ages 5 and 14 maintained a 75% attendance rate. That year, student registration equaled 6.3% of the regular school enrollment, a heady figure for an incipient summer program. After 1886, Newark's network of vacation schools expanded rapidly. By 1894, summer enrollment had doubled and included nearly 10% of all Newark public school students. In 1901, enrollment broke 5,000; in 1907 it reached over 10,000; and in 1914 over 21,000 students attended thirty-one vacation schools across the city. By then, summer enrollment reached 31.5% of the regular term.[17] An additional 4,000 entered Newark's six path-setting all-year schools. All totaled, Newark's vacation schools drew a larger percentage of school children than in most cities.

In beginning vacation schools, Newark's educators shared similar motivations as their predecessors in Providence. Primarily, school officials feared the unhealthy influences of "the street" on children whose families could not afford to go away during the summer. They also hoped "to preserve their [children's] school habits" and foster proclivities for "punctual and regular attendance, obedience, cleanliness, promptness, and industry well directed."[18] Yet Newark's vacation schools diverged from Providence's in several ways. First, they grew steadily for thirty years and endured, without interruption, until the Great Depression. Second, they preserved some of the regular school curriculum. Newark's vacation schools generally avoided the typical academic course of study, but they still taught reading, writing, arithmetic, and language in addition to music, sewing, and manual work.[19] Finally, they were full-fledged extensions of the public schools: located in public school buildings, taught and administered by public school personnel and financed with public money from the outset.[20]

Taken together, the experiences of Providence and Newark illustrate the malleability of the overtaxation ideology. Administrators in both cities countered potential opposition through the shape they gave to vacation schools. Providence superintendents always noted that their summer students functioned "without any strain upon the brain" because "no hard study was required." Because summer vacation lasted nine weeks in Providence and the term ran for six weeks, school officials argued that the remaining three weeks, "in which to enjoy perfect rest from books," left children enough time for rejuvenation.[21] Even as Newark's Superintendent Barringer proposed vacation schools, he recognized that "it would be unwise to keep up the regular schools during this heated period. It would soon break down the teachers and many of the students." Therefore, he assured readers that the proposed schools "would not undertake the regular school course."[22] Although Newark's program incorporated some English instruction, it was carefully balanced with more typical vacation school activities.

Despite local success and national recognition, the summer classes in Providence and Newark did not match their sponsors' hopes and spur imitation by many other cities. In Providence, the superintendent of schools expressed the desire that "the attention of educators and philanthropists in other principal cities of our country" would lead to their adoption in all "thickly settled areas."[23] Newark's administrators saw themselves as the vanguard of an unstoppable momentum toward summer education. Superintendent Barringer optimistically stated that soon vacation schools "will be organized in most of our large cities" and saw Newark as "the pioneer in this movement." His prediction, to his later dismay, proved to be premature. By 1895, he noted accurately that Newark remained the only city with publicly run summer sessions. While children and teachers were willing participants, he found that among some of his peers old fears of overstudy retained their potency.[24] Indeed it remained for the AICP in New York to spark other philanthropic groups to launch vacation schools in their cities after 1894. Nevertheless, Providence and Newark laid the groundwork for the movement. They originated the ideological constructs and school structures that educators and reformers in other cities would eventually adopt and maintain throughout the twentieth century.

The Diffusion of Vacation Schools across the United States

Providence and Newark trailblazed the two basic paths for the formation, development, and spread of vacation schools: private and public sponsorship. The earliest cities to initiate summer education followed Providence's example. External social organizations started the schools and eventually the public education systems took them over. By 1910, the public realm had assumed control over most pre-existing private vacation schools and had begun to substitute an academic curriculum for the original recreative and industrial course of studies. After that, Newark's model stood out as cities without charity vacation schools simply started summer schools on their own. These later adopters like Richmond and Kansas City never experienced an alteration of their vacation schools because they immediately instituted a public program with an academic curriculum. Signifying the transformation in control and curriculum, the institution's name changed as well. By 1920, vacation schools were more commonly known as summer schools and existed in scores of communities.

A host of private endeavors launched the earliest vacation schools. Women's groups were active in many areas, but civic clubs, churches, and charities also took the lead in some municipalities. Table 5.1 identifies the founding organizations in eighteen of the twenty-two major cities containing vacation schools by 1901. It highlights that private institutions had started all but Newark's schools: women's clubs in Chicago, Cincinnati, and Milwaukee, civic clubs in Philadelphia and Pittsburgh, principals' and teachers' associations in Buffalo, churches in Boston and Cleveland, and charities in New York and Indianapolis. These organizations typically set up special committees or associations to run the vacation schools. Their members compiled detailed records of their work and publicized it through in a variety of manners. Although they did not form their own national organization, vacation school advocates participated in the kindred Playground Association, distributed their annual reports as widely as possible, contributed articles to popular and educational journals, and piqued scholarly interest that resulted in several formal studies of vacation schools. Collectively, these efforts ignited a movement that reached a wide swath of American communities.

As vacation schools dispersed across the country, how far did they extend? In general, vacation schools expanded considerably though not uniformly to numerous American communities over the first thirty years of the twentieth century. Table 5.2 presents the aggregate national data to illustrate the breadth of vacation school diffusion. Early cumulative records are infrequent, but a 1912 survey conducted by Clarence Arthur Perry for the Russell Sage Foundation found that the number of American municipalities reporting vacation schools increased from 56 in 1909 to 141 in 1912. The United States Bureau of Education gave further legitimacy to the movement when it began collecting data on vacation schools shortly thereafter. In a 1917 bulletin, it

Table 5.1. *First adopters and founding organizations of vacation schools (cities over 100,000 in 1900)*

City	Population	Year	Founding Institution
Boston	560,892	1866	First Church of Boston; College Settlements Association
Providence	175,597	1868	Citizens Committee on Vacation Schools
Newark	246,070	1886	Newark Board of Education
Brooklyn[a]	1,166,582	1887	Unknown
New Haven	108,027	1888	Unknown
New York[a]	1,850,093	1894	Association for Improving the Condition of the Poor
Cleveland	381,768	1895	Ladies' Aid Society of Old Stone Church; Day Nursery and Free Kindergarten Association
Chicago	1,698,575	1896	Civic Federation; Permanent Vacation Schools Committee of Women's Clubs
Indianapolis	169,164	1897	Public Recreation Committee of the Children's Aid Association
Philadelphia	1,293,697	1898	Civic Club
Baltimore	508,957	1898	Unknown
Buffalo	352,387	1898	Principals' Association; Women Teachers' Association
Minneapolis	202,718	1898	Improvement League
Syracuse	108,374	1898	Mother's Club
Cincinnati	325,902	1899	Women's Club
Milwaukee	285,325	1899	Women's Club of Wisconsin
Rochester	162,608	1899	Women's Educational and Industrial Union
Washington	278,718	1899	A local merchants association
Pittsburgh	321,616	1900	Civic Club; Pittsburgh Playground Association
Louisville	204,731	1900	Unknown
Kansas City	163,752	1901	The Athenaeum
Toledo	131,822	1901	City Federation of Women's Clubs

Sources: See Appendix.

[a] The consolidation of New York City, which joined together Brooklyn, Queens, Manhattan (New York), Staten Island, and the Bronx, occurred in 1898, after the cities of Brooklyn and New York started vacation schools.

Table 5.2. *Aggregate national data for public summer schools, 1909–34*

Year[a]	Cities Reporting Summer Schools	Biennial Change in Number of Cities (%)	Student Enrollment	Number of Personnel	Expenditures	
					Actual	Real[b]
909–10	56	....	....	....	....	....
911–12	141	152.8	....	....	$300,000	$434,153
917–18[c]	211	14.4	124,252	4,269	$362,577	$308,576
921–22	231	4.7	280,507	9,748	$1,652,981	$1,693,628
923–24	346	49.8	355,266	11,747	$1,970,630	$1,958,876
925–26	392	13.3	421,867	13,291	$2,578,381	$2,491,189
927–28	447	14.0	456,099	14,377	$3,242,665	$3,399,020
929–30	374	-16.3	492,638	14,481	$4,043,433	$4,242,847
931–32	278	-25.7	439,030	13,253	$3,755,821	$5,144,960
933–34	160	-42.2	109,844	3,317	$602,363	$914,056

Sources: Clarence A. Perry, *American Vacation Schools of 1912*, pamphlet no. R133 (New York: Russell Sage Foundation, 1913); W. S. Deffenbaugh, "Summer Sessions of City Schools." *U.S. Bureau of Education Bulletin, 1917*, no. 45. (Washington: Government Printing Office, 1918); U.S. Bureau of Education, *Biennial Survey of Education* (1920–34).

[a] The Bureau of Education Reports did not identify which summer was reported. Moreover, its data from 1912 through 1916 is omitted here because it did not distinguish between vacation schools (either public or private) and summer sessions at colleges or private preparatory schools.

[b] These expenditures are adjusted for cost of living (1926 = 100).

[c] The expenditures for this school year is substantially underestimated. Of the 152 districts with publicly funded vacation schools, thirty did not report their expenditures.

identified 211 towns and cities that operated summer classes. These communities employed over 4,000 teachers and educated nearly 125,000 students even though spending had not risen much since 1912 and had probably declined in real terms during World War I. The unstable economic conditions that followed the Great War may have initially limited the extension of vacation schools, but by 1921 their growth nationwide proceeded unabated.[25] In ten years the number of cities opening summer programs doubled, reaching 447 in 1927–28, while the numbers of teachers employed and students taught more than tripled, peaking at 14,481 teachers and 492,638 students in 1929–30.[26] Not surprisingly, the Great Depression precipitated a huge retrenchment in the number of communities maintaining vacation schools as well as ending the first wave of vacation school diffusion, though as the data in Table 5.2 indicate, the severe cutbacks did not come immediately. By 1933–34, real expenditures had declined by 73% since 1927–28 and only 160 cities still ran summer schools.

These aggregate figures obscure the full extent of the spread of vacation schools in two significant ways. First, the vacation schools spread down the urban hierarchy, from the largest cities to the smallest towns. By 1927, though most American communities did not sponsor vacation schools, the majority of the nation's greatest and many of its mid-sized cities did. That year, two thirds of all the cities with over 100,000 inhabitants ran vacation schools, including twelve of the thirteen cities with populations over 500,000.[27] Table 5.3 divides urban communities with populations over 25,000 into four cohorts at roughly ten-year intervals from 1900 to 1927 and tabulates the percentages of cities with vacation schools in each group. It indicates that in any given year, the cohorts of larger cities contained a greater percentage of vacation school cities than the groups with smaller urban populations. For example, in 1921 the figures for the four population size cohorts were as follows: 92% for cities over 500,000, 77% for cities between 250,000 and 500,000, 49% for cities between 100,000 and

Table 5.3. *Percentage of American cities with vacation schools, 1900–1927*

City Size	1900[a]	1912	1921	1927
25,000–99,999	. . . .	25 (N = 179)	33 (N = 218)	42 (N = 284)
100,000–249,999	22 (N = 23)	52 (N = 31)	49 (N = 43)	61 (N = 56)
250,000–499,999	67 (N = 9)	73 (N = 11)	77 (N = 13)	67 (N = 24)
≥ 500,000	83 (N = 6)	75 (N = 8)	92 (N = 12)	92 (N = 13)
Total	. . . .	33 (N = 229)	40 (N = 286)	48 (N = 377)

Sources: For 1900 vacation school data, see Appendix. For 1912, see Clarence A. Perry, *American Vacation Schools of 1912*. New York: Russell Sage Foundation, 1913. Pamphlet no. R133. For 1921, see U.S. Bureau of Education, *Biennial Survey of Education* (1920–22) and for 1927 see U.S. Bureau of Education, *Biennial Survey of Education* (1926–28). Population cohorts based on U.S. Census data from 1900, 1910, 1920 and 1930.

Note: Figures in parentheses are base Ns for the adjacent percentages. Figures for 1900 and 1910 include both public and private schools; figures for 1920 and 1930 only include public schools.

[a] Data on vacation schools for cities in the 25,000–100,000 category in 1900 are too sketchy to tabulate. No national data exist and reliance on contemporary portraits and local reports probably underestimates the totals. Some cities of this size in New England, such as Cambridge, Hartford, and New Haven, clearly had already begun vacation schools. Perry's 1912 data probably undercount the number of cities and towns maintaining as well.

250,000, and 33% for towns between 25,000 and 100,000. In short, vacation schools were typically located in cities and more likely found in larger ones.

The data in Table 5.3 also demonstrate that vacation schools extended their reach in each cohort over time. Although there are a few short-term decreases in percentage evident, the number of cities with vacation schools rose in every year reported for each cohort. For example, for cities between 250,000 and 500,000 inhabitants, the percentage declined from 77 to 67 between 1921 and 1927, but the actual number of cities with vacation schools rose from ten to sixteen. This contraction in percentage but not number suggests that the increase in cities running vacation schools simply did not always keep pace with the continued urbanization and population growth in America. Indeed, the number of cities falling into the 250,000–500,000 cohort nearly doubled in that same interval. Overall, the key moments of vacation school diffusion occurred first and only became complete in the nation's metropolises.

A second manner in which the combined totals conceal the full extent of vacation schools from 1900 to 1927 is that they do not indicate the continuity in an individual city's summer program. In fact, vacation schools held a precarious position in many city school systems and often ran irregularly.[28] Municipalities tended to follow one of four patterns of uneven maintenance. Some cities, such as Hartford, Philadelphia, Providence, and Springfield (MA), opened vacation schools sporadically rather than consistently over the twenty-eight year period. Others, including Boston, Houston, and Worcester, experienced only temporary interruptions of an otherwise annual school program. Third, cities like Grand Rapids and San Francisco only attempted vacation schools for one or two summers. Finally, some cities with long-established vacation school programs stopped running them during the 1920s before the Great Depression began. Indianapolis, Memphis, Rochester, and Syracuse fall into this last category.

Given these four trends, the actual number of municipalities that attempted vacation schools during the first three decades of the twentieth century is easily underestimated. In 1927, 181 of the 377 cities in the United States with populations over 25,000 in 1930 maintained summer schools, but another 96 with previous vacation school experience were not currently running them. Combining past and present vacation school locations, these 277 municipalities constituted 72% of the urban areas with populations over 25,000 in 1927. Table 5.4 breaks down these cumulative totals into the four cohorts used in Table 5.3

Table 5.4. *Cumulative percentage of American cities with vacation schools, 1900–1927*

City Size	1900–1927[a]	1927
25,000–99,999	67 (N = 284)	42 (N = 284)
100,000–249,999	86 (N = 56)	61 (N = 56)
250,000–499,999	92 (N = 24)	67 (N = 24)
≥ 500,000	100 (N = 13)	92 (N = 13)
Total	72 (N = 377)	48 (N = 377)

Sources: For the 1927 data, see U.S. Bureau of Education, *Biennial Survey of Education* (1926–28). Cumulative data culled from the following sources: Appendix; Clarence A. Perry, *American Vacation Schools of 1912*. New York: Russell Sage Foundation, 1913. Pamphlet no. R133; U.S. Bureau of Education, *Biennial Survey of Education* (1916–18, 1920–22, 1922–24, 1924–26, 1926–28).

[a] Cumulative totals indicate all communities that had launched a vacation school at any time from 1900–1927 but were not necessarily running them in 1927. Figures in parentheses are base Ns for the adjacent percentages.

and highlights a substantial rise in each group when compared to the actual figures just from 1927. When every vacation school site from 1900 to 1927 is considered, the participation levels are as follows: 100% for the 13 cities over 500,000, 92% for those in the 250,000 to 500,000 group, 86% for those in the 100,000 to 250,000 group, and 67% for those towns between 25,000 and 100,000 inhabitants. Thus Curtis comes reasonably close to his prediction of "every city" over 20,000 with a vacation school when adoption is considered cumulatively. By the 1920s, public summer education was a widespread though still fragile urban educational innovation.

Returning to Curtis one last time, how regionally based were vacation schools? Curtis stated in 1903 that vacation schools were a phenomenon of "the North," which certainly appeared true at the time. Contemporary accounts of the vacation school movement discussed with good reason cities in the Northeast and Midwest—an overwhelming number of the original adopters of vacation schools lay north of the Mason-Dixon Line and east of the Mississippi River. Of the twenty-two earliest cities with vacation schools identified in Table 5.1, eleven were located in the Northeast and eight in the Midwest. In fact, New England, New York, and New Jersey contained the first six cities listed. Kansas City was the city furthest to the west, and all three southern cities mentioned—Louisville, Baltimore, and Washington—are situated near the South's northern borders. This regional predomi-

Table 5.5. *Regional distribution of vacation schools in cities over 25,000*

Region[a]	Percentage of a Region's Cities With Vacation Schools		
	1912	1922	1928
Northeast	38 (N=97)	47 (N=108)	52 (N=131)
New England	36 (N=42)	35 (N=46)	51 (N=55)
Mid-Atlantic	40 (N=55)	56 (N=62)	53 (N=76)
Midwest	31 (N=70)	44 (N=94)	52 (N=124)
East North Central	35 (N=51)	42 (N=76)	53 (N=100)
West North Central	21 (N=19)	50 (N=18)	50 (N=24)
South	30 (N=44)	29 (N=59)	39 (N=84)
Southeast	25 (N=20)	42 (N=31)	41 (N=41)
East South Central	55 (N=11)	9 (N=11)	38 (N=16)
West South Central	15 (N=13)	18 (N=17)	37 (N=27)
West	17 (N=18)	24 (N=25)	39 (N=38)
Mountain	17 (N=6)	43 (N=7)	70 (N=10)
Pacific	17 (N=12)	17 (N=18)	29 (N=28)
Total	33 (N=229)	40 (N=286)	48 (N=377)

Source: *Biennial Reports of the Bureau of Education*, 1921–22 and 1927–28; Clarence A. Perry, *American Vacation Schools of 1912*, pamphlet no. R133 (New York: Russell Sage Foundation, 1913); U.S. Bureau of the Census, *Abstract of the Census of the United States* (1910, 1920, 1930).

[a] The United States Census Bureau divided the nation into nine geographic regions identified in italics. The four general regions are comprised of two or three of these census regions as indicated. Figures in parentheses are base Ns for the adjacent percentages.

nance is not surprising given that the nation's urban industrial centers developed in the Northeast and Midwest.

The initial regional imbalance in vacation school location gave way to a more broadly based national movement. Table 5.5, which breaks down the diffusion by general and more specific regional cohorts, demonstrates that the underrepresented South and West never closed yet substantially narrowed the gap by 1928. By 1912, the South's proportion of cities with vacation schools (30%) had nearly reaching the Midwest's, and though stagnating for a decade, it enjoyed another growth spurt in the 1920s. Vacation schools in the West increased at an even faster rate, equaling the South's 39% by 1928. Nevertheless, the proportion for these two regions remained much smaller than the 52% figure for both the Northeast and the Midwest. Thus the Northeast

Table 5.6. *Stages of vacation school transformation in cities over 100,000 in 1900*

Cohort A: Four-Stage Development

Average Population Rank: 15.2

Rank	City	Date 1	Date 2	Date 3	Date 4
2	Chicago	1896	1903	1909	1911
14	Milwaukee	1899	1904	1905	1914
15	Washington	1899	1901	1918	1914
19	Minneapolis	1898	1903	1908	1911
20	Providence	1868	1900	1901	....
21	Indianapolis	1897	1898	1910	1913

Cohort B: Three-Stage Development

Average Population Rank: 10.7

Rank	City	Date 1	Date 2	Date 3	Date 4
1	New York	1894	1898	1898	1906
3	Philadelphia	1898	1898	1901	1922
4	St. Louis	1905	1907	1907	1911
5	Boston	1866	1900	1900	1909
7	Cleveland	1895	1903	1904	1903
8	Buffalo	1898	1900	1900	1911
10	Cincinnati	1899	1906	1906	1908
11	Pittsburgh	1900	1905	1911	1911
12	New Orleans	1904	1904	1907	1910
13	Detroit	1903	1903	1905	1912
24	Rochester	1899	1907	1910	1910
30	Syracuse	1898	1906	1906	1915

Cohort C: Two-Stage Development

Average Population Rank: 24.7

Rank	City	Date 1	Date 2	Date 3	Date 4
6	Baltimore	1898	1911	1911	1911
16	Newark	....	1886	1886	1910
18	Louisville	1900	1913	1913	1913
22	Kansas City	1901	1911	1911	1911
23	St. Paul	1908	1908	1909	1909
28	Columbus	1912	1917	1917	1917
31	New Haven	1888	1914	1914	1914
32	Paterson	1909	1913	1913	1909
33	Fall River, MA	....	1910	1910	1911
38	Scranton	....	1914	1914	1919

Cohort D: One-Stage Development					
			Average Population Rank: 30.0		
Rank	City	Date 1	Date 2	Date 3	Date 4
17	Jersey City	. . . .	1911	1911	1911
25	Denver	. . . .	1902	1902	1902
35	Omaha	. . . .	1913	1913	1913
36	Los Angeles	. . . .	1911	1911	1911
37	Memphis	. . . .	1909	1909	1909

Sources: See Appendix.

Note: DATE1 is the first year of philanthropic vacation schools (no record found in several cities). DATE2 is the first year of initial public funds for vacation schools. DATE3 is the first year of complete public funds for vacation schools. DATE4 is the first year classes for academic credit were introduced to vacation schools.

remained dominant in sheer vacation school numbers and in proportion until the end of the 1920s, when the Midwest nearly equaled it.[29]

As they spread across the country, vacation schools entered individual urban school systems over a period of stages that marked their transformation into academic, credit-bearing summer classes. Four distinct moments in the transition process stand out: the year of the first record of any private philanthropic vacation school, the year some public money was first provided for vacation schools, the year public money first accounted for all vacation school expenditures, and the year academic classes were first offered for credit in a vacation school. Table 5.6 identifies these four years for the thirty-eight cities with populations over 100,000 in 1900. It groups them into four cohorts determined by how many stages of vacation school development they underwent.

The nation's largest cities typically started vacation schools prior to 1900 and experienced three or all four stages of development. Every city listed in cohort A and B began with a charitable enterprise in which local citizen groups instituted recreative and manual arts classes for the children of the urban immigrant poor. These urban areas were also among the earliest to commence the transition to summer schools, generally initiating the process before 1905. While some of the cities in cohort C also had philanthropic vacation schools early on, they did not usually experience the shift until after 1910. For the cities in cohort D, no record of any private philanthropic origins was located.

The change from vacation to summer schools mostly occurred in the first decade of the twentieth century. The structural metamorphosis occurred in two ways. First, the public school authority of a city would assume control over the administration of the vacation schools from the philanthropic or women's club committees. Sometimes a swift shift in control occurred, as the boards of education in Boston, Buffalo, Cincinnati, New York, St. Louis, and Syracuse completed the take over in a single year. Other cities blurred the boundaries between public and private. The Cleveland Board of Education, for example, contributed funding to the vacation schools in 1903 and entirely financed and managed them the following summer. Some cities stretched out the process even further. Chicago's school board began making monetary contributions in 1903, but its vacation schools remained under the guidance of its woman's clubs until 1909. The transition took five years in Minneapolis and six years in Pittsburgh. Still, in nearly all of the cities from cohorts A and B, the transfer of vacation schools to the public sector occurred by 1910.

Second, the curriculum of the vacation school evolved from a recreational and industrial focus to an academic one. In 1902, Denver introduced a short-lived vacation school with both play and regular school subjects.[30] The next year Cleveland added academic classes to its vacation schools, with New York and Cincinnati following in 1906 and 1908, respectively (See Table 5.6). Over the ensuing five years, most cities already running vacation schools (cohorts A and B) began the transition. In addition, most municipalities first starting vacation schools after 1908 skipped the first two stages of development and immediatedly set up public summer schools with an academic program.[31] Thus cohort D cities like Jersey City, Los Angeles, Memphis, and Omaha never experienced a philanthropic origin, while some, such as Baltimore, Kansas City, and Louisville, with early but long-lasting private vacation schools underwent a complete and simultaneous switch to public administration and to academic courses.

By 1912, the momentum of summer education in the nation's largest cities had clearly shifted to regular schoolwork. The vacation school survey conducted by Clarence Arthur Perry that year went out to superintendents, not private organizations, and Perry found that the vast majority of vacation programs offered academic studies.[32] The introduction of this coursework did not precipitate the immediate elimination of the recreative and manual work of vacation schools. Many were merged with afternoon playground programs, and in some communities private organizations reemerged to run summer play schools.[33] As most cities took as long as a decade to remove the original activities, vacation schools temporarily bifurcated around these academic and non-academic purposes. In 1914, the United States Commissioner of Education noted that "there were two types of vacation schools: one aims to educate through play and to keep the children off the street, the other to help children who have lost time or who are capable of gaining a grade."[34] Three years earlier he had observed that the former were more numerous and better known than the latter, but three years later a 1917 Bureau of Education report indicated a complete turnaround. It found that 66% of vacation schools were free and publicly funded, 31% depended on student tuition, and that less than 2% relied on private financing. It also corroborated the prevalence of academic summer classes by using labels such as "failures," "exceptionally bright," and "normal" to identify the "classes of children in summer school."[35] Summer education now largely relied on public expenditures and served students who needed to make up a failure or who wanted to move ahead in the graded curriculum.

Together, the data presented here illuminate noteworthy patterns of vacation school diffusion. Vacation schools enjoyed an overall rise in their number, size, and resources the first three decades of the twentieth century until the Great Depression. During those years they extended down the urban hierarchy through national, regional, and statewide networks. They also evolved through a series of stages from recreational to academic programs run by public not private entities. Despite their widespread diffusion, vacation schools remained fragile in many cities and towns nationwide. Often communities discontinued vacation schools for a summer or more while in some they never restarted during the period. Thus the number of cities to experiment with vacation schools in the first three decades of the twentieth century far surpassed the number that supported them in any one year.

The precarious existence of vacation schools may have contributed to their transformation. The urban conditions, rural curatives, and pedagogical concerns typically identified as reasons to start vacation schools constitute an incomplete explanation for both their spread and evolution. To highlight the plight of the immigrant working-class in areas starting vacation schools before 1900 makes sense. Providence, Newark, New York, and Chicago were cities in the vanguard—they had few models to follow and chose to act against prevailing conceptions of the summer in order to address a perceived social problem. Subsequent adopters shared similar urban anxieties, but communication about prior decisions made elsewhere had narrowed the range of actions they might take.[36] The unusual candor of one Buffalo superintendent hints at the competitiveness and symbolic value that also lay behind vacation school adoption. "All of these forms of educational effort [vacation schools, evening schools, and playgrounds]," he crowed, "are already well established in the world's great industrial centers, and it is in the manifest destiny of Buffalo to take rank with the greatest of these."[37] This sort of frankness was hardly usual, but civic rivalries were rampant and reached into public school organizations. After 1900, the bandwagon was headed towards public summer schools awarding academic credit. This chapter now to turns to Chicago to follow its progress more closely.

The Bureaucratic Transformation of Summer Education in Chicago

Chicago's vacation schools are ripe for study. Although other cities began vacation schools earlier, Chicago's program was quite large and path setting.[38] It also provided an alternative model of summer education, as its schools diverged from eastern cities in several important areas including curriculum, organization, and most relevant here, the shift to summer schools. As Table 5.6 indicated, some cities converted vacation schools to public entities in a single year while others took a year or two to complete the process. In contradistinction, Chicago's public schools embarked on a gradual six-year takeover of the private vacation schools. The Chicago Woman's Club founded vacation schools in 1898, first accepted public money in 1903, and retained administrative control over them until 1909. These women were conversant with the ideas and supportive of the projects of Jane Addams, John Dewey, and Francis Parker, and they produced highly detailed reports on their programs that have survived. In short, the large-scale, well-chronicled, and slow-changing vacation programs in Chicago are especially suitable for an inquiry into institutional transformation.

The extent to which the vacation schools changed under public control is readily apparent if certain aspects of the program are assessed. When it launched vacation schools, the Woman's Club faced a series of questions about their purposes, management, staffing, curriculum, and resources: Who would teach in them and who would they teach? How would they be administered? What studies and activities would they offer? How would they be financed? From 1898 to 1902, the club settled these questions in ways that it hoped would prove popular with citizens and educators alike. On a shoe-string budget it instituted a summer program girded by a solid organizational structure, a multifaceted course of study, and a diverse faculty. Simultaneously, the club worked towards convincing Chicago's board of education to assume control, but engineering a public takeover presented several difficulties. The women maneuvered around political, legal, and financial obstacles that took until 1909 to overcome entirely. In the meantime, once the board of education started contributing money to the vacation schools in 1903, it returned to the questions posed above and began offering its own set of answers to them. When the private to public transition was complete, school officials had to consider to what extent these schools would connect to other components of the school system. The assumption that they needed to fit smoothly underlay the modern summer school's emergence from the Woman's Club vacation program.

That this transformation occurred in the Windy City is all the more noteworthy because turn-of-the century Chicago was the site of heated school politics as well as innovative schools receiving national acclaim. The battles over superintendencies, budgets, and centralization, the rise of the Chicago Teachers' Federation, and the institutions of Addams, Dewey, and Parker are well narrated elsewhere and form an important backdrop to the development of vacation schools in Chicago.[39] Nevertheless, rather than completely retelling much-told stories, they are briefly referred to here only when directly relevant to vacation schools. For despite the overlaps with the larger tensions in public schools, there is a narrative to the Chicago vacation school movement that is somewhat removed from the city's school wars. Chicago's vacation schools had an identifiable birthplace and mother, nursery and nursemaid, and not so many years later, a cemetery plot and caretaker.

The Chicago Woman's Club and summer vacation schools

Chicago's vacation schools originated in the city's intertwined philanthropic and education communities. They started in 1896 but only became firmly established two years later under the direction of the Chicago Woman's Club. In fact, the first two vacation schools did not last beyond an inaugural summer. In 1896, the Civic Federation, a loosely knit organization of Chicago charities dominated by business leaders, launched vacation classes in the Joseph Medill School. The federation's education committee, chaired by Sadie American and aided by University of Chicago President William Rainey Harper, requested and received from the Chicago Board of Education the use of the school building, its equipment, and its janitorial staff. John Dewey, duplicating elements of the curriculum at his own recently started University

Elementary School, arranged a course of study that emphasized industrial subjects, used no textbooks, and held weekly excursions. The Education Committee selected the Medill School as the site for the summer classes due to its location in a Russian and Jewish neighborhood. The school proved extremely popular from the outset, as 1,000 elementary aged children applied for the 360 available spots. The board of education, however, required the federation to post a $1,600 bond to cover the school's expenses, which pushed the initial school into debt and caused the Civic Federation not to repeat its attempt in 1897. Instead, women of the University of Chicago Settlement House gained permission from the board of education and started a vacation school at the Seward School. The school's recreation and sewing classes served a Bohemian, German, and Polish population. Despite its apparent success, the settlement house did not attempt to reopen its school the following July.[40]

By then, Sadie American had thrown her energies into the cause of summer education. Young and unmarried, American had joined the Woman's Club in December of 1895 and two years later was still a newcomer who had yet to assume any position of responsibility within the group. Nevertheless, American led an "active campaign" to persuade the club to assert leadership over the foundering vacation school movement. With a bent towards social activism, a long-standing involvement in other educational projects, and typical middle-class concerns about summer crime and student atrophy, she convinced its members that the Woman's Club would serve the vacation school cause better than the Civic Federation or any other organization.[41] Moreover, she pushed the club to move quickly—in time for the summer of 1898.

The vacation school program initiated by the Chicago Woman's Club achieved a measure of longevity. Spurred by American, the club petitioned the board of education for the use of two schools sites. American coordinated a successful publicity campaign for vacation schools and raised nearly $10,000 through a sale of flag pins in schools that capitalized on jingoistic fervor in the aftermath of the destruction of the *U.S.S. Maine.* As a result, five schools selected by the Woman's Club opened in July 1898, and they enrolled more than 2,000 immigrant children.[42] Encouraged by the schools' popularity, American formed and headed the Chicago Permanent Vacation School and Playground Committee [hereafter Permanent Committee] in 1899. Fifty-three local woman's clubs joined, and for the next few years this committee spearheaded Chicago's vacation schools through its fundraising

Table 5.7. *Financial contributors to the Chicago Woman's Club vacation schools*

Contributor	1900	1902	1903	1905	1906	1908
Woman's Clubs	$2,874	$3,495	$4,199	$4,321	$4,313	$4,765
Individuals	$646	$3,870	$2,722	$1,711	$2,303	$2,772
Business Groups	$0	$110	$65	$0	$0	$1,170
Bd. of Education	$0	$0	$1,000	$5,000	$10,000	$15,000
Miscellaneous	$0	$1,175	$52	$252	$32	$370
Unknown	$2,925	$316	$0	$0	$0	$0
Balance	$0	$0	$205	$131	$308	$405
Total Raised	$6,445	$8,965	$8,243	$11,414	$16,955	$24,483
Total Spent	$6,445	$8,965	$6,869	$10,741	$16,403	$23,218

Sources: Chicago Board of Education. *Annual Report* 47–55 (1900–1908); Chicago Woman's Club. "Report of the Chicago Permanent Vacation School and Playground Committee" (1900–1908).

and publicity efforts. To actually design the curriculum, hire the staff, and administer the program, the committee created a Vacation School Board consisting of both women philanthropists and educators.[43] With this organizational structure, the Woman's Club ran and expanded Chicago's largest network of vacation schools for over a decade.[44]

The Permanent Committee encountered difficulties in raising money for the schools. Despite its success in 1898, donations for vacation schools declined. The committee raised only $6,445 in 1900 and $8,243 in 1903 (see Table 5.7). In the latter year, vacation school Superintendent William Bogan noted that "the financial problem, which is always staring vacation schools in the face, seemed unusually complex" in light of substantially reduced donations early on in the year. Although sufficient funds arrived by the summer, the schools followed austere measures already implemented, and the committee held over surplus monies for the following summer.[45] Table 5.7 indicates that the largest bulk of annual vacation school funds typically came from local chapters of the Woman's Club, and their contributions rose only slightly over the years. Individual benefactors also accounted for substantial amounts of the total funds raised, but their donations fluctuated widely. The business community provided very little, much to the chagrin of the Permanent Committee. The apparent lack of interest from Chicago's prominent businessmen left its leading women even more desirous of public financial support.[46] Only after the board of education authorized the use of public funds did vacation schools' total expenditures rise substantially.

The curriculum designed by the Vacation School Board reflected the broader social and pedagogical aims of the movement. At first, the program concentrated as much on setting as on content. Removing a child "from the hot, dirty streets and crowded houses to spacious and airy rooms" was a key if pedagogically unambitious goal of the first summer program. Its leaders assumed that only in a wholesome environment could the child's intellect, body, and emotions develop. Once the children arrived in great numbers, the need for carefully planned activities became more apparent and helped shift the emphasis from keeping children off the streets to offering them enriching experiences. "The child himself," American noted, "and how to expand and develop the good and beauty in him, was the central thought influencing the 'board' in arranging the curriculum."[47] Done right, such a program "gave the children a sense of freedom and also of personal responsibility hitherto unknown, and filled them with a new thought of the immensity and beauty of the world.[48]

Chicago's vacation schools offered a program steeped in the "new education" promoted by Dewey and Parker. The daily schedule included music, manual training, and sewing, but nature study centered the curriculum. All weekly excursions occurred in the outdoors, as students visited parks and collected material, drew scenes, and frolicked. Back in school, they studied the plants, insects, and animals they had seen without using books, which remained barred from the summer coursework. The children also enjoyed gymnastics and recreative games. Some activities were segregated by sex. In sewing, girls learned to darn hose, mend tears, and make aprons while the boys produced kites and ornaments from raphia, cardboard, wood, and paper. Unlike others of its era, the manual training classes were not explicitly offered to prepare future industrial workers for specific jobs. The Woman's Club viewed them in the Deweyan sense as a means to an intellectual end—"developing the slumbering faculties of the child." Overall, the curriculum changed little in subsequent years of the club's direction. Mostly, it just added additional subjects and activities: vegetable gardens and advanced work in cooking in 1902; basketry, ironwork, and other forms of manual training in 1903; and house-keeping in 1905.[49]

Chicago vacation schools also bore the imprint of Jane Addams' considerable influence. As they occasionally cited her, school leaders explained that the schools aimed to Americanize immigrant children but not demonize them. One vacation school superintendent praised

teachers for espousing "a rare sociological opportunity" to stir a melting pot by inculcating American values and habits. The schools hoped
to fuse "all of our nationalities into one new municipal family, with
common human aims and a single municipal destiny to work out." To
this end, the school day began with a salute to the flag and the repetition of a civic creed. The music program taught "songs of devotion,
patriotism and industry." Nevertheless, the vacation schools did not
attempt to make over entirely the culture of their students. They also
sought to develop in all nationalities "an encouraging and appreciative
receptivity for the best each nationality has to give to America." To
that end, the schools introduced story-telling to the curriculum in
1906, which included classic tales from the students' native lands.[50]

The Americanization efforts reflected the heavily immigrant make
up of Chicago's vacation school population during the Woman's Club
years. Unlike most counterparts in other cities, the Vacation School
Board kept annual records of the ethnic origins of the enrolled students
(see Tables 5.8, 5.9).[51] These data reveal three important traits. First,
Table 5.8 indicates that native-born American students were noticeably
absent from Chicago's vacation schools. In 1899, only 16.0% of the

Table 5.8. *Chicago vacation school enrollment by nationality: annual aggregate percentages*

Nationality	1899	1902	1905	1908
African American	3.2	....	0.4	4.0
Native-born American	16.0	4.3	5.7	7.2
Bohemian	2.2	....	10.2	12.5
German	15.8	13.9	16.3	10.9
Irish	7.8	7.9	6.6	11.4
Italian	5.4	10.9	21.6	11.2
Jewish	22.3	42.9	21.4	26.1
Polish	....	6.6	3.3	10.4
Swedish/Scandinavian[a]	15.5	11.4	4.1/8.5	1.8/2.6
Others	11.8	2.8	6.0	3.7
	N = 1,753	N = 2,577	N = 4,360	N = 6,003

Sources: Chicago Woman's Club. "Report of the Chicago Permanent Vacation School
and Playground Committee" (1899–1908).

[a] In 1899, the school census used the category of Scandinavian, but Swedes were predominant. In 1902, the label Swedish was used. In 1905 and 1908 separate populations were listed for Swedes, Norwegians, Finns, and Danes. The first figure is just
of the percentage of Swedes, the second a combined figure for all four groups.

vacation school population claimed an American background, a proportion which would recede in subsequent years to 4.3% in 1902. Thereafter, the percentage of American-born children slowly rose but remained small: 5.7% in 1905, 7.2% in 1908. Second, vacation schools served certain ethnic populations in particular. The national groups most consistently well represented were Jews, Germans, and Scandinavians. In a typical summer Jews had the largest number of students, ranging from 21.4% to 26.1% of the total number, though in 1902, Jews accounted for a phenomenal 42.9% of the vacation school students. Germans usually ranked either second or third with around 14% of the students. Scandinavians, primarily Swedish, were early patrons of the vacation schools (15.5% in 1899), but their participation steadily tailed off (2.6% by 1908). In contradistinction, enrollments for Italians and Bohemians increased during the same decade. In 1899 they, respectively, had made up 5.4% and 2.2% of the student body. In 1905, Italians peaked at 21.6% and formed the largest national group in vacation schools. The following summer, Bohemians constituted 20.6% of the summer students.

Table 5.9 illustrates the third characteristic of vacation school student populations: that certain ethnic groups dominated each vacation school.[52] In thirteen of the thirty summer schools listed for 1899, 1902, 1905, and 1908, one group accounted for at least 50% but often 90% of the total enrollment. For example, the Foster, Goldsmith, and Smyth Schools were overwhelmingly Jewish; the Adams School was predominantly Swedish; and the Dante School was mainly Italian. By 1908, expansion of Chicago's vacation schools gave more groups a building of their own: Keith School for African Americans, Jungman School for Bohemians, and Graham School for the Irish. The seventeen other schools served more mixed populations in which two or three nationalities predominated. Groups like Germans and Bohemians shared the Hamline, Froebel, and Pickard Schools, and Poles attended the Burns and Burr Schools in large numbers.[53] The predominance of specific groups, of course, reflected the tight ethnic neighborhoods that permeated Chicago. Ironically, for institutions intending to Americanize their students, a school's dense ethnic make up in the summer could well have had the opposite impact. It certainly made the selection of schools sites an issue of no small importance to most ethnic groups.

The early vacation schools hired faculty from a variety of teaching backgrounds. Most teachers came from outside of the public schools. In 1898, only twenty-nine of the seventy teachers in the Woman's

Table 5.9. *Individual vacation school enrollment by nationality, Chicago, 1899–1908*

Year	School	Primary Nationality Group (%)	Secondary Nationality Group (%)
1899	Adams	Scandinavian (24.6)	American (22.1)
	Carpenter	Scandinavian (40.5)	German (25.5)
	Foster	Jewish (71.0)	....
	Haven	American (29.0)	German (21.3)
1902	Adams	Swedish (53.0)	Irish (16.0)
	Burns	German (45.0)	Polish (30.0)
	Foster	Jewish (88.0)	....
	Goldsmith	Jewish (93.0)	....
	Washington	Italian (40.0)	German (17.0)
1905	Adams	Swedish (30.2)	Italian (25.4)
	Dante	Italian (87.8)	....
	Foster	Jewish (87.3)	....
	Froebel	German (30.8)	Bohemian (30.6)
	Hamline	German (34.3)	Bohemian (27.9)
	Jones	Italian (48.4)	Jewish (22.4)
	Medill	Jewish (38.1)	Russian (25.3)
	Washington	Italian (39.9)	Norwegian (32.1)
1908	Burr	Polish (33.4)	Jewish (26.6)
	Dore	Italian (79.8)	....
	Foster	Jewish (88.4)	....
	Graham	Irish (88.9)	....
	Hamline	Bohemian (24.4)	German (22.7)
	Holden	Polish (34.0)	German (26.2)
	Jenner	Italian (61.3)	American (19.2)
	Jungman	Bohemian (91.4)	....
	Keith	African Amer. (91.4)	....
	Pickard	Bohemian (27.8)	German (27.3)
	Smyth	Jewish (90.7)	....
	Thorpe	Polish (26.2)	Irish (18.4)
	Washington	Italian (53.2)	German (12.9)

Source: Chicago Woman's Club. "Report of the Chicago Permanent Vacation School and Playground Committee" (1899–1908).

Note: Groups are omitted for schools in which the second largest nationalities constituted less than 10% of the school's summer population.

Club vacation schools taught in Chicago's public schools. Thirty came from private schools, settlement houses, or training schools, and eleven held no other teaching positions at all.[54] This diversity stemmed from the private sector origins of the vacation schools and the social as well as educative aims of the program. Vacation schools sought teachers more for their personal characteristics than for their specialized knowledge. No examination scores or teacher ratings were used in selection because the qualities administrators desired in their teachers were not easily measurable or discernible. One early vacation schools superintendent ranked academic qualifications third for ideal vacation school teachers. Most essential were "everlasting cheerfulness and unselfishness, sympathy and love for children, refinement and culture that will be wholesome as an example for the children." Next in importance were "a ready adaptability to new situations and ability to overcome obstacles." Only after these characteristics was proficiency "in a special line of work pursued in the schools" considered.[55]

In Chicago, the difficulty in obtaining a vacation school position varied greatly from year to year. The job supply usually increased each summer but remained small in comparison to the number of potential teachers in Chicago.[56] Initially, there was a high demand for teaching positions in vacation schools. In the early years, superintendents reported and counted on the tremendous enthusiasm for the work by teachers from all over Chicago, which "more than anything else keeps up attendance in the schools throughout the summer." They gushed over the cooperation and cordiality among the teaching staff, often seen in abundance at weekly faculty social gatherings. In one year as many as five people applied for each available position. The teaching environment of the vacation school alone may have attracted more than enough qualified applicants, for the pay scale certainly did not. While hoping that poor pay could weed out all but the most idealistic teachers, superintendents viewed the low salaries as an overall impediment to attracting a quality staff.

Over time, demand for summer teaching jobs appears to have flagged. By 1907, the list of applicants for vacation schools was often "not a large one to draw from, and for some of the positions it is almost impossible to secure good teachers." In those instances, teachers were chosen blindly, and principals had to live with selections that proved inadvisable. A 1908 increase in compensation for teachers and administrators helped renew interest. "As a result," noted John Shoop, the current superintendent of the vacation schools and future superintendent of Chicago public schools, "many competent and forceful teachers are offering their services to the Vacation Schools." Of course, additional routes to summer employment existed. Recognizing the occurrence of nepotism in hiring, principals were cautioned to resist "the temptation to appoint teachers for other reasons than those of actual policy."[57]

Aside from such abuses, vacation school superintendents deemed the autonomy granted throughout the summer system to be beneficial. This independence stemmed from the top of the hierarchy of authority. The Permanent Committee of the Woman's Club steered clear of the Vacation School Board's oversight of the schools. Likewise, the board initially shaped the school program and served as a "court of last resort" but gave principals immediate direction of their schools and respected their autonomy.[58] Each principal chose his own faculty, and this practice enabled him to stamp his school with his own signature. Because so much variation existed between each school's program and experience, vacation school superintendents regularly included separate accounts for each school in their annual reports. Principals, in turn, allowed vacation school teachers a fair amount of liberty. Vacation schools intentionally offered a "free [opportunity] for the teacher to develop," and teachers planned their own classroom agendas in pre-summer session meetings. One exception was in sewing, which was the only subject area that originally had a centrally outlined curriculum. However, Superintendent Bogan abolished the supervisor of sewing position in 1903 and encouraged each sewing teacher to chart her own course.[59] In short, the autonomy built into the vacation school program at all levels was highly valued. Even with the risk of favoritism in the hiring of faculty, another superintendent reasoned that "any system for selection [of teachers] which would in any way restrict the selection would destroy the efficiency of the schools."[60]

The public takeover and reformulation of Chicago's vacation schools

Despite a highly successful philanthropic program, the Woman's Club considered vacation schoolwork to lay within the domain of public education. From the inception of vacation schools, it intended to transfer financial and administrative control of them to the board of education. "Let us hope," wrote Sadie American, in 1900, "that the wishes of all may be realized and the new century [will] find Chicago with this unique and valuable addition to its school system." American and her successors articulated several reasons why the board of education could run the vacation schools more effectively. They believed it would offer financial stability, allow for the program's continued expansion, and strengthen administration of the schools. One active committee member and future chairperson summed up the basis of their advocacy of a public takeover: "to provide permanency and improve efficiency."[61] A public takeover, however, did not swiftly occur. The club faced political, legal, and towering financial barriers that took a full decade to surmount.

The Woman's Club never faced strong personal or public opposition to their vacation schools. Nevertheless, it still had to cultivate political support from the doubters as well as the enthusiasts on the Chicago Board of Education. This was no easy task in the 1890s, when public and board assaults on "fads and frills" in the curriculum began in 1893 and never completely subsided.[62] In that context, Sadie American's assessment of the members' initial response to her vacation school efforts is not surprising, as she noted in 1896 that "they had neither comprehension of the work, nor understanding of its purpose and need."[63] The board turned down the club's earliest petitions for administrative and financial support of vacation schools and some of its members hesitated to lend any support to the woman's clubs. In 1898, one board member initially blocked the club from using public school buildings, though he eventually withdrew his opposition.

To sway the skeptics, the Woman's Club published detailed reports on the vacation schools, emphasized their popularity and success, and highlighted Chicago's leadership of a national trend. As elected officials, such arguments induced some board members to view public vacation schools more favorably.[64] By 1900, the club had some but not enough allies on the board of education willing to make appropriations for vacation schools. After 1900, these supporters spoke more forcefully for vacation schools. Chicago superintendents began reporting on the "sympathy" held for the vacation school movement and advocated that the public schools assume control. Superintendent Edwin Cooley became an especially vocal proponent for vacation schools, joining the vacation school board and proclaiming in 1905 that Chicago needed fifty vacation schools to serve 50,000 children in Chicago. That same year, reform Mayor Edward Dunne's appointment of Jane Addams and six others to the board of education further aided the cause. By then, vacation school leaders recognized the growing popular acceptance of and board acquiescence to vacation schools and grew confident of an eventual public takeover.[65]

Another stumbling block the Woman's Club ran into was legal in nature. In 1898, Illinois state law required school years to last between five and nine months. As such, state law not only prevented the public adoption of vacation schools but any allocations of public school money as well. In 1899, the club launched a campaign to enable public vacation schools to comply with state law. At its bequest, a local judge drew up an amendment that allowed cities over 100,000 to establish and administer vacation schools and playgrounds under their own rules. The woman's club found sponsors in both the Illinois House and Senate, and American and other women traveled to Springfield to testify in favor of the bill. It passed the house unanimously and passed the senate with only a slight delay. The testimony and lobbying of the Chicago women proved crucial in securing its passage.[66]

With ideological, political, and legal barriers removed, the financial difficulties remained formidable. Year after year, board of education members pleaded budgetary constraints when they rejected a financial contribution to the vacation schools.[67] In 1900, the board's Committee on School Management approved a proposal to take over the preexisting vacation schools and run them solely. The board of education referred this and subsequent resolutions to its Committee on Finance, where they languished. The finance committee proclaimed its sympathy with the idea but found it "unwise at the present time to assume the control and management of the vacation school" because the next year's school appropriation would not allow for it. The board of education refused to deplete other departments in order to fund vacation schools. A change in revenue laws in 1900 also created financial difficulties for the board for the next few years. Thus the first board member motion for an appropriation (of $6,000) and public control of vacation schools met with defeat in 1900.[68]

Despite this resistance on financial grounds, the Chicago Board of Education gradually upped its stake in the vacation schools after the turn of the century. In 1901, the board contributed additional supplies and allowed the Permanent Committee of the Woman's Club to take up a collection among public school children that netted $630.[69] In 1903, these women maneuvered the board of education into finally allocating money for vacation schools. Just weeks before the summer began, the committee informed the board that it had not raised enough money to maintain the usual vacation school in "the Ghetto." Rather than face the discontinuance of a popular and already established institution, the board decided unanimously to appropriate $1,000 from an unspent balance in the education fund to run a school in that neighborhood.[70] With a precedent set, the board's appropriations for vacation schools rose steadily over the next few years. The Committee of Finance, long the guardian of the board's purse strings, increased the 1904 allocation from $3,000 to $5,000, and an initial appropriation of

$8,000 for 1906 was raised to $10,000 shortly before the onset of summer. In 1908, the $15,000 in public money accounted for 65% of the vacation school expenditures. When the board doubled that allocation for 1909, it assumed full control over the vacation schools as well.[71]

Public takeover of Chicago's vacation schools in the summer of 1909 did not immediately alter them. The transformation that occurred began well before and stretched well beyond the final transition of authority in 1909. The board always intended that control of the vacation schools "under its own auspices" would accompany public financing. Moreover, the Vacation School Board willingly relinquished its authority in a number of areas—curriculum, hiring, school selection—prior to 1909 in order to achieve the seemingly elusive goal of complete public administration of vacation schools. With its very first contribution to the Woman's Club in 1903, the board of education asserted and achieved some disposition over the schools when it mandated that its $1,000 allocated for the vacation schools be spent "under the direction of the Superintendent of Schools."[72] The $1,000 covered less than 15% of the vacation school expenses, and the superintendent merely applied it to teachers' salaries, but the following summer the board imposed further restraints on the Woman's Club. It demanded and received the right to determine the location of any additional vacation schools, to approve the course of study and the program of exercises, and to set the requirements for vacation schoolteachers.[73] Having gained this power, the board did not use it to make significant changes in the curriculum or the school sites during the first decade of the twentieth century. Most notably, it did not add academic classes, although one board member advocated such a course of action as early as 1905.[74] Thus it is likely that even with public oversight of the school's subject matter, the Woman's Club members and Vacation School Board retained much influence and some autonomy.

In contrast, the board of education quickly exerted control over the hiring of school personnel. It clearly disapproved of the high number of nonpublic schoolteachers who worked in the vacation schools but struggled with the Woman's Club over the removal of those teachers. Criticizing the existing process for involving "too much guess work," in 1904 it required—as the price of its financial support—that all new vacation school teachers have board certification.[75] As for previously employed vacation school staff members without board of education certificates, it decreed that they be paid out of private funds. The following year, the board sought and received a commitment from the Woman's Club to hire only staff who held certificates from the Chicago public schools. As the summer of 1905 and the impending dismissal of personnel outside the school system approached, the club's Vacation School Board negotiated a last-minute stay. Vacation schools Superintendent William Bogan pleaded for the retention of the nine teachers and one principal threatened with removal, noting that loss of these vacation school veterans would leave the program without personnel of their skill and experience. The board relented and decided not to make the requirement for certificates retroactive but set the conditions for the eventual removal of noncertified teachers. As these ten staff members left the vacation schools, they would only be replaced by public school certified teachers.

In the end, public school officials lacked the patience to wait for this gradual transition to a certified teaching staff. In 1908, Shoop announced that the schools would hire only applicants eligible for appointment in city schools. Noting that this action was "a departure from previous policies," he defended the change because "nearly the entire amount paid for salaries was contributed from the Public School Treasury."[76] As a result of these policies, the makeup of the faculty had visibly shifted. By the time the school system completed its takeover in 1909, Chicago's vacation schools were staffed only by public school teachers.

As the sole proprietor of vacation schools, the board of education wielded its authority and began to refocus the summer curriculum. In the industrial courses, the emphasis had moved away from countering negative street influences and toward fitting children into the general educational process. Recreation programs and games remained, but schools limited the amount of time devoted to such pursuits. Nature study grew harder to maintain as qualified teachers and adequate facilities became more difficult to find.[77] Although Superintendent Shoop still praised the vacation schools for "liberating the children from a conventional atmosphere in the school-room," he and Chicago Superintendent Ella Flagg Young introduced "academic review classes" to Chicago's vacation schools in 1911. That summer, three vacation schools added classes that registered 640 students needing to make up course work. In addition, one summer high school opened to serve the same purpose for older students.[78]

Academic classes steadily assumed a larger role in Chicago's summer schools. Claiming widespread success with the inaugural effort, Shoop recommended them as a permanent addition to the vacation school work. In 1912, two more high schools were added, the number of elementary schools doubled, and the number of students enrolled in the latter more than tripled to 2,165. In each subsequent summer, academic review classes became more numerous at the expense of the industrial and particularly the recreational classes. In 1915, Shoop observed that "the trend has been toward a type of school that correlates with and supplements the usual work of the regular class-room."[79] Still, the academic classes did not instantaneously replace Chicago's traditional vacation program. Shoop retained a sense of the experimental role of the vacation schools. His 1914 report observed that "there are still many suggestive lines that may be followed in the Vacation Schools that will supplement and add to the range of action of the regular schools."[80] Indeed the complete transformation to an academic program in Chicago summer schools evolved over a ten-year period. Nevertheless, Shoop pushed for the further expansion of the academic role of summer education by allowing superior students to enroll in an accelerated course of study. Chicago was hardly in the vanguard of the movement towards academic summer schools, but by 1915 it was well on its way.[81]

The last vestige of Chicago's original vacation schools was their immigrant student population. In all likelihood, the schools continued to primarily serve foreign-born Americans through at least World War I. Certainly school leaders retained the vacation schools' focus on eastern and southern Europeans. Superintendent Shoop continued to publicize vacation schools as a program for the disadvantaged classes through "efforts to create and maintain an equilibrium of opportunity in the rank and file of the social order."[82] He also suggested that immigrants attended vacation schools with more constancy and with more pronounced interest than American-born children. Finally, data he published in 1914 identified students from the same long-standing ethnic users of vacation schools: Italians, Jews, Russians, Poles, Germans, and Bohemians. Combined, these nationalities accounted for 65% of the entire vacation school enrollment that summer.

Despite the strong presence of immigrant children, vacation schools increased their representation of native-born children of native-born parents in the early 1910s. The 1914 ethnic survey demonstrated that the number of American-born students had more than doubled since 1908. That year, enrollments of native-born Americans were 5% and 4% for whites and blacks, respectively. In 1914, nearly 20% of the vacation school enrollment came from children of native-born Americans of all races.[83] What's particularly of interest is why this increase most likely took place. In this six-year span, the number of school sites jumped from thirteen to twenty-nine and student enrollment from 10,687 to 17,263. Much of the rise coincided with the start and expansion of the review classes cited above. Incorporating an academic curriculum and selecting sites all over the city may have helped Chicago schools officials reach out to an American-born population.

Bureaucracy meets contingency: an explanation of the vacation school transformation

Why were Chicago's vacation classes so thoroughly remade into summer schools? The two-phased transformation of Chicago's vacation schools suggests giving bureaucratic impulses substantial explanatory weight. In the Windy City, shifts in curricular offerings and student ethnic identities stemmed from decisions made only after the board of education gained control of the vacation schools. School leaders reconstituted the makeup of the faculty even earlier, once their initial financial contributions gave them some leverage. Even within the public domain, there were struggles for control of the vacation schools—particularly between the superintendent and the board of education. They clashed, for example, in 1909 over the finalization of public administration of the Woman's Club vacation schools. The superintendent's office "recommended that the vacation schools be conducted under the direction of the superintendent's office as in the case of the other departments of the schools," but after "a lively executive session," the board instead designated Shoop as superintendent of a separate organizational structure for vacation schools.[84] The results of that decision may have been marginal. No matter which component of the public school system ran them, vacation schools felt pressure to meld smoothly with the regular school program.

Knowing the shortcomings of a functionalist explanation, were there pressures external to the school system faced by Chicago's vacation classes? It is easy to imagine three outside scenarios that might have pushed Chicago school leaders to alter their vacation program. First consider a demographic perspective. The Chicago school system, like most others in urban areas, suffered from insufficient space and an excess of overage students.[85] Its average daily attendance increased by 47% in the twenty years after 1900 and in sheer numbers needed to school nearly 100,000 more children on a daily basis in 1920. A 1904 study found that while its eighth grade graduates averaged 14.5 years of age, they ranged from age 12 to age 19, with substantial numbers between 13 and 17. Ten years later, Young raised similar concerns during her tenure as superintendent.[86] While Chicago's school system initiated certain policies to grapple with these conditions, its officials never articulated how vacation schools might alleviate them nor suggested that academic review classes in fact served to do so. These new classes had a limited reach considering that in 1914 they served under 2,500 students in a system approaching 275,000 on a daily basis during the regular school year.[87]

Second, how did Chicago's immigrant population react to the transformation of vacation schools? Foreign-born children attended vacation classes in large numbers both before and after they became academic in nature. Moreover, no indicators of strong ethnic discontent or advocacy were found in the popular press, the Chicago school records, or the extensive secondary literature on Chicago's ethnic communities.[88] Summer schools functioned as a form of child care for immigrant communities whether the students studied nature or mathematics. What's more, classes for credit in core subject areas served children eager to receive as much schooling as possible before they had to enter the work force permanently. For native citizens eager to Americanize newcomers, both permutations of summer education served admirably—especially at a minimal expense. Thus these communities remained publicly silent about schools that enjoyed widespread acclaim.

Finally, what role did budget considerations play in the remaking of summer education in Chicago? Initially, the vacation schools received fairly smooth financial backing from the public sector. The Woman's Club had experienced difficulty in soliciting charitable gifts from 1898 to 1902, but its funding difficulties eased after the board of education began to contribute in 1903. Board allocations for vacation schools steadily increased until the 1909 takeover, and its budget deliberations never generated attacks on vacation schools for profligacy. The familiar criticism of "fads and frills" never included vacation schools in Chicago as it did in other cities.[89] In fact, at times the board demonstrated outright generosity. In 1907, when last-minute private donations left the club's Permanent Committee only $550 short of opening two more vacation schools, the board immediately voted to increase its previously determined appropriation by that amount.[90] Such beneficence would not last.

Chicago's vacation schools eventually faced financial cutbacks that hastened their makeover. After nearly a decade of steady increases, they suffered a 28% reduction in expenditures in 1911. How this budget crisis did and did not affect summer education in Chicago is quite revealing. The schools experienced the negative impact in two ways: supplies were scarcer and classes were held only four days a week. In this way, Shoop attempted to distribute the hardship rather evenly and managed to open only four fewer schools than the previous summer. He also retained the essential character and conditions of the vacation schools. Thus excursions remained a part of the program, special summer schools still served the tubercular, deaf, and crippled children, and teacher and principal salaries stayed the same.[91] But what seemed most impervious to the ups and downs of school fiscal policy were the academic review classes.

Despite the loss of funds in 1911, Young and Shoop chose to introduce these classes into three elementary vacation programs and one high school. The high school was a last-minute budget item that likely came out of the board of education's contingency fund—a surprising decision in a year of retrenchment. Was there a link between these two events? It is possible that he thought the review work would fare better in any budget negotiations than manual or recreational activities, but Shoop left no written record suggesting that the timing of the academic review classes was related to the loss of funds. Nor did he appear to add academic work in order to curry favor or mobilize support from the board of education, for in 1911 it still appeared content with the traditional curriculum of the Woman's Club vacation schools. Most likely, Shoop was swayed by the trends in other cities of which he was well aware.[92] Future budget developments, however, would highlight the extent of Shoop and the board of education's commitment to the summer schools' academic classes.

The allocations for vacation schools were nearly restored in 1912. Rather than return to a five-day-per-week session, Shoop expanded the number of schools to thirty, a new high for Chicago. In so doing, he extended the reach of vacation schools into areas with larger American populations, whose numbers in the vacation schools more than doubled in that one year. Whether or not this action—like the new review classes—was intended to broaden the appeal of the vacation schools to secure them against future cut backs is unclear. But Shoop was unwilling to sacrifice the growth of what he increasingly saw as the most important feature of vacation schools to insufficient funds. While expenditures remained below their levels in 1910, the review classes attracted hundreds more students than anticipated. Faced with this influx, Shoop reported that "the importance of this work is of such nature that the management of the schools did not feel justified in turning these children away." As a result of the unintended growth, vacation school expenditures in 1912 exceeded their budget by $1,300. Forced to ask the board of education to cover the deficit from its contingency fund, Shoop found his request easily granted without contention. Later that year, the board used that same source to finance the growing summer high school program. In both these cases, the board's generosity appears unusual for a body grappling with tight budgets.[93]

The new academic credit priority for summer education was laid bare in 1915. By then, the makeup of the board of education had changed substantially. Dominated by fiscal conservatives growing more and more hostile to Young's superintendency, the summer of 1915 witnessed the highly charged conflict over the Loeb Rule that eventually ended Young's tenure as superintendent of schools.[94] Prior to that monumental blow-up, signs of changing agendas were evident even in the relative backwater of Chicago's vacation schools. Vacation schools had finally begun to shed some aspects of their recreational and industrial program. Most notably, some resources were diverted from the summer day trips, and even more were reoriented toward the summer high schools. From 1912 to 1914, vacation school expenditures held steady in the low $30,000 range. Summer high schools, having just begun in 1911, received more than $25,000 in 1914. In both 1913 and 1914, they were initially granted $10,000 per summer, received a subsequent appropriation of another $10,000, and in the latter summer were permitted to expend 25% more than budgeted.[95]

In 1915, a large financial crunch dealt the Chicago vacation schools a blow from which they were never to recover. In the fall of 1914, the board of education anticipated a budget squeeze and among its austerity measures was a slight reduction in both the vacation and summer high school allocations. By the spring of 1915, the deficit had grown much larger than anticipated, and in an extremely contentious meeting, the board of education voted to cut teacher salaries by 7.5%. In a less publicized decision, the board recommended the abolishment of summer classes in the elementary vacation schools with the exception of the six review schools for academic make-up work. While some board members initially objected to this cut, the conservative businessman Jacob Loeb engineered a 15–3 vote in favor of it.[96] While vacation school expenditures dropped to under $10,000, the summer high school program was left alone. Thus faced with a hard choice of resource allocation and increasingly antipathetic to any school activities with insufficient "economy," Chicago school leaders abandoned the original vacation school curriculum of recreational and industrial work and focused the summer classes on moving students through the graded subject matter.

Chicago's vacation schools recouped their funding the next year but not their non-academic or experimental emphasis. In 1916, Shoop replaced Young as superintendent of the Chicago schools, and he kept the vacation program oriented towards academics. When expenditures returned to their previous levels, the number of children attending did not, as the summer review classes never served as many students as the vacation schools. The average daily attendance peaked at 11,609 children in 1914. By the early 1920s, that figure hovered around 4,000. In the meantime, the summer high schools had been receiving a larger appropriation than the elementary schools, and they too offered mostly academic coursework, though at least one school focused on commercial subjects and domestic science.[97] Thus vacation elementary schools lost their formative characteristics and their place as the predominant summer option offered by the public school system.

The metamorphosis of vacation programs into summer schools did not make recreation and industrial work completely unavailable to the children of Chicago's urban immigrant poor. Playgrounds and other philanthropic vacation activities flourished in the Windy City until the Great Depression.[98] Moreover, the Woman's Club tried to return to its roots when its Education Committee convinced the board of education to set up summer recreational centers in 1917. In a near repetition of events from twenty years earlier, four school buildings opened in congested areas of the city and gathered children from streets and alleys to provide plays, games, physical training, story telling, singing, and "Penny Lunch" service.[99] The irony of this course of action seemed lost on Superintendent Shoop, who reported well attended centers that probably reduced juvenile delinquencies in their neighborhoods and recommended their continuation and expansion in number. Shoop highlighted the contrasts to Chicago's now primarily academic vacation schools but overlooked the recreation centers' similarity to the original vacation schools of the 1890s. Chicago, it seems, was prepared to reinvent the wheel.

Conclusion

Vacation schools reintroduced formal summer education to America's cities. Initially launched in Providence and Newark, vacation schools began to generate national attention when the Association for Improving the Condition of the Poor started three schools in New York in

1894. Offering a curriculum steeped in the manual arts, nature study, and recreation, vacation schools spread down the urban chain until most large and mid-sized American cities had experimented with them by 1927. Concurrent to this diffusion, the philanthropists and reformers who first opened vacation schools eagerly transferred control of them to urban school systems. In Chicago, the Woman's Club engineered a gradual public takeover of its program but soon found out that public control was no panacea. Public management, in Chicago and most cities, thoroughly altered the character of vacation schools. What emerged by 1920 were twentieth-century summer schools devoted to offering remediation and enrichment for academic credit.

The budgetary crises encountered by Chicago's vacation schools illustrated some of the contradictions of public control. First, their very occurrence refuted one of the chief justifications for public administration of vacation schools, namely to ensure stability in the program. Second, the ill effects of too much learning continued to be both accepted and discounted. In Chicago, Shoop explained his trimming the 1912 vacation school session to four days per week through these long-standing notions. He justified this course of action by noting that "the plan reduces the draft on the vitality of both teachers and pupils during the warm summer months and provides a larger portion of the vacation period for recreation."[100] At the same time, the addition of the academic review classes challenged adherents of the overstudy ideology by incorporating the book work removed from the urban summer during the nineteenth century and studiously avoided in the Woman's Club's vacation activities.

Shrinking budgets prodded Chicago's vacation schools towards change already well in progress. From the outset, the women who founded these recreative and industrial programs in working-class immigrant neighborhoods wanted them to become a part of the public school system. After the board of education began to contribute money for their staffing in 1903, it exerted control over who could teach in them. When it completed its takeover in 1909, it soon opened schools in more middle-class and native-born American neighborhoods. It also added an academic component that eventually dominated summer education in Chicago public schools. The previous offerings of the vacation schools were relegated to playgrounds and recreation centers and summer classes evolved to look much like the regular school coursework—similar on paper though not always in practice. While both shared the function of pushing students through a series of grade levels, summer schools—even in their latest reincarnation as academic institutions—may have retained traces of the tone set by the earlier non-academic activities.

Certainly the addition of academic review classes helped solidify the role of summer education in Chicago's school system; nevertheless its place remained suspect. Now firmly linked with the coursework of the regular school year, summer schools struggled to gain acceptance for the quality of their work and in several aspects lacked autonomy. The summer high schools immediately encountered the criticism that an entire term's worth of material could not be learned over a few short weeks. Lengthening the summer term from five to seven to eight weeks over two summers hardly resolved the concern nor ended the deliberation of the proper length of the summer school.[101] With these and other doubts about summer coursework, regular schools were fiercely protective of their right to determine student movement through the graded system. As early as 1912, Shoop assured his principals that the summer review classes did not assume the right to recommend promotion. Instead, they were instructed to send certified statements on the amount of work done and an application for promotion to the regular schools, whose principals would then test the summer students and ascertain their fate.[102]

Such concerns, among others, would plague summer academic programs in Chicago and elsewhere almost from their inception. The transformation of vacation into summer schools—without eliminating financial instability—created new questions about their academic quality. These misgivings tarnished the schools' reputation and became the gravest problem facing summer programs in the 1920s. In Chicago, school administrators appeared only mildly attentive in addressing them. Given that Chicago experienced some turmoil in its municipal governance and its public schools in the years following World War I, a more stable school system offers a less obstructed look at the efforts to confront the quality and reputation of summer schools. In Detroit, Superintendent Frank Cody headed a nationally acclaimed system that recognized and attempted to resolve the contradictions in using summer school as an extension of the regular school program.

CHAPTER SIX

"Easy Credit": *The Limits of Reputation and the Structure of Summer Schools in Detroit, 1901-39*

"The lady doth protests too much, methinks."
—Shakespeare, *Hamlet* (Act III, Scene ii)

There is great wisdom in Shakespeare's words. This line from *Hamlet* sheds light on the suspiciously repetitive statements of urban school administrators about the high quality of summer school coursework. Why did so many school officials emphasize that "summer school promotions, by authority of the superintendent, have the same validity as regular school promotions"?[1] Why did large majorities of summer school administrators surveyed in the 1920s claim to achieve academic outcomes comparable to regular schools?[2] Indeed, why were they queried so often and why did they sound so defensive when providing statistical evidence about the performance of summer teachers and students? The answers to these questions lie in the stigma that attached itself to summer schools as they evolved into academic programs linked to the regular school year. By the 1920s, many school personnel and constituents viewed the summer schools as more lax about attendance, discipline, and learning than their regular school counterparts. This negative image was a significant internal issue within the burgeoning urban school systems, whose leaders worked hard to improve the reputation of summer schools but achieved limited success. As two Brooklyn summer administrators lamented in 1923, "Many do not look with favor upon summer high schools, believing that most of the boys and girls simply go there to have a good time."[3]

Such criticisms of summer schools are surprising in light of their continued growth nationwide. Not a highly visible or vocal bunch, the detractors did not deter and perhaps enhanced the public popularity of summer schools doling out supposedly easy academic credit. As Chapter Five depicted, summer schools expanded to dozens of new cities and reached thousands of additional students during the 1920s. From 1918 to 1928, the number of cities with summer schools doubled from 211 to 447; the number of teachers tripled from 4,269 to 14,377; and the number of students in attendance nearly quadrupled, rising from 124,252 to 456,099.[4] Whether or not they had a weak reputation or program, teachers and students eagerly participated in summer schools, and city school systems readily appropriated funds for them in the 1920s. This depiction is certainly true of Detroit, whose summer school enrollment and expenditures grew by over 200% during the 1920s. By 1930, one-sixth of all elementary students and one-fifth of all high school students in Detroit enrolled in summer schools.[5] This chapter examines how in Detroit—amid all this plenty—administrators attempted to enhance the standing of summer schools within the larger system.[6]

The Detroit case study demonstrates widespread derision of summer schools, tensions between these and regular school programs, and a concerted effort to respond to them. In the Motor City, summer schools struggled to raise standards, resolve internal bureaucratic tensions, and maintain financial backing despite tremendous popular support and system-wide expansion. The central issue addressed here is why summer schools were seen as inferior elements of the school system. Was the perception, in fact, true? How did administrators try to overcome the structural and attitudinal obstacles to effective summer education? Why did summer schools never become fully integrated into the school program even after they offered regular academic courses for credit?

These questions are answered through four lines of inquiry on how summer schools functioned in relation to regular schools: student admissions and promotions policies; personnel selections; administrative relationships; and organizational structure. In so doing, this chapter traces the educational background of students using summer schools; it describes the staffs teaching and the subjects taught in them; and it assesses the way in which summer schools were arranged and administered. In the end, it argues that through the negotiations over the relationship between summer and regular schools, institutional identities developed that largely contributed to the stigma associated with summer school. At the same time, it suggests that the content and structure of summer school in Detroit also yielded a reputedly inferior educational product.

Vacation Schools: Origins and Transformation

Like most American industrial cities, Detroit's modern form of public summer education originated in the vacation school movement. The city's board of education first opened vacation schools as an offshoot of pre-existing afternoon playgrounds, which had opened in 1901. When the vacation schools began two years later, they too offered children supervised play opportunities, but several characteristics distinguished these new programs from the playgrounds: vacation schools used the schoolhouse as well as its grounds; they opened during the mornings in addition to the afternoons; and most importantly, they offered work in manual training through classes in benchwork, basketry, and sewing.[7] Nevertheless Detroit's playgrounds and vacation schools remained intertwined after 1903. Superintendent Wales Martindale stressed the link between them: "The proper connection of recreation with the vital pursuits of life must come through the amalgamation of the vacation school with the public playground."[8] A notable example of this connection was the annual Playgrounds and Vacation Schools Field Day. Held since 1904 at the city's public recreation facilities on Belle Isle, the event brought together children from all of its summer activities for a day of patriotic revelry, athletic competition, and arts and crafts displays.[9]

As in most communities, vacation schools in Detroit were a success. Whether or not they functioned as intended by contributing to safer streets, more skilled workers, or more assimilated newcomers, vacation schools were clearly popular with a number of constituencies.[10] Teachers wanted to work in them; parents scrambled to register their children; and students attended these voluntary classes with great regularity. Enrollment figures are sketchy from the early years, but the sessions attracted hundreds of children in increasing numbers each year. For example, the number of students taking basketry city-wide rose from 2,008 in 1906 to over 10,000 in 1910.[11] What made this growth possible was a steady rise in expenditures during this period (in spite of the board of education's almost annual failure to obtain its requested level of funding). In 1903, the board allocated $1,200 to open

its first three vacation schools; by 1911, $17,715 paid for sixteen
schools (See Table 6.1). By then, the length of the summer sessions had
also increased from forty to fifty days, and schools were open five and
a half days a week.[12]

Summer vacation schools had expanded for nearly a decade in Detroit when in 1912 Superintendent Martindale introduced classes for
academic credit into two vacation schools. Several factors seem to have
influenced this process. First, he grew increasingly dissatisfied with the
work in some of the crafts and industrial classes, particularly sewing
and lacemaking.[13] Second, even after nine years of existence, the vacation schools remained similar to but dwarfed by the playground program. By 1911, between 15,000 and 30,000 used the playgrounds
weekly, far more than were taking vacation school classes.[14] Therefore,
the transformation of the vacation schools to an academic curriculum
would not leave Detroit youth bereft of summer recreational activity.
Third, Martindale was no doubt aware of and influenced by the transition occurring in other cities. He was active in the school extension
movement, spoke at an annual meeting of the Playground Association
of America, and returned deeply impressed by Chicago's recreation
program.[15] Detroit's 1912 adoption of academic classes occurred after
the innovation appeared in other cities with which it might compare
itself: including Cleveland (1903), New York (1906), Cincinnati (1908),
Chicago (1911), and Pittsburgh (1911).

The transformation from vacation to summer schools was gradual.
In 1912, the board of education spent nearly twice as much money to
run the original vacation school programs as it did to fund the two
academic schools. Classes in industrial and aesthetic arts continued for
several years, and the schools also retained the annual Playgrounds and
Vacation Schools Field Day. Although not immediate, the transition to
summer schools was steady. Allocations for the academic classes regularly increased, from $5,592 in 1912 to $23,458 in 1917, and student
enrollments rose accordingly (See Table 6.1). Moreover, after 1913 the
annual reports of the superintendents made little mention of the original vacation schools. Their subsequent data and comments about
summer education referred only to the new academic classes. Eventually, the Detroit public schools experienced an institutional memory
loss about the recreational vacation schools. In his annual report for
the 1929–1930 school year, Superintendent Frank Cody brushed aside
their origins when he noted that "summer schools in Detroit are a development of the last ten years although existing in a rudimentary way
for a few years before 1919." Five years earlier, a history of public

Table 6.1. *Detroit vacation and summer schools, 1903–30*

Year	No. of Schools	Students Enrolled	Average Attendance	Teaching Expenditures	Real Expenditures[a]
1903	3	. . . .	. . . .	$1,200	$2,013
1904	5	. . . .	. . . .	$2,000	$3,350
1905	6	. . . .	. . . .	$2,000	$3,328
1906	6	. . . .	. . . .	$2,000	$3,236
1907	8	. . . .	. . . .	$4,500	$6,902
1908	9	. . . .	. . . .	$10,225	$16,256
1909	11	. . . .	. . . .	$8,629	$12,765
1910	12	. . . .	. . . .	$11,539	$16,391
1911	16	. . . .	. . . .	$17,715	$27,296
1912[b]	18	668	. . . .	$16,447	$23,802
1913	3	943	. . . .	$7,898	$11,315
1914	3	1,442	. . . .	$9,418	$13,830
1915	5	2,210	. . . .	$16,470	$23,698
1916	6	2,287	. . . .	$15,131	$17,697
1917	11	4,143	. . . .	$23,458	$19,964
1919[c]	13	6,510	5,620	$75,416	$54,413
1920	13	10,188	8,417	$124,078	$80,361
1921	27	16,369	13,562	$162,975	$166,983
1922	31	16,109	12,731	$148,846	$153,296
1923	34	17,876	14,693	$155,509	$154,582
1924	38	21,113	18,122	$179,544	$183,021
1925	40	24,601	20,506	$208,873	$201,810
1926	52	29,312	24.092	$248,309	$248,309
1927	55	31,978	26,646	$272,471	$285,609
1928	58	32,656	26,802	$293,471	$303,486
1929	58	31,247	26,083	$308,156	$323,353
1930	56	33,654	29,171	$315,267	$364,892

Sources: Detroit Board of Education. *Annual Report* (1903–31); U.S. Department of Commerce, Bureau of the Census, *Historical Statistics of the United States: Colonial Times to 1970.* Washington: Government Printing Office, 1975, p. 200.

Notes: Enrollment figures do not include summer students at Detroit's junior colleges. Expenditures do not include administrative or operational costs. Starting with 1920, the school number and enrollment figures are grand totals. They include elementary, high school, college, and special schools.

[a] These expenditures are adjusted for cost of living (1926 = 100).

[b] The 1912–30 figures for students and teachers only represent the two summer schools that introduced academic classes that year. The expenditures include costs for all vacation classes.

[c] No data reported in 1918 due to World War I.

education in Detroit recognized that vacation schools began as early as 1903 but claimed that their purpose was always to provide academic credit for accelerated and retarded students.[16]

Summer sessions generally ran for eight weeks and offered a wide array of courses. The elementary curriculum included five basic subject areas: composition, spelling, arithmetic, history, and geography. For older students, Detroit opened high schools for academic, technical, and commercial work. Academic coursework included algebra, chemistry, English, French, geometry, history, Latin, and trigonometry. Bookkeeping, shorthand, and typewriting were offered as commercial subjects. Cass Technical High School held regular academic courses as well as pattern making, mechanical drawing, machine shop, printing, automobile service, gas engine mechanics, foundry practice, pharmacy, sheet metal work and other technical classes.[17] Summer classes did not last all day; for the elementary grades, a single session ran from 8:00 A.M. to noon. The high school day lasted one hour longer and held courses for 90 or 135 minutes. Detroit's summer schools were free to city residents but charged a fee to the few non-Detroit children who attended. Detroit also ran open air schools, continuation schools, teachers colleges, and junior colleges during the summer.[18]

Detroit's incipient summer schools served a wide range of children. Classes started at fifth grade and went up to the senior high school level, though most children who attended were between ages 11 and 15. The omission of grades 1–4 from summer schools is not surprising. For young children, a summer of recreation remained a viable option in the minds of educators; in contradistinction, older youth were admonished not to "waste the entire summer in play." Moreover, vestiges remained of nineteenth-century medical theory on the dangers of overstimulaton, and young children were always deemed particularly vulnerable to mental fatigue. Even in the 1910s, Detroit school officials were wary of criticism that summer schools harmed health and specifically deflected it in their annual reports. They also reported that girls predominated in summer classes, but both boys and girls attended in large numbers. Girls were slightly overrepresented in the early years— in both 1916 and 1917, girls accounted for 54% of all summer school students—but by the 1920s there were more boys than girls during some summers. The superintendents did not survey the occupational backgrounds of the students' families, but one did note that "the large majority of the summer school students come from families who are not too well fixed economically. Their parents are largely industrial workers." In 1917, future superintendent Frank Cody estimated that

70% of summer school children came from families of moderate or straitened means. At the same time, he did acknowledged that some "better-to-do parents" sent their children as well—a trend which probably gained momentum during the 1920s.[19]

Detroit's summer schools also taught immigrant children of diverse nationalities. The initial vacation programs were not intended to benefit the city's established populations, as Superintendent Martindale explained: "I do not believe that every neighborhood would profit largely by having its school open for the same sort of work during vacations."[20] Instead, like Newark and Chicago, Detroit launched vacation schools to aid and influence newcomers to the United States, and Danish, Norwegian, Russian Jewish, and Hungarian students attended in substantial numbers. The early academic summer schools continued to open in neighborhoods inhabited by these ethnic groups, but they did not necessarily serve the most targeted populations. Superintendent Charles Chadsey observed in 1916 that Jewish, German, and Scandinavian children still predominated in the summer classrooms, but he noted that students were typically second- or third-generation descendants of immigrants.[21] Apparently, many of the first-generation immigrant families from Southern and Eastern Europe that poured into Detroit in the 1890–1924 period did not send their children to summer schools in large numbers. Indeed, of the three groups Chadsey mentioned, only the Jews represented the "new immigrant" of the post-1890 era.

After 1916, the ethnic makeup of Detroit's summer school population began to change. For one thing, Martindale's successors abandoned his view of limited vacation school service and sought to diffuse summer school buildings throughout the city in an effort to reach and satisfy all populations. Arguing that the schools' success and popularity justified an expanded scope, they opened them in middle-class areas that had once lacked summer programs. Detroit school officials chose centrally located summer schools and used high school buildings for elementary classes to reach a variety of neighborhoods. Frederick De Galan, who ran the city's summer programs during the 1920s and 1930s, even hoped to extend summer schools to every school building.[22]

How much did this expansion alter the ethnic group makeup among summer students? Unfortunately, this question is impossible to measure precisely as the public schools never classified summer students by nationality. However, the results of a 1921 nationality survey of the regular school population suggest that at the least, summer

Table 6.2. *Projected nationality distribution at summer school sites, 1921 and 1922*

School	Primary Nationality Group (%)	Secondary Nationality Group (%)	Tertiary Nationality Group (%)
Bishop	Russian (45.8)	U.S. black (19.1)	Polish (10.8)
Cass Technical High School	U.S. white (51.4)	Russian (13.1)	Canadian (9.3)
Central H.S.	U.S. white (39.2)	Russian (21.1)	Polish (7.4)
Davison	U.S. white (22.1)	Polish (13.7)	U.S. black (9.7)
Eastern[a]	U.S. white (60.3)	German (11.7)	Canadian (11.4)
Ellis	Polish (59.5)	U.S. white (17.6)	German (8.9)
Franklin	U.S. white (65.1)	Canadian (14.8)	Maltese (1.9)
Garfield	Polish (12.1)	Roumanian (7.9)	Austrian (7.2)
Greenfield Park	U.S. white (46.3)	English (10.0)	Canadian (8.2)
Hely	U.S. white (46.4)	Polish (15.9)	German (9.9)
Longfellow	U.S. white (49.6)	Canadian (6.8)	U.S. black (5.6)
Marr	U.S. white (73.8)	Canadian (12.1)	English (3.9)
Northern[a]	U.S. white (57.6)	Canadian (8.9)	Russian (7.8)
Northwestern[a]	U.S. white (65.3)	Canadian (13.7)	English (4.5)
Ruthruff	U.S. white (62.0)	Canadian (10.5)	English (7.2)
Southeastern[a]	U.S. white (64.0)	Canadian (9.5)	German (7.2)
Southwestern[a]	U.S. white (47.1)	Hungarian (15.4)	German (11.2)
Webster	U.S. white (62.1)	Canadian (12.8)	English (6.5)

Sources: Detroit Board of Education. *Educational Bulletin* 5, spec. no. 5 (May 1922), pp. 1–2; *Research Bulletin* 5, no. 7 (January 1922), pp. 21–24.

[a] These high school buildings hosted elementary summer programs.

schools were increasingly placed in areas with large Anglo-American populations. The 1921 study provided an ethnic profile of each Detroit school during the regular year, and Table 6.2 identifies the dominant nationalities in buildings used as summer schools in 1921 and 1922. First, it demonstrates that most summer schools, 15 out of 18, were located in sites that regularly served native-born American populations. Of course, including high schools skews the figures because they typically underrepresented immigrant populations, but without them, 73% of the elementary schools still had a plurality of white, native-born Americans. This figure is identical to the proportion of Detroit's

141 elementary schools with a dominant Anglo-American student body during the September to June school year. Second, Table 6.2 indicates that when secondary, tertiary and quaternary groups are considered, older immigrant groups—such as the English, Scottish, and Canadians—and African-American migrants from the South were as common as more recent arrivals from Poland, Russia, and Hungary. Finally, the four schools that were specifically added in 1921 all contained large Anglo-American populations from the United States, Canada, and England. Thus the table suggests that summer schools now reflected the city's population as a whole. Given the widespread placement of summer schools among native-born American neighborhoods during the 1920s, it seems likely that the schools were accommodating larger numbers of nonimmigrant children. Ironically, this change occurred even as foreign-born immigrants grew predominant in Detroit schools.[23]

One characteristic that had not changed with the transformation from vacation to summer schools was the discourse of needs used to justify them. Like other urban superintendents across the nation, Superintendent Martindale had started vacation schools in Detroit to occupy idle immigrant children who clogged the streets and engaged in reckless activity during the summer. Writing of the early vacation schools in 1906, he noted that "the greatest need is felt in the crowded districts where policemen have the difficult duty of repressing the natural and laudable desire felt by every healthy boy to play some, in itself, harmless game."[24] Martindale also proffered a human capital formation motive for vacation schools. Summer activities included benchwork, basketry, sewing, and other "such useful occupations as to encourage habits of thrift and develop the necessary skill to perform useful manual work."[25]

In adopting academic summer classes, Martindale's successors retained the same rationale. To Frank Cody, who became superintendent in 1919, the issue of occupying urban youth during the summer remained predominant:

> The long summer vacation in a large industrial city like Detroit presents a social problem of importance, releasing as it does, thousands of children from the mild and wholesome discipline of school and turning them over to the doubtful freedom of the streets.[26]

Here, Cody implies that Detroit's summer schools befit a city of its magnitude; elsewhere he expanded on the "habits of laziness, petty vice, and mental sloth" that developed on the street.[27] Fearing rises in juvenile delinquency and noting the impact of child labor laws, Cody suggested that "children should be kept busy. Unless they have something to do in which they can use their native energy they may find things with which to occupy themselves that are harmful or unsafe."[28] As late as 1929, Cody incorporated the same logic that was used by the earliest vacation school advocates of the nineteenth century even though the institution he administered was vastly different.

Detroit school officials also drew upon the contemporary language of social efficiency. Embracing the value of wider functions for school buildings, Cody regularly reported the number of permits granted for use of school premises and repeatedly praised his city's "maximum utilization of the school plant through the summer months."[29] Administrators also had to rationalize the new academic subjects of summer school, and the saving of time and money served as nicely in Detroit as in other cities. School managers typically cited the large number of summer graduates and the high percentage of promoted students to justify the programs. For advanced students, passing summer school twice allowed high school graduation one semester early. For students going to work instead of to high school, summer school enabled them at least to graduate from the eighth grade. Elementary students could make up one half a grade through summer work.[30] In fact, many students in Detroit did follow these paths. The number of eighth grade graduates, for example, rose from 613 to 1,545 from 1923 to 1927. Moreover, from 1919 to 1928, passing percentages for various summer school cohorts ranged from 68% to 92% and averaged over 80%.[31] Thus summer schools helped speed thousands of students through the graded public school system, a fact that educators publicized in order to promote the summer work.

Superintendent Cody emphasized the economic value of the summer schools as well. In a promotional article highlighting the progressive nature of Detroit's school system, Cody identified vacation schools as the most cost effective of all of Detroit's education programs.[32] In fact, he reported annually the per-capita costs of all forms of schooling in Detroit, data that are presented in Table 6.3. In 1921–22, the per-capita costs of summer schools in Detroit were $13.50, slightly less than the $13.61 for evening schools but substantially lower than the figures for regular elementary schools ($70.00), intermediate schools ($110.54), and high schools ($162.92). The yearly computations followed these patterns until the end of the 1920s, when evening schools recorded lower per-capita costs than summer schools. Cody used these statistics to calculate an actual amount of money that sum-

Table 6.3. *Per-capita cost of instruction for Detroit schools, 1920–31*

Year	Summer	Evening	Elementary	Intermediate	High School
1920–21	$20.62	$22.05	$71.18	$113.41	$165.23
1921–22	$13.50	$13.61	$70.09	$110.54	$162.92
1922–23	$12.40	$13.54	$70.43	$113.48	$145.59
1923–24	$12.49	$13.12	$71.93	$106.84	$141.30
1924–25	$10.58	$16.05	$71.66	$104.34	$123.38
1925–26	$11.33	$16.83	$70.63	$101.10	$126.26
1926–27	$14.98	$16.24	$75.74	$100.94	$140.85
1927–28	$13.37	$16.10	$77.75	$117.01	$133.71
1928–29	$14.67	$18.57	$74.80	$113.64	$132.02
1929–20	$17.01	$13.58	$76.06	$119.01	$128.84
1930–31	$15.71	$15.27	$77.53	$121.40	$125.86

Sources: Detroit Board of Education. *Annual Report* 78–88 (1920–31).

mer schools saved the public school system. For example, in 1931 he argued that an investment of $18,000 in the 1,850 students who earned promotion credits saved the city $70,000. Cody, of course, recognized that these eliminated expenditures existed only in theory, but he claimed that "the saving of time and morale of the pupils is real and substantial, and, in the aggregate, of transcendent importance."[33] By saving students time, he argued, summer schools avoided additional expenditures during the regular school year.

With these well-received justifications supporting them, Detroit's summer schools were poised for tremendous expansion by 1920. That summer's enrollment surpassed 10,000 for the first time, an enlargement of over 1000% since 1912 (see Table 6.1). Likewise, instructional costs increased by 65% from 1919, when they constituted 1.2% of all system-wide instructional outlays. As a result, expenditures surpassed the $100,000 level for the first time. Total expenditures topped $162,000 in 1920, which enabled the city to open 13 schools. But these figures were just the starting point for sustained growth during the upcoming decade. By the eve of the Great Depression, the Detroit public school system administered summer schools in 58 locations. The schools now cost well over $400,000 and attracted over 30,000 students each year (see Table 6.1).[34] Yet amid this expansion and popularity, summer schools proved to be an awkward fit with the rest of the school system. Even as they grew similar to regular schools, summer classes were never equal to them in the minds of administrators, teachers, and students.

Summer Schools: Reputation and Administration

The origins and transformation of Detroit's vacation schools share much in common with the experiences of Chicago and other American cities. Once the academic schools became the dominant form of summer education, urban school systems struggled to make them function in relation to the regular schools. From reading the surviving documents from Detroit, it is clear that summer schools were generally seen as deficient by many observers. Contemporary school administrators often dismissed such perceptions through repetitive statements about the "special standards for admission and passing," that ultimately ring hollow.[35] Was summer education in Detroit the weakest component of the school year? Why was it perceived as such? Did the quality and or image of summer schools improve due to the strenuous efforts of administrators in Detroit? To answer these questions four more will be addressed: How was the academic performance of summer school students, and what was its impact on their progress through the school system? What was the level of quality of the teachers hired to work in summer schools? How was the authority over summer school grades and promotions distributed between summer and regular school principals? How were summer schools organized within the Detroit school system? Surprisingly, the answers to these queries do not reveal uniform inadequacy but rather depict a system struggling to overcome powerful limits of time and weakness of organization.

The unfavorable reputation of summer schools is not supported by the statistical profile of the students. First, consider the educational background of the summer student. Detroit started its academic classes in 1912 primarily to serve failed students, and the schools originally only admitted passing students if vacancies existed. By 1916, advanced students registered in greater numbers than remedial students, as nearly 64% of the summer students attempted to skip half a grade that summer (see Table 6.4). This reversal did not stem from any official change in policy; instead, it "was due to the demand of parents that their children, bright and industrious enough to avail themselves of the new opportunities, be given a chance."[36] Student registrations continued to strengthen the academic makeup of Detroit's vacation schools. In 1917, less than one-fourth of the summer students came to make up failed work, and as Table 6.4 indicates, during the 1920s the figure dropped

Table 6.4. *Detroit summer school enrollment by student classification, 1916–28*

Year and School Type	Students Taking New Work		Students Repeating Old Work	
	Number	%	Number	%
1916	776	64	438	36
1920	4,657	85	828	15
1924	13,795	88	2,022	13
1924–elementary	10,532	91	1,007	9
1924–high school	3,263	76	1,015	24
1928	21,854	86	3,554	14
1928–elementary	15,535	92	1,335	8
1928–high school	6,319	74	2,219	26

Sources: Detroit Board of Education. *Annual Report* 74–86 (1916–28).

to about 15 percent. Table 6.4 also separates figures for high school and elementary students to show that a larger block of remedial students were present in the former, but both school types were overwhelmingly comprised of advanced students. Thus summer schools in Detroit contained mostly children eager to skip a grade and not the system's backward and delinquent students as many believed.

The selection process for summer students did present some problems for school officials. Even though most summer school students had not failed a course the previous term, administrators found that a loose admissions policy marred the quality and reputation of the summer program by allowing undeserving students to move ahead too quickly. At first, admission to Detroit's summer schools was open to any interested students and not dependent on a recommendation from a teacher or principal. Despite the official encouragement of consultations with school personnel and the limitation on how many classes students could take, the lack of restrictions led many marginal students to enter summer programs in order to quicken their progress through school.[37] To remedy this practice, the school system adopted a more restrictive and selective registration policy in the early 1920s. The new process allowed only unconditionally passed students who maintained a minimum grade point average to try for promotion. Initiated partially in order to keep summer school expenditures within the budget appropriation, the selective registration policy became a key component in administrators' efforts to prop up the summer school work and was maintained throughout the 1920s.[38]

Not all aspects of the selection process could be reformed so successfully. With the academic purpose of summer school entrenched by 1920, Detroit's schools and their admissions process emphasized learning for credit more than learning for its own sake. While the schools freely registered both failures and skippers after 1916, students who wanted to attend merely to improve their knowledge and skills were only accepted if room permitted. This group of students attended summer school "to strengthen their future marks" without expecting to receive a pass slip, but few actually came for this purpose.[39] "Strengthening" was only a second tier goal of the summer school—an acceptable by-product for students who did not pass their coursework. Although the city's school system was designed to produce knowledge as well as credentials, Detroit's summer schools primarily embodied the former function. No change in admissions policy could alter the role they played in awarding credentials. Even when "pupils who have barely passed and generally weak pupils" were admitted to summer school as readily as students who failed or passed easily, they did not attend in great numbers. Summer schools might allow students seeking strengthening, but most attended in order to pass classes and pass them they did. This overt form of credentialism, unrecognized by contemporaries, lay behind much of the summer school's academic woes.[40]

Summer school students' passing rates provide less surety of the high quality of summer programs than their attendance patterns. Detroit superintendents were not perfectly diligent in reporting annual summer school promotion rates during the 1916 to 1928 period. One might assume that the records did not survive or were inexplicably or even intentionally omitted from the city's annual reports. But the missing data might also reflect an ambivalence about passing percentages held by summer school administrators who faced dual considerations about student promotions. Passing too many students might indicate the ease of the summer school program to observers, while promoting too few learners would undermine the claims of efficiency that underlay its very existence.

In fact, school policy on this issue was quite contradictory. Over the course of the 1920s, Superintendent Cody regularly reported on "efforts to ... maintain high standards" and that these "special standards for passing" remained unchanged.[41] Yet while Cody listed the "imposition of high promotion standards rigidly maintained" as one of the accomplishments of the summer school program, the promotion standards were not so inflexible. In 1923, the minimum grade-point total for promotion was actually lowered; this reduced level lasted through

Table 6.5. *Detroit summer school passing rates by student classification,*
1916–28

Year and School Type	Students Taking New Work		Students Repeating Old Work	
	Number	%	Number	%
1916	776	73	438	77
1920	4,657	80	828	77
1924	13,795	79	2,022	73
1924–elementary	10,532	75	1,007	61
1924–high school	3,263	92	1,015	85
1928	21,854	82	3,554	83
1928–elementary	15,535	80	1,335	81
1928–high school	6,319	88	2,219	84

Sources: Detroit Board of Education. *Annual Report* 74–86 (1916–28).

the 1926 summer, after which the minimum returned to what it had been at the start of the 1920s.[42] Furthermore, the superintendent's office had little ability to control the assignment of grades. As a result, its claims that summer grades had the same validity as those of the regular schools appear spurious especially because promotion rates for summer school students tended to be high. Table 6.5 presents the passing rates from 1916 to 1928 over four-year intervals. It displays aggregate annual passing percentages ranging from 73 to 83, and this steadiness of the yearly rates suggests that promotions did not become easier or more difficult to earn over time. Thus neither the changing type of student attending nor the regular appearance of policy bulletins from the superintendent's office appear to affect the passing rates of students. Finally, the figures did not substantially differ for students taking old and new subjects, but when data is broken down between high school and elementary students, the table demonstrates higher passing rates for the latter. These differences were especially evident in the 1924–28 interval and may stem from the greater restrictions that were placed on what high school students could take during the summer.[43] High school subjects may also have been particularly susceptible to the drive for high standards.

The best opportunity for educators to demonstrate statistically the worthiness of summer school lay in follow-up studies of their students. How students performed once they were back in the regular school program greatly concerned school administrators. One of the first in-

Table 6.6. *Average student grades in basic subjects during 1922 summer and fall terms*

Type of Pupil	June GPA	Summer GPA	January GPA	Summer School Population (%)
Advancing	2.10 P	2.13 P	2.46 P	69
Strengthening	2.66 P	4.06 N	2.66 P	20
Making up a Failure	3.63 N	2.63 P	2.83 P	9
Unsuccessful Attempt to Make up a Failure	3.86 N	4.16 N	2.90 P	2

Sources: Detroit Board of Education. *Annual Report* 80 (1922–23), pp. 53–54.

Notes: P = Passed, N = not passed. Lower numbers indicate higher grades on a scale of 1–5.

vestigations in Detroit tracked the progress of three groups of 1921 summer students: (1) pupils promoted in June who earned an extra promotion in August; (2) pupils promoted in June who did not make the extra promotion in August; (3) pupils who failed in June and then earned promotion in August. The results reported by Superintendent Cody highlighted the role of summer school in providing credentials. He found that remedial students of group 3 benefited the most, as 42% improved upon their June marks in August, and of them 88% were promoted again after the fall marking period. Group 1 also displayed follow-up success, gaining nearly as high marks in the fall as in previous terms. For these advanced students, higher grades in June correlated with greater likelihood of success in the August and January marking periods. Only students from group 2, who were awarded certificates of strengthening, did not earn improved grades in the following January. Cody's conclusion that attending summer school simply to enhance one's knowledge and skills was not profitable reinforced the program's credentialing aspects.[44]

Subsequent data from the 1920s mostly corroborated the research from 1921. Table 6.6 presents the findings from a 1923 investigation of 1,000 summer school students classified into four groups: the three from the 1921 study as well as students who unsuccessfully attempted to make up a failure during the summer. The first three groups performed as they did in 1921, that is students who earned advancement or made up credit during the summer sustained their work in the fall. The June failures were once again particularly successful as they improved a 3.63 June average to a 2.83 January mark.[45] Advanced students still tended to pass in January, but with a less impressive average (2.46) than in June (2.10), a finding which likely fueled suspicion that too many marginal students were promoted in the summer. On the other hand, promoted students supposedly strengthened through summer work again showed no improvement in the fall. However, students who failed in both June and August did find themselves strengthened, as they significantly elevated their grade performance from a 3.86 average in June to 2.90 in January. Nearly a decade later, a cohort of students who had failed in June and passed in August was tracked through the ensuing fall term, during which 88% of them passed again in January.[46] In the interim, the numbers were less impressive. In 1925, for example, students who maintained a 2.36 average in the summer only averaged 2.62 per subject in the fall term.[47] Overall, these figures offered mixed results for summer school proponents, but they presented them to show that summer work was at least comparable to the regular term curriculum. The data were meant to counter the pervasive negative stereotypes about summer school.

The characteristics of the teaching pool also belie the notoriety of the summer school academic program. Detroit administrators established several requirements in order to guarantee a distinctive group of teachers for its summer schools. Qualifications included regular employment by the Detroit public schools, a teaching evaluation score of at least a B and teaching experience in the subject matter. In order to prevent burnout, teachers were prohibited from working more than four consecutive summer sessions. While this last regulation was not always maintained, Detroit did succeed in attracting its better teachers to the summer schools.[48] In 1925, 61% of the summer elementary and 32% of the summer high school teachers were graded an A, compared to only 7% of the entire teaching staff city wide. The cohort of summer teachers continued to rate highly overall and only occasionally included teachers below a B. In addition, more summer high school teachers displayed A rankings by the end of the decade.[49] By then, these highly evaluated summer teachers were paid $150.00 and $180.00 per month for elementary and high school work, respectively. These salaries coupled with the benign working conditions accounted for the great demand for summer school positions, which enabled the schools to hire such well-rated teachers. Eventually, summer school Director Frederick De Galan attempted to appoint summer teachers in proportion to a school's number of summer students. This policy proposal suggests the ongoing demand for the summer jobs, as well as the efforts to set bureaucratic guidelines for their distribution.[50]

The relationship between regular and summer school principals offers the strongest evidence of weakness in the summer school program. In a system with sharply drawn bureaucratic lines like Detroit's, it is easy to imagine that issues of control would arise between summer and regular term employees. The reputations of summer schools, however, only intensified the problem, and regular school principals generally believed that the summer programs were tainted by lower standards. The lack of confidence in summer coursework intensified conflict with summer school principals over the disposition and promotion of summer students. Aware of this discord, Superintendent Cody and Director De Galan directed most of their summer school improvement measures at the behavior of regular school principals. By 1925, Cody reported success in this endeavor, stating that "efforts to elevate summer schools and maintain high standards were continued with a resulting increase in the support of regular principals."[51] Despite this optimism, however, tension between the two groups remained tangible throughout the decade.

The most divisive internal strife surfaced over linking the summer and regular schools at the beginning and end of the summer. Regular elementary school principals resisted giving up control of their students to the summer school principal for the July-August session. Before the summer term, they often interfered with the placement of summer students in a course of study. A technical administrative problem stemmed from regular school principals' habit of granting passing certificates to some students without placing them on their school's promotion lists. As a result of this practice, there were often discrepancies between the official school promotion lists and the students' report cards. By assigning these "conditional" passes to students, regular school principals attempted to influence the summer course of study of their students. In some cases, they planned to have these students repeat the same class in the fall, but in most they simply gave recommendations or placed conditions on summer school enrollment. In this way they deliberately forced summer school principals to seek their advice in the ordering of summer classes.[52]

The practice of awarding conditional promotions placed both symbolic and palpable burdens on summer school personnel. On the one hand, these contingent marks signified the limited authority and expertise of the summer administrators—an ironic message considering that many also served as principals during the regular school year. However, they also encumbered summer principals with students who arrived on the first day of classes only to find that their promotion in

June was not as straightforward as it had appeared. No doubt angered at this infringement upon their authority, summer principals often moved these students ahead anyway without consulting the regular school principals. This reaction only exacerbated tensions between these different supervisors, and the discord did not dissipate by the end of the summer. Since regular school principals denigrated the work of the summer schools, they were not always eager to honor promotion certificates awarded to students during the summer. They often placed conditions in "the disposition of summer school attendants upon their return," especially if the summer school principals had not followed their earlier recommendations.[53] Given these substantial divisions between the summer and regular school programs, both sets of principals appealed to the superintendent's office for direction.

Superintendent Cody and Director De Galan proffered solutions that decidedly supported the summer school program. First, they emphasized that conditional passes were intended as an exceptional and not a normal course of action. In extreme cases the regular school principals could advise the summer school administrator on the disposition of a student (and expect their wishes to be followed). However, De Galan warned that "such recommendations should be carefully stated and should not be so numerous as to amount to a private and general restriction upon summer school entrance."[54] As the conflict between principals persisted throughout the 1920s, the superintendent's office required regular school principals to pass and fail students unconditionally to insure consistency between student certificates and school promotion rolls. Finally, if they continued to place restrictions on students' promotions, regular principals were alternatively told that these students would be treated as failures in the summer schools or that the "recommendations" would be seen as "strictly advisory—not mandatory."[55] As for the return to school in September, students passing summer classes were to receive full academic credit upon returning to their regular school.

In all of these cases, De Galan tried to shore up the credibility of the summer school principal by affirming a simple principle. "In general," he wrote, "summer principals have the right to determine the disposition of their pupils and to issue passing, strengthening, or failing certificates with the same validity as attaches to the certificates of the regular schools."[56] But in asserting the authority of the summer principal, he acknowledged the shortcomings of the summer school. While regular school staff were constantly instructed to fulfill their administrative responsibilities towards the summer school and to limit their efforts at control, they were also told that "the summer schools, in turn, will put forth every endeavor in their work with the pupils furnished, to maintain their severe scholarship standards and to deserve the continued support of the regular schools."[57] It is not clear, however, that such a bargain was ever reached to the satisfaction of all participants. The repetition of these reminders and decrees suggests that inter-school tension remained a problem for the administrators of Detroit's school system throughout the 1920s. It also hints at the way in which the bureaucratic structure of summer schools affected their quality.

The key dilemma about summer school organization in Detroit arose from a perennial question facing school systems: where to centralize and where to localize control over schools. In the case of summer education, its features and purposes pointed to a system-wide management because only a fraction of schools were used to serve the city's entire student population. In addition, the transformation from vacation to academic summer schools required the central office to link the summer programs to the regular system. Thus many of the basic procedures necessary for summer academic classes were centrally run from their inception in 1912. For example, city superintendents recommended and the board of education approved of all summer teachers and administrators and set the curriculum.[58] Once the summer session began, the schools were run with only nominal supervision from the superintendent's office. Each building had a full-time principal in charge of a cohort of teachers and one clerk, and the high schools had librarians as well. The regular elementary principal usually served as head of the summer school in his building. In the high schools, an assistant principal took charge of the summer, evening, and other programs and oversaw department heads during summer months.[59] All summer school heads reported to the deputy superintendent since there was no lower-level administrator directly responsible for the summer program.

The central coordination of summer education tightened during the 1920s. A new layer was added to the school bureaucracy when De Galan was appointed director of the summer schools, and he supervised them more closely. Other system-wide positions were created as well, including a mental examiner, clinical psychologist, supervisor of health education, supervisor of research, and assistants in the building and equipment departments.[60] As a result, spending on administrative costs increased. Table 6.7 shows that at the start of the 1920s, the bulk of summer expenses went to pay for staff salaries. However, in 1926

Table 6.7. *Summer school expenditures in Detroit: 1920–29*

Year	Teaching Costs		Operating and Administrative Costs		Total ($)
	($)	(%)	($)	(%)	
1920	124,078	76.3	38,612	23.7	162,690
1921	162,975	92.7	12,750	7.3	175,725
1922	148,846	92.9	11,448	7.1	160,294
1923	155,509	93.5	10,837	6.5	166,346
1924	179,544	94.9	9,564	5.1	189,108
1925	208,873	94.4	12,375	5.6	221,248
1926	248,309	72.2	95,503	27.8	343,812
1927	272,471	71.9	106,523	28.1	378,994
1928	293,471	67.3	142,901	32.7	436,372
1929	308,156	65.9	159,429	34.1	467,585

Sources: Detroit Board of Education. *Annual Report* 78–86 (1920–29), pp. 53–54.

De Galan's office began to finance and oversee many of the nonteaching aspects of the program. Most of these costs went for the operation of summer schools: keeping the building open, providing books and supplies, paying janitorial staffs, but separate expenditures for administration and supervision were also recorded.[61] As De Galan looked back in 1932 on the developments of the previous decade, he recognized that "the summer organization tended to become a miniature replica of the regular organization."[62] As such, it began to suffer from many of the foibles of a modern bureaucratic school system. The Detroit summer schools became standardized and regimented to deliver an established curriculum without very much flexibility in how to do it. This centralized organization hampered individual schools from overcoming the largest barrier to summer school efficacy: the lack of sufficient time to accomplish the task of providing academic credentials backed by knowledge.

Insufficient Time and Other Summer School Dilemmas

Ultimately, the reputation of summer schools suffered due to a number of factors. First, by design summer schools taught the same subjects as the regular schools in far less time. Since a normal term lasted twenty weeks and the summer term only eight, Detroit administrators limited the number of subjects students studied and lengthened the daily class meetings to compensate for the deficiency. Early on, many assumed that this practice worked. In 1920 the *Detroit Education Bulletin* reported that "experience has proved that in eight weeks, with ninety minute recitation periods five days a week, a pupil, by concentrating on only two subjects can master these subjects just as well as he can in the regular semester when he studies four or five subjects."[63] Yet looking back in 1932, De Galan offered a more forthcoming appraisal of the issue to a national audience. "The brevity of time available for covering courses," he wrote, "was an embarrassment." He admitted that teachers must cut material out of courses and retain only the core, sometimes reducing them "below a reasonable minimum." Finally, he recognized that while follow-up studies demonstrated that summer students achieved satisfactory results, the summer schools were still plagued by "an impression of inadequacy."[64] De Galan's solution to the dilemma—to subdivide the regular school term into two ten-week halves and expand the summer term to ten weeks as well—was never seriously considered in these Great Depression years.[65]

The connection between summer school deficiency and sufficient time drew the interest of researchers in education. A Detroit summer school, intact throughout the Depression, was the site of a major investigation from 1929–37 conducted by Rolland Nancarrow and Claude Nemzek. Their study examined how the summer program could teach twenty weeks of school work in eight weeks. Its very hypothesis— "that so much must be covered in a short period of time may hinder the achievement of pupils"—indicates a traditional approach towards education where learning was measured by the amount of material committed to memory.[66] The researchers also tested another common sentiment among educators, that "summer school work is not of the same quality as work in regular school sessions," by comparing the grades for intermediate students seeking promotion before, during and after summer school.[67] The authors' findings supported popular beliefs about summer schools by showing higher average marks for the summer term and lowest for the fall term after the summer. Thus they concluded that standards were lower during the summer, and that summer school work had a detrimental effect on subsequent educational output.[68]

An additional sixty years of hindsight suggests that while Nancarrow and Nemzek's figures are not conclusive, their argument is persuasive. The question of coverage greatly contributed to the undoing of the summer school's reputation. As vacation schools, Detroit's recreational summer classes were not burdened by expectations of delivering a curriculum and promoting students. The academic program that began in 1912 was directly linked to the graded school program of the regular schools, which demanded a certain passage of time as well as a learning of knowledge. Even the brightest of students, the ablest of teachers, and the most intense concentration of study could not completely compensate for the far fewer number of weeks in the summer session when the standard of achievement was knowledge acquisition. That summer education was placed in this bind reflects larger trends in the social construction of time, particularly in the growth of time discipline and the commodification of time in the social and economic life of England and later the United States.[69] Spurred by the ideologies and habits of Protestantism and capitalism, time became a resource to spend and not to waste.[70] Many historians have shown how schools in the United States taught these values overtly through pedagogy and curricula. This case study of Detroit details how schools embedded this time sense indirectly through the very way in which they structured the use of summer school.

Within these temporal parameters, summer school in Detroit became a focal point of conflict between different groups of educators. Although school administrators tended to share a similar social class background, internal fissures stemmed from their distinct locations within Detroit's public education system.[71] On the one hand, principals of regular schools fiercely guarded their turf: control of their buildings and their students. As a result, they often resisted relinquishing their students to summer classes and accepting the validity of summer promotions. Summer school administrators, comprised of regular principals and vice principals, resented the marginalization of their programs and contested encroachments on their authority. Officials from the superintendent's office attempted to mediate such disputes and legitimize the summer academic work, yet even the centralization of summer school control under De Galan's leadership did little to breach the discord or repair the wounds.

Centralization did, however, add another layer to the administrative capacities and removed some individuality from the Detroit summer schools. By 1930, school personnel had completed the transformation of the original vacation schools from experimental recreational classes into regimented credit-bearing institutions. Administrative fiat introduced academic classes in 1912 and bureaucratic squabbling in the 1920s hardened the incipient structure of summer school, leaving a form of summer education that has remained essentially intact for the remainder of the twentieth century. In Detroit, the stigma of summer school originated more from the growth of the public sector than from the attitudes of students who attended summer schools. The classes may have been considered easier to take or teach, but to a public concerned with earning school credentials in a timely fashion, there was still little stigma to attendance despite any weak public reputation summer schools may have developed. Like their predecessors in the nineteenth century, it was schoolmen from the vantage point of a particular institutional position who found the summer school classes unworthy.

Finally, ever-present climatic conditions posed problems for summer schools. The summer was an undeniably difficult season in which to undertake study, especially in buildings not well designed for sweltering heat. While administrators tried to add time to the summer course of study, they were limited by the prospect of too much time spent in stifling summer classrooms. De Galan conceded as much and noted that as a result the impact of the summer curriculum lessened: "It is found absolutely necessary to make concessions to the heat in framing the program of courses for the summer term, thus losing the equality of content among the terms, and so a considerable part of those who pass in the summer term fail in the fall term." De Galan's negative assessment about subsequent summer student performance notwithstanding, he hoped to overcome the barriers presented by heat and poor ventilation. After some consideration of Newark and Nashville's all-year plans, which used four terms of twelve weeks each, De Galan rejected it because "it does not repeal the weather nor change the disposition of the bulk of the people who take their vacations during the hot summer."[72]

Climate inhibited the work of summer schools through its social as well as its material impact. In particular, De Galan blamed the family vacation for reducing the effect of the program by drawing children away early. The summer vacation—itself a response in part to the summer weather—had become entrenched behavior of the middle class and had seeped into working-class lifestyles as well by the 1920s.[73] Summer attendance percentages, often reported at well over 90%, were deceptive because they were based on average, not total enrollments. In fact, as early as 1917 Cody had reported a continual tailing off of attendance during the summer term. In the first couple of weeks, many repeating high school students dropped out in discouragement over the rapid pace of the summer work or because industrial jobs became available. Later on in the summer term, more children left when their families embarked on a vacation outside of Detroit. Finally, some children dropped out near the end of the term in anticipation of failure.[74] These patterns continued during the 1920s, as De Galan observed that only "a disappointingly small proportion of the summer enrollment continues through to the end of the term, and only a part of these pass."[75] Such a claim, however, appears exaggerated. In fact, average attendance typically ran only a few thousand below total enrollment, and most of those who did attend ended up passing. Summer schools in 1928, for example, experienced a total enrollment of 32,656, an average attendance of 26,802, and granted 20,934 promotions. That 64% of all the students who at least partially attended summer school passed at the end of the summer hardly seems like a disappointing or small proportion. While Detroit's summer programs were successful on paper, and most likely in the minds of teachers and students who participated, they nevertheless developed a reputation for inferior scholarship that restricted admissions, tightened standards, or centralized control could not dispel. In this regard, the persistent subordinate status of Detroit's summer schools was typical of urban school systems.

Conclusion

Summer schools in Detroit were representative in many respects, but in particular for the ambivalence with which many observers viewed them. On the one hand, they formed an inexpensive means of pushing students through the graded system. On the other, they had to deliver a curriculum amid conditions of uncomfortable climate, irregular attendance, and bureaucratic tension. Even more challenging, they needed to achieve student mastery of a subject in a truncated period of time. These issues proved formidable for administrators in small communities as well as in large cities. As a summer school director from Bay City, Michigan, admitted, "the question is often asked whether we do not have lost time during the summer school." Like his counterparts in Detroit, he emphasized the ways in which the summer program compensated for insufficient time—through longer class sessions, Saturday meetings, and smaller class sizes.[76] Similarly, summer schools in Mount Vernon, New York, used only experienced teachers, limited the subjects offered, and substituted individualized instruction for the "old-fashioned method of class instruction" to counter the distractions of summer.[77] Many localities sought to buttress the validity of a summer school promotion and dispel the beliefs that summer schools were disorderly and run by inexperienced faculty.[78] Thus the struggle over the quality and reputation of summer education concerned many public school systems in the 1920s.

By the end of the decade, however, disparagement of the summer schools arose from an additional source: Deweyan theorists. These university-based educators took a completely different tack than those in Detroit, who lambasted summer schools for failing to equal the ordered academic environment of the regular term. Progressives attacked summer schools for the opposite reason—because they too closely resembled the usual school program. William Kilpatrick, as chair of a 1933 White House meeting on summer vacation activities, criticized the evolution of the vacation school into an extension of the traditional school program and methodology. In his report, he laid out a philosophy of education that centered on the "self-directed experience" that rejected the "authoritative handing down" of knowledge. His evaluation of summer schools compared them to this standard and found them lacking: "Judged in the light of the philosophy presented at the beginning of this report, the vacation school, considered as a separate enterprise, is falling woefully short of giving to girls and boys a wholesome enriched and integrated educational experience."[79] Kilpatrick harked back to the earliest vacation school founders when he invoked the idea that vacation schools should be the site of experimentation in the schools, and he highlighted the summer projects that drew upon Deweyan ideals.[80] Their trenchant critique notwithstanding, Progressives failed to change the dominant patterns of summer education found in Detroit and other cities. Though well publicized, their programs remained a small minority among traditional summer academic schools and were unable to alter the overall notoriety of summer school.

In short, summer schools became perhaps the most maligned component of public school systems for several reasons. By the 1920s, vacation was ensconced in American culture, and the power of traditional and modern expectations for the summer was formidable.[81] Academic schooling conflicted with the older medical fears and newer leisure activities of many families in a way that the earlier recreational vacation schools did not. Summer schools, unlike their predecessors, also required a level of centralized control that limited the opportunity for individual principals, parents, and teachers to shape their programs. Nor did the original vacation schools embrace a task that was based on time, whereas achievement of the basic summer school goal—to impart a subject well enough to grant academic credit—faltered in face of eight- or ten-week sessions. In many ways, these shortcomings appear ironic. Educators set up a system in which credentialism mattered as much as learning and then complained when students blatantly used summer school to obtain such credentials and summer staffs lowered learning standards for them. Even more ironic, the solution favored by administrators in Detroit was the intensification of the credentials purpose through an all-year school schedule. The city never adopted one, and the movement for year-round schools only took hold in a small number of districts. Fiscal restraints were the most obvious reason why, but the presentation of the year-round school as a logical extension of summer program was actually a weak argument given the powerful popular prejudices against summer education. Of course, most administrators ignored the Progressive critique of summer education as well. Since the summer schools failed to reform themselves substantially in either direction, both their academic purpose and their weak reputation have lasted throughout the twentieth century.

EPILOGUE

Summer School in the Service of National Education Aims, 1930-2000

The aim of this book was to outline and account for the extent of and limits to summer education in American public schools. It has shown that summer education has always occupied a significant place in public schooling but that it has not been a wholesale component since before the Civil War. At the dawn of the common school movement, rural and urban areas maintained public schools during the summer. The schools attracted large numbers of students and taught standard subjects, yet were the bane of reformers who wanted to extend district school years while excluding the summer term. Hoping to carve out time for the professional development of teachers and, in the case of cities, fearing that too much schooling would wear on the fragile minds and bodies of children, the incipient schoolmen achieved substantial calendar reform by 1890. To do so, they used newly created or honed state policies—from constitutional clauses to legislative mandates to financial mechanisms—to alter rural school calendars. In the cities shorter school years stemmed from efforts to accommodate yet standardize local practices.

Even as summer terms disappeared and annual school year lengths converged towards a 180-day standard, another key shift in the educative role of summer occurred. Reformers of the late nineteenth century began to articulate a new vision for summer education as a response to urban environments transformed by industrialization and immigration. Their concern that overstudy injured children's health abated; instead, vacation school leaders contended that "the environment of children living in the poorest wards causes physical, mental, and moral degeneration."[1] In particular, they bemoaned city streets crowded with idle children prone to commit mischief or worse and lamented the removal of the natural world from the lives of the urban immigrant poor. They also grew to deplore the disuse of summer time and school facilities and the loss in learning that resulted. Starting in the nation's largest cities and roughly spreading down the urban hierarchy, mixtures of private women's, civic, church, and business groups started vacation programs in neighborhoods of the immigrant poor.

Early twentieth-century vacation schools were immensely popular with the people they attracted. Working parents welcomed the opportunity of some structured summer activity for their children. Students enjoyed the vacation school's relaxed tone and texture that was fostered by a curriculum based on recreation, manual training, excursions, and nature study. Teachers benefited from administrative encouragement to try innovative teaching methods. Thus vacation schools served the needs of their consumers even as their founders wielded them as an instrument of social control. In the end, however, vacation schools were appropriated more by the public school systems than by any other group. Philanthropic reformers looked to the city schools to take over the programs primarily in order to stabilize their funding, but superintendents were inclined to do so for their own purposes. As vacation schools became public entities, they changed dramatically. School administrators tightened organizational control, broadened their extent by opening schools in middle-class areas, and most importantly added academic classes for school credit.

With new management, functions, and clientele in place by 1920, the programs adopted a new name: summer schools. Now serving both elementary and high school students, summer schools allowed them to make up work they had failed in June or to take advanced work and try to skip ahead of their age-grade cohort. Caught up in a system that produced credentials as well as knowledge, summer schools continued to draw large numbers of students because they awarded academic credit. But they were not quite as popular as vacation schools. They lost the many qualities that made them distinct from the regular schools: flexible organization, an eclectic collection of teachers, relaxed discipline, and warm interpersonal relations. Now administrators judged them by the standards of the regular schools, yet here too they were deemed insufficient: they admitted too many marginal scholars, they promoted students too easily, and they lacked enough time to cover a school subject fully. From the perspective of the student to that of the superintendent, they developed a stigma that no effort at removal ever erased.

This dilemma encapsulates the historical paradox of summer education: the alternating and sometimes dueling forces driving its presence and absence from public schools. To some extent, nineteenth-century schoolmen like John Pierce were correct—for a variety of reasons the summer term was weaker than the rest of the school year despite its ubiquitous presence. On the other hand, by 1900 educators soon learned that to do nothing in the summer was equally problematic for many children. It is not hard to see, then, that there was a *via media* for summer education to take. The history of the vacation school in the early twentieth century is the story of charting that pathway, but by 1930 certain routes had become closed. By then, neither univeral diffusion nor elimination of summer education was a likely occurence. For the duration of the twentieth century, the entrenchment of summer vacation and the disreputable image and additional cost of summer school would line up well against any reconceptualization of social or educational needs that called for an increase or enhancement of summer education. Over the last seventy years, the federal government has provided much of the impetus for expanding summer education and so has encountered the historic limitations narrated in this study.

The Federal Government and Summer Education in the Twentieth Century

When Grant Venn of the United States Office of Education invoked the slogan "summer is cool in summer school" in 1968, he perhaps unknowingly tapped into several historically grounded meanings for summer education.[2] On one level, he suggested that school buildings were now better equipped to negate the summer heat—most likely through better means of ventilation and perhaps air conditioning. These were no small improvements, as summer education in the United States had traditionally suffered because the weather often was simply too hot to conduct school effectively. In the nineteenth century, summer was removed from the school year of rural and urban communities in part because the summer climate made learning and even city life difficult. Turn-of-the-century vacation schools avoided complaints about the heat by adopting a recreational program, but the academic summer schools that replaced them by 1920 suffered because their traditional subjects and methods were much less suited for the warm temperatures.

More importantly, one could infer from Venn's words that—contrary to public perception—summer school attendance should not have any association with failure. In the nineteenth century, summer sessions had gained notoriety among educators, but the typically younger children who attended them were not seen as inferior students when compared to the older winter scholars. The vacation schools' service of urban immigrants and poor might have potentially tainted their reputation, but the schools became popular because they were fun and very unlike the regular public school. With the advent of academic summer schools for failed students to make up work, the "uncool" of summer school came into full force. Despite a variety of efforts by administrators to bolster the image of summer schools during the 1920s and beyond, they remained poorly regarded—with a low status that no Office of Education motto could alter. Thus Venn's declaration alluded to a central problem facing summer school in the twentieth century.

In writing that summer is "cool" Venn also had a very specific context in mind. Taken narrowly, the slogan aimed to inspire city school districts to run programs during July and August of 1968. It claimed that summer schools would deter urban unrest and so help prevent another "long hot summer" from occurring. Venn favored work-study for disadvantaged youth to better their prospects, but the thrust of his argument was that simply removing teenagers "with nothing to do but brood on the injustice of their plight" from ghetto streets would eliminate one key ingredient of urban riots—adolescent participants. In the 1960s, the federal government did more than suggest that localities launch job training summer programs. Legislation from the Vocational Education Act of 1963 to the Elementary and Secondary Education Act of 1965 provided financial and technical assistance for communities to initiate summer schools, and many did.[3] Symbolically, the Office of Education's efforts to defuse riotous conditions signified a larger trend in education since 1930 that has especially influenced summer schooling. The last seventy years witnessed the entrance of national needs into the discourse on summer education and the intervention of the federal government into the summer use of public schools. In particular, the New Deal, World War II, the Cold War, and the War on Poverty each provided distinct moments for summer education initiatives.

In 1933, the Roosevelt White House convened the Conference on Child Health and Protection. As part of the meeting, the Subcommittee on Summer Vacation Activities of the School Child assessed the reach of playgrounds, summer schools, day camps, Bible schools, and play schools. Its report urged an increase of summer educational programs for children: "The field of vacation time lies before us. The ground may be hard to break, but the soil is fertile and can be readily adapted to present day needs."[4] What is incongruous about the document is that this major call to arms by the White House occurred in the midst of the Great Depression. With the Roosevelt administration unwilling and unable to provide federal aid directly to local systems that faced severe budget constraints, an overall retrenchment occurred in public education during the 1930s that did not spare summer programs. In fact, they were specifically targeted, along with other "fads and frills," for closure.[5] In order to save expenses, cities curtailed their summer schools in numerous ways. Many, including Chicago, Cleveland, Detroit, Philadelphia, Richmond, and St. Louis, eliminated some

Table E.1. *Aggregate national data for public summer schools, 1927–56*

Year	Cities with Summer Schools	Student Enrollment	Number of Personnel	Expenditures Actual	Real[a]
1927–28	447	456,099	14,377	3,242,665	3,399,020
1929–30	374	492,638	14,481	4,043,433	4,242,847
1931–32	278	439,030	13,253	3,755,821	5,144,960
1933–34	160	109,844	3,317	602,363	914,056
1935–36	155	117,176	3,779	666,158	832,697
1937–38	135	106,270	3,661	771,305	893,749
1939–40	170	127,452	3,938	847,428	1,099,128
1941–42	....	....	....	....	....
1943–44	220	159,818	....	....	....
1945–46	173	215,254	5,402	....	....
1947–48	278	264,651	8,042	....	....
1949–50	304	300,657	9,134	....	....
1951–52	265	326,906	....	....	....
1953–54	286	288,519	....	....	....
1955–56	323	383,918	....	....	....

Sources: U.S. Bureau of Education, *Biennial Survey of Education* (1926–56).

[a] These expenditures are adjusted for cost of living (1926 = 100).

or all summer schools. Others, such as Hartford, Louisville, San Antonio, Seattle, and Syracuse, instituted charges for tuition. A few reduced the rate of pay for summer school teachers.[6] A 1932 poll of superintendents for cities over 100,000 revealed that among fifty-five respondents, fourteen eliminated certain or all summer schools, ten began charging enrollment fees (nine had pre-existing fees but may have raised them), and five limited enrollments and course offerings.[7]

The aggregate impact of these individual decisions was tremendous. Table E.1. reveals the extent to which the Great Depression clipped the summer school movement. The number of communities running vacation schools dropped precipitously from 447 to 160 between 1928 and 1934. The number of students plummeted from 439,030 in 1932 to 109,844 in 1934. Likewise, the number of teachers fell from 13,253 to 3,317, and real expenditures declined from over $5,000,000 to under $1,000,000 in those same years.[8] These figures suggest that most cities abandoned vacation programs completely, while in other municipalities summer schools survived but barely stayed intact. Detroit's summer program, for example, experienced a reduction in summer expenditures by more than two-thirds from 1930 to 1936. By 1934, only 8,195 students attended—a substantial decline from an enrollment total of 33,654 in 1930.[9] Table E.1 demonstrates that nationally, summer school activity remained at lower levels throughout the Depression, World War II, and beyond. By the mid-1950s, when the U.S. Office of Education stopped tabulating national aggregate data, summer schools had substantially bounced back but still had not reached their pre-Depression levels.

These declines of the Great Depression were well reported in city newspapers and education journals.[10] Both the press and the profession, however, ignored two ironies of summer school retrenchment. First, summer programs had become more like regular school in part to avoid the "fad and frill" charge that precipitated the termination of some earlier vacation schools. Despite their transformation into credit granting institutions, summer schools never fully removed this derisive label. Therefore, they were among the earliest programs eliminated or cut back during the Depression. Second, the scaling back of summer schools occurred "at a time when so many unemployed could take advantage of them."[11] If anything, the social conditions that sparked the turn-of-the-century vacation school movement were much worse during the 1930s. While most cities could not maintain let alone extend summer school spending, a few took the opposite path in the midst of the Depression. In the 1932 survey mentioned above, 17 of the 55 communities reported no significant changes or in a few cases, increased activity from 1930 to 1932.[12]

The Great Depression initiated the federal government as a major player in the realm of education. As a response to the national crisis, many of the New Deal work programs contained an educational component that circumvented state and local school bureaucracies. Between the Public Works Administration [PWA] and the Work Progress Administration [WPA], nearly 20,000 new schools were built. Among the over four million workers hired by the Civil Works Administration [CWA] were thousands of teachers, while the Civilian Conservation Corps [CCC] and later the National Youth Administration [NYA] targeted 16- to 20-year-olds with work projects and part-time jobs to enable students to remain in high school and college.[13] The jobs provided by the CCC and NYA were not seasonal, so the summer became an integral part of their activities. Beyond the economic crisis of the 1930s, the federal government continued to incorporate summer into its efforts to fight World War II, the Cold War, and the War on Poverty. As a result, additional types of summer education periodically appeared in the second half of the twentieth century. They did not replace the academic remedial and enrichment classes—which remained the dominant form of summer education—but more often supplemented or expanded them.

As the United States became embroiled in World War II, federal officials identified a number of ways in which schools could provide summer education to help combat the enemy. With few resources and no enabling legislation passed, the U.S. Office of Education could only encourage local educators to take action. To do so, in 1942 it replaced its biweekly publication, *School Life*, with *Education for Victory*. Intended only for the duration of the war, the journal consisted of just three volumes.[14] As the mouthpiece for the federal government on education, it outlined a war strategy of extended school services. One area in which it encouraged and recorded expansion was the summer. The journal reported that 270 communities ran summer programs in 1942, marking a 59% jump from the 170 localities listed by the Office of Education in 1940 (see Table E.1).[15] This war-driven enlistment of summer education is particularly notable for three reasons.

First, most of these new programs did not represent a return to the academic summer schools. Instead, they offered extended school services especially geared toward the child care needs of mothers working in war industries. Although held in and run by the public schools, the programs looked and felt nothing like the regular school year and instead recalled the original vacation schools. For example, a program in Wilmington, Delaware, included "crafts, music, outdoor games, baseball, special events such as pet, doll, amateur and minstrel shows, picnics, swims, and trips to interesting points." This "varied and interesting program" was seen as the key to a summer program's success and its popularity with both working mothers and children. The programs were also viewed as opportunities for teachers to experiment with less traditional methods and activities, but in the eyes of *Education for Victory* their ultimate purpose lay in their contribution to the war effort. The journal lauded the play school work of the Child Study Association for its service to children of working mothers and low-income groups. It presented as the greatest proof of summer school success the anecdotal evidence that "another mother said her production in the munitions plant went up when she knew her children were happy and well cared for at the center."[16]

A second way in which federal education officials hoped for assistance from the summer schools was through war service training courses. *Education for Victory* recommended classes in business, trade, and clerical occupations for girls who would replace men entering the armed forces. For the future soldiers, the journal suggested physical fitness; for the adult civilians, it promoted training for air raid wardens, auxiliary fire fighters, and police offices. It advised educators to expand vocational training in agriculture and industry as well. Even the traditional classes in math, science, English, and social studies were to be "adapted to the specific needs of the armed forces and war production."[17] Overall, the Office of Education favored extending schools in any way during the summer in order to provide skills and promote attitudes useful to the war effort. Thus it reported with approval that some wartime summer school curricula included aviation education, home nursing, nutrition, and first aid.[18]

Third, summer school openings occurred extensively in areas that had traditionally not adopted them. Geared towards the war needs, many communities with defense plants started summer schools. As a result, the regional distribution of summer education in 1942 was quite different from the diffusion thirty years earlier (see Table E.2). At the turn of the century, vacation schools began in the Northeast and were disproportionately located there and in the Midwest. In 1912, over three-fourths of the nation's reported vacation schools lay in these two regions, but by 1942, that percentage fell to under one-half. As the site of many wartime factories, the South now held a plurality (37.6%) of summer programs and the West's proportion had also increased,

Table E.2. *Regional distribution of vacation and summer schools*

Region	1912 (%)		1924 (%)	
Northeast	41.1	(N=58)	24.0	(N=63)
New England	19.9	(N=28)	13.7	(N=36)
Mid-Atlantic	21.3	(N=30)	10.3	(N=27)
Midwest	35.5	(N=50)	25.1	(N=66)
East North Central	26.2	(N=37)	14.1	(N=37)
West North Central	9.2	(N=13)	11.0	(N=29)
South	16.3	(N=23)	37.6	(N=99)
Southeast	7.1	(N=10)	19.0	(N=50)
East South Central	6.4	(N=9)	11.0	(N=29)
West South Central	2.8	(N=4)	7.6	(N=20)
West	7.1	(N=10)	13.3	(N=35)
Mountain	3.5	(N=5)	1.9	(N=5)
Pacific	3.5	(N=5)	11.4	(N=30)
Total	100.0	(N=141)	100.0	(N=263)

Sources: Clarence A. Perry, *American Vacation Schools of 1912.* New York: Russell Sage Foundation, 1913. Pamphlet no. R133; "Summer Programs in Extended School Services," *Education for Victory* 2 (August 16, 1943), p. 22.

Note: Figures in parentheses are base Ns for the adjacent percentages.

though less dramatically. Thus in the 1940s, the needs for and uses of summer education were quite particular to the wartime conditions.

Education for Victory also touched on familiar rationalizations for summer school. Like the first vacation school advocates, it stressed the waste of idle school resources, the benefits of planned recreational activities to the "total well-being" of children, and the "rising tide of juvenile delinquency" stemming from crowded neighborhoods and absentee parents.[19] But the journal had a much more comprehensive vision for an all-day summer program than most existing summer schools. Its ideal day care center would develop from the child care committee of local defense councils and incorporate all agencies responsible for child welfare. It also envisioned funding from a variety of sources: not just the local public schools, but state departments of education and federal grants, welfare and recreation agencies, local PTAs, business, labor, and women's groups, churches, and parents.[20] The schools would include strenuous morning activity, quiet games and stories after lunch, and group projects in drama, music, or nature. The journal stressed the inclusion of games in the program because in addition to enjoyment and physical growth, they would develop qualities of cooperation, initiative, and fair play.[21]

To what extent did summer programs fulfill the war-time hopes of the Office of Education? At times, individuals and groups with strong ties to the local school system or firm beliefs in traditional practice resisted some of the federal policy initiatives for wartime education. For example, professional educators sometimes rebuffed calls to close the school year early "to release youth for industry," and they might have resented demands that they either teach or find other employment during the summer to contribute to manpower shortages.[22] Furthermore, it is clear just from the curriculum descriptions provided by *Education for Victory* that most summer schools did not directly adopt the war subjects outlined by federal education officials. However, some did add on small war-effort activities such as paper collection drives and salvaging operations.[23] Others expanded efforts to provide academic credits so that high school seniors one semester short could finish up school in the summer before they joined the army.[24] Finally, many schools moved beyond the purely academic coursework and reintroduced play and crafts into summer school. As a result, many summer schools functioned as day care centers—to the great delight of working mothers.[25] At least in these activities, the federal government successfully encouraged local schools systems to incorporate summer education for victory.

During the 1950s, the federal government's role in education expanded in several ways. Most significantly, the Supreme Court's 1954 decision in *Brown v. Board of Education* involved the federal government in the desegregation of the nation's schools and issues of equity in general. Post-war economic and social conditions impelled members of the universities, foundations, and the government to reassess the quality of America's schools as well. In the midst of this rethinking, the Soviet Union's launching of *Sputnik* in October, 1957 precipitated a national education crisis. After *Sputnik* there was, as Diane Ravitch has noted, a general consensus "that the national interest depended on improving the quality of America's schools."[26] As a result, Congress passed the National Defense Education Act [NDEA] in 1958. The law promoted the study of mathematics, science, and foreign languages through federally funded fellowships, grants, and loans.[27] A number of these new programs provided monies for summer educational activities.

Many educators viewed summer as the best time to advance the purposes of the NDEA. Since federal money could only be expended for supplemental, not general, education spending, summer was ideal for providing advanced studies for gifted pupils and useful for teachers and administrators seeking to strengthen overall academic standards. In the aftermath of *Sputnik*, many communities launched summer programs that focused on science, mathematics, and foreign language training for talented students.[28] They relied on the financial resources of several entities, including the NDEA programs, private foundations, universities, school systems, and student tuition. For example, the Mark Twain Summer Institute, a school serving the St. Louis area, offered language courses in English, Russian, German, and Greek, advanced mathematics and economics, and several branches of science including physics, chemistry, behavioral science, and experimental zoology. Like many such programs, it was funded through a combination of public and private sources.[29]

Did the spate of summer enrichment programs for advanced students that opened in the late 1950s mark a transition in the purpose and use of summer education? Certainly many contemporaries of the post-*Sputnik* era thought so. Looking back from 1965, one contributor to the *American School Board Journal* reported "a quiet, almost unnoticed, revolution" in summer schools because they were now "attracting some of the brightest, most capable high school students."[30] In a 1960 research bulletin, the National Education Association reported the result of a survey of 302 school districts on summer schools. It found 256 districts with some sort of program, of which 80% claimed that enrichment was a key goal. The study concluded "that the emphasis in summer school programs is shifting from help only for the slower students to a broader concept which includes something of value for all students."[31]

This new emphasis on advanced students in summer schools did not, however, transform the summer school. First, summer schools always contained a large enrichment component, and at times, as in Detroit during the 1920s, a majority of students attended summer schools to try skip a grade. Second, the remedial component remained a vital part of summer programs even in the 1950s. While courses in Russian, rapid reading, and calculus were added to the summer curriculum, classes in basic reading and math skills were not removed. Even with a slew of new programs like the Mark Twain Summer Institute, most formal summer learning still occurred under the auspices of the regular school system. Finally, by the mid-1960s, the Civil Rights movement and the Great Society programs returned the national focus to the remedial needs of poor and minority students.

When the federal government declared War on Poverty in 1964, it again enlisted the summer school as a key weapon in its battles. The campaign centered on bridging the gaps between disadvantaged youth and middle-class America through education and job training for the poor. Its framers hoped that federal programs would teach them skills and impart values to counteract a "culture of poverty." While initially the War on Poverty comprised projects funded by the newly created Office of Economic Opportunity [OEO], a myriad of federal initiatives embodied the effort to erase learning deficits of students raised in poverty: the Extended School Program, Head Start, Upward Bound, Great Cities, school lunch programs, and most importantly, Title I of the Elementary and Secondary Education Act.[32] Many of these programs contained significant summer components. For example, Title I programs aided 2.7 million children in the summer of 1966, funding school projects for enrichment, cooperative work-study, migrant education, guidance and counseling services, instruction in English as a Second Language, and staff development. In justifying expenditures for these activities, the Office of Education reiterated the same points that vacation school advocates had first made nearly one hundred years earlier. Summer education allowed for "experimentation and innovation," more careful selection of teachers, "warmer classroom relationships," "time for intensive programs of teacher training," "de-emphasis on grades," and could have "special beneficial effects on the year round success of Title I programs."[33]

Head Start projects manifested many similar summer characteristics as Title I programs. The program's ideological underpinnings directed its "comprehensive child welfare services" toward preparing "culturally deprived," lower-income participants to enter school on an equal footing with more affluent youth. Unlike Title I, it was originally conceived and first initiated as a summer program for children entering kindergarten or first grade. In 1965, the inaugural year of the program, Head Start provided summer activities for 560,000 children.[34] After 1965, the OEO funded Head Start services year-round, but summer projects remained in areas lacking adequate facilities. Due to the "maximum feasible participation" clause of the Economic Opportunity Act, local communities were quite active in the design of many projects. This involvement led to a tremendous variety in the type of programs run in each city. Still, like Title I undertakings, most resembled the vacation schools of the 1890s in spirit and form. A Head Start project in Los Angeles, for example, was initiated and run by local chapter members of Delta Sigma Theta, a national sorority of women.

Its project members also commended the use of empty school plants, as one participant recalled, "Fortunately for us, Head Start occurred during summer months when the buildings which we selected had only limited use."[35] A project in Detroit offered many of the same activities as the turn-of-the-century vacation schools: "The seven-week summer Head Start program gave youngsters for five days, three hours a day, healthy doses of the arts, games, and field trips in an attempt to orient them towards school, oral expression, muscle coordination, and getting along with other youngsters."[36] This Detroit project also provided medical and dental examinations as well as breakfasts to its children. Ironically, neither the national or local officials demonstrated much awareness of the fact that Head Start was a summer program with significant antecedents as such.

A final example of the federal government's involvement in supplemental summer educational projects lies in a much smaller program than either Title I or Head Start. In the summer of 1963, President Kennedy funded a $250,000 Dropout Campaign through an emergency fund. With this money, the U.S. Office of Education launched a national publicity campaign against dropping out of school and spread the funds across 63 cities. These communities then enlisted school counselors to identify and contact potential or actual dropouts during August. Within broad federal guidelines, participating cities employed a variety of approaches: Detroit ran an "extensive promotions campaign" and screened dropouts to "encourage the most able to return" to school; Los Angeles started a pilot project to reach 100 "hard core" dropouts; in New York, "September evening guidance and testing centers provided educational and vocational counseling for dropouts up to age twenty as a supplement to an August counseling program" for over 3,500 youth.[37] Overall, the Office of Education reported that nearly 1,400 school personnel communicated with almost 60,000 students and achieved mixed results. While only slightly more than half actually reentered school, over 92% of the returnees were still in school by November 1963.

As a result of all of these summer projects, the participation of urban youth in summer programs rose substantially in the 1960s. Consider the case of Detroit. By 1967, Detroit Superintendent Norman Drachler hoped to involve over 100,000 Detroit children in summer activities that included the regular summer schools and federally funded projects and scholarships. At the end of July, Drachler could look back and smile. Detroit's regular summer schools matriculated 96,000 students that year; Head Start attracted 6,000 children; Great

Cities Projects enrolled 4,700 pupils; the Youth Training Program recruited 1,900 teenagers; and a state special education program drew in
512 youngsters.[38] While Detroit's academic summer schools brought in
over three times as many students as they ever registered in the 1920s
(see Table 6.1), the federally funded projects of the 1960s provided a
substantial complement by offering many projects that harked back to
the early vacation schools.

Persistent Historical Patterns and Summer Education Today

For all of its repeated and diverse efforts of the last seventy years, the
federal government has been no more successful than early twentieth-
century vacation school reformers at making summer education universal or permanent. Thus federal initiatives in education highlight
some dominant features of summer schooling largely established between 1840 and 1930. While drafting summer school to address national interests was largely new, the more localized social misgivings of
citizens and professional aspirations of educators have shaped discussions about the summer for 160 years. These concerns have become
remarkably consistent over time. The nineteenth-century medical belief that overstudy made children and even teachers vulnerable to ill
health persists in less overdrawn statements about fatigue and burnout. Juvenile delinquency and inactivity during the summer have troubled generations of urban inhabitants. The potential for curricular and
pedagogical experimentation has always drawn educators to the summer. Teachers' anecdotal evidence that over the summer students forget what they learn dates to the antebellum era. Finally, the possibilities for the cost-efficient use of time and space in crowded districts
have enticed administrators for a century.

   While these issues are likely to appear in any late twentieth-
century discussion of summer education, one idea invariably arises: the
natural existence of summer vacation. Nineteenth-century Americans
knew full well that summer was a season for schooling, yet their twentieth-century descendents regularly claim that summer vacation was
"handed down by an early American agricultural society."[39] To many,
the rhythms of farm life dictated the scheduling of school around the
summer. A central aim here has been to dispel this myth by depicting
substantial summer terms held during the antebellum era and by tracing the conscious creation of summer vacation by nineteenth-century
educators. Nevertheless, the fallacious explanation for the origins of
summer vacation became in the twentieth century a powerful intellec-

tual limit to creating or expanding special summer programs and to lengthening the regular school year. Once the 180-day, September-to-June school calendar became the norm, any attempt to alter significantly the duration of the school year contended with the powerful position of summer vacation in this nation's culture, economy, and historical memory.

What has remained largely intact since 1920 is a summer school designed to produce academic promotions through advanced and repeated coursework. The summer curriculum has swayed between tendencies towards basic scholarship and supplemental activities. Periodic flirtations with less traditional subjects notwithstanding, the summer school is rooted in the age-graded structure of American public schools. Such grounding has not freed the summer school from its reputation as something gratuitous and inferior, and these labels have made it inherently susceptible to cuts during budget crises. In several different times and settings, the availability of funds proved to be a singularly important material condition determining the extent of summer education. Thus aggregate spending for and participation in summer school during the twentieth century have been punctuated by ebbs and flows. Beyond issues of cost, opposition to the major changes in the educational use of summer stemmed from larger issues about the control and purpose of schools.[40] Today, summer schools are riding another burst of growth, but they remain sites for conflict and consensus over the direction of public education.[41] Over the last five years, educators and policymakers have earmarked substantial expenditures for a number of recent proposals to expand summer education—recent, but not truly new.

The most notable trend is the hitching of summer school onto the bandwagon to eliminate social promotion. In Chicago, New York, and other communities, school systems have initiated draconian measures to fail all students not achieving new and presumably more rigorous academic standards. The impetus to do so has come in large part from the long-standing national discourse about the quality of public education resparked by the 1983 publication of *A Nation at Risk* and rekindled by Goals 2000 and the national standards movement. As state and eventually local bodies produced their own sets of academic standards, focus has shifted to holding students (and teachers and principals) accountable for reaching them. In the present climate of school reform, proponents of social promotion are lying low, but since at least the 1980s, even they have argued that summer school was a viable option to increase passing rates.[42] Politicians and policymakers advocating an "end [to] social promotion" appear to have listened.[43] As a result, summer school has become a key component in the fight to enforce academic standards. In keeping with its historical role in remediation, summer school theoretically serves as a last resort for failing students. In practice, the results are less clear cut.

In the summer of 1999, New York City expanded its summer school classes to include all third, sixth, and eighth grade students who had failed a city-wide standardized test administered in June. As a result, thousands attended, and 64.2% passed an August test and earned promotion. In September, however, two revelations indicated that summer school was no more immune from glitches than other forms of public education. First, out of 35,000 students who should have attended summer school, 14,000 did not. When these absentees were included in the data on promotions, only 40% of all intended summer students were eligible to move on to the next grade.[44] A second and ultimately more embarrassing revelation came when then New York City Schools Chancellor Rudy Crew reported errors in the scoring of the initial June examinations. As a result, more than 8,500 students were mistakenly assigned to summer school in the first place. Subsequent allegations that teachers fudged their students' test scores, though in this case not summer school tests, further undermined public confidence in these measurements.[45] At one level, these errors are mere red herrings; they don't necessarily reflect inadequacy in the premise behind mandatory summer school, just the implementation, and thus can be easily rectified. Or can they? New York City planned to proceed with expansion for summer school to all students in the year 2000, placing some estimates at student enrollment as high as 360,000 students.[46] Thus the burden of finding the necessary funds, teachers, and space only grew heavier on the school system.

The summer of 2000 brought to New York an even larger, yet slightly less troubled, summer school session. First, the city was aided by a total enrollment of 319,000—higher than the 228,000 from 1999 but lower than originally anticipated. Of these, 63,000 were K-8 students required to attend—an 80% increase but also less than estimated earlier in the year. While the public schools avoided the previous summer's debacle of thousands of no shows, they struggled to maintain a strong attendance rate and to keep students from withdrawing entirely. By the end of the summer, over 4,000 of the elementary students mandated to attend had left, as well as an additional 47,000 high school students. Attendance rates stood at 77% for elementary students and ranged from 50% to 61% for high schoolers.[47] Absenteeism and withdrawals occurred despite efforts of school officials to contact parents about summer attendance, and School Chancellor Harold Levy spoke of lobbying the state to change its education code "to make summer school mandatory for all students who fail during the regular school year."[48] Finally, the 63% promotion rate for the required elementary school attendees left room for some pessimistic interpretations. Only 40% had actually passed the end-of-summer exams, as classroom teachers promoted the rest. Thus skeptics wondered whether the allowance for teachers' discretion would undermine the academic standards and foster the very social promotions that the summer program was intended to address.[49] These and other concerns remained intact after the summer of 2001, as New York City's summer schools experienced familiar administrative difficulties and similar levels of student registration, attendance, and achievement.[50]

Not all of the issues that arose contained elements that were particular to summer school, but those related to attendance notably were. City schools struggle with absenteeism year round, but the problem is particularly acute during the summer term. While critics of the board of education blamed hasty preparation and poor communication for the high rate of absenteeism, it is not self-evident that all parents would have sent their children if they had received enough notice or clearly understood the consequences of non-attendance. Powerful beliefs and habits of summer, solidified over one hundred years of summer recreation, must not be discounted by educators and politicians.[51] In New York City, most of the summer students came from low- or middle-income, working-class backgrounds, but if the academic standards proponents have their way, new rigor will enter the "shopping mall high" as well as the inner city elementary school.[52] What middle-class or affluent parents will say when their children's promotions are dependent on summer school attendance, thus threatening family travel or summer camp plans, remains to be seen. Already, however, there are reports of some backlash against the standards movement from these folk.[53]

Nor is it evident that these efforts can avoid the fundamental problem of time faced by summer school administrators since the beginning of the century. Can summer schools adequately provide a year or even a semester's work in two months or, in the case of New York, in five weeks? Some of those who recognize that the answer is no might argue that summer schools could more easily prepare children for an exam in that short duration and so justify the approach taken in New York and other cities today. This response is also problematic for its embracing of high-stakes standardized tests—whose eternal shortcoming is that they determine pedagogical and curricular decisions as much as they reflect them. Too often, these means of measuring some levels of student achievement become the goal of a student's class, school, or system. At the very least, programs constituted to redress academic failure leave the stigma of summer school intact.

These concerns form a large part of the debates surrounding the extended school year and year-round schooling. Some educators and politicians have suggested lengthening the school term to 200 or 220 days. The backlash against shortened urban terms first began in the 1890s and occasionally flared again in the twentieth century without having any impact on the actual lengths of the city school years.[54] The issue was raised anew in *A Nation at Risk*. Essentially, the document linked lower student achievement in the United States to, among other variables, insufficient time spent on learning, especially in comparison to other industrial nations. It therefore endorsed restructuring the use of school time and lengthening the school day and year.[55] Eleven years later, the *Prisoners of Time* report echoed these recommendations for more school time and better use of it.[56]

The extended school year could manage to avoid many of the concerns regarding the attendance, coverage, and reputation of summer schools. Rather than relying on summer school as a safety net for failure, it would provide more time initially to get struggling students to reach acceptable levels of academic performance. The likely reluctance of school personnel and the obvious financial barriers notwithstanding, critics also see no point in lengthening the school year without fundamentally changing how school time is spent.[57] One increasingly popular device for restructuring the school calendar and including the summer in it is year-round schooling (YRS). Across the nation, the number of year-round-schools jumped from 287 in 1980 to over 1,900 in 1994.[58] Many YRS are a stop-gap solution to district overcrowding, and these simply rearrange the shape of the school year without increasing the amount of time each student attends class. Those that have added school days as well as restructured them perhaps come closest to resolving the historic limitations of summer school but do so at the expense of summer vacation. Is the YRS a model for all schools to emulate? What is needed to answer this question are two types of appraisals: an evaluation of the research on whether such summer schooling produces its intended outcomes in achievement and a value judgment about whether this is the type of learning desirable for schools in the summer.

For much of the twentieth century, there was substantial scholarly interest in the educational results of summer. This body of research essentially raises two related questions: What is the impact of summer school and what is the effect of summer vacation on learning?[59] Regarding the first issue, many evaluations of summer programs (often reaching at-risk students) tend to be negative, indicating that educational undertakings in the summer seemingly do not provide much help for the participants.[60] However, the recently published *Making the Most of Summer School* suggests that there is some academic gain, which is somewhat dependent on the student's social class and the program's design.[61] Research on the second question shows that children—particularly those from lower socioeconomic strata—learn at a slower rate during summer vacation, and some actually regress when they are not attending school. Dubbed "summer setback" by scholars, studies of this problem date back to 1906.[62] Thus while current summer programs may achieve inadequate or at best limited promotion rates and long-term results, the alternative of no summer school is worse for many children. Because research has found that summer is a key moment in cognitive development, some type of formal education should occur during the long vacation, even if its sole purpose is to turn failing test scores into passing ones. In fact, a summer school program need not reach the same degree of achievement that the regular schools do; simply arresting academic decline would be an important contribution.[63]

To suggest that summer education in any form is better than none at all will no doubt raise some eyebrows. The values embedded in policy choices for summer school tap into larger societal debates about schooling. Some educators object to the reorientation of summer schools around examination preparation because they reject the standards movement's top-down implementation and its reliance on high-stakes testing. Their position on summer education is not to bother to give students more time in school if it is not going to be used wisely. Or as Harvard's Gary Orfield has put it, "It's just a very simple-minded addition to a poorly designed system of instruction and assessment."[64] This argument is powerful but not entirely pursuasive. It not only ignores the research findings on summer setback, but it also misses a social context that earlier generations understood. Summer schools have always served purposes far beyond just the cognitive development of children. In this era of two working parents and latch-key children, longer school years may be worth implementing independently of, although one hopes concurrent to, efforts to improve the quality of education. Nevertheless, it is easy to see the inadequacies of the current approach to summer school and is therefore worthwhile to push for better and not just more educational opportunities for children during the summer.

Conclusion

What then would a model summer school program look like? Foremost, it would offer something distinct from the regular school year. Summer school would become far more attractive if it could engage students in learning without seeming quite so like school. Particularly for those students who need help with basic literacy and numeracy skills, summer schools should seek alternatives to the methods that have so far failed to reach them. What shape those approaches take should not be dictated by distant administrative, scholarly, or political figures but rather should come from the people working directly with students: principals and teachers. Given the long-standing seasonal patterns to schooling, parental involvement is also key in developing and selecting school calendar and summer school options. Publicly sponsored summer educational activies can but need not be located in an actual school building, but they should be available for all students and targeted at those who lack options of travel, summer camp, employment, or family time. Of course, to use summer vacation for this purpose requires citizens to have the will to enact social policies for the specific benefit of its least powerful and most impoverished members.

More than one policy can fulfill these overarching values. Extending the school year to make it comparable with those of other industrial nations would be an improvement for many students by truncating yet keeping the summer vacation. Year-round schooling can break up entirely the learning loss associated with ten weeks of summer vacation, but it should neither assimilate the summer into its regular curriculum nor treat it as solely as a means to ease overcrowding. Separate summer programs could perhaps most easily retain a unique flavor. While many are stagnant from years of remediation and grow further corrupted by test preparation, others do offer engaging yet substantive educational activities—from to chess to cooking to computer skills to nature study.[65] Finally, school systems could embrace summer programs as sources of teacher professional development and curricular development.

These suggestions are informed by the history presented in this book, but there is a danger in expecting a blueprint for public policy from the study of the past. While historical developments often narrow current options, knowledge of the past can help to broaden future possibilities. This is not to say that forms of summer education in the nineteenth century are retrievable or even desirable today. Rather, this study has shown that the school calendar and summer school structures which seem embedded are really only creations of the past one hundred and fifty years. They are in no way natural and therefore are malleable by citizens, politicians, educators, and scholars with the imagination to think boldly about summer learning as good educational and social policy. There certainly is no "golden age" of summer education to return to—early summer sessions and vacation schools had their own shortcomings—but the past serves as a vivid reminder that summer can and should play a vital and special role in public education today.

APPENDIX

The Origins of Vacation Schools in the United States

Rank and City	Population in 1900	Date 1	Date 2	Date 3	Date 4	Source
1. New York	3,437,202	1894	1898	1898	1906	Perry, *Wider Use of the School Plant*, 134; New York City Department of Education, *Eighth Annual Report of the City Superintendent of Schools* (1906), 352.
2. Chicago	1,698,575	1896	1903	1909	1911	Chicago Board of Education, *Annual Report* 50 (1903), 123; 49 (1902), 23; 56 (1909) 103; 58 (1911), 128.
3. Philadelphia	1,293,697	1898	1901	1901	1922	Lee, "Preventive Work," 590; Philadelphia Superintendent of Public Schools, *Annual Report* 22 (1923), 26–28.
3A. Brooklyn	1,166,582	1887	1898	1898	....	Robinson, "Vacation Schools," 254; Lee, "Preventive Work," 590.
4. St. Louis	575,278	1905	1907	1907	1911	St. Louis Board of Education, *Annual Report* 56 (1909), 169; 53 (1906), 308–13; 57 (1910), 107–13.

Rank and City	Population in 1900	Date 1	Date 2	Date 3	Date 4	Source
5. Boston	560,892	1866	1900	1900	1909	Boston Schools Superintendent, *Annual Report* 25 (1905), 46–47; 30 (1910), 128–31; *Report of the Commission on Vacation Schools* (1901), 3.
6. Baltimore	508,957	1898	1911	1911	1911	Baltimore Board of School Commissioners, *Annual Report to the Mayor and City Council of Baltimore* 70 (1899), 59; 83 (1912), 18.
7. Cleveland	381,768	1895	1903	1904	1903	Cleveland Board of Education, *Annual Report of the Public Schools* 67 (1903), 31, 35; 73 (1909), 51–52.
8. Buffalo	352,387	1898	1900	1900	1911	Buffalo Superintendent of Education, *Annual Report* (1900), 25–26; (1901), 76, (1912), 31.
9. San Francisco	342,782	....	....	....	....	San Francisco Superintendent of Schools and Board of Education, *Annual Report* (1897, 1899–1901, 1907–12, 1924–29).
10. Cincinnati	325,902	1899	1906	1906	1908	Cincinnati Public Schools, *Annual Report* 72 (1900) 61–62; 77 (1905), 73; 80 (1908), 62–64; (1909), 68–69.
11. Pittsburgh	321,616	1900	1905	1911	1911	Pittsburgh Playground Association, *Annual Report* 12 (1907), 6; Pittsburgh Board of Public Education, *Annual Report.* n.s. 1 (1911), 69–70.

Rank and City	Population in 1900	Date 1	Date 2	Date 3	Date 4	Source
12. New Orleans	287,104	1904	1904	1907	1910	New Orleans Board of Directors and of the Superintendent of the Public Schools, *Annual Report* (1907), 18; (1911), 48.
13. Detroit	285,704	1903	1903	1905	1912	Detroit Board of Education, *Annual Report* 61 (1904), 96; 65 (1908), 102–5; Detroit Board of Education, *Education in Detroit, 1916,* 70–71.
14. Milwaukee	285,325	1899	1904	1905	1914	Reese, *Power and the Promise of School Reform,* 153, 160; Milwaukee Board of Education, *Annual Report,* 48 (1907), 66–67; 56 (1915), 22; Lee, "Preventive Work," 591.
15. Washington	278,718	1899	1901	1918	1914	District of Columbia Board of Education, *Annual Report* (1899), 49; (1902), 42–43; (1920), 69; (1916), 203.
16. Newark	246,070	. . . .	1886	1886	1910	Newark Board of Education, *Annual Report* 30 (1886), 81; 54 (1910), 57.
17. Jersey City	206,433	. . . .	1911	1911	1911	Jersey City Board of Education, *Annual Report* 44 (1912), 100–102.
18. Louisville	204,731	1900	1913	1913	1913	Houston, "Bibliography of Playgrounds and Vacation Schools," 359; Board of Education of Louisville, Kentucky. *Annual Report* 2 (1912), 51–54.

Rank and City	Population in 1900	Date 1	Date 2	Date 3	Date 4	Source
19. Minneapolis	202,718	1898	1903	1908	1911	Minneapolis Board of Education, *Annual Report* 28 (1905), 50–51; 32 (1909), 145; 34 (1911), 104–5.
20. Providence	175,597	1868	1900	1901	. . . .	Providence School Committee, *Annual Report* (1900), 6–8; (1901), 9–11.
21. Indianapolis	169,164	1897	1898	1910	1913	Robinson, "Vacation Schools," 258; Lee, "Preventive Work," 591; *Indianapolis Public Schools, Annual Report* (1916), 52–53.
22. Kansas City	163,752	1901	1911	1911	1911	Reese, *Power and the Promise of School Reform*, 153; Kansas City Board of Education *Annual Reports* 40 (1911), 32–33; 43 (1914), 56–57.
23. St. Paul	163,065	1908	1908	1909	1909	St. Paul Board of School Inspectors, *Biennial Report* 51–52 (1910–12), 53–54; Perry, *Wider Use of the School*, 138–39.
24. Rochester	162,608	1899	1907	1910	1910	Reese, *Power and the Promise of School Reform*, 153,160; Rochester Board of Education, *Report for the Years 1907–1908*.
25. Denver	133,859	. . . .	1902	1902	1902	Denver Board of Education, *Annual Report of School District One* n.s. 15 (1917), 73.

Rank and City	Population in 1900	Date 1	Date 2	Date 3	Date 4	Source
26. Toledo	131,822	1901	....	1910	1910	Reese, *Power and the Promise of School Reform*, 153; Board of Education of the Toledo City School District, *Annual Report* 28 (1901–02), 126.
27. Alleghany	129,896	1905	....	....	....	Perry, *Wider Use of the School*, 137.
28. Columbus	125,560	1912	1917	1917	1917	Columbus Board of Education. *Annual Report of the Public Schools* (1918–23), 124–25; Perry, *American Vacation Schools of 1912*, 6.
29. Worcester	118,421	1899	1906	1906	....	Worcester Board of Education, *The Annual Report of the Public Schools* 71 (1907), 135.
30. Syracuse	108,374	1898	1906	1906	1915	Lee, "Preventive Work," 591; Syracuse Board of Education, *Annual Report* (1905–07), 83; (1915–16), 98.
31. New Haven	108,027	1888	1914	1914	1914	Houston, "Bibliography of Playgrounds and Vacation Schools," 359; New Haven Board of Education, *Annual Report* (1914), 18–19.
32. Paterson	105,171	1909	1913	1913	1909	Paterson Public Schools, *Annual Report* (1908–09), 123–24; (1914), 41.
33. Fall River	104,863	....	1910	1910	1911	City of Fall River, *Annual School Report* (1910), 28; (1911), 20.
34. St. Joseph	102, 979	....	....	....	....	St. Joseph Board of Education, *Annual Report* (1900–1914).

Rank and City	Population in 1900	Date 1	Date 2	Date 3	Date 4	Source
35. Omaha	102,555	....	1913	1913	1913	Omaha Board of Education, *Annual Report* (1913), 27.
36. Los Angeles	102, 479	....	1911	1911	1911	Los Angeles Board of Education, *Annual Report* (1913–14), 129.
37. Memphis	102,320	....	1909	1909	1909	Memphis Board of Education, *Annual Report* (1911–12), 24–25.
38. Scranton	102,026	....	1914	1914	1919	Scranton Board of Education, *Survey of the Scranton Public Schools* (1914–15), 66; *Survey of the Scranton Public Schools* (1918–20), 89–90.
39. Lowell	94,969	....	1901	....	....	Massachusetts Board of Education, *Annual Report* 66 (1901–02), 206.
41. Cambridge	91,886	1896	1900	1900	1910	Cambridge School Committee, *Annual Report* (1901), 71; (1910), 52.
43. Atlanta	89,872	....	1915	1915	1915	Ecke, *From Ivy Street to Kennedy Center* (1972), 101–2.
46. Richmond	85,050	....	1911	1911	1911	Richmond Superintendent of the Public Schools, *Annual Report* 43 (1911), 13.
48. Seattle	80,671	....	1918	1919	1918	Seattle Public Schools, *Annual Report* 34 (1916–21), 85–86.
49. Hartford	79,580	1897	1899	1901	1918	*Report of the Board of School Visitors of the Town of Hartford* (1900–1901), 36–38; (1918–19), 26.

Rank and City	Population in 1900	Date 1	Date 2	Date 3	Date 4	Source
50. Reading	78,961	....	1922	1922	1922	Reading School District, *Report of the Superintendent* (1925), 14.
52. Camden	75,935	....	1933	1933	1933	Camden Board of Education, *Annual Report* (1933), 27.
54. Bridgeport	70,996	1923	1924	1924	1924	Bridgeport Superintendent of Schools, *Annual Report* 47 (1922–23), 16–18.
55. Lynn	68,513	....	1913	1913	1913	Lynn Department of Schools, *Annual Report* (1914), 13.
58. New Bedford	68,442	....	1910	1910	1911	New Bedford School Committee, *Annual Report* (1912), 70.
59. Des Moines	62,139	....	1909	1909	1909	Des Moines Public Schools, *First Annual Report of the Des Moines Vacation Schools* (1909).
61. Somerville	61,643	....	1901	1901	1929	Somerville School Committee, *Annual Report* 30 (1901), 36.
70. Salt Lake City	53,531	1906	1918	1918	1918	Salt Lake City Public Schools, *Twenty-Ninth Annual Report* (1918), 64–65.
72. Duluth	52,969	....	1912	1912	1912	Duluth Board of Education, *Annual Report* (1915–16), 6.
92. Brocton	40,063	1905	1911	1911	1911	Brocton Public Schools, *Annual Report* (1911).
96. Pawtucket	39,231	....	1925	1925	1925	Pawtucket School Board, *Annual Report* (1925–26), 9.
97. Altoona	38,973	1912	1923	1923	1923	Altoona School District, *Report* (1938–39), 129.

Notes

Introduction

1. NCES, *The Condition of Education 1998*, Supplemental Table 5–2. http://nces.ed.gov/pubs98/condition98/c9805d02.html; NCES, *Digest of Educational Statistics, 1998*, Table 161. http://nces.ed.gov/pubs99/digest98/d98t161.html. At ten weeks, the American summer vacation is also one of the longer ones among developed countries. France, Germany, and the United Kingdom have six weeks; Denmark and the Netherlands have seven weeks; and Austria and Norway have eight weeks of summer vacation. Conversely the United States' 180-day school year is shorter than the "international average of 180 to 190 days for nations with five day weeks." Nations such as Japan, Italy, and parts of Germany have school years with more than 200 days that include Saturday mornings. F. Howard Nelson, *How and How Much the U.S. Spends on K–12 Education: An International Comparison* (Washington D.C.: American Federation of Teachers, 1996). http://www.aft.org/research/reports/interntl/sba.htm.

2. *New York Times*, September 2, 1999; August 11, 2000.

Chapter One: "A Time to Reap and a Time to Sow?"

1. Michigan Superintendent of Public Instruction, *Annual Report* 33 (1869), 137.

2. Had Wheeler served a generation earlier, he still would have made the same inspections. For sample descriptions of such visits, see the *American Annals of Education* 1 (October 1831), 472; New York Superintendent of the Common Schools, *Annual Report* (1842–43), 445.

3. These shifts are largely unstudied outside of Massachusetts, and even there the research findings on school years are limited. In their detailed quantitative history, Carl Kaestle and Maris Vinovskis only discuss the first shift—the aggregate school year length in Massachusetts rose from 150 days in 1840 to 192 days in 1880—and not the second. Carl F. Kaestle and Maris A. Vinovskis, *Education and Social Change in Nineteenth-Century Massachusetts* (Cambridge: Cambridge University Press, 1980), 38–39, 81, 258–61.

4. Most historians of nineteenth-century American public education recognize the existence of rural summer terms, but many tend to marginalize their importance. For example, see Clifton Johnson, *Old-Time Schools and School-Books* (Gloucester, Massachusetts: Peter Smith, 1963); Lawrence Cremin, *American Education: The National Experience, 1783–1876* (New York: Harper & Row, Publishers, 1980); David Nasaw, *Schooled to Order: A Social History of Public Schooling in the United States* (New York: Oxford University Press, 1979); Elwood Cubberley, *Public Education in the United*

States: A Study and Interpretation of American Educational History, 2d ed. (Boston: Houghton Mifflin Company, 1934); Robert L. Church, *Education in the United States: An Interpretive History* (New York: The Free Press, 1976).

5. Carl Kaestle, *Pillars of the Republic: Common Schools and American Society, 1780–1860* (New York: Hill and Wang, 1983), 15.

6. Charles W. Odell, "Summer Work in Public Schools," *University of Illinois Bulletin no. 49*, xxvii (22 April 1930), 11; Lee Soltow and Edward Stevens, *The Rise of Literacy and the Common School in the United States: A Socioeconomic Analysis to 1870* (Chicago: University of Chicago Press, 1981), 122. Soltow and Stevens note that some schools offered special vacations for harvesting during the summer, but this was not typical. Odell observed that toward the end of the century, new and improved roads contributed to the disappearance of the summer term. Nineteenth-century contemporaries recognized these patterns of school term attendance by age and season as well. For example, see the *American Journal of Education* 2 (April 1827): 197; the Michigan Superintendent of Public Instruction, *Annual Report* 27 (1863), 180; and the New York Superintendent of Public Instruction, *Annual Report* 16 (1870), 315.

7. Kaestle, *Pillars of the Republic*, 15.

8. Michigan Superintendent of Public Instruction, *Annual Report* 5 (1841), 52.

9. Kaestle and Vinovskis, *Education and Social Change*, 133–34. The strong relationship between agrarian life and school year length was negative: the larger the number of farm acres per capita in a district, the shorter the school term. The best predictor of a lengthy school year was the percentage of merchants in a town rather than the level of industrialization. A town's wealth (as measured by assessed valuation per capita) was a less useful determinant once the other variables were controlled in the regression, whereas the percentage of foreign born had a strong positive correlation to the length of public schooling. Population size, though it showed a high correlation to school year length, was a weaker predictor than agricultural and commercial factors. Overall, 52.1% of the variation in school year length found in Massachusetts towns was explained by the group of independent variables tested.

10. John L. Rury, "The Variable School Year: Measuring Differences in the Length of American School Terms in 1900," *Journal of Research and Development in Education* 21 (Spring 1988), 29–36. Rury's data demonstrated less pronounced but still considerable urban/rural patterns beyond the nineteenth century, and he too discovered that country or city residence was not the most useful indicator of school year length. After occupation as a farmer, the second most powerful predictor was region, with immigrant status, occupations as laborers or professionals, and residence in the Northeast proving ineffective as independent variables.

11. Kaestle, *Pillars of the Republic*, 105–6.

12. Horace Mann, in an 1847 circular, questioned groups of experienced teachers on how much improvement in morals and conduct to expect "if all our common schools were what they should be." His ideal school conditions included trained teachers, organized curricula, and ten-month school years. Jonathan Messerli, *Horace Mann: A Biography* (New York: Alfred A Knopf, 1972), 443–44. Henry Barnard proposed lengthening Connecticut's minimum school year by at least two months. Commissioners of Common Schools in Connecticut, *Second Annual Report of the Secretary to the Board*, (1840), 24–25.

13. Michigan Superintendent of Public Instruction, *Annual Report* 6 (1842), 28, *Annual Report* 51 (1889), 297; Virginia Superintendent of Public Instruction, *Annual Report* 1 (1871), 173; *Annual Report* 21 (1891), 78. These statewide figures tend to underrepresent the increased duration of rural terms because, as Chapter Two demonstrates, urban term lengths generally declined over the same intervals.

14. U.S. Commissioner of Education, *Annual Report 1867–1868* (Washington: Government Printing Office, 1868), 92.

15. Cremin, *American Education: The National Experience*, 151; The University of the State of New York, *Education in New York State, 1784–1954*, comp. and ed. Harlan Hoyt Horner (Albany, New York: State Education Department, 1954), 50; Samuel S. Randall, *The Common School System of the State of New York* (Troy, N.Y.: Johnson and Davis, Steam Press Printers, 1851), 5–8.

16. Cremin, *American Education: The National Experience*, 151–53; Elsie Garland Hobson, "Educational Legislation and Administration in the State of New York, 1777–1850" (Ph.D. dissertation: University of Chicago, 1918), 31–34; *American Annals of Education*, 5 (April 1835): 171; Randall, *The Common School System*, 9–13. The law and subsequent revisions passed by 1814 created a three-tiered system: local districts (created by towns), which maintained school buildings; towns, which employed and managed schoolteachers; and the state, which aided local efforts through the dispersion of information and interest from school funds. In 1814, the state created the rate bill system that authorized localities to make up a deficit in the annual school budget by taxing parents of schoolchildren (though it exempted the poor and indigent). This funding mechanism eventually earned the ire of common school reformers seeking to extend the school year.

17. Kaestle, *Pillars of the Republic*, 10–11, 24–25. For a discussion of the impact of the 1795 act on Westchester County in particular, see Robert Francis Seybolt, *The Act of 1795 for the Encouragement of Schools and the Practice in Westchester County* (Albany: The University of the State of New York), 1919. As Kaestle and Vinovskis argued for Massachusetts, the nature of the common school movement in New York was about educational intensification more than expansion of reach. Kaestle and Vinovskis, *Education and Social Change*, 5–6.

18. New York Superintendent of the Common Schools, *Annual Report* (1836–37), 4; *Annual Report* (1837–38), 5; *Annual Report* (1838–39), 3.

19. The high figures for the 1840s and 1850s are suspect, however, because early state superintendents readily acknowledged that their figures were exaggerated due to the often unreliable reports of local schools and their own practice of rounding up to whole numbers. New York Superintendent of the Common Schools, *Annual Report* (1836–37), 4; New York Superintendent of Public Instruction, *Annual Report* 3 (1857), 7–8; *Annual Report*, 7 (1861), 7.

20. New York Superintendent of the Common Schools, *Annual Report* (1842–43), 35–36.

21. Bedford, N.Y. *Bedford School Report*, 1842, 1843.

22. New York Superintendent of the Common Schools, *Annual Report* (1842–43), 175, 191.

23. *American Journal of Education* 2 (April 1827), 197; *American Annals of Education* 6 (June 1836), 260–63; *District School Journal for the State of New York* 2 (1841–42),

5; New York Superintendent of the Common Schools, *Annual Report* (1842–43), 134, 663, 670.

24. New York Superintendent of the Common Schools, *Annual Report* (1843–44), 324.

25. *District School Journal for the State of New York* 2 (1841–42), 4–5; New York Superintendent of the Common Schools, *Annual Report* (1842–43), 9; *Annual Report* (1843–44), 35. Attendance in the summer of 1844 was only 60% of the winter term, but the summer figures were incomplete with six counties missing, including Westchester. Since the superintendents reported data by county, rural totals were determined by subtracting from the state totals the eight counties that contained communities larger than 10,000 inhabitants: Erie, Kings, Monroe, New York, Oneida, Onondaga, Queens, and Richmond.

26. New York Superintendent of the Common Schools, *Annual Report* (1843–44), 133–34. The following data do not include figures for New York City, which were unavailable to the state superintendent but would have slightly raised the percentages for the higher-length categories.

27. New York Superintendent of the Common Schools, *Annual Report* (1842–43), 7–9. The 1844 data yielded a larger number of responses yet are less complete because several counties did not report summer term data. Despite a greater number of courses recorded for 1844, the distribution of them is similar to that of 1843. The superintendent did not continue to report this data after 1844.

28. The 1844 figure, 41.3%, is only slightly lower. New York Superintendent of the Common Schools, *Annual Report* (1843–44), 33–42.

29. The 1844 data confirms the above findings. Language and mathematics skills predominated in both sessions, with the summer students focused slightly more on basics like spelling and word definitions. One puzzling difference between the two data sets is in the geography figures, which inexplicably fell to 1.5% of the total in 1844. New York Superintendent of the Common Schools, *Annual Report* (1843–44), 33–42.

30. New York Superintendent of the Common Schools, *Annual Report* (1842–43), 8–9; *Annual Report* (1843–44), 33–42. In 1844, there were 6,843 summer term teachers and 6,407 winter term teachers.

31. New York Superintendent of Public Instruction, *Annual Report* 23 (1877), 419.

32. New York Superintendent of the Common Schools, *Annual Report* (1842–43), 7–9.

33. Kaestle, *Pillars of the Republic*, 124. Geraldine Clifford has suggested two additional factors that drew women into teaching: demographic changes in women's reproduction patterns and the incipient public schools' creation of a female teaching labor pool. Clifford, "'Daughters into Teachers': Educational and Demographic Influences on the Transformation of Teaching into 'Women's Work' in America," in *Women Who Taught: Perspectives on the History of Women and Teaching*, eds. Alison Prentice and Marjorie R. Theobald (Toronto: University of Toronto Press, 1991), 115–35. For additional perspectives on this topic, see Donald Warren, ed., *American Teachers: History of a Profession at Work* (New York: Macmillan, 1989).

34. This finding differs slightly from Kaestle, who emphasizes the brevity of employment faced by women. Kaestle, *Pillars of the Republic*, 126.

35. Data from 1844 corroborates this portrait: female summer teachers working at a younger age, with less experience, and for less money than their male counterparts in the winter. New York Superintendent of the Common Schools, *Annual Report* (1843–44), 42–56.

36. New York Superintendent of the Common Schools, *Annual Report* (1842–43), 670. Westchester's attendance in the summer (4,070) was also substantially lower than in the winter (7,300) that year. On the other hand, the schools taught essential skills in reading, arithmetic, geography, and English grammar, engaged a few students in the higher branches, and hired more men (sixty-five) then women (fifty-two).

37. New York Superintendent of the Common Schools, *Annual Report* (1842–43), 444–45.

38. U.S. Commissioner of Education, *Annual Report 1867–1868* (Washington: Government Printing Office, 1868), 92.

39. The University of the State of New York, *Education in New York State, 1784–1954*, 50. The 1795 law apportioned school fund money among towns willing to tax themselves for the maintenance of schools. It based distribution of the school fund within towns on the total number of days attended by children over age four. Thus in theory school attendance and school year length both factored into the apportionment equation, but the actual law had little impact on schooling. Hobson, "Educational Legislation and Administration," 29.

40. Hobson, "Educational Legislation and Administration," 31–34, 136.

41. Hobson, "Educational Legislation and Administration," 136.

42. New York Superintendent of Public Instruction, *Annual Report* 7 (1861), 24; *Annual Report* 36 (1890), 85–86.

43. New York Superintendent of Public Instruction, *Annual Report* 12 (1866), 13.

44. There were certainly no large district bureaucracies in place yet, but each county was typically divided into two or three districts with their own inspector and trustees. New York Superintendent of Public Instruction, *Annual Report* 13 (1867), 285.

45. New York Superintendent of Public Instruction, *Annual Report* 36 (1890), 54.

46. New York Superintendent of Public Instruction, *Annual Report* 36 (1890), 85–86.

47. New York Superintendent of Public Instruction, *Annual Report* 38 (1891), xv.

48. For a discussion of these social indicators, see Kaestle and Vinovskis, *Education and Social Change* and Rury, "The Variable School Year," 29–36.

49. New York Superintendent of Public Instruction, *Annual Report* 17 (1871), 21.

50. Hobson, "Educational Legislation and Administration," 34–36; For discussion on the conflict over school taxes in New York, see Nasaw, *Schooled to Order*, 53–59.

51. Nasaw, *Schooled to Order*, 55–56. See also Kaestle, *Pillars of the Republic*, 117, 149–51.

52. Nasaw, *Schooled to Order*, 56–57; New York Superintendent of the Common Schools, *Annual Report* (1850–51), 144. The drop was not as widespread as Nasaw suggests. While many districts did lower their school years to the four-month minimum, the statewide average only fell from eight to 7.6 months. In other educational measurements, the superintendent recorded no drops at all.

53. Nasaw, *Schooled to Order*, 58; Samuel S. Randall, *History of the Common School System of the State of New York*, (New York: Ivison, Blakeman, Taylor and Co., 1871), 288–90.

54. The University of the State of New York, *Education in New York State, 1784–1954*, 50–51; New York Superintendent of Public Instruction, *Annual Report* 8 (1862), 388. Of course Westchester experienced less "deficiency" than most counties. One of the reasons why Westchester's school terms remained higher than average was because many of its schools were organized not through rate bills but under the alternative union free school legislation passed in 1853. New York Superintendent of Public Instruction, *Annual Report* 8 (1862), 387.

55. New York Superintendent of Public Instruction, *Annual Report* 8 (1862), 390; *Annual Report* 11 (1865), 106, 140, 142, 262; *Annual Report* 13 (1867), 53; *Annual Report* 17 (1871), 57. Educators also attributed irregular attendance and inadequate textbooks to the reliance on rate bills.

56. The University of the State of New York, *Education in New York State, 1784–1954*, 50–51.

57. New York Superintendent of Public Instruction, *Annual Report* 15 (1869), 11–12, *Annual Report* 16 (1870), 9. Average and aggregate attendance also increased noticeably after 1867.

58. New York Superintendent of Public Instruction, *Annual Report* 17 (1871), 306; *Annual Report* 19 (1873), 344.

59. New York Superintendent of the Common Schools, *Annual Report* (1836–37), 6.

60. New York Superintendent of the Common Schools, *Annual Report* (1836–37), 6.

61. New York Superintendent of Public Instruction, *Annual Report* 17 (1871), 25.

62. It is, however, difficult to pinpoint the law's impact as the state term length data for this period are very rough and incomplete. Table 1.1 indicates only a minor rise from 1850 to 1855, but a more immediate surge seems unlikely given that the state average only rose from 7.9 months in 1852 to 8.0 months in 1854. New York Superintendent of the Common Schools, *Annual Report* (1852–53), 4; New York Superintendent of Public Instruction, *Annual Report* 1 (1855), 7.

63. New York Superintendent of Public Instruction, *Annual Report* 7 (1861), 24.

64. New York Superintendent of Public Instruction, *Annual Report* 21 (1875), 396; *Annual Report* 36 (1890), 358.

65. New York Superintendent of Public Instruction, *Annual Report* 31 (1885), 473. Like other advocates of calendar reform, the Schenectady superintendent noted that the county's districts could now hire teachers for the full year.

66. New York Superintendent of Public Instruction, *Annual Report* 34 (1888), 508.

67. New York Superintendent of Public Instruction, *Annual Report* 31 (1885), 5–6; *Annual Report* 27 (1881), 594; *Annual Report* 34, (1888), 508. Of course some districts resented the change for the havoc it caused with local statutes on and practices of filing reports.

68. New York Superintendent of Public Instruction, *Annual Report* 36 (1890), 52.

69. Bedford, N.Y. *Bedford Historical Records*. vol. v: Minutes of Town Meetings, 1784–1841 (1976), vi–vii.

70. Donald W. Marshall, *Bedford Tricentennial: 1680–1980* (Katonah, N.Y.: Katonah Publishing Corp., 1980), 54–55.

71. *Attendance Data from Cantatoe School*, Schools Folder, Bedford Town Archives; *School District No. 6, Bedford, 1843–1844*. Westchester County Historical Society [WCHS], Bedford Schools—Vertical File.

72. Bedford N.Y. *Document No. 29, School District No. 2, Minutes*, June 10, 1826. See also October 23, 1835.

73. Bedford School Commissioners, *Annual Report*, 1830–62 (not inclusive), WCHS.

74. Marshall, *Bedford Tricentennial: 1680–1980*, 55; Bedford School Commissioners, *Annual Report*, 1830–62 (not inclusive), WCHS.

75. Of the several Westchester towns researched, Bedford had the most extensive archival material.

76. Bedford N.Y. *Document No. 29, School District No. 2, Minutes*, June 10, 1826; Dec. 9, 1826; Nov. 8, 1828; Nov. 17, 1828; April 30, 1829; Dec. 26, 1850.

77. Bedford N.Y. *Document No. 29, School District No. 2, Minutes*, Oct. 10, 1871; Bedford School Commissioners, *Annual Report*, 1870–74, WCHS.

78. Bedford N.Y. *Document No. 29, School District No. 2, Minutes*, Dec. 26, 1850; Oct. 12, 1860; Oct. 10, 1871; Oct. 28, 1872; Oct. 14, 1873.

79. Bedford N.Y. *Document No. 29, School District No. 2, Minutes*, Oct. 12, 1860.

80. Bedford N.Y. *Document No. 29, School District No. 2, Minutes*, Oct. 10, 1882; Oct. 9, 1883; Aug. 26, 1884; Aug. 25, 1885; Aug. 31, 1886; Aug. 30, 1887; Aug. 28, 1888; Aug. 6, 1889; Aug. 5, 1890.

81. New York Superintendent of Public Instruction, *Annual Report* 38 (1891), xv.

82. John C. Springman, *The Growth of Public Education in Michigan* (Ypsilanti, Michigan: Michigan State Normal College, Division of Field Services, 1952), 19.

83. Cremin, *American Education: The National Experience*, 161–62.

84. Springman, *The Growth of Public Education in Michigan*, 13–14.

85. Cremin, *American Education: The National Experience*, 162.

86. Michigan Superintendent of Public Instruction, *Annual Report* 6 (1842), 19, 26–28.

87. Michigan Superintendent of Public Instruction, *Annual Report* 9 (1845), 26.

88. Michigan Superintendent of Public Instruction, *Annual Report* 5 (1841), 50–54.

89. Michigan Superintendent of Public Instruction, *Annual Report* 1 (1837), 60; *Annual Report* 2 (1838), 73; *Annual Report* 5 (1841), 54.

90. Kaestle and Vinovskis, *Education and Social Change*, 132–35; Rury, "The Variable School Year," 29–36.

91. Detroit, with a population just over 9,000 in 1840, was far smaller than hinterland cities like Pittsburgh, Cincinnati, and St. Louis as well as the centers of the eastern seaboard. U.S. Bureau of the Census, *Abstract of the Fifteenth Census of the United States, 1930*, Washington: Government Printing Office, 22–23.

92. Of these seventy-two districts, two ran schools for twelve months, one for eleven months, five for over ten months, sixteen for exactly ten months, and another forty-eight for nine months. The distribution of school year lengths by district size (children between five and seventeen) was as follows: 1 to 30 children—18 districts; 31 to 60 children—26 districts; 61 to 90 children—14 districts; 91–120 children—3 districts; 121–150 children—4 districts; 151–180 children—1 district; 181–210 children—1

district; and no record—5 districts. Michigan Superintendent of Public Instruction, *Annual Report* 6 (1842), 26–28.

93. Michigan Superintendent of Public Instruction, *Annual Report* 5 (1841), 50–56. Spearman's R = .294.

94. Michigan Superintendent of Public Instruction, *Annual Report* 27 (1863), 59.

95. U.S. Commissioner of Education, *Annual Report 1867–1868* (Washington: Government Printing Office, 1868), 111; David Tyack, Thomas Hames, and Aaron Benavot, *Law and the Shaping of Public Education, 1785–1954* (Madison, Wisconsin: University of Wisconsin Press, 1987), 56–58.

96. Mary Rosalita, *Education in Detroit Prior to 1850* (Lansing: Michigan Historical Commission, 1928), 334.

97. Tyack, Hames, and Benavot, *Law and the Shaping of Public Education*, 83.

98. Michigan Superintendent of Public Instruction, *Annual Report* 5 (1841), 31.

99. Michigan Superintendent of Public Instruction, *Annual Report* 5 (1841), 35–43.

100. Michigan Superintendent of Public Instruction, *Annual Report* 17 (1853), 6.

101. In the antebellum era, school superintendents typically calculated a school month as 22 days. After the Civil War, they usually equated a month with 20 days. Thus Figure 1.3 overstates the increase in the actual number of school days.

102. Tyack, Hames, and Benavot, *Law and the Shaping of Public Education*, 84.

103. Michigan Superintendent of Public Instruction, *Annual Report* 17 (1853), 1–7.

104. National Education Association, *Addresses and Proceedings* 19 (1880), Appendix B, 133.

105. Michigan Superintendent of Public Instruction, *Annual Report* 51, (1887), ix.

106. Michigan Superintendent of Public Instruction, *Annual Report* 51, (1887), ix–x.

107. Michigan Superintendent of Public Instruction, *Annual Report* 51, (1887), ix–x.

108. Michigan Superintendent of Public Instruction, *Annual Report* 51, (1887), ix.

109. For example, in 1843, its average length of student attendance was 20 weeks, the highest in Michigan. Michigan Superintendent of Public Instruction, *Annual Report* 7 (1843), 15. After Wayne County, Washtenaw had the largest population of school-aged children in Michigan, and so was an obvious leader in school enrollments and school spending. Michigan Superintendent of Public Instruction, *Annual Report* 8 (1844), 29.

110. Michigan Superintendent of Public Instruction, *Annual Report* 8 (1844), 3; *Annual Report* 50 (1888), ii–vii. Looking backward, Superintendent of Public Instruction John M. Gregory noted that township districts led to raised school-year lengths, reduced costs per pupil, equalized school access and local school taxes, more uniform textbooks, and reduced numbers of school officers.

111. Michigan Superintendent of Public Instruction, *Annual Report* 22 (1858), 140.

112. Charles O. Hough and R. Clyde Ford, *John D. Pierce, Founder of the Michigan School System: A Study of Education in the Northwest* (Ypsilanti, Michigan: Scharf Tag, Label & Box Company, 1905), 130–41; Michigan Superintendent of Public Instruction, *Annual Report* 31 (1867), 18–22.

113. Michigan Superintendent of Public Instruction, *Annual Report* 34 (1870), 140; *Annual Report* 35 (1871), 133. In 1871, 158 winter teachers and 148 summer teachers were hired.

114. Michigan Superintendent of Public Instruction, *Annual Report* 37 (1873), 193.

115. Pierce did claim, in his 1867 diatribe, that summer attendance totals were only 30% of those for the winter. However, he only cited data from two schools, which combined drew 94 students in the winter and only 30 in the summer. While attendance was probably lower in the summer, it is unlikely that Pierce used representative examples. Even if they were, they might just indicate that degree to which summer school was already declining by 1867 and do not negate the larger argument that summer school in the antebellum period was substantial. Michigan Superintendent of Public Instruction, *Annual Report* 31 (1867), 20.

116. Michigan Superintendent of Public Instruction, *Annual Report* 34 (1870), 140; *Annual Report* 35 (1871), 133.

117. The average earnings for the summer term were converted from weeks ($3.33 per week). The superintendent did not explain why different standards were used, but it may indicate that summer terms were noticeably shorter than winter terms by 1871.

118. Michigan Superintendent of Public Instruction, *Annual Report* 37 (1873), 194.

119. Cornelius J. Heatwole, *History of Education in Virginia* (New York: The Macmillan Company, 1916), 44–58.

120. Heatwole, *History of Education in Virginia*, 58. See also Edgar W. Knight, ed., *A Documentary History of Education in the South Before 1860*, Vol. 1 (Chapel Hill: The University of North Carolina Press, 1949), 664.

121. D. E. Gardner, "History of Public Education in Henrico County," in Virginia Superintendent of Public Instruction, *Annual Report* 16 (1885), 198–99.

122. Heatwole, *History of Education in Virginia*, 100–105.

123. A. J. Morrison, *The Beginnings of Public Education in Virginia, 1776–1860* (Richmond: David Bottom, Superintendent of Public Printing, 1917), 7–16; Heatwole, *A History of Education in Virginia*, 124–36.

124. Tyack, Hames, and Benavot, *Law and the Shaping of Public Education*, 56; Heatwole, *A History of Education in Virginia*, 216–21.

125. Virginia Superintendent of Public Instruction, *Annual Report* 1 (1870), 9; "Appendix B," *NEA Addresses and Proceedings* 19 (1880), 134.

126. Virginia Superintendent of Public Instruction, *Annual Report* 7 (1877), 9; *Annual Report* 2 (1872), x. Ruffner linked an additional enrollment of 35,000 to this increase. Both improvements ultimately came from "the increased liberality of the people," who raised county and district contributions as the state fund waned.

127. Virginia Superintendent of Public Instruction, *Annual Report* 7 (1877), 9; *Annual Report* 10 (1880), 120.

128. Virginia Superintendent of Public Instruction, *Annual Report* 7 (1877), 9; *Annual Report* 10 (1880), 120.

129. Virginia Superintendent of Public Instruction, *Annual Report* 3 (1873), 165.

130. Virginia Superintendent of Public Instruction, *Annual Report* 2 (1872), x; *Annual Report* 5 (1875), 52; *Annual Report* 19 (1889), 23.

131. Virginia Superintendent of Public Instruction, *Annual Report* 20 (1890), 89–96. The County Superintendents also repeatedly wished for larger appropriations, better teachers, better school buildings, and higher standards.

132. Poor roads and farm work remained deterrents of school attendance throughout the nineteenth century. Virginia Superintendent of Public Instruction, *Annual Report* 18 (1888), 25.

133. Virginia Superintendent of Public Instruction, *Annual Report* 16 (1886), 116.

134. Heatwole, *A History of Education in Virginia*, 222–27.

135. Virginia Superintendent of Public Instruction, *Annual Report* 8 (1878), 5–7; *Annual Report* 9 (1879), 4–5. By 1890, Virginia's average school session length of 5.8 months was one of the longest among the old states of the Confederacy. For comparison, southern states reported the following average lengths for white schools in 1890: Alabama, 3.7 months; Kentucky, 5.0 months; Louisiana, 5.2 months; North Carolina, 3.0 months, and Texas, 5.9 months. For blacks, the figure was the either the same or lower: Virginia, 5.8 months; Alabama, 3.6 months; Kentucky, 5.0 months; Louisiana, 4.7 months; North Carolina, 3.0 months, and Texas, 5.6 months. U.S. Commissioner of Education, *Annual Report 1890–1891* (Washington: Government Printing Office, 1893), 961.

136. Virginia Superintendent of Public Instruction, *Annual Report* 8 (1878), 5–7; *Annual Report* 4 (1874), 46.

137. Virginia Superintendent of Public Instruction, *Annual Report* 8 (1878), 5–7; *Annual Report* 7 (1877), 26; *Annual Report* 8 (1878), 71.

138. Virginia Superintendent of Public Instruction, *Annual Report* 16 (1886), 13.

139. Virginia Superintendent of Public Instruction, *Annual Report* 16 (1886), 13.

140. Virginia Superintendent of Public Instruction, *Annual Report* 7 (1877), 8.

141. Virginia Superintendent of Public Instruction, *Annual Report* 7 (1877), 8.

142. Michigan Superintendent of Public Instruction, *Annual Report* 31 (1867), 19.

143. Cubberley, *Public Education in the United States*, 289, 326; Odell, "Summer Work in Public Schools," 15; Johnson, *Old-Time Schools and School-Books,* 130.

144. See, for example, Kaestle, *Pillars of the Republic*, 111; Soltow and Stevens, *The Rise of Literacy and the Common School in the United States*, 109–11.

Chapter Two: "No More Rulers, No More Books"

1. U.S. Commissioner of Education, *Annual Report 1891–1892* (Washington: Government Printing Office, 1894), 664.

2. U.S. Commissioner of Education, *Annual Report 1891–1892* (Washington: Government Printing Office, 1894), 665.

3. Studies of nineteenth-century schooling that either gloss over or completely ignore the developments in the school year calendar include Selwyn Troen, *The Public and the Schools: Shaping the St. Louis System, 1838–1920* (Columbia, Missouri: University of Missouri Press, 1975); Diane Ravitch, *The Great School Wars: New York City, 1805–1973: A History of the Public Schools as Battlefield of Social Change* (New York: Basic Books, Inc., 1974); Michael B. Katz, *The Irony of Early School Reform: Educational Innovation in Mid-Nineteenth Century Massachusetts* (Cambridge, Massachusetts: Harvard University Press, 1968); Stanley K. Schultz, *The Culture Factory: Boston Public Schools, 1789–1860* (New York: Oxford University Press, 1973); Carl F. Kaestle, *The Evolution of an Urban School System* (Cambridge, Massachusetts: Harvard University Press, 1973). To be fair, these studies were more concerned with the intersection of class, culture, race, and politics in the incipient school systems rather than their structural development.

4. One study that details the shortened urban school year is the excellent social history by Carl F. Kaestle and Maris A. Vinovskis, *Education and Social Change in nineteenth-century Massachusetts* (Cambridge: Cambridge University Press, 1980), 39,

82, 118–20, 133–34, 250, 259. In it, Kaestle and Vinovskis delineated a substantial mid-nineteenth-century decline in the length of the school years in three Essex County cities of 15,000–20,000 people in 1860 (Lawrence, Lynn, and Salem). In 1840, they averaged 269 days per year; in 1860 the figure was 238, by 1880 it dropped to 224. In contradistinction, the authors traced a 40-day rise in school year length for five towns of about 1,000 inhabitants in the same time span. Thus Kaestle and Vinovskis recognized that the growth in school terms occurred only at the rural level. They also offered multifarious interpretations about school calendar patterns that explain why urban terms were longer than rural terms as well as why most rural terms expanded over the century. They do not, however, account for why urban term lengths declined, the question that is at the heart of this chapter.

5. Michigan Superintendent of Public Instruction, *Annual Report* 5 (1841), 43.

6. Detroit Board of Education, *Annual Report* 2 (1843), 1; *Annual Report* 3 (1844), 1; *Annual Report* 6 (1847), 2. Most, but not all, of Detroit's schools opened for all four quarters. In 1847, 12 of Detroit's 14 schools ran 4 quarters while the other two taught for three, including the summer quarter.

7. Michigan Superintendent of Public Instruction, *Annual Report* 17 (1853), 147–55; Detroit Board of Education, *Annual Report* 8 (1849), 2.

8. Michigan Superintendent of Public Instruction, *Annual Report* 17 (1853), 153. In 1850, attendance on the last day of the spring-summer term was 2,267, compared two 2,620 for the winter term and 2,372 for the fall term.

9. Michigan Superintendent of Public Instruction, *Annual Report* 14 (1850), 59.

10. The spring term began the second Monday after the third Saturday in April and closed the fourth Saturday in July. Detroit Board of Education, *Annual Report* 18 (1860), 76.

11. Detroit Board of Education, *Annual Report* 25 (1867), 74, 81.

12. See Kaestle, *Evolution of an Urban School System* and Ravitch, *Great School Wars*.

13. Kaestle, *Evolution of an Urban School System*, 80–88; Edwin G. Burrows and Mike Wallace, *Gotham: A History of New York City to 1898* (New York: Oxford University Press, 1999), 499–500.

14. Kaestle, *Evolution of an Urban School System*, 149–51; Ravitch, *Great School Wars*, 67–76, 79.

15. Thomas Boese, *Public Education in the City of New York* (New York: Harpers Brothers, 1869), 68–84; Kaestle, *Evolution of an Urban School System*, 160; Ravitch, *Great School Wars*, 79–83; Public School Society, "Report of the Committee Appointed to Make the Necessary Arrangements for Terminating its Existence: Dissolution of the Public School Society," 1853.

16. Kaestle, *Evolution of an Urban School System*, 182.

17. Public School Society, *Twenty-Eighth Annual Report* (1833), May 3 Minutes; *Thirty-Eighth Annual Report* (1843), May 5 Minutes.

18. New York Board of Education, *Annual Report* 1 (1842), 8.

19. The three-week recess in August was established by the Free School Society at least as far back as 1818. A Emerson Palmer, *Being a History of Free Education in the City of New York* (London: Macmillan & Co., Ltd., 1905), 41; Burrows and Wallace, *Gotham*, 488; Alice Morse Earle, *Colonial Days in Old New York* (New York: Charles Scribner's Sons, 1896), 32.

20. Burrows and Wallace, *Gotham*, 178–79, 374. 718–20; Kaestle and Vinovskis, *Education and Social Change*, 38–39, 82; Public School Society, *Thirtieth Annual Report* (1835), 16; *Thirty-First Annual Report* (1836), 15.

21. New York Superintendent of the Common School. *Annual Report*, 1851–52, 159. Data from the early and mid-1840s were tabulated by county, not city, and not tabulated at all for New York City. Figures from Kings County (Brooklyn today) in 1844 show slightly greater numbers in attendance for ten months or longer than the Brooklyn data from 1850. Brooklyn existed as an independent city until its consolidation with New York in 1898. New York Superintendent of the Common Schools, *Annual Report* (1843–44), 30.

22. Westchester County regularly reported better than average attendance for the categories above six months. In 1856, for example, it had a larger proportion (4.5%) of its students attending school year round than any other non-urban county in the state, which reported a figure of 1%. New York Superintendent of Public Instruction, *Annual Report* 4 (1857), 6.

23. Statewide in 1850, over one half of New York students attended school for fewer than four months per year while a meager 6.3% came for ten months or longer. New York Superintendent of the Common Schools, *Annual Report* (1849–50). A similar pattern existed in Massachusetts cities, Kaestle and Vinovskis, 118–120.

24. Total attendance figures are used because average attendance was not tabulated by the PSS. Although the data end with the 1842, there is no indication that seasonal attendance patterns changed much in the subsequent decade.

25. When the state collected data comparing the curriculum and teaching cohorts of summer and winter terms in 1843 (discussed in Chapter One), New York City provided the exact same figures for each term. New York Superintendent of the Common Schools, *Annual Report* (1843–44), 30.

26. New York Board of Education, *Annual Report* 12 (1853), 5–6.

27. New York Board of Education, *Annual Report* 4 (1845), 4; 10 (1851), 9–13.

28. Public School Society, *Thirty-Seventh Annual Report* (1842), May 6 Minutes; *Thirty-Eighth Annual Report* (1843), May 5 Minutes.

29. Boese, *Public Education in the City of New York*, 70.

30. Boese, *Public Education in the City of New York*, 73. See also Ravitch, *Great School Wars*, 84–85.

31. New York Board of Education, *Report of the Free Academy* (1850), 12; (1851), 4.

32. Special Committee of the New York Board of Education, *Report on the System of Popular Education in the City of New York* (New York: William C. Bryant & Co., 1851), 32.

33. New York Board of Education, "Document No. 1: Inaugural Address of Andrew H. Green, President," Documents (1857), 4–5; Boese, *Public Education in the City of New York*, 69; Ravitch, *Great School Wars*, 83–87.

34. New York Board of Education, *Annual Report* 12 (1853), 5–6.

35. New York Board of Education, *Journal* (1855), 48, 247–48.

36. Kaestle, *Evolution of an Urban School SystemI*, 182.

37. Ravitch, *Great School Wars*, 86.

38. New York Board of Education, *Annual Report* 15 (1856), 7.

39. New York Board of Education, *Annual Report* 15 (1856), 6–7. Randall reasoned that the Commencement holiday was desirable at first "to give all possible *eclat* to its anniversary," but now that the school was established the holiday was no longer needed.

40. New York Board of Education, *Annual Report* 19 (1860), 19–20; *Journal* (1860), 359.

41. New York Board of Education, *By-Laws and General Rules and Regulations* 1858 (New York: Pudney & Russell, Printers, 1859), 17; *Annual Report* 19 (1860), 19–20; *Journal* (1860), 359.

42. In 1861, the Board of Education voted to close all schools on January 3rd and 4th to honor President Buchanan's plea for a day of national prayer. New York Board of Education, *Journal* (1860), 367–368.

43. New York Board of Education, *Journal* (1869), 138; (1872), 167, 221, 904; Ravitch, *Great School Wars*, 92–99.

44. New York Board of Education, *Journal* (1877), 481–84.

45. New York Board of Education, *Journal* (1865), 118, 195, 382–83; (1873), 274.

46. New York Board of Education, *Journal* (1861), 40; (1869), 303; (1875), 307.

47. New York Board of Education, *Journal* (1865), 195; (1867), 173; (1872), 167.

48. *New York Times*, June 22, 1865; New York Board of Education, *Journal* (1872), 221.

49. New York Board of Education, *Journal* (1866), 140.

50. New York Board of Education, *Journal* (1869), 111, 138.

51. Neither the board's *Journal* nor the local press depicted any debate over the issue. New York Board of Education, *Journal* (1866), 140; *New York Times*, May 17, 1866; *New York Tribune*, May 17, 1866.

52. New York Board of Education, *Journal* (1869), 138; *New York Herald*, July 22, 1869; *New York Times*, July 22, 1869.

53. *New York Herald*, July 22, 1869; *New York Times*, July 22, 1869. It seems likely that some members supported the resolution not on its merits but only because they believed the board's by-laws had not been followed when the initial vacation period was determined. Initially appointed for his reform credentials, Sands' links to Tammany were eventually uncovered. Ravitch, *Great School Wars*, 92–97.

54. New York Board of Education, *Journal* (1870), 183.

55. *New York Times*, June 1, 1871, June 15, 1871; *New York Herald*, June 15, 1871; *New York Tribune*, June 15, 1871; New York Board of Education, *Journal* (1871), 118–19, 142.

56. New York Board of Education, *Journal* (1872), 203; *New York Herald*, March 7, 1872.

57. On this issue, however, Smyth voted with the majority. New York Board of Education, *Journal* (1872), 219–21.

58. Cindy S. Aron, *Working at Play: A History of Vacations in the United States* (New York: Oxford University Press, 1999), 15–44. Antecedents for such vacationing date back to the seventeenth century. Barbara G. Carson, "Early American Tourists and the Commercialization of Leisure," in *Of Consuming Interests: The Style of Life in the Eighteenth Century*, eds. Cary Carson, Ronald Hoffman, and Peter J. Albert (Charlottesville: University Press of Virginia, 1994), 376, 380–81.

59. I thank the late David Angus for his persistence in suggesting this line of inquiry to me.

60. Howard P. Chudacoff and Judith E. Smith, *The Evolution of American Urban Society*, 5th ed. (Upper Saddle River, N.J.: Prentice Hall, 2000), 38, 54; U.S. Bureau of the Census, *Abstract of the Fifteenth Census of the United States, 1930*, Washington: Government Printing Office, 22–23.

61. In New York, twenty years of school construction and extension brought in many private school students but did not increase the percentage of children going to school. In fact, the percentage decreased from 58.2% to 55.1% from 1829 to 1850. Kaestle, *Evolution of an Urban School System*, 89.

62. New York Board of Education, *Annual Report* 13 (1854), 10–16; *Journal*, (1854), 7–8.

63. New York Board of Education, *Annual Report* 12 (1853), 6.

64. New York Board of Education, *Annual Report* 4 (1845), 4.

65. See for example New York Board of Education, *Annual Report* 3 (1844), 4; 6 (1847), 8–9.

66. Public School Society, *Twenty-Eighth Annual Report* (1833), May 3 Minutes.

67. New York Board of Education, *Annual Report* 8(1849), 6. See Charles E. Rosenberg, *The Cholera Years: The United States in 1832, 1849, and 1866* (Chicago: University of Chicago Press, 1987), 108.

68. New York Board of Education, *Journal* (1866), 218–19; *New York Herald*, July 8, 1869.

69. New York Board of Education, *Annual Report* 12 (1853), 22–30; 13 (1854), 18–30; 16 (1857), 11–20.

70. The board argued that it was legally entitled to additional funds, and public sentiment on its side caused the city's Common Council to require the comptroller to provide the money. The controversy did not die, however, as the next year's conflict arose over whether the rescue money was an advance on the 1855 allocation or part of the legal expenditures for 1854. New York Board of Education, *Annual Report* 15 (1856), 25–30. Another shortfall that did not lead to a reduced school year occurred in 1871. New York Board of Education, *Annual Report* 30 (1871), 46–51.

71. Ravitch, *Great School Wars*, 95.

72. *New York Times*, July 22, 1869; *New York Herald*, July 22, 1869; May 19, 1870.

73. Kaestle, *Evolution of an Urban School System*, 136–81; William J. Reese, *The Origins of the American High School* (New Haven: Yale University Press, 1995), 68–70.

74. Passed in 1874, New York State's compulsory education legislation remained essentially unenforced for at least two decades. Likewise, centralization of the city's system did not occur until 1896. Ravitch, *Great School Wars*, 112, 134–58, 168.

75. Superintendent of Public Schools in the City of Brooklyn, *Annual Report* o.s. (1853), 4; 1 (1856), 4; 6 (1861), 56–57; 18 (1872), 45; 29 (1883), 10, 178, 186.

76. Carl F. Kaestle, *Pillars of the Republic: Common Schools and American Society, 1780–1860* (New York: Hill and Wang, 1983), 198–201.

Chapter Three: "School's out for Summer"

1. Carl F. Kaestle, *Pillars of the Republic: Common Schools and American Society, 1780–1860* (Hill and Wang: New York, 1983), 76.

2. Kaestle, *Pillars of the Republic*, 112–35; William J. Reese, *The Origins of the American High School* (New Haven: Yale University Press, 1995), 38–49.

3. Caroline Winterer, "Avoiding a 'Hothouse System of Education': Nineteenth-Century Early Childhood Education from the Infant Schools to the Kindergartens," *History of Education Quarterly* 32 (Fall 1992), 289–314.

4. Stanley K. Schultz, *The Culture Factory: Boston Public Schools, 1789–1860* (New York: Oxford University Press, 1973), 92–100; John Duffy, "School Buildings and the Health of American School Children in the Nineteenth Century," in *Healing and History: Essays for George Rosen* ed. Charles Rosenberg (New York: Dawson, Science History Publications, 1979), 161–78; Kaestle, *Pillars of the Republic*, 122.

5. Brian Gill and Steven Schlossman, "'A Sin against Childhood': Progressive Education and the Crusade to Abolish Homework, 1897–1941," *American Journal of Education* 105 (November 1996), 31–34; Reese, *Origins of the American High School*, 201.

6. These new understandings of time should not simply be subsumed under Protestantism and particularly capitalism because they are too often excluded entirely. For example, even Carl Kaestle's outstanding treatment of common school ideology highlights the value placed on personal thrift and industry without explicitly including the reconception of time even though the emphasis on spending and not wasting time is connected to the work ethic encouraged by Protestant and capitalist thought. Kaestle, *Pillars of the Republic*, 82–83.

7. Kaestle, *Pillars of the Republic*, 111.

8. Carl F. Kaestle and Maris A. Vinovskis, *Education and Social Change in Nineteenth-Century Massachusetts* (Cambridge: Cambridge University Press, 1980), 134.

9. Most debates usually reflected larger issues related to the entire common school movement. In particular, interested parties contended over the locus of rural school control (whether it would be local or state centered), of urban school authority (whether it would be based in wards or a central board), and over the financing of school innovations (whether additional school taxes would be needed to add school days).

10. Jonathan Messerli, *Horace Mann: A Biography* (New York: Alfred A Knopf, 1972), xii.

11. Messerli, *Horace Mann*, 247, 455; Kaestle, *Pillars of the Republic*, 76, 104–27.

12. Massachusetts Board of Education, *Sixth Annual Report* (1842), 24.

13. Massachusetts Board of Education, *Sixth Annual Report* (1842), 24. For an excellent review of the literature on summer setback, see Harris Cooper, Barbara Nye, Kelly Charlton, James Lindsay and Scott Greathouse, "The Effects of Summer Vacation on Achievement Test Scores: A Narrative and Meta-Analytic Review," *Review of Educational Research*, (December, 1996), 227–68.

14. Messerli argues that in his first three years as secretary, Mann's circuits through Massachusetts took on an almost evangelical feel as he articulated humanitarian impulses behind the common school movement. Messerli, *Horace Mann*, 251–308.

15. Massachusetts Board of Education, *Sixth Annual Report* (1842), 25.

16. Massachusetts Board of Education, *Sixth Annual Report* (1842), 25.

17. Massachusetts Board of Education, *Sixth Annual Report* (1842), 25–26.

18. Massachusetts Board of Education, *Sixth Annual Report* (1842), 26–27.

19. Massachusetts Board of Education, *Sixth Annual Report* (1842), 26–27.

20. Mann did repeat his concerns about excess mental effort causing ill health in a section on physical education found in his final annual report. Moreover, his private correspondence with physicians like Edward Jarvis, John Warren, and J. B. Woodward addressed health concerns as well. Massachusetts Board of Education, *Twelfth Annual Report* (1848), 33–36; 27 Horace Mann to J. B. Woodward, November, 1840, Edward Jarvis to Horace Mann 19 April, 1852, Horace Mann Papers, Massachusetts Historical Society.

21. "Neglect of Schools in Summer," *American Annals of Education*, 8 (May 1838): 260–61.

22. Connecticut Superintendent of Common Schools, *Second Annual Report* (1840), 24–25; Michigan Superintendent of Public Instruction, *Annual Report* 37 (1873), 193.

23. Detroit Board of Education, *Annual Report* 17 (1853), 155; New York Board of Education, *Report of the Free Academy* (1850), 12; (1851), 4.

24. Providence School Committee, *Annual Report* (1872), 8.

25. Committee of the Society for the Improvement of Common Schools in Connecticut, *Report* quoted in the *American Annals of Education* 2 (April 1832): 202.

26. Michigan Superintendent of Public Instruction, *Annual Report* 21 (1857), 71; *The American Educational Monthly* 10 (1873): 391.

27. Schultz, *The Culture Factory*, 92–100.

28. *The American Educational Monthly* 1 (1864): 269–70.

29. *Pennsylvania School Journal* 3 (1854): 219.

30. Michigan Superintendent of Public Instruction, *Annual Report* 21 (1857), 66–71.

31. Virginia Superintendent of Public Instruction, *Annual Report* 4 (1874), 174.

32. *Pennsylvania School Journal* 3 (1854): 219; *The American Educational Monthly* 1 (1864): 269–70. In this instance, the author's ground plan for an ideal structure also included windows "hung with weights and pulleys, if possible, so that the upper sash can be lowered to permit the more rapid escape of the heated and vitiated air, during hot weather."

33. Schultz, *The Culture Factory*, 93.

34. *The American Educational Monthly* 6 (1869): 29; *The American Educational Monthly* 2 (1865): 177.

35. *Common School Journal* 2, (15 June 1840), 219.

36. Michigan Superintendent of Public Instruction, *Annual Report* 21 (1857), 65. Mayhew felt the ventilation problem was worst in the winter because windows and doors needed to remain shut.

37. Schultz, *The Culture Factory*, 96; *Common School Journal* 1, (15 October 1839), 316; *Common School Journal* 2 (15 July 1840), 316.

38. Michigan Superintendent of Public Instruction, *Annual Report* 5 (1841), 31. Much medical practice in the nineteenth century also assumed that bilious diseases such as malaria were seasonal. Carl. J. Pfeiffer, *The Art and Practice of Western Medicine in the Early Nineteenth Century* (Jefferson, North Carolina: McFarland & Company, Inc., Publishers, 1985), 156–63.

39. *Massachusetts Teacher* 25 (August 1872): 332.

40. *Lancaster Examiner* cited in the *Pennsylvania School Journal* 8 (1859): 48.

41. *Pennsylvania School Journal* 8 (1859): 48. Most educators also distinguished between males and females with regard to the dangers of too much schooling. In general, educators who noted distinctions feared that "girls suffer most from injurious influences" of schooling. *Massachusetts Teacher* 9 (1856), 560.

42. *Massachusetts Teacher* 25 (August 1872): 332.

43. *The American Educational Monthly* 2 (1865): 176.

44. Bernard Wishy, *The Child and the Republic: The Dawn of Modern American Child Nurture* (Philadelphia: University of Pennsylvania Press, 1968), 70–72; *Massachusetts Teacher* 25 (August 1872): 332; *The American Educational Monthly* 2 (1865): 177; *The American Educational Monthly* 11 (1874): 419.

45. *Massachusetts Teacher* 3 (November 1850): 351.

46. When considering the nature of the learning experience, educators regularly indicated the importance of lesson content and teaching methodology in relation to students' health. One contributor to the *American Educational Monthly* even suggested that the danger of too much schooling would disappear if proper pedagogy were the norm, noting that "if quality as well as quantity is included in the development, no limit can be assigned to the extent of the latter, and consequently no limit to the manifestations of intellectual and spiritual power that may pour through the brain." *The American Educational Monthly* 11 (1874): 419.

47. *The Massachusetts Teacher* 26 (1873): 332.

48. *Massachusetts Teacher* 16 (1863): 32.

49. Francis F. Packard, *History of Medicine in the United States*, vol. 2 (New York: Paul B. Hoeber, 1931), 954–67.

50. Richard Harrison Shryock, *Medicine and Society in America: 1660–1860* (New York: New York University Press, 1960), 68.

51. Shryock, *Medicine and Society in America*, 69.

52. There was, however, substantial regionalism in adherence to medical ideas. For example, physicians in Philadelphia and Charleston were more likely than those in Boston to follow the Scottish school of thought. John Harley Warner, *The Therapeutic Perspective: Medical Practice, Knowledge, and Identity in America, 1820–1885* (Cambridge: Harvard University Press, 1986; reprint, Princeton: Princeton University Press, 1997), 22–23.

53. Shryock argues that Brown ended up exaggerating the influence of capillary tension by claiming that it caused all illness and that therefore there was really only one disease in the world. His practice of bleeding as a remedy was also overdone, leading to a reaction against him in some medical circles and its disuse in therapeutic practice in antebellum America. Shryock, *Medicine and Society in America*, 69–70; Warner, *The Therapeutic Perspective*, 5. For an articulation of the resiliency of bloodletting, see John S. Haller, Jr., *American Medicine in Transition, 1840–1910* (Urbana: University of Illinois Press, 1981), 66.

54. Warner, *The Therapeutic Perspective*, 37–57; Shryock, *Medicine and Society in America*, 70–75. See also John Harley Warner, *Against the Spirit of System: The French Impulse in Nineteenth-Century American Medicine* (Princeton: Princeton University Press, 1997). Shryock suggests that the history of medicine has followed rough cycles between specific and universal approaches to health and illness.

55. John C. Warren, *Physical Education and the Preservation of Health* 2d ed. (Boston: William D. Ticknor & Company, 1846).

56. Warren, *Physical Education and the Preservation of Health*, 6, 8–9.

57. J. G. Barford, M.D., "Over-Pressure in Schools," *The Lancet* 2 (27 Septembeı 1884): 570.

58. U.S. Commissioner of Education, *Annual Report, 1870–71* (Washington: Government Printing Office, 1871), 544.

59. Robert T. Edes, "High-Pressure Education; Its Effects," *The Boston Medical & Surgical Journal* 106 (1882): 221.

60. Clement Dukes, *Health at School: Considered in its Mental, Moral, and Physical Aspects* 4th ed. (London: Rivingtons, 1905), 583. Although Dukes primarily addressed English boarding (public) schools, here he included both England's public schools and its new, state-funded ones.

61. Barford, "Over-Pressure in Schools," 570. Educators also questioned the pedagogical value of emulation. See Reese, *Origins of the American High School*, 132–35.

62. "London," *The Lancet* 2 (1884): 484; Dukes, *Health at School*, 218–23.

63. *The American Educational Monthly* 7 (1870): 422–23. Virginia Superintendent of Public Instruction, *Annual Report* 4 (1874), 174.

64. Daniel Clark, "Education in Relation to Health," *American Journal of Insanity* 43 (1886): 45; Horatio Charles Wood, *Brain-work and Overwork* (Philadelphia: Presley Blakiston, 1880), 69; Dukes, *Health at School*, 236–51.

65. Frederick MacCabe, "On Mental Strain and Overwork," *The Journal of Mental Science* 21 (1875): 388–402; Barford, "Over-Pressure in Schools," 570; Dukes, *Health at School*, 282.

66. MacCabe, "On Mental Strain and Overwork," 393–402.

67. Wood, *Brain-work and Overwork*, 66–69. Wood, like most of his profession at this time, did not discount physical causes outside of the workplace. Although Wood emphasized the various types of mental stress, he still acknowledged poor hygiene, undernourishment, overexposure to alcohol, tobacco, coffee, and tea, as important factors in nervous disorders.

68. Edes, "High-Pressure Education; Its Effects," 220–22. Edes wrote of specific cases of neurasthenia in women. He attributed the association to differences in behavior between boys and girls. A boy, noted Edes, was likely to "content himself with such moderate scholastic honors as are easily within his reach, and to get his sleep and recreation even at the expense of class standing." Edes claimed that girls worked tirelessly until they dropped, explaining that "it seems to be a compound of conscience, ambition, and a desire to please, in varying proportions with a peculiar feminine sort of obstinacy which, in a better cause, and reasonably directed, would demand admiration rather than pity." A discussion of "Overstrain in Female Education" identified the problem's source as the "unremitting continuance [of learning] during the menstrual periods." See "Overstrain in Female Education," *The Lancet* 2 (1884): 73.

69. Barford, "Over-Pressure in Schools," 570.

70. "London," *The Lancet* 1 (1884): 261, 410, 445, 455, 635, 947; "London," *The Lancet* 2 (1884): 73, 284, 547, 616, 662, 698, 879, 977–78, 1016, 1113.

71. "London," *The Lancet* 2 (1884): 284.

72. "London," *The Lancet* 2 (1884): 547.

73. Dukes, *Health at School*, 264.

74. MacCabe, "On Mental Strain and Overwork," 392.

75. Wood, *Brain-work and Overwork*, 16.

76. Edes, "High-Pressure Education; Its Effects," 220; MacCabe, "On Mental Strain and Overwork," 393; Wood, *Brain-work and Overwork*, 124; Dukes, *Health at School*, 258.

77. Barford, "Over-Pressure in Schools," 570; Dukes, *Health at School*, 259. Cachexia is a general wasting of the body during a chronic disease.

78. Wood, *Brain-work and Overwork*, 74.

79. Winterer, "Avoiding a 'Hothouse System of Education'," 291, 296–97; Kaestle, *Pillars of the Republic*, 109; Maris Vinovskis and Dean May, "A Ray of Millennial Light: Early Education and Social Reform in the Infant School Movement in Massachusetts, 1826–40," in Maris Vinovskis, *Education, Society, and Economic Opportunity: A Historical Perspective on Persistent Issues* (New Haven: Yale University Press, 1995), 17–44. Winterer argues that "support for the infant schools quickly flagged in the wake of Brigham's publication," and Kaestle notes that the alarm especially pertained to very young children. See also Norman Dain, *Concepts of Insanity in the United States, 1789–1865* (New Brunswick, N.J., 1964).

80. U.S. Commissioner of Education, *Annual Report, 1870–1871* (Washington: Government Printing Office, 1871), 542.

81. U.S. Commissioner of Education, *Annual Report, 1870–1871* (Washington: Government Printing Office, 1871), 544.

82. Wood, *Brain-work and Overwork*, 76–84, 110–21.

83. MacCabe, "On Mental Strain and Overwork," 392–93.

84. Dukes, *Health at School*, 324–26.

85. Edes, "High-Pressure Education; Its Effects," 223; Reese, 134.

86. Clark, "Education in Relation to Health," 53–54.

87. Clark, "Education in Relation to Health," 53–54.

88. *The American Educational Monthly* 7 (1870): 420–21.

89. Dukes, *Health at School*, 583. See also Barford, "Over-Pressure in Schools," 570.

90. Dukes, *Health at School*, 582–90.

91. Wood, *Brain-work and Overwork*, 85–106. Wood also printed an informal list of do's and don'ts. Included among the latter were excessive travel, summer resort visits, games of chess, and bible study classes which repeated the methods of the grammar schools. What activity was most beneficial? Wood claimed that "camping out is by far the best way of procuring a healthful summer rest," (p. 106).

92. "London," *The Lancet*, 2 (1884): 978.

93. *Pennsylvania School Journal* 22 (1873): 130–31; U.S. Commissioner of Education, *Annual Report, 1870–1871* (Washington: Government Printing Office, 1871), 544.

94. Wood, *Brain-work and Overwork*, 74.

95. Edward. H. Clarke, *The Building of a Brain* (Boston: James Osgood & Co., 1874), 44–45.

96. *The American Educational Monthly* 11 (1874): 419.

97. Clarke, *The Building of a Brain*, 29.

98. U.S. Commissioner of Education, *Annual Report, 1870–1871* (Washington: Government Printing Office, 1871), 544.

99. U.S. Commissioner of Education, *Annual Report, 1870–1871* (Washington: Government Printing Office, 1871), 544. See also *The American Educational Monthly* 7 (1870): 72.

100. *Pennsylvania School Journal* 22 (1873): 130–31.

101. *Massachusetts Teacher* 10 (1857), 130; *Massachusetts Teacher* 9 (1856), 553. See also *Massachusetts Teacher* 25 (1872), 332 for an especially biting criticism of the over-taxation theory.

102. *Pennsylvania School Journal* 15 (1866): 206. His plea received no immediate gratification. Pennsylvania increased its minimum to five months in 1872, where it remained until at least after 1880. (Department of Superintendence, *Addresses and Proceedings of the National Education Association* appendix B, 19 (1880), 106.

103. *Massachusetts Teacher* 14 (1861): 309.

104. *Pennsylvania School Journal* 31 (1882): 37.

105. *Massachusetts Teacher* 14 (1861): 309–10.

106. *Pennsylvania School Journal* 31 (1882): 37.

107. *Massachusetts Teacher* 14 (1861): 309–10.

108. *The American Educational Monthly* 2 (1865): 43.

109. *The American Educational Monthly* 2 (1865): 245.

110. New York Superintendent of Public Instruction, *Annual Report* 8 (1861), 14.

111. New York Superintendent of Public Instruction, *Annual Report* 23 (1876), 419.

112. *Massachusetts Teacher* 9 (1856): 470.

113. *Pennsylvania School Journal* 7 (1858): 14; *Pennsylvania School Journal* 15 (1866–67), 206. Teachers themselves reflected on the professional difficulties in being hired by term. See A. H. Nelson's recollections of his first teaching stint for a winter term in Maine in 1858–59 in "The Little Red Schoolhouse," *Educational Review* 23 (May 1902): 304–15.

114. Michigan Superintendent of Public Instruction, *Annual Report* 37 (1873), 194.

115. *Pennsylvania School Journal* 7 (1858): 14.

116. *Massachusetts Teacher* 23 (1870): 296.

117. *Pennsylvania School Journal* 8 (1859): 344; *Pennsylvania School Journal* 19 (1870): 6.

118. *The American Educational Monthly* 4 (1867): 320.

119. *The American Educational Monthly* 2 (1865): 246; *The American Educational Monthly* 5, (1868): 328.

120. *The American Educational Monthly* 2 (1865): 43, 245.

121. *The American Educational Monthly* 3 (1866): 311.

122. *The American Educational Monthly* 3 (1866): 311.

123. *The American Educational Monthly* 2 (1865): 245.

124. *The American Educational Monthly* 2 (1865): 246.

125. *Massachusetts Teacher* 6 (1853): 161.

126. For an excellent discussion of this "cult of domesticity," see Nancy F. Cott, *The Bonds of Womanhood: "Woman's Sphere" in New England, 1780–1835* (New Haven: Yale University Press, 1977).

127. Henry G. Schneider, "The Summer School and the Teacher," *Education* 17 (December 1896): 230–31.

128. *The American Educational Monthly* 1 (1864): 211.

129. Schneider, "The Summer School and the Teacher," 230–31.

130. *Massachusetts Teacher* 6 (1853): 162–63.

131. *Massachusetts Teacher* 10 (1857): 400.

132. *Pennsylvania School Journal* 35 (1886): 64.

133. *Massachusetts Teacher* 10 (1857): 400.

134. *Massachusetts Teacher* 10 (1857): 400.

135. *Pennsylvania School Journal* 7 (1858): 14.

136. *Massachusetts Teacher* 6 (1853): 166.

137. *The American Educational Monthly* 3 (1866): 272–73.

138. *Massachusetts Teacher* 6 (1853): 163–64.

139. *Massachusetts Teacher* 6 (1853): 166.

140. *Massachusetts Teacher* 14 (1861): 310; *Massachusetts Teacher 16* (1863): 287.

141. *Massachusetts Teacher* 23 (1870): 297.

142. Schneider, "The Summer School and the Teacher," 230–31.

143. One perennial scholarly question—whether time cycles are internalized in most organisms (called circadian rhythm) or are driven from outside cosmic sources (called celestial rhythm)—grapples with the biological and physical elements of time. Anthony Aveni, *Empires of Time: Calendars, Clocks, and Cultures* (New York: Basic Books, 1989), 5, 23–25.

144. Aveni, *Empires of Time*, 85.

145. Edward Thompson, "Time, Work-Discipline, and Industrial Capitalism," *Past and Present* 38 (December 1967): 61; Aveni, *Empires of Time*, 84, 207.

146. Aveni, *Empires of Time*, 51.

147. David S. Landes, *Revolution in Time: Clocks and the Making of the Modern World* (Cambridge, Massachusetts: The Belknap Press, Harvard University Press, 1983), 189; Thompson, "Time, Work-Discipline, and Industrial Capitalism," 56; Aveni, *Empires of Time*, 6–7, 146.

148. Landes, *Revolution in Time*, 40.

149. Landes, *Revolution in Time*, 7. Landes' presentation of causality is not one-sided. Although he sees the impact the clock had on western sense of time, he notes that "the clock did not create an interest in time measurement; the interest in time measurement led to the invention of the clock." This concern developed from several sources: the Catholic Church and monasteries in particular, courtly life, the new urban bourgeoisie, and burgeoning textile industries. See Landes, *Revolution in Time*, 58–73.

150. Thompson, "Time, Work-Discipline, and Industrial Capitalism," 66–84. Schools were a "universe of disciplined time" in the ways they demanded punctual attendance, adopted timed schedules, and relied on military style discipline of the master.

151. David Brody, "Time and Work During Early American Industrialism," *Labor History* 30 (Winter 1989): 19–22; Thompson, "Time, Work-Discipline, and Industrial Capitalism," 95. Thompson labels Puritanism as the "agent of conversion" to new valuations of time.

152. Brody, "Time and Work During Early American Industrialism," 36. Paul B Henley disputes the Thompson/Brody interpretation in "Time, Work, and Social Context in New England," *The New England Quarterly* 65 (December 1992): 531–59. Henley argues that the productive use of time was well established in Puritan economic and family life, and therefore underplays the importance of the factory in the development of time discipline. Even more recently, Mark M. Smith has argued that the slave South also developed a "modern clock consciousness" in which slaveholders imposed and slaves resisted time discipline. Mark M. Smith, "Old South Time in

Comparative Perspective," *American Historical Review* 101 (December 1996): 1432–69. Neither Henley's nor Smith's findings undermine the purpose here, since they contend that time discipline developed earlier than Brody suggested.

153. Brody, "Time and Work During Early American Industrialism," 39–46; Thompson, "Time, Work-Discipline, and Industrial Capitalism," 85; Landes, *Revolution in Time*, 74.

154. Brody, "Time and Work During Early American Industrialism," 45.

155. *The American Educational Monthly* 4 (1867): 320.

156. *Massachusetts Teacher* 16 (1863): 287.

157. *The American Educational Monthly* 6 (1869): 324; *The American Educational Monthly* 4 (1867): 320; *Massachusetts Teacher* 6 (1853): 163; *Pennsylvania School Journal* 9 (1860): 344.

158. Michigan Superintendent of Public Instruction, *Annual Report* 31 (1867), 19.

159. *The American Educational Monthly* 1 (1864): 225–26.

160. Massachusetts Board of Education, *Sixth Annual Report* (1842), 24.

161. Massachusetts Board of Education, *Sixth Annual Report* (1842), 24; Commissioners of Common Schools in Connecticut, *Second Annual Report of the Secretary to the Board* (1840), 25; Michigan Superintendent of Public Instruction, *Annual Report* 8 (1845), 26.

162. *The American Educational Monthly* 6 (1869): 324.

163. Massachusetts Board of Education, *Sixth Annual Report* (1842), 25.

164. *The American Educational Monthly* 1 (1864): 225.

165. *Pennsylvania School Journal* 8 (1859): 48.

166. "Vacations," *The American Educational Monthly* 2 (1865): 246.

167. Massachusetts Board of Education, *Sixth Annual Report* (1842), 25.

168. *The Massachusetts Teacher* 26 (1873): 333, 334.

169. Virginia Superintendent of Public Instruction, *Annual Report* 7 (1877), 9.

170. Aveni argues that these seasonal cycles, driven by societal life patterns, are not truly natural. Aveni, *Empires of Time*, 123.

171. Virginia Superintendent of Public Instruction, *Annual Report* 7 (1877), 8.

172. Michigan Superintendent of Public Instruction, *Annual Report* 41 (1877), 173.

173. Medical therapeutics and indeed the very professional identity of physicians transformed in the decades following the Civil War. See Warner, *The Therapeutic Perspective*.

174. U.S. Commissioner of Education, *Annual Report, 1891–1892* (Washington: Government Printing Office, 1894), 664–65. They were not able to halt the decline of the urban school term. The retraction slowed after the turn of the century but continued over the next four decades until the length reached the current standard of 180 days. In that same period of time, rural terms maintained their growth until they too arrived at the 180-day school year.

175. Educators began to speak of a more effective use of time—of the school day as well as the school year. In the nineteenth century, this meant incorporating elements other than book learning, particularly recreational or athletic activities. *American Annals of Education* 3 (September 1833): 433.

Chapter Four: "Mitigating Mental and Moral Stagnation"

1. The importance of the Progressive Era for public education is chronicled most prominently by Lawrence Cremin and David Tyack. William Reese has ably treated the vacation school's significance as a Progressive movement. Lawrence Cremin, *The Transformation of the School: Progressivism in American Education, 1876–1957* (New York: Alfred A. Knopf, 1961; Vintage Books, 1964); David Tyack, *The One Best System: A History of American Urban Education* (Cambridge, Massachusetts: Harvard University Press, 1974); William J. Reese, *Power and the Promise of School Reform: Grassroots Movements during the Progressive Era* (Boston: Routledge & Kegan Paul, 1986), 148–163.

2. One of Cremin's basic assumptions was that "progressive education began as Progressivism in education." Cremin, *The Transformation of the School*, viii.

3. Robert Wiebe, *The Search for Order, 1877–1920* (New York: Hill and Wang, 1967); Tyack, *The One Best System*, 3–6.

4. Peter Filene launched this revision of the historiography on progressivism in 1970 and set off a contentious debate over the very existence of a singular movement. More recently, the backlash against its place in the periodization of American history has subsided. Richard L McCormick has argued persuasively that "we cannot avoid the concept of progressivism—or even a progressive movement—because, particularly after 1910, the terms were deeply embedded in the language of reformers and because they considered the words meaningful." Such usage and understanding of the term was certainly the case with vacation schools advocates and officials. Indeed, the report that "nearly every progressive city in the United States now opens its schools for about six weeks each summer" was quite typical in education journals. Peter Filene, "An Obituary for the 'Progressive Movement'," *American Quarterly* 22 (Spring 1970): 20–34; Richard L. McCormick, *The Party Period and Public Policy: American Politics from the Age of Jackson to the Progressive Era* (Oxford: Oxford University Press, 1986), 268. See also John D. Buenker, "The Progressive Era: A Search for a Synthesis," *Mid-America* 51 (1969): 175–93; John D. Buenker, John C. Burnham, and Robert M. Crunden, *Progressivism* (Cambridge, Massachusetts: Schenkman Pub. Co., 1977); and Richard L. McCormick, *From Realignment to Reform: Political Change in New York State, 1893–1910* (Ithaca: Cornell University Press, 1981). Historians of education have participated in this interpretive revision through a number of fine monographs tracing pluralistic school politics in individual cities. See for example, Paul Peterson, *The Politics of School Reform, 1870–1940* (Chicago: University of Chicago Press, 1985); Julia Wrigley, *Class Politics and Public Schools, Chicago, 1900–1950* (New Brunswick: Rutgers University Press, 1982); Ronald Cohen, *Children of the Mill: Schooling and Society in Gary, Indiana, 1906–1960* (Bloomington, Indiana: Indiana University Press, 1990); Jeffrey Mirel, *The Rise and Fall of an Urban School System: Detroit, 1907–1981* (Ann Arbor: The University of Michigan Press, 1993); Reese, *Power and the Promise of School Reform*.

5. McCormick, *The Party Period and Public Policy*, 275.

6. Daniel T. Rodgers, "In Search of Progressivism," *Reviews in American History* 10 (December 1982), 115–16.

7. Rodgers, "In Search of Progressivism," 114–17.

8. U.S. Bureau of the Census, *Abstract of the Fifteenth Census of the United States, 1930* (Washington: Government Printing Office, 1933), 22–23.

9. U.S. Bureau of the Census, *Abstract of the Twelfth Census of the United States, 1900,* 3d ed. (Washington: Government Printing Office, 1904), 100–102.

10. Zane L. Miller and Patricia McLain, *The Urbanization of Modern America,* 2d ed. (San Diego: Harcourt Brace Jovanovich, 1987), 25–96; Howard P. Chudacoff and Judith E. Smith, *The Evolution of American Urban Society,* 5th ed. (Upper Saddle River, N.J.: Prentice Hall, 2000), 86–115; David R. Goldfeld and Blaine A. Brownell, *Urban America: A History,* 2d ed. (Boston: Houghton Mifflin, 1990), 178–236.

11. Goldfeld and Brownell, *Urban America: A History,* 1–9, 178–84.

12. Gunther Barth, *City People: The Rise of Modern City Culture in Nineteenth-Century America* (New York: Oxford University Press, 1980). While Barth argues that modern city culture was egalitarian at the core, Alan Trachtenberg suggests that many of these same cultural forms exemplify a new cultural hegemony of business elites that helped consolidate their economic and political victories. Francis Couvares' study of industrialization in Pittsburgh traces the development of a mass culture that both empowers and co-opts the working class. See Alan Trachtenberg, *The Incorporation of America: Culture and Society in the Gilded Age* (New York: Hill and Wang, 1982); Francis G. Couvares, *The Remaking of Pittsburgh: Class and Culture in an Industrializing City, 1877–1919* (Albany: State University of New York Press, 1984).

13. Jon Teaford, *The Twentieth-Century American City: Problem, Promise, and Reality* (Baltimore: Johns Hopkins University Press, 1986).

14. The characterization of social reform as motivated by concerns for control or justice has been long contended by historians. Thomas Haskell's essay and David Brion Davis' response in the *American Historical Review* get at the heart of this debate. See Thomas Haskell, "Capitalism and the Origins of Humanitarian Sensibility," *American Historical Review* 90 (1985): 339–61, 547–66 and David Brion Davis et al., "Forum on Capitalism, Hegemony, and Humanitarianism," *American Historical Review* 92 (1987): 797–878. For a useful treatment of this issue in the Progressive Era, see Arthur S. Link and Richard L. McCormick. *Progressivism* (Arlington Heights, Illinois: Harlan Davidson, Inc., 1983), 67–104.

15. As Stanley Schultz has argued, ideas about improving the physical environment of cities mostly stemmed from a desire to rectify the moral nature of human beings. Stanley K. Schultz, *Constructing Urban Culture: American Cities and City Planning, 1800–1920* (Philadelphia: Temple University Press, 1988). David Scobey also considers social reform through urban design movements in David Scobey, "Empire City: Politics, Culture, and Urbanism in Gilded-Age New York City" (Ph.D. diss., Yale, 1989). For an excellent treatment of the charity organizations of that time, see Paul Boyer, *Urban Masses and Moral Order in America, 1820–1929* (Cambridge, Massachusetts; Harvard University Press, 1978).

16. Goldfeld and Brownell, *Urban America: A History,* 236–83. The historiographic debate of the last twenty-five years over the adequacy of the term "progressive" will not be addressed here. Clearly as a catchall phrase it has its limits. For example, Howard Chudacoff distinguishes between civic and social reform, while Daniel Rodgers identifies three distinct languages of reform. Still, the vast differences in the reforms and reformers of this era notwithstanding, the myriad of reform impulses all stemmed from the industrial transformation of America. See Filene, "An Obituary for the 'Progressive Movement,'" 20–34; Rodgers, "In Search of Progressivism," 113–32; Chudacoff and Smith, *The Evolution of American Urban Society,* 183–205.

17. Cremin, *The Transformation of the School*, 11–12, 90–126; Barbara Beatty, *Preschool Education in America: The Culture of Young Children from the Colonial Era to the Present* (New Haven: Yale University Press, 1995), 9–12, 75–76, 116–117; Clarence J. Karier, *Scientists of the Mind: Intellectual Founders of Modern Psychology* (Urbana, IL: University of Illinois Press, 1986), 6–7; Clarence J. Karier, *The Individual, Society, and Education: A History of American Educational Ideas* 2d ed. (Urbana, IL: University of Illinois Press, 1986), 150–182.

18. Called the "aristocracy of character" by David Tyack, these mostly white, native born, Protestant, middle-aged men served, on boards of education, as superintendents, and in other administrative positions. As "managers of virtue," they shared the typical assumptions of other nineteenth-century urban reformers. Their visions of social welfare and control survived the twentieth-century transformation of educational professionals into experts through training. David Tyack, "Pilgrims Progress: Toward a Social History of the School Superintendency 1860–1960," in *The Social History of American Education*, eds. Edward McClellan and William Reese (Urbana, Ill.: University of Illinois Press, 1988); David Tyack and Elisabeth Hansot *Managers of Virtue: Public School Leadership in America, 1820–1980* (New York: Basic Books, 1982), 5–7.

19. Henry S. Curtis, "Vacation Schools, Playgrounds, and Settlements," *Report of the US. Commissioner of Education of 1903* (Washington: Government Printing Office, 1905) vol. I, 3.

20. Francis L. Cardozo Jr., "Vacation Schools" *Education* 22 (November 1901): 141–150. Providence School Committee, *Annual Report* (1873), 66; Sadie American, "Vacation Schools and Their Function," *Kindergarten Magazine* VIII (June 1896): 701. At the lowest part of the labor force, mobility for work not leisure was quite typical. Tramping too, became a common, if not romanticized way of life—especially during economic downturns. Summer vacations for the working class only became more common in the 1920s and 1930s. Eric H. Monkkonen, ed., *Walking to Work: Tramps in America, 1790–1935* (Lincoln: University of Nebraska Press, 1984); Cindy S. Aron, *Working at Play: A History of Vacations in the United States* (New York: Oxford University Press, 1999), 67–68.

21. T. P. Bailey, "Vacation Schools" *Journal of Education* 71 (12 May 1910), 522; Sadie American, "Vacation Schools and Their Function," 702; "Vacation Viewed as an Interruption," *Elementary School Teacher* XI (September 1910) 38.

22. Curtis, "Vacation Schools, Playgrounds, and Settlements," 3.

23. Sadie American, "Vacation Schools and Their Function," 702.

24. Clarence Arthur Perry, *Wider Use of the School Plant* (New York City: Russell Sage Foundation, 1910), 117–18.

25. Curtis, "Vacation Schools, Playgrounds, and Settlements," 3.

26. Perry, *Wider Use of the School Plant*, 121.

27. Perry, *Wider Use of the School Plant*, 117–18.

28. C. J. Walter, "Continuation Classes," *Journal of Education* 78 (28 August 1913): 177.

29. Curtis, "Vacation Schools, Playgrounds, and Settlements," 4.

30. See also Sadie American, "Vacation Schools and Their Function," 702; Perry, *Wider Use of the School Plant*, 117–18; Nina C. Vandewalker, "The Social Settlement Vacation School," *Kindergarten Magazine* X (1897–98): 75–76.

31. Joseph Lee, "Preventive Work," *Charities Review* 10 (February 1901): 587.

32. Cardozo Jr., "Vacation Schools," 141.

33. Sadie American, "Vacation Schools and Their Function," 703; Sadie American, "The Movement for Vacation Schools," *American Journal of Sociology* 4 (November 1898): 310.

34. Cardozo Jr., "Vacation Schools," 141–50.

35. *New York Times*, September 17, 1898.

36. Lee, "Preventive Work," 592. For a similar claim, see Cardozo Jr., "Vacation Schools," 141.

37. Samuel T. Dutton and David Snedden, *Administration of Public Education in the United States,* 3d ed. (New York: Charles Macmillan Company, 1924), 701. For other references to and discussions of the need for vacation schools to improve urban conditions, see "Idea of Vacation Schools," *Charities* 9 (6 September 1902): 220; I.S. Blackwelder, "Report of the Chicago Vacation School," *Elementary School Teacher* V (March 1905): 432; Gertrude Blackwelder, "Chicago Vacation Schools," *Elementary School Teacher* VI (December 1905): 211–14; C. J. Walter, "Continuation Classes," *Journal of Education* 78 (28 August 1913): 179; Richard Waterman Jr., "Vacation Schools," *Addresses and Proceedings of the National Education Association* 37 (1898), 404.

38. "Editorial," *Education* 21 (May 1901): 569.

39. Perry, *Wider Use of the School Plant,* 365.

40. Curtis, "Vacation Schools, Playgrounds, and Settlements," 2.

41. Evangeline Whitney, "Vacation Schools, Playgrounds, and Recreation Centers," *Addresses and Proceedings of the National Education Association* 43 (1904), 298.

42. Beatty, *Preschool Education in America,* 11–13.

43. Curtis, "Vacation Schools, Playgrounds, and Settlements," 2–3.

44. For a discussion of class and urban public parks, see Roy Rosenzweig and Elizabeth Blackmar, *The Park and the People: A History of Central Park* (Ithaca: Cornell University Press, 1992); and David Schuyler, *The New Urban Landscape: The Redefinition of City Form in Nineteenth Century America* (Baltimore: Johns Hopkins University Press, 1986); as well as Schuyler's *Creating Central Park, 1857–1861* (Baltimore: Johns Hopkins University Press, 1982).

45. American, "The Movement for Vacation Schools," 309.

46. For a discussion of how this ideology—that the city was a harmful place to learn and the country was a natural learning environment—shaped curricular developments in schools, see Herbert Kliebard, *The Struggle for the American Curriculum, 1893–1958* (Boston: Routledge & Kegan Paul, 1986), 54–55. Kliebard shows how the beliefs of G Stanley Hall, among others, were infused with this romantic notion of nature.

47. Caroline M. Hill, "Extension of the Vacation School Idea," *Elementary School Teacher* V (January 1905): 301.

48. American, "The Movement for Vacation Schools," 309.

49. "Recreation Plus Education: Vacation Schools in New York," *Municipal Affairs* 2 (September 1898): 438.

50. Hill, "Extension of the Vacation School Idea," 299.

51. New York City Department of Education, *Fifth Annual Report of the City Superintendent of Schools* (1902–03), 174. Clarence Arthur Perry wrote of this experience in *Wider Use of the School Plant,* 118.

52. Helen C. Putnam, "Vacation Schools and Playgrounds in Providence, R.I.," *Report of the U.S. Commissioner of Education of 1899–1900* (Washington: Government Printing Office, 1900) vol. I, 901. For additional citations on nature study, see I. S. Blackwelder, "Report of the Chicago Vacation School," 432; and Lee, "Preventive Work," 592.

53. Detroit Board of Education, *Annual Report* 62 (1904–05), 85.

54. "Recreation Plus Education: Vacation Schools in New York," 438.

55. NYC Department of Education, *Fourth Annual Report* (1901–02), 156.

56. American, "Vacation Schools and Their Function," 704.

57. New York State Education Department, *Annual Report* 6 (1910), 30. See also Waterman Jr., "Vacation Schools," 406.

58. Charles Mulford Robinson, "Vacation Schools," *Educational Review* 17 (March 1899): 250.

59. "Vacation School in Los Angeles," *Journal of Education* 77 (3 April 1913): 373.

60. Cardozo Jr., "Vacation Schools," 147, 150.

61. Robinson, "Vacation Schools," 258.

62. Vandewalker, "The Social Settlement Vacation School," 77–78

63. Waterman Jr., "Vacation Schools," 407–8. Like many vacation school programs, the Clean City League served multiple purposes by encouraging both civic participation and sanitary habits.

64. Whitney, "Vacation Schools, Playgrounds, and Recreation Centers," 305.

65. Developed in Sweden, sloyd was a system of manual training that employed wood carving and joinery (cabinetmaking) to prepare students in the use of tools.

66. NYC Department of Education, *Eleventh Annual Report* (1908–09), 554.

67. "Editorial," 569.

68. NYC Department of Education, *Fourth Annual Report* (1901–02), 159.

69. New York City Department of Education for Manhattan and the Bronx, *Report on Vacation Schools and Playgrounds* (1899), 38–40.

70. See Martin Sklar, *Corporate Reconstruction of American Capitalism, 1890–1916: The Market, the Law, and Politics* (Cambridge: Cambridge University Press, 1988).

71. NYC Department of Education, *Fourth Annual Report* (1901–02), 156.

72. J. H. Beveridge, "Vacation-Club Work," *Addresses and Proceedings of the National Education Association* 54 (1916), 1061.

73. "Editorial," 569.

74. "Recreation Plus Education: Vacation Schools in New York," 433.

75. NYC Department of Education for Manhattan and the Bronx. *Report on Vacation Schools and Playgrounds* (1899), 6.

76. Hill, "Extension of the Vacation School Idea," 300; "Vacation Viewed as an Interruption," 36.

77. Providence School Committee, *Annual Report* (1875), 25–29; "Lengthening the School Year," *Elementary School Teacher* 14 (May 1914): 409.

78. Newark Board of Education, *Annual Report* 30 (1886), 82; *Annual Report* 32 (1888), 66. See also *Annual Report* 31 (1887), 58; and *Annual Report* 33 (1889), 82.

79. *New York Times*, January 5, 1901; February 4, 1902; February 6, 1902.

80. Providence School Committee, *Annual Report* (1875), 25–29.

81. *New York Times*, January 5, 1901; February 4, 1902; February 6, 1902; John R. Kirk, "Against Long Vacations," *Journal of Education* 74 (28 September 1911), 314.

82. Kirk, "Against Long Vacations," 314; Aron, *Working at Play*, 6–9.

83. Lee, "Preventive Work," 592–93.

84. American, "Vacation Schools and Their Function," 703.

85. Perry, *Wider Use of the School Plant*, 144.

86. "Vacation Viewed as an Interruption," 37.

87. Newark Board of Education, *Annual Report* 50 (1906), 97.

88. Walter, "Continuation Classes," 177.

89. W. H. Elson, "All-year School Plan in Cleveland," *Journal of Education* 73 (5 January 1911), 12.

90. J. H. Harris, "Vacation Schools," *Journal of Education* 78 (21 August 1913), 149.

91. Kirk, "Against Long Vacations," 315.

92. Karl L. Alexander and Doris R. Entwisle, "Summer Setback: Race, Poverty, School Composition, and Mathematics Achievement in the First Two Years of School," *American Sociological Review* 57 (February 1992): 72–84; Barbara Heyns, "Schooling and Cognitive Development: Is There a Season for Learning," *Child Development* 58 (October 1987): 1151–60.

93. Providence School Committee, *Annual Report* (1875), 13.

94. Cardozo Jr., "Vacation Schools," 147.

95. American, "The Movement for Vacation Schools," 312.

96. "Vacation Viewed as an Interruption," 36.

97. Walter, "Continuation Classes," 177. See also Perry, *Wider Use of the School Plant*, 140.

98. J. M. Greenwood, "Vacation Schools," *Independent* 54 (1902), 1793.

99. Providence School Committee, *Annual Report* (1873), 13.

100. U.S. Commissioner of Education, *Annual Report, 1891–92* (Washington: Government Printing Office, 1894), 664–65.

101. Herbert Kliebard, "Keeping Out of Nature's Way: The Rise and Fall of Child-Study as the Basis for Curriculum, 1880–1905," in *Forging the American Curriculum: Essays in Curriculum History and Theory* (New York: Routledge, Chapman and Hall, Inc., 1992), 51–65.

102. "Vacation Viewed as an Interruption," 37.

103. For example, one administrator offered the following plan to reform the school schedule: "School work can be much better done during these [morning] hours in the summer than in the present school hours of the winter months. Attendance is easier and buildings do not need to be heated. Where such a program is organized, it may be found necessary to change the school work so as to give more laboratory and shopwork during the summer session than in the winter and less of the ordinary bookwork.", "Lengthening the School Year," 409.

104. Dutton and Snedden, *Administration of Public Education*, 701; "The Waning School Term of the Cities," *Los Angeles School Journal* VII (5 November 1923): 15.

105. Cardozo Jr., "Vacation Schools," 147; "Idea of Vacation Schools," 220–24; Denver Board of Education, *Annual Report of School District One*, o.s. 28 (1901–02), 28. See also Robinson, "Vacation Schools," 250.

106. American, "Vacation Schools and Their Function," 704.

107. NYC Department of Education for Manhattan and the Bronx, *Report on Vacation Schools and Playgrounds* (1898), 20.

108. Diane Ravitch, *The Great School Wars: A History of the New York City Public Schools* (New York: Basic Books, 1974), 118.

109. California Superintendent of Public Instruction, *Biennial Report for the Years 1876 and 1877,* 7–8.

110. These differences were regularly noted by vacation school chroniclers. For example, Newark primarily conducted nature study for primary grade children; New York highlighted industrial education; Boston's schools remained recreational for several years; Chicago's adopted Deweyan philosophies. Waterman Jr., "Vacation Schools," 405–6.

111. Denver Board of Education, *Annual Report* 28 (1901–02), 29.

112. Compulsory attendance is rejected in "Idea of Vacation Schools," 224.

113. Greenwood, "Vacation Schools," 1792.

114. Blackwelder, "Report of the Chicago Vacation School," 432.

115. "Idea of Vacation Schools," 224.

116. Vandewalker, "The Social Settlement Vacation School," 77.

117. Denver Board of Education, *Annual Report* 28 (1901–02), 29.

118. Putnam, "Vacation Schools and Playgrounds in Providence, R.I.," 902.

119. "Idea of Vacation Schools," 221.

120. Greenwood, "Vacation Schools," 1792.

121. Dutton and Snedden, *Administration of Public Education,* 701.

122. Cardozo Jr., "Vacation Schools," 144, 146. Cardozo did believe in some relation to the regular schoolwork, but in a thematic, not an organizational sense.

123. Association for Improving the Condition of the Poor, *Fifty-Second Annual Report, 1896,* 75.

124. Perry, *Wider Use of the School Plant,* 140; Greenwood, "Vacation Schools," 1793.

125. Greenwood, "Vacation Schools," 1793.

126. Cuban's research has suggested that despite the pervasiveness of Progressive rhetoric and ideology, teaching methods have changed very little over the last 100 years. The majority of teachers continued to employ traditional, teacher-centered, mimetic classroom practices and only incorporated more open, child-centered methods in ways that diffused their transformative potential. Larry Cuban, *How Teachers Taught: Constancy and Change in American Classrooms 1890–1990,* 2d ed. (New York: Teachers College Press, 1993).

127. "Idea of Vacation Schools," 220.

128. Cremin, *The Transformation of the School,* viii–ix.

129. Cremin, *The Transformation of the School,* 88; David Tyack, *The One Best System,* 3–6.

130. Rodgers, "In Search of Progressivism," 123. Rodgers jettisons the notion of uniform and coherent Progressive ideology. Instead, he posits that there were three distinct social languages from which Progressives borrowed: a language of anti-monopolism, of social bonds and social nature, and of social efficiency. These tropes were not inherently linked, and the origins and peak of each language varied.

131. Rodgers, "In Search of Progressivism," 126.

132. Superintendent of the City of Lynn, Massachusetts, *Annual Report* (1914), 13.

133. Clarence Arthur Perry, *Wider Use of the School Plant* (New York: Russell Sage Foundation, 1910).

134. Perry, *Wider Use of the School Plant,* 359, 365.

135. U.S. Commissioner of Education, "Wider Use of the School Plant," *Annual Report, 1910–1911* (Washington: Government Printing Office, 1912), 151–54; Curtis, "Vacation Schools, Playgrounds, and Settlements," 2–4; Dutton and Snedden, *Administration of Public Education,* 701; Reese, *Power and the Promise of School Reform,* 148–176. An earlier edition of Dutton and Snedden's classic work discussed vacation schools in a chapter titled "The Widening Sphere of Public Education." More recently, Reese's monograph contained a chapter entitled "Vacation Schools, Playgrounds, and Educational Extension."

136. Kirk, "Against Long Vacations," 315. See also Walter, "Continuation Classes," 179.

137. Cleveland Board of Education, *Annual Report of the Public Schools* 67 (1902–03), 19; New York City Department of Education, *Sixth Annual Report of the City Superintendent of Schools* (1903–04), 145.

138. Waterman Jr., "Vacation Schools," 404.

139. Baltimore's totals do not include summer or evening schools, Richmond's includes the former. Baltimore Board of School Commissioners, *Annual Report to the Mayor and City Council of Baltimore,* 83 (1911–12), 8; Richmond Superintendent of the Public Schools, *Annual Report* 55 (1923–24), 41.

140. Dutton and Snedden, *Administration of Public Education,* 701.

141. Both provided organized play outdoors in the schoolyard, although most vacation schools involved additional elements. Lee, "Preventive Work," 587.

142. Pittsburgh Playground Association, *Annual Report* 14 (1909), 16; *Annual Report* 16 (1911), 12. In fact, the Pittsburgh Playground Association continued to run its own vacation schools several years after the Board of Education launched its own schools in 1911.

143. Cincinnati Public Schools, *Annual Report* 81 (1909–10), 66.

144. Charles W. Odell, "Summer Work in Public Schools," *University of Illinois Bulletin no. 49* xxvii (22 April 1930), 12–13. William Wirt was the innovative Bluffton superintendent who moved on to greater fame in educational circles as superintendent of schools in Gary, Indiana, and achieved notoriety when his "Gary Plan" was dabbled with in New York. Ravitch, *The Great School Wars,* 203–18.

145. Hebb, "All-Year Schools Have Many Advantages," 198.

146. J. W. Kennedy, "The All-Year School." *Addresses and Proceedings of the National Education Association* (Washington: National Education Association, 1917), 796.

147. Elson, "All-year School Plan in Cleveland," 12. W. E. Chancellor, also a school superintendent, makes a similar link between vacation and year-round schools in "Forty-eight Week's School Year," *Journal of Education* 73 (12 January 1911): 35–36.

148. Perry, *Wider Use of the School Plant,* 142.

149. Cleveland Board of Education, *Annual Report of the Public Schools* 72 (1907–08), 64–65. For more on the educational and economic value of summer academic classes, see volumes 73 and 68.

150. Massachusetts Board of Education, *Eighty-Seventh Annual Report* (1923–24), 22.

151. Pittsburgh Board of Public Education, *Annual Report* 2 (1913), 102; Walter, "Continuation Classes," 177.

152. Thorton S. Alexander, *Vacation Schools* (Cambridge: The Cooperative Press, 1901), 3.

153. "Lengthening the School Year," 408–9.

154. See, for example, J. Leroy Thompson, "Is This Education?" *American School Board Journal* 98 (June 1939): 43–45; C. R. Murphy, "How One City Conducts a Summer School Without Public Expense," *American School Board Journal* 84 (1932): 51.

155. "Idea of Vacation Schools," 222.

Chapter Five: "Keeping up with Superintendent Jones"

1. Henry S. Curtis, "Vacation Schools, Playgrounds, and Settlements," *Report of the U.S. Commissioner of Education of 1903* (Washington: Government Printing Office, 1905) vol. I, 4. For another example of such optimism, see Samuel T. Dutton and David Snedden, *Administration of Public Education in the United States*, 3d ed. (New York: Charles Macmillan Company, 1924), 701.

2. In 1894, vacation schools already existed in Boston and Newark. See Appendix for the source of information for each city, as well as a more comprehensive breakdown of the origins of vacation schools in each municipality.

3. Sadie American, "The Movement for Vacation Schools," *American Journal of Sociology* 4 (November 1898): 311.

4. As William Reese has observed, "This change has generally been ignored by historians, who have treated vacation schools as a static institution." Reese's own work, of course, brought attention to this oversight, but his focus is on the grassroots origins of vacation schools, not the process of becoming a public entity. William J. Reese, *Power and the Promise of School Reform: Grassroots Movements During the Progressive Era* (Boston: Routledge & Kegan Paul, 1986), 161. Public schools, of course, have remade many school innovations. For a general discussion of this pattern, see David Tyack and Larry Cuban, *Tinkering Toward Utopia: A Century of Public School Reform*, (Cambridge, Massachusetts: Harvard University Press, 1995), 60–84.

5. See, for example, the recommendation of Nathaniel H.R. Dawson in U.S Commissioner of Education, *Annual Report, 1887–1888* (Washington: Government Printing Office, 1890), 213–14, and that of the Superintendent of Public Instruction for Cambridge, Massachusetts, *School Committee Report* (1872), 27.

6. Boston School Committee, *Proceedings* (1878), 33, 38–39, 130.

7. Already by the first decade of the twentieth century, the exact origins of vacation schools were blurred in the writings of their chroniclers. For contemporary accounts, see Curtis, "Vacation Schools, Playgrounds, and Settlements," 3–11; Lee, "Preventive Work," 586–92; American, "The Movement for Vacation Schools," 309–325; Robinson, "Vacation Schools," 250–60; K. A. Jones, "Vacation Schools in the United States," *Review of Reviews* 17 (June 1898): 710–16.

8. Providence School Committee, *Annual Report* (1870), 10–11, 33–34.

9. Providence School Committee, *Annual Report* (1876), 175.

10. Rhode Island Board of Education and Committee of Public Schools, *Annual Reports* 33 (1877), 173; Edward Martin Stone, *A Century of Education: Being a Concise History of the Rise and Progress of the Public Schools of the City of Providence* (Providence: Providence Press Co., 1876), 74.

11. Providence School Committee, *Annual Report* (1875), 6.

12. Providence School Committee, *Annual Report* (1873), 20–21.

13. Providence School Committee, *Annual Report* (1876), 44.

14. Providence School Committee, *Annual Report* (1876), 7.

15. Rhode Island Board of Education and Committee of Public Schools, *Annual Reports* 30 (1874), 164; Stone, *A Century of Education*, 74; Providence School Committee, *Annual Report* (1873), 20–21; (1875), 13.

16. Providence School Committee, *Annual Report* (1879), 3–4, 7. The *Annual Report* did note that 1878 presented Providence's schools with grave difficulties. Faced with the impact of depression on local businesses and several outbreaks of illness among children, Providence most likely closed the summer schools in the wake of declining revenues. A later annual report, in a history of Providence's summer schools, notes that in 1878, the vacation schools were "discontinued for lack of funds." Providence School Committee, *Annual Report* (1900), 145.

17. Newark Board of Education, *Annual Report* 30 (1886), 79–83; *Annual Report* 38 (1894), 95–96; *Annual Report* 45 (1901), 135–36; *Annual Report* 51 (1907), 287–89; *Annual Report* 59 (1914–15), 72–79.

18. Newark Board of Education, *Annual Report* 29 (1885), 83; *Annual Report* 35 (1891), 83.

19. Newark Board of Education, *Annual Report* 29 (1885), 82–83.

20. Newark Board of Education, *Annual Report* 29 (1885), 82–83; *Annual Report* 30 (1886), 79–83. With an initial appropriation of $1,300, subsequent expenditures reached $54,154 in 1914 but still constituted a tiny portion of Newark's school money.

21. Providence School Committee, *Annual Report* (1879), 87; *Annual Report* (1873), 20–21; *Annual Report* (1878), 39–40.

22. Newark Board of Education, *Annual Report* 29 (1885), 83.

23. Providence School Committee, *Annual Report* (1875), 6.

24. Newark Board of Education, *Annual Report* 34 (1890), 90; *Annual Report* 35 (1891), 84; *Annual Report* 39 (1895), 100. Barringer derided those who claimed it was "a great crime to attend school [during the summer]."

25. U.S. Bureau of Education, *Bulletin of 1919*, no. 91 (Washington: Government Printing Office, 1920).

26. These figures may appear unimpressive when considering the total number of municipalities and students in the United States in those years, but they expanded enough to carve a real niche in public school systems. The 447 urban communities (using the U.S. Census definition of population greater than 2,500) with vacation schools in 1927 constituted nearly 16% of the 2,855 city school systems existing nationwide. Admittedly, summer programs contained far smaller percentages of students enrolled, teachers employed, and resources consumed. Even at their peak, vacation classes never even accounted for 1% of the total expenditures of urban public school systems, and the number of students and teachers each totaled almost 4% of the regular school figures. Yet as the cases of Providence and Newark demonstrate, these percentages were typically much higher in individual cities. In addition, the aggregate figures are more likely to be underestimated rather than overestimated. First, some districts remained negligent in reporting data to the state superintendency. Second, these data are for official urban areas (towns or cities over 2,500), but some smaller units had clearly experimented with them by then. U.S. Bureau of Education, *Biennial Survey, 1926–1928* (Washington: Government Printing Office, 1930), 504–6.

27. U.S. Bureau of Education, *Biennial Survey, 1926–1928*, 561–574; U.S. Bureau of the Census, *Abstract of the Fifteenth Census of the United States, 1930* (Washington: Government Printing Office, 1933), 22–33.

28. For example, the figures in Table 5.3 imply that in each year presented, one or two cities with over 500,000 inhabitants did not run vacation schools. The actual cities lacking them differed in each year—demonstrating the impermanence of vacation schools in specific locales. St. Louis had not yet initiated vacation schools in 1900. Baltimore and Philadelphia had halted their vacation schools by 1912. Philadelphia remained without vacation schools in 1921, and by 1927 San Francisco had discontinued its late starting program.

29. Viewed another way, vacation schools were overrepresented in the Northeast and underrepresented in all three of the other regions. In 1912, the Northeast contained 42% of the nation's cities and towns with over 25,000 people and 49% of the vacation schools in towns of that size. The comparable 1912 figures for the Midwest were 30% to 29%, for the South, 20% to 18%, and for the West, 8% to 4%. The figures for vacation schools in the Midwest and South were underrepresented in 1912, but only slightly so. In 1928, the South (cities–22%, vacation schools–18%), and West (cities–10%, vacation schools–8%) remained underrepresented, while the Northeast (cities–35%, vacation schools–38%) and the Midwest (cities–33%, vacation schools–36%) were overrepresented.

30. Denver School District One, *Annual Report* 28 (1901–02), 28. Newark's vacation schools had always included instruction in reading, writing, and mathematics, but the work was very light and not for academic credit. In 1901, the summer schools targeted backward students, but the following year the Newark program reemphasized manual training. Academic credit was finally offered in 1910. Newark Board of Education, *Annual Report*, 29 (1885), 3; 41 (1897), 60–62; 45 (1901), 60; 46 (1902), 72; 48 (1904), 100; 54 (1910), 57.

31. This change in vacation school origins was observed by contemporaries. See for example Samuel T. Dutton and David Snedden, *Administration of Public Education in the United States*, 3d ed. (New York: Charles Macmillan Company, 1924), 701.

32. Clarence A. Perry, *American Vacation Schools of 1912*, pamphlet no. R133 (New York: Russell Sage Foundation, 1913). Perry's list does not distinguish between private and public vacation schools. Still, it is reasonable but not foolproof to claim that most of the vacation schools in the 141 towns uncovered by Perry were publicly run. On the other hand, many superintendents had always reported on their city's private vacation schools because they were typically held in public school buildings, and Perry's list definitely contains both types. Perry's survey results on the nature of the vacation school were quite clear. 114 vacation schools reported providing academic work in addition to manual work whereas only 26 reported handwork alone (one city did not report) based on a survey sent to 774 cities with 382 respondents.

33. "Summer Play Schools," *School and Society* 31 (21 June 1930): 833–834; "Summer Play Schools in New York City," *School and Society* 32 (6 September 1930): 316; Lucy Retting, "Summer Vacation, a Problem and a Privilege," *Progressive Education* 8 (May 1931): 379–87; R. I. Denny et al., "Accepting the Challenge," *Childhood Education* 8 (May 1932): 484–87.

34. U.S. Commissioner of Education, *Annual Report, 1913–1914* (Washington: Government Printing Office, 1915), vol. 1, 92.

35. After 1917, the Bureau of Education did not provide that information again in its sections on summer education, suggesting that the sources of funding and types of students no longer varied. U.S. Commissioner of Education, *Annual Report, 1910–1911* (Washington: Government Printing Office, 1912), vol. 1, 150; W.S. Deffenbaugh, "Summer Sessions of City Schools," *U.S. Bureau of Education Bulletin 1917* (Washington: Government Printing Office, 1918).

36. Word of vacation school development passed through urban governments, education organizations, philanthropic circles, and other social networks. This phenomenon is explored through the cross-disciplinary subfield of diffusion analysis. Geographers, economists, and other social scientists have studied topics ranging from the spread of public policies to the adoption of new farm technology. Everett Rogers offers a definition that is most useful, treating diffusion as "the process by which an innovation is communicated through certain channels over time among members of a social system." Everett M. Rogers, *Diffusion of Innovations*, 3d ed. (New York: The Free Press, 1983). One of the earliest works is Gabrielle Tarde's *Laws of Imitation* (New York: Holt, 1903). Torsten Hagerstrand's *The Propagation of Innovation Waves* (Royal University of Lund: Department of Geography, 1952) ignited the research of the last forty years. Influential diffusion case studies include James Coleman, Elihu Katz, and Herbert Menzel. *Medical Innovation: A Diffusion Study* (Indianapolis: Bobbs-Merrill Company, Inc., 1966); J. C. Hudson, "Diffusion in a Central Place System," *Geographical Analysis* 1 (January 1969), 45–58; G. F. Pyle, "The Diffusion of Cholera in the United States in the Nineteenth Century," *Geographical Analysis* 1 (January 1969), 59–75; and Gudmund Hernes, "Structural Change in Social Processes," *American Journal of Sociology* 82 (November 1976), 513–47. For a critique of traditional models of diffusion, see Laurence A. Brown, *Innovation Diffusion: A New Perspective* (New York: Methuen & Co., 1981). G. Clark, *Innovation Diffusion: Contemporary Geographical Approaches*, Concepts and Techniques in Modern Geography, no. 40 (Norwich: Geo Books, 1984) and Richard Morrill, Gary L. Gaile and Grant Ian Thrall, *Spatial Diffusion* (Beverly Hills and London: Sage Publications, 1988) present diffusion from a geographic perspective. For a highly mathematical treatment, see Vijay Mahajan and Robert A. Peterson, *Models for Innovation Diffusion*, Quantitative Applications in the Social Sciences, eds. John L Sullivan and Richard G. Nieme (Beverly Hills and London: Sage Publications, 1985). The highly readable work of George W. Downs Jr., *Bureaucracy, Innovation, and Public Policy* (Lexington, Mass.: Lexington Books, DC Heath, 1976) isolates diffusion within the public domain. Erik Monkkonen's *Police in Urban America: 1860–1920* (Cambridge: Cambridge University Press, 1981) employed the techniques of diffusion analysis with great effect in his historical analysis of the origins of urban police bureaucracy. For a diffusion analysis of vacation schools, see Kenneth Gold, "'Mitigating Mental and Moral Stagnation': Summer Education and American Public Schools, 1840–1990" (Ph.D. diss., University of Michigan, 1997), 191–97.

37. Buffalo Superintendent of Education, *Annual Report* (1905–06), 26.

38. Reese's monograph used four medium-sized cities as his case studies: Kansas City, Milwaukee, Rochester, and Toledo. Reese, *Power and the Promise of School Reform*, 148–63.

39. David Hogan, *Class and Reform: School and Society in Chicago, 1880–1930* (Philadelphia: University of Pennsylvania Press, 1985); Julia Wrigley, *Class Politics and*

Public Schools: Chicago, 1900–1950 (New Brunswick: Rutgers University Press, 1982); Paul E. Peterson, *The Politics of School Reform, 1870–1940* (Chicago: University of Chicago Press, 1985); Marjorie Murphy, *Blackboard Unions: The AFT & the NEA, 1900–1980* (Ithaca: Cornell University Press, 1990); Richard J. Storr, *Harper's University, The Beginnings: A History of the University of Chicago* (Chicago: University of Chicago Press, 1966).

40. The Civic Federation was also known as the Associated Charities. It was started by Jane Addams and others in response to the depression of 1893 and was a key organization behind Progressive reform in Chicago. Chicago Woman's Club, "Report of the Chicago Permanent Vacation School and Playground Committee" (1899), 7–8; Chicago Board of Education, *Annual Report* 45 (1898–99), 146; American, "The Movement for Vacation Schools," 27–29, 320–21; I. S. Blackwelder, "Report of the Chicago Vacation School," *Elementary School Teacher* V (March 1905): 432; Katherine Camp Mayhew and Anna Camp Edwards, *The Dewey School: The Laboratory School of the University of Chicago, 1896–1903* (New York: D. Appleton-Century Company, 1936), 391–92; Hogan, *Class and Reform*, 31–40; Storr, *Harper's University*, 186–87. Mary McDowell, the head resident of the University Settlement and the organizer of the Seward Vacation School, did not remain active in the subsequent vacation schools. The Settlement House financed their school primarily through two donations by wealthy female benefactors, whereas the Civic Federation had relied on smaller subscriptions from a broader base.

41. Henriette Greenebaum Frank and Amalie Hofer Jerome, comps., *Annals of the Chicago Woman's Club for the First Forty Years of Its Organization* (Chicago: The Libby Company, Printers, 1916), 182, 207–9; Chicago Woman's Club, *The Twenty-First Annual Announcement, 1897–1898* (Chicago: Wm. C. Hollister & Bro., 1898), 30, 38.

42. American, "The Movement for Vacation Schools," 322; Chicago Board of Education, *Proceedings*, May 4, 1898, 424–25; June 15, 1898, 495.

43. Sadie American led both groups as the chairperson of the Permanent Committee and as president of the Vacation Board. She served through the summer of 1900. Membership in the Permanent Committee expanded as seventy-five local woman's clubs participated by 1902. The Vacation School Board's membership included educators affiliated with the Chicago Normal School, the University of Chicago, the Chicago Training School, and the Kindergarten Training School. Jane Addams of Hull House, and later Chicago Schools Superintendent Edwin Cooley also served on the board. The Woman's Club was also active in a host of other "child-saving" reforms. Blackwelder, "Report of the Chicago Vacation School," 432; Chicago Woman's Club, "Report of the Chicago Permanent Vacation School and Playground Committee" (1899), 8; (1900), 3; (1902), 7; (1905), 5. For a discussion of kindergartens, playgrounds, and other "child-saving" activities, see Hogan, *Class and Reform*, 51–95.

44. Although the Woman's Club remained the primary institution behind Chicago's vacation schools, other groups and individuals regularly requested and received permission to use a public school building for a vacation school. In 1898, Cyrus McCormick Jr. funded an additional program at the Hammond School while his sister and future benefactoress of Francis Parker, Mrs. Emmons Blaine, sponsored five programs not located in public school buildings. By 1900, several groups and individuals outside of the Chicago Woman's Club ran vacation schools, including the principal of the John Spry School, the Little Dear Child League, and the South Side Club. Like the

Woman's Clubs, all petitioners agreed to bear all the expenses incurred. Chicago Board of Education, *Proceedings*, June 15, 1898, 495; May 29, 1900, 453; June 27, 1900, 534; Jack K. Campbell, *Colonel Francis W. Parker: The Children's Crusader* (New York: Teachers College Press, 1967), 200–201.

45. As will be discussed shortly, the board of education made its first contribution in 1903 to help the Permanent Committee alleviate this financial crisis. Chicago Woman's Club, "Report of the Chicago Permanent Vacation School and Playground Committee" (1903), 6–7.

46. Chicago Woman's Club, "Report of the Chicago Permanent Vacation School and Playground Committee" (1905), 8. David Hogan has portrayed the business community ambivalence and opposition to several aspects of Progressive reform in Chicago. Hogan, *Class and Reform*, 43–44.

47. Chicago Board of Education, *Annual Report* 45 (1898–99), 145; American, "The Movement for Vacation Schools," 322–24.

48. Chicago Woman's Club, "Report of the Chicago Permanent Vacation School and Playground Committee" (1899), 32.

49. Chicago Board of Education, *Annual Report* 45 (1898–99), 207–8; Chicago Woman's Club, "Report of the Chicago Permanent Vacation School and Playground Committee" (1899), 13; (1900), 5; (1902), 12; (1903), 8; (1905), 9–10; Hogan, *Class and Reform*, 83–85. For Dewey's early conception of vocational education, see *The School and Society*, rev. ed. (Chicago: University of Chicago Press, 1915), 5–12, 17–20; Mayhew and Edward, *The Dewey School*, 262.

50. Chicago Woman's Club, "Report of the Chicago Permanent Vacation School and Playground Committee" (1900), 25; (1905), 19–20; (1906), 9–11; (1907), 37–38; Chicago Board of Education, *Annual Report* 45 (1898–99), 207–8.

51. While these data are atypical and valuable, one superintendent rightfully cautioned that the data "are of qualitative rather than quantitative value" because of discrepancies in reporting and in definition of nationality. With the figures that follow, it is most probable that nationality was defined as the birthplace of the parent. Chicago Woman's Club, "Report of the Chicago Permanent Vacation School and Playground Committee" (1900), 31.

52. Of course, this clustering was also a feature of the regular year schools. It is not clear whether vacation schools were more or less segregated. Given the fewer number of vacation schools, they might be less segregated, but on the other hand, school sites were selected with specific immigrant populations in mind.

53. Chicago Woman's Club, "Report of the Chicago Permanent Vacation School and Playground Committee" (1899), 31; (1902), 33; (1905), 31; (1906), 29; (1908), 43.

54. American, "The Movement for Vacation Schools," 324. The vacation schools also employed recent graduates of Parker's Chicago Normal School and other teacher training institutions as cadets to assist in the classroom.

55. Chicago Woman's Club, "Report of the Chicago Permanent Vacation School and Playground Committee" (1902), 12.

56. The number of teachers in the Woman's Club vacation schools increased from 70 in 1898 to 250 ten years later. American, "The Movement for Vacation Schools," 324; Chicago Board of Education, *Annual Report* 54 (1907–08), 280.

57. Chicago Woman's Club, "Report of the Chicago Permanent Vacation School and Playground Committee" (1902), 12–13, (1903), 16–17, (1908), 8. Another recom-

mendation for the selection of teachers came from Superintendent Bogan, who suggested choosing the vacation school faculty earlier in the year in order to avoid the poor choices that occurred at the last minute. The late date for the organization of the vacation schools was a general complaint of the superintendents.

58. Chicago Woman's Club, "Report of the Chicago Permanent Vacation School and Playground Committee" (1899), 9; (1906), 20.

59. Bogan reported favorably on the move, noting that the sewing work was "remarkably varied and successful," in an area which had previously earned some criticism for its work. Chicago Woman's Club, "Report of the Chicago Permanent Vacation School and Playground Committee" (1903), 8.

60. Chicago Woman's Club, "Report of the Chicago Permanent Vacation School and Playground Committee" (1900), 5; (1902), 12–13, 17; (1903), 8.

61. Chicago Woman's Club, "Report of the Chicago Permanent Vacation School and Playground Committee" (1899), 8–10; 1900, 4, 29; Blackwelder, "Report of the Chicago Vacation School," 432, 437; Frank and Jerome, *Annals of the Chicago Woman's Club,* 182.

62. Peterson, *The Politics of School Reform,* 57–60; Hogan, *Class and Reform,* 99–100.

63. Chicago Woman's Club, "Report of the Chicago Permanent Vacation School and Playground Committee" (1899), 8.

64. In 1900, over 500 registered visitors from 32 states and territories as well as Canada observed the Woman's Club vacation schools. Chicago Board of Education, *Proceedings,* May 4, 1898, 424–25; Chicago Woman's Club, "Report of the Chicago Permanent Vacation School and Playground Committee" 1900, 33.

65. Chicago Board of Education, *Proceedings,* December 27, 1899, 221–22; Chicago Woman's Club, "Report of the Chicago Permanent Vacation School and Playground Committee" (1899), 10; (1902), 7; Chicago Board of Education, *Annual Report* 45, (1898–99), 146; *Annual Report* 47 (1900–1901), 112; *Annual Report* 48 (1901–02), 79. Gertrude Blackwelder, "Chicago Vacation Schools" *Elementary School Teacher* VI (December 1905): 214; Jane Addams, *Twenty Years at Hull-House* ed. with and intro by Victoria Bissell Brown (Boston and New York: Bedford/St. Martin's, 1999), 169.

66. Chicago Woman's Club, "Report of the Chicago Permanent Vacation School and Playground Committee" 1899, 9–10; Chicago Board of Education, *Annual Report* 45 (1898–99), 146; Frank and Jerome, *Annals of the Chicago Woman's Club,* 209.

67. This refrain was a familiar one to Chicago's Progressive educators, as Francis Parker could well attest. Campbell, *Colonel Francis W. Parker,* 157–61, 177–87.

68. Chicago Board of Education, *Proceedings,* December 27, 1899, 221–22; January 23, 1901, 353; April 17, 1901, 560; Blackwelder, "Chicago Vacation Schools," 214; Chicago Woman's Club, "Report of the Chicago Permanent Vacation School and Playground Committee" 1900, 4.

69. The money raised equaled 12% of vacation school expenditures that summer. Chicago Board of Education, *Annual Report* 48 (1901–02), 79–80.

70. Although only discussed as "the Ghetto," the school which opened as a result of the board's financial intervention served a predominantly Jewish population. Vacation School Superintendent Frank Darling observed in 1902 that the demand for vacation schools at the predominantly Jewish Foster and Goldsmith schools was by far the highest in Chicago. In the final wording of the June 24 resolution, the word Ghetto

was stricken. Chicago Board of Education, *Proceedings*, June 10, 1903, 608; June 24, 1903, 613; Chicago Woman's Club, "Report of the Chicago Permanent Vacation School and Playground Committee" 1902, 9–10.

71. Chicago Board of Education, *Proceedings*, April 27, 1904, 649; May 11, 1904, 686–687; June 6, 1906, 858, 861; Chicago Board of Education, *Annual Report* 54 (1907–08), 281; *Annual Report* 56 (1909–10), 103; *Annual Report* 58 (1911–12), 128; "Chicago Permanent School Extension Report," 1909–1910, 18. After the transition was finally completed in 1909, the renamed Vacation School Committee remained involved with the vacation schools for several years but gradually moved into other areas of school extension. It redoubled its efforts in playground use and opened the schools for story telling and civic activities.

72. The Board also inserted this language to forestall legal stipulations prohibiting the outright donation of public money to a private venture. Chicago Board of Education, *Annual Report* 45 (1898–99), 146; Chicago Board of Education, *Proceedings*, June 10, 1903, 608.

73. Chicago Board of Education, *Proceedings*, June 8, 1904, 733.

74. His May 1905 motion to form two vacation school classes that prepared pupils who failed academic examinations was referred to a committee and never enacted. Chicago Board of Education, *Proceedings*, May 24, 1905, 712.

75. Chicago Woman's Club, "Report of the Chicago Permanent Vacation School and Playground Committee" 1903, 17; Chicago Board of Education, *Proceedings*, June 8, 1904, 733.

76. Chicago Board of Education, *Proceedings*, April 12, 1905, 590, 712, 715; Chicago Board of Education, *Annual Report* 54 (1907–08), 278, 280–81; *Annual Report* 60 (1913–14), 391; In fact, the board's 1908 contribution of $15,000 accounted for 65% of the total vacation school costs and 94% of the amount expended for teaching. Since board policy already prohibited the use of its money for non-certified teachers, in practical terms Shoop only pronounced a policy shift due to occur shortly anyway.

77. Chicago Board of Education, *Annual Report* 56, (1909–10), 104; *Annual Report* 58, (1911–12), 128.

78. Chicago Board of Education, *Annual Report* 58, (1911–12), 108, 128–29; *Annual Report* 59, (1912–13), 202; John T. McManis, *Ella Flagg Young: and a Half-Century of the Chicago Public Schools*, (Chicago: A. C. McClurg & Co., 1916), 180–81.

79. Chicago Board of Education, *Annual Report* 59 (1912–13), 202, 263; *Annual Report* 60, (1913–14), 393; *Annual Report* 62, (1915–16), 13; *Annual Report* 66 (1921–22), 13–14. Summer high schools also proved popular with students, despite the fact that they charged enrollment fees per class.

80. Chicago Board of Education, *Annual Report* 60, (1913–14), 392.

81. Shoop certainly knew how other cities had transformed their vacation school curricula and actually traveled to observe academic summer schools at least once prior to 1911. Chicago Board of Education, *Proceedings*, July 14, 1909, 854.

82. Chicago Board of Education, *Annual Report* 56 (1909–10), 105.

83. The 1914 data did not list African Americans as a separate category, but the overwhelming majority would fall into the native-born category. Also, over half of the children labeled foreign were in fact born in America, even if their parents were not. All totaled, 64% of the 17,263 enrolled vacation school students were born in the United States in 1914. "Chicago Woman's Club, "Report of the Chicago Permanent

Vacation School and Playground Committee" 1908, 43; Chicago Board of Education, *Annual Report* 61, (1914–15), 38–42.

84. *Chicago Tribune*, April 22, 1909, 3; Chicago Board of Education, *Proceedings*, April 21, 1909, 906. The board's resolve was made easier for having occurred during the six-month interim between Cooley's resignation and Young's surprise appointment as city superintendent. In general, the board retained a hand in some of the often minute details of running a summer program while at other times serving to rubber stamp actions already undertaken. Wrigley, *Class Politics and Public Schools*, 121; Hogan, *Class and Reform*, 207; Chicago Board of Education, *Proceedings*, July 20, 1910, 45–46; June 28, 1911, 1074, September 4, 1912, 139.

85. See Jeffrey E. Mirel, "Progressive School Reform in Comparative Perspective," in *Southern Cities, Southern Schools: Public Education in the Urban South*, ed. David Plank and Rick Ginsburg (New York: Greenwood Press, 1990), 160–63; David L. Angus, Jeffrey E. Mirel, and Maris A. Vinovskis, "Historical Development of Age Stratification in Schooling," in Maris A. Vinovskis, *Education, Society, and Economic Opportunity: A Historical Perspective on Persistent Issues* (New Haven: Yale University Press, 1995), 171–93.

86. Ira Katznelson and Margaret Weir, *Schooling for All: Class, Race, and the Decline of the Democratic Ideal* (New York: Basic Books, 1985; Berkeley: University of California Press, 1988), 97; Chicago Board of Education, *Annual Report* 50 (1903–04), 129–133; McManis, *Ella Flagg Young*, 198.

87. Chicago Board of Education, *Annual Report* 61, (1914–15), 39; Peterson, *The Politics of School Reform*, 157.

88. James R. Grossman, *Land of Hope: Chicago, Black Southerners, and the Great Migration* (Chicago: The University of Chicago Press, 1989), 246–58; Andrew T. Kopan, *Education and Greek Immigrants in Chicago, 1892–1973* (New York: Garland Publishing, Inc., 1990), 209; Louis Wirth, *The Ghetto* (Chicago: University of Chicago Press, 1928), 153–240; Dominic A. Pacyga, *Polish Immigrants and Industrial Chicago: Workers on the South Side, 1880–1922* (Columbus: Ohio State University Press, 1991), 56–59, 144–48.

89. Such an episode partially aimed at vacation schools and other school extensions took place in New York in 1903. In Chicago, attacks on "fads and frills" focused on additions to the curriculum, such as music, art, and foreign languages. Kenneth Gold, "From Vacation to Summer School: The Transformation of Summer Education in New York City, 1894–1915," *History of Education Quarterly* 42 (Spring 2002), 40–41; Wrigley, *Class Politics and Public Schools*, 128.

90. Chicago Board of Education, *Proceedings*, July 17, 1907, 35.

91. Chicago Board of Education, *Proceedings*, January 25, 1911, 576–77, 579; April 19, 1911, 833; *Annual Report* 58 (1911–12), 127.

92. Chicago Board of Education, *Proceedings*, July 14, 1909, 27; January 25, 1911, 579; February 7, 1912, 832; *Annual Report* 58, (1911–12), 127–128; 59 (1912–13), 202.

93. Chicago Board of Education, *Annual Report* 58, (1911–12), 128; 59 (1912–13), 202; *Proceedings*, February 21, 1912, 686; September 18, 1912, 253; February 26, 1913, 902; May 14, 1913, 1247; May 28, 1913, 1301.

94. While there were many issues between the board and Young, her allegiance to the teachers and their union proved to be the most contentious. The Loeb Rule forbade any Chicago teacher's membership in a labor union. For the unfolding drama

surrounding Young's resignation, see Wrigley, *Class Politics and Public Schools*, 121–33 and Hogan, *Class and Reform*, 208–10; Murphy, *Blackboard Unions*, 81–83.

95. The data did not differentiate between the academic and non-academic components of the vacation schools, though the latter consumed an increasing proportion of the total expenditures. *Annual Report* 66 (1921–22), 163, 165; *Proceedings*, February 26, 1913, 902; May 14, 1913, 1247, 1301; May 13, 1914, 1226–27; July 8, 1914, 50, 53.

96. Chicago Board of Education, *Proceedings*, September 30, 1914, 247; October 14, 1914, 344; May 12, 1915, 1128; Hogan, *Class and Reform*, 208; *Chicago Tribune*, May 13, 1915, 3.

97. Chicago Board of Education, *Proceedings*, May 13, 1914, 1226–27; July 7, 1915, 2.

98. Three sponsors of vacation classes after the public takeover of the Woman's Club program included the Women's Trade Union League, the prominent McCormick family, and the Polish National Alliance. Chicago Board of Education, *Proceedings*, July 20, 1910, 15–16; September 4, 1912, 139; June 9, 1915, 1225.

99. Chicago Board of Education, *Annual Report* 64 (1917–18), 122.

100. Chicago Board of Education, *Annual Report* 59 (1912–13), 200.

101. Chicago Board of Education, *Proceedings*, May 28, 1913, 1301; May 13, 1914, 1226–27; May 10, 1916, 2817; *Annual Report* 68 (1923–1924), 28.

102. Chicago Board of Education, *Annual Report* 59 (1912–13), 202.

Chapter Six: "Easy Credit"

1. Detroit Board of Education, *Educational Bulletin* 14, no. 1 (September 1930), 11.

2. In one study, nearly 70% of the superintendents queried claimed as good results in summer school as in regular school. R. H. Bush, "Current Practices in Summer School," *School Review* 32 (February 1924): 145. In a 1930 survey of the summer school literature, another concluded that "on the whole, the quality of summer work is probably as high as that of work done during the regular school year." Charles W. Odell, "Summer Work in Public Schools," *University of Illinois Bulletin no. 49*, xxvii (22 April 1930), 42.

3. Carl A. Krause and Alfred L. Hoffman, *The Organization and Administration of a City Vacation High School* (New York: New York City Board of Education, 1923), 16.

4. In 1927–28, 361,314 teachers employed and 12,273,412 students enrolled in 2,855 city school systems across the United States during the regular school year. Thus 16% of the nation's cities ran summer schools by 1928, though just under 4% of their teachers and students could be found in them. W. S. Deffenbaugh, "Summer Sessions of City Schools," *U.S. Bureau of Education Bulletin of 1917*, no. 45 (Washington: Government Printing Office, 1918), 30–45; U.S. Bureau of Education, *Biennial Survey of Education, 1926–1928* (Washington: Government Printing Office, 1930), 508.

5. Detroit Board of Education, *Annual Report* 88 (1930–31), 18, 84.

6. The Motor City is an excellent case study for a number of reasons. Detroit had a large and expanding summer school program in the 1920s. It also had a well–respected Progressive school administration that addressed the topic of summer education in both local and national forums. Finally, there is an excellent extant secondary literature on Detroit schools, highlighted by the award-winning monograph by Jeffrey

Mirel, *The Rise and Fall of an Urban School System: Detroit, 1907–1981* (Ann Arbor: University of Michigan Press, 1993).

7. Detroit Board of Education, *Annual Report* 61 (1903–04), 96.

8. Detroit Board of Education, *Annual Report* 64 (1906–07), 100.

9. Detroit Board of Education, *Annual Report* 67 (1909–10), 131; *Annual Report* 70 (1912–13), 109–110.

10. Despite efforts to Americanize immigrants, the vacation school setting fostered space in which non-native heritage could at times flourish in an uneasy balance with Wasp culture. Consider the 1913 Field Day. The program included athletic contests held in the morning and a pageant entitled 'Liberty's Fete' in the afternoon. The latter event, "symbolic of the Old World coming to the New," featured a procession of children dressed in "peasant costumes of Ireland, England, Italy, Russia, Hungary, Bohemia, Holland, and Scotland." Later, the students performed folk dances, from the Russian Komarinskaia to the Italian Tarantella. Detroit Board of Education, *Annual Report* 70 (1912–13), 105.

11. Vacation school enrollments were tabulated by type of class and do not account for any overlap among students. Detroit Board of Education, *Annual Report* 65 (1907–08), 111; *Annual Report* 68 (1910–11), 179; *Annual Report* 69 (1911–12), 125.

12. Detroit Board of Education, *Annual Report* 64 (1906–07), 102–4; *Annual Report* 65 (1907–08), 102–6, 111; *Annual Report* 67 (1909–10), 131; *Annual Report* 68 (1910–11), 179.

13. Detroit Board of Education, *Annual Report* 70 (1912–13), 106–7.

14. Detroit Board of Education, *Annual Report* 70 (1912–13), 109–10.

15. Detroit Board of Education, *Annual Report* 64 (1906–07), 95–96.

16. Detroit Board of Education, *Annual Report* 87 (1929–30), 86; Arthur B. Moehlman, *Public Education in Detroit* (Bloomington, Indiana: Public School Publishing Company, 1925), 163.

17. In 1927, Detroit summer schools began incorporating film into their classes. Detroit Board of Education, *Educational Bulletin* 3, no. 2 (October 1919), 4–5; *Educational Bulletin* 3, no. 9 (May 1920), 5; *Educational Bulletin* 13, no. 4 (December 1929), 8.

18. Detroit Board of Education, *Educational Bulletin* 6, no. 1 (September 1922), 24; *Educational Bulletin* 12, no. 2 (October 1928), 12. Over the course of the 1920s, the tuition rates ranged from $13.50 to $15.00 for the elementary, intermediate, and high school summer terms.

19. Detroit Board of Education, *Annual Report* 74 (1916–17), 16–18; *Annual Report* 75 (1917–18), 145–48; *Annual Report* 82 (1924–25), 53; Detroit Board of Education, *Educational Bulletin* 1, no. 3 (April 1918), 3; Detroit Board of Education, *Educational Bulletin* 3, no. 2 (October 1919), 5.

20. Detroit Board of Education, *Annual Report* 64 (1906–07), 101.

21. Detroit Board of Education, *Annual Report* 75 (1917–18), 146–47.

22. Detroit Board of Education, *Annual Report* 74 (1916–17), 5, 11, 16; Detroit Board of Education, *Educational Bulletin* 4, no. 9, (May 1921), 12; *Educational Bulletin* 10, special no. 1 (May 1927), 2; *Educational Bulletin* 13, no. 7 (March 1930), 4; *Educational Bulletin* 12, no. 9 (June 1929), 2.

23. From 1920 to 1921, the total percentage of non-American white students rose from 49.4% to 53.5%, a figure that continued to rise in the 1920s. Detroit Board of Education, *Educational Bulletin* 5, research bulletin no. 7 (January 1922), 20.

24. Detroit Board of Education, *Annual Report* 62 (1904–05), 84; *Annual Report* 64 (1906–07), 94.

25. Detroit Board of Education, *Annual Report* 62 (1904–05), 85.

26. Detroit Board of Education, *Educational Bulletin* 12, special no. 1 (May 1929), 1.

27. Detroit Board of Education, *Educational Bulletin* 1, no. 3 (April 1918), 3.

28. Detroit Public Schools Superintendent, *Monthly Letter* 1, no. 1 (October 1921), 1.

29. Detroit Board of Education, *Annual Report* 81 (1923–24), 22; Detroit Board of Education, *Educational Bulletin* 10, special no. 1 (May 1927), 6; *Educational Bulletin* 11, special no. 1 (May 1928), 6; *Educational Bulletin* 12, special no. 1 (May 1929), 1.

30. Detroit Board of Education, *Educational Bulletin* 3, no. 9 (May 1920), 5; Detroit Board of Education, *Annual Report* 82 (1924–25), 53.

31. Detroit Board of Education, *Annual Report* 77 (1919–20), 99; *Annual Report* 78 (1920–21), 50; *Annual Report* 81 (1923–24), 70; *Annual Report* 82 (1924–25), 53; *Annual Report* 84 (1926–27), 91–92; *Annual Report* 85 (1927–28), 92; *Annual Report* 86 (1928–29), 95.

32. Frank Cody, "A Representative City School System," *School Life* 8 (February 1923): 124.

33. Detroit Board of Education, *Educational Bulletin* 15, no. 1 (September 1931), 6.

34. Detroit Board of Education, *Annual Report* 77 (1919–20), 112; *Annual Report* 78 (1920–21), 94; Detroit Board of Education, *Annual Report* 87 (1929–30), 173.

35. Detroit Board of Education, *Annual Report* 81 (1923–24), 70; *Annual Report* 83 (1925–26), 58; *Annual Report* 86 (1928–29), 94–95.

36. Detroit Board of Education, *Annual Report* 75 (1917–18), 145.

37. Detroit Board of Education, *Educational Bulletin* 2, no. 10 (June 1919), 3.

38. Detroit Board of Education, *Educational Bulletin* 5, special no. 5 (May 1922), 2; Detroit Board of Education, *Annual Report* 80 (1922–23), 53–54; *Annual Report* 81 (1923–24), 70; *Annual Report* 83 (1925–26), 58; *Annual Report* 84 (1926–27), 91; *Annual Report* 85 (1927–28), 92; *Annual Report* 86 (1928–29), 94.

39. Detroit Public Schools Superintendent, *Monthly Letter* 1, no. 9 (June 1922), 3.

40. For a potent historical and contemporary critique of credentialism in education, see David Labaree, *How to Succeed in School Without Really Learning: The Credentials Race in American Education*, (New Haven: Yale University Press, 1997).

41. Detroit Board of Education, *Annual Report* 82 (1924–25), 53; *Annual Report* 83 (1925–26), 58; *Annual Report* 84 (1926–27), 92; *Annual Report* 86 (1928–29), 94.

42. Detroit used a 1–5 grading scale with the following meanings: 1 - excellent; 2 - good; 3 - fair; 4 - poor (but passed) and 5 - failed. Until 1923, summer students needed to total nine points or less in their three summer subjects in math, English, and history (with no 5's and only one 4 permitted). From 1923 to 1926, students needed to total ten points or less, and in 1927 the limit returned to nine points. Detroit Board of Education, *Annual Report* 80 (1922–23), 53–54; *Annual Report* 81 (1923–24), 70; *Annual Report* 83 (1925–26), 58; *Annual Report* 87 (1929–30), 87.

43. High school students could take no more than 2 subjects. Only good or excellent students could take two classes for advancement, and extremely poor students

were encouraged to register only for one class. Detroit Board of Education, *Educational Bulletin* 12, special no. 1 (May 1929), 4.

44. Of course Cody used a credential—a passing grade—as his standard of evaluation. Detroit Board of Education, *Annual Report* 79 (1921–22), 51–52.

45. These figures are based on a 1–5 grading scale (see fn. 42).

46. Frederick De Galan, "Summer School Pupils' Progress Study," in Detroit Board of Education, *Educational Bulletin* 15, no. 5 (April–June 1932), 6. See also the Detroit Board of Education, *Annual Report* 86 (1928–29), 94–95.

47. In 1926, the figures were nearly identical: the cohort averaged 2.38 for the summer term and 2.61 for the fall, while in 1928 the gap closed slightly, with the same classification of students averaging 2.52 for the summer term and 2.67 for the fall term. Detroit Board of Education, *Educational Bulletin* 9, no. 9 (May 1926), 6; *Educational Bulletin* 10, no. 8 (April 1927), 8; *Educational Bulletin* 11, no. 9 (May 1928), 14.

48. Detroit Board of Education, *Educational Bulletin* 7, no. 8 (April 1924), 7; *Educational Bulletin* 7, no. 9 (May 1924), 7; Detroit Board of Education, *Educational Bulletin* 11, no. 1 (September 1927), 11.

49. Detroit Board of Education, *Educational Bulletin* 9, no. 1 (September 1925), 17. In 1928, for example, over 58% of the summer high school teachers were rated an A. Detroit Board of Education, *Educational Bulletin* 10, no. 1 (September 1926), 15; *Educational Bulletin* 11, no. 1 (September 1927), 2; Detroit Board of Education, *Annual Report* 86 (1928–29), 86.

50. Detroit Board of Education, *Educational Bulletin* 11, no. 1 (September 1927), 11; *Educational Bulletin* 12, no. 9, (May 1929), 15.

51. Detroit Board of Education, *Annual Report* 82 (1924–25), 53.

52. Detroit Board of Education, *Educational Bulletin* 9, no. 1 (September 1925), 3; *Educational Bulletin* 9, no. 9 (May 1926), 6; *Educational Bulletin* 10, no. 8 (April 1927), 14.

53. Detroit Board of Education, *Educational Bulletin* 10, no. 1 (September 1926), 15; *Educational Bulletin* 11, no. 1 (September 1927), 6; Detroit Board of Education, *Educational Bulletin* 8, no. 1 (September 1924), 31.

54. Detroit Board of Education, *Educational Bulletin* 8, no. 1 (September 1924), 31; *Educational Bulletin* 9, no. 9, (May 1926), 6.

55. Detroit Board of Education, *Educational Bulletin* 10, no. 1 (September 1926), 15; *Educational Bulletin* 10, special no. 1 (May 1927), 2; *Educational Bulletin* 11, no. 9, (May 1928), 14; *Educational Bulletin* 11, special no. 1 (May 1928), 2; *Educational Bulletin* 12, special no. 1, (May 1923), 3.

56. Detroit Board of Education, *Educational Bulletin* 8, no. 1 (September 1924), 31.

57. Detroit Board of Education, *Educational Bulletin* 8, no. 10 (June 1925), 3; For similar comments, see *Educational Bulletin* 9, no. 9, (May 1926), 6; and *Educational Bulletin* 11, no. 9, (May 1928), 14.

58. Detroit Board of Education *Proceedings* (1917–18), 565–67.

59. Detroit Board of Education, *Annual Report* 78 (1920–21), 63–71.

60. Detroit Board of Education *Proceedings* (1925–26), 3–5.

61. In 1929, the $467,585 in expenditures for summer schools in Detroit was spent as follows: $308,156 for teachers' salaries; $129,973 for operation, $13,045 for administration, $6,367 for supervision; and $10,044 for fixed charges from auxiliary agencies. Detroit Board of Education, *Annual Report* 87 (1929–30), 173.

62. F. S. De Galan, "Some Thoughts on Summer Schools," *Clearing House* 6 (May 1932): 525.

63. Detroit Board of Education, *Educational Bulletin* 3, no. 9 (May 1920), 6.

64. De Galan reasoned that summer elementary schools most commonly faced this problem. High school summer courses used almost the same amount of hours as the regular semester, so the only loss was in the number of courses taken. Elementary schools not only discarded all but the basic courses in English, mathematics, and social science, but spent only about two-thirds the amount of time on them as the regular school program. De Galan, "Some Thoughts on Summer Schools," 525–26.

65. In Detroit, Depression retrenchment meant that teacher salaries stayed low; new schools were not constructed; and old schools remained overcrowded. While the board of education avoided layoffs and large budget cuts, the school system was in no financial position to embark on a plan like De Galan's. Mirel, *The Rise and Fall of an Urban School System*, 129–30.

66. Rolland J. Nancarrow and Claude L. Nemzek, "Influence of Summer-School Attendance upon the Achievement of Intermediate-School Pupils," *School and Society* 52 (12 October 1940), 341.

67. Nancarrow and Nemzek, "Influence of Summer-School Attendance," 341.

68. Nancarrow and Nemzek, "Influence of Summer-School Attendance," 342–44.

69. David Brody, "Time and Work During Early American Industrialism," *Labor History* 30 (Winter 1989): 5–46; Edward Thompson, "Time, Work-Discipline, and Industrial Capitalism," *Past and Present* 38 (December 1967): 56–97; Paul B. Henley, "Time, Work, and Social Context in New England," *The New England Quarterly* 65 (December 1992): 531–559; David S. Landes, *Revolution in Time: Clocks and the Making of the Modern World* (Cambridge, Massachusetts: The Belknap Press of Harvard University Press, 1983); Steven Carter, "On American Time: Mythopoesis and Marketplace," *Journal of American Culture* 17 (Summer 1994): 35–39.

70. For a good comparative treatment of developments in time sense, see Mark M. Smith, "Old South Time in Comparative Perspective," *American Historical Review* 101 (December 1996): 1432–1469.

71. For a traditional statement of the social identity of professional educators, see Paul Mattingly, *The Classless Profession: American Schoolmen in the Nineteenth Century* (New York: New York University Press, 1975). A more recent formulation is found in David Tyack's article "Pilgrims Progress: Toward a Social History of the School Superintendency 1860–1960," in *The Social History of American Education*, eds. Edward McClellan and William Reese (Urbana, Ill.: University of Illinois Press, 1988); or David Tyack and Elisabeth Hansot, *Managers of Virtue: Public School Leadership in America, 1820–1980* (New York: Basic Books, 1982). In Tyack's words, superintendents formed an "aristocracy of character" based on a Protestant middle-class background.

72. De Galan, "Some Thoughts on Summer Schools," 526.

73. Cindy Aron, *Working at Play: A History of Vacations in the United States* (Oxford: Oxford University Press, 1999), 3–4.

74. Detroit Board of Education, *Annual Report* 75 (1917–18), 147–48.

75. De Galan, "Some Thoughts on Summer Schools," 526.

76. C. R. Murphy, "How One City Conducts a Summer School Without Public Expense," *American School Board Journal* 84 (1932): 51.

77. Mount Vernon Department of Public Instruction, *Annual Report*, (1925), 76; *Annual Report*, (1926), 86.

78. Krause and Hoffman, *The Organization and Administration of a City Vacation High School*, 16; Cincinnati Public Schools, *Annual Report* 81 (1909–10), 68; Gold, "Summer Education and American Public Schools," 338–49.

79. William Kilpatrick, "Summer Vacation Activities of the School Child," *Report of the Subcommittee on Summer Vacation Activities of the School Child* White House Conference on Child Health and Protection, Section III: Education and Training, Committee C: The School Child (New York: The Century Company, 1933), 6–7, 13–14, 26.

80. Lawrence Cremin, *The Transformation of the School: Progressivism in American Education, 1876–1957* (New York: Alfred A. Knopf, 1961; Vintage Books, 1964), 173, 215–216. Tarrytown, New York, opened summer schools in the midst of the Depression that were admittedly experimental in adopting "the progressive ideal." The schools took no attendance, issued no reports, awarded no credits, relied on no age-grading, and offered classes in academic and nonacademic areas. J. Leroy Thompson, "Is This Education?" *American School Board Journal* 98 (June 1939): 43–45. The Child Study Association of America also ran play schools in New York, Cleveland, and Detroit. "Summer Play Schools" *School and Society* 31 (21 June 21 1930): 833–34.

81. Aron, *Working at Play*, 3–4.

Epilogue

1. Helen C. Putnam, "Vacation Schools and Playgrounds in Providence, R.I.," *Report of the U.S. Commissioner of Education of 1899–1900* (Washington: Government Printing Office, 1900), vol. I, 898.

2. Grant Venn, "A Remedy for Ghetto Unrest" in *American Education* U.S. Department of Health, Education and Welfare, Office of Education (Washington: May 1968), 24.

3. Venn, "A Remedy for Ghetto Unrest," 23–24.

4. William Kilpatrick, "Summer Vacation Activities of the School Child," *Report of the Subcommittee on Summer Vacation Activities of the School Child* White House Conference on Child Health and Protection, Section III: Education and Training, Committee C: The School Child (New York: The Century Company, 1933), 5.

5. "Closing of Summer Schools," *School and Society* 35 (23 April 1932): 556–57.

6. Denver Public Schools, Department of Research, "Study Relating to Curriculum Organization, and to Elimination and Curtailment of Departments, Evening Schools, and Summer Schools in Cities of Population 100,000 and Over" (Denver, 1932), 10.

7. Denver Public Schools, "Elimination and Curtailment of Summer Schools," 2.

8. U.S. Bureau of Education, *Biennial Survey of Education, 1926–1928* (Washington: Government Printing Office, 1930), 506–12; *1932–34* (Washington: Government Printing Office, 1935), 480–86.

9. Detroit Board of Education, *Annual Report* 96 (1938–39), 7, 94–95; *Annual Report* 97 (1939–40), 39–40.

10. Historians nevertheless have disputed the extent of the Great Depression's impact, particularly whether or not the educational contractions marked a "watershed" in public schooling. The long-standing answer was yes, but in 1984, David Tyack, Robert

Lowe, and Elizabeth Hansot challenged the watershed interpretation with the publication of *Public Schools in Hard Times: The Great Depression and Recent Years*. In it, they argued that there were few basic changes in the government and finance of public education, that most educators were not progressive innovators let alone political radicals, that retrenchment was uneven not uniform, and that the Depression interrupted but did not deflect long-term trends of higher rates of high school enrollment and graduation. Other recent scholarship contradicts these suppositions. Julia Wrigley uncovered significant retrenchment in public school expenditures and programs during the 1930s. Ira Katznelson and Margaret Weir found minimal retrenchment in school provisions, but they identified a significant reversal in school governance reforms which they attributed to working-class withdrawal from school politics. Jeff Mirel counted the formation of teachers' political consciousness, the influx in working-class students, the implementation of the general curriculum track, the elimination of long-term school construction and shifts in political coalitions as significant developments stemming from the Great Depression. David Tyack, Robert Lowe, and Elizabeth Hansot, *Public Schools in Hard Times: The Great Depression and Recent Years* (Cambridge: Harvard University Press, 1984); Julia Wrigley, *Class Politics and Public Schools; Chicago 1900–1950* (New Brunswick, New Jersey: Rutgers University Press, 1982), 218–27; Ira Katznelson and Margaret Weir, *Schooling For All: Class, Race, and the Decline of the Democratic Ideal* (Berkeley: University of California Press, 1985), 121–41; Jeffrey Mirel, *The Rise and Fall of an Urban School System: Detroit, 1907–1981* (Ann Arbor: University of Michigan Press, 1993), 89–137.

11. "Closing of Summer Schools," 556–57.

12. For example, Everitt, Massachusetts, first opened public summer schools in 1931 and Oakland, California, in 1932. Denver Public Schools, "Elimination and Curtailment of Summer Schools," 2.

13. William Leuchtenburg, *Franklin D. Roosevelt and the New Deal, 1932–1940* (New York: Harper & Row Publishers, Inc., 1963), 121–33, 174; Lawrence Cremin, *The Transformation of the School: Progressivism in American Education, 1876–1957* (New York: Alfred A. Knopf, 1961: Vintage Books, 1964), 318–24.

14. "Summer Programs in Extended School Services," *Education for Victory* 2 (16 August 1943): 22.

15. "Summer Programs in Extended School Services," 22.

16. "Summer Programs in Extended School Services," 22.

17. "Summer Mobilization of School Services," *Education for Victory* 1 (15 May 1942): 5.

18. "Summer Mobilization of School Services," *Education for Victory* 1 (15 May 1942): 5–9. Wartime morale was a large concern of *Education for Victory*, as the following passage suggests: "In days like these, how parents feel about air raids and war, how they feel about working or not, what they should tell their children about our enemies, are of vital concern because children reflect parental attitudes." "Summer Play School," *Education for Victory* 1 (1 September 1942): 20.

19. "Summertime in the All-Day School Program," *Education for Victory* 1 (15 March 1943): 3.

20. "Summertime in the All-Day School Program," 3.

21. "Summertime in the All-Day School Program," 4.

22. "What They are Doing to Win the War," *Education for Victory* 1 (15 May 1942): 10; "Summer Employment of Teachers," *Education for Victory* 2 (20 May 1944): 16–17.

23. "Summer Salvage Programs," *Education for Victory* 3 (4 June 1945): 22–23.

24. "What They are Doing to Win the War," 9. At the private level, fifty elite preparatory schools were running summer sessions by 1945 as part of a "wartime acceleration program" to allow boys to finish their secondary education and enter college before service in the armed forces. "Some Wartime Summer Sessions in Independent Schools Will Continue," *School and Society* 62 (20 October 1945): 246.

25. See for example an account of summer school in Rochester: "School Recreation Program in Rochester, NY," *Education for Victory* 3 (3 November 1944): 28–29.

26. Diane Ravitch, *The Troubled Crusade: American Education: 1945–1980* (New York: Basic Books, 1983), 229.

27. For a thorough treatment of the NDEA, see Barbara Barksdale Clouse, *Brainpower for the Cold War: The Sputnik Crisis and the National Education Defense Act of 1958* (Westport, Connecticut: Greenwood Press, 1981).

28. O. Meredith Parry, "Use Summer School to Broaden Your Curriculum," *High School Journal* 42 (January 1959): 116–20; Christine Burger, "Summer Program for Talented Children," *Instructor* 70 (June 1961): 22; Joe Zafforoni, "Summer Science Activities," *Instructor* 71 (June 1962): 64–65, 78; Frank M. Muth, "Quiet! Scientists at Work," *Industrial Arts and Vocational Education* 51 (January 1962): 23; Frank E. Granucci and Robert J. Griffin, "Enrichment Program for an Elementary Summer School," *Peabody Journal of Education* 38 (May 1961): 353–58; V. Durham, "English Enrichment: Challenging the Talented before Junior High," *Clearing House* 34 (February 1960): 333–36; "Yale Summer School," *School and Society* 88 (5 November 1960): 408.

29. Robert F. Lemen, "Summer School for the Gifted: Mark Twain Summer Institute, Clayton, Missouri," *School and Society* 89 (Summer 1961): 270–71.

30. Marvin Miller, "Scholars in Shirt Sleeves: Summer School Comes of Age," *American School Board Journal* 150 (April 1965): 21.

31. "Summer Schools = Opportunity," *National Education Association Research Bulletin* 38 (February 1960): 23–24.

32. The Great Cities program, started in 1959, foreshadowed the focus of the War on Poverty. The historical debate over the War on Poverty in general mirrors differences between liberal and radical politics. While many treat the Great Society as the shining liberal moment of the late twentieth century, New Left historians are critical of the focus of many programs, which targeted the poor themselves and not underlying structural causes of poverty. The following works present the flavor of this debate. For a cogent thematic treatment of the War on Poverty, see Ira Katznelson, "Was the Great Society a Lost Opportunity?" in *The Rise and Fall of the New Deal Order, 1930–1980*, ed. Steve Fraser and Gary Gerstle (Princeton: Princeton University Press, 1989), 185–211. For a more liberal yet still critical interpretation, see Allen Matusow, *The Unraveling of America: A History of Liberalism in the 1960s* (New York: Harper & Row, 1984), 97–127, 217–71. For a less liberal focus on the educational components, see Ravitch, *The Troubled Crusade*, 148–61; and Hugh Graham Davis, *The Uncertain Triumph: Federal Education Policy in the Kennedy and Johnson Years* (Chapel Hill: University of North Carolina Press, 1984). For a concise summation of the revisionist

perspective on the education programs, see Joel Spring, *The American School: 1642–1993*, 3d ed. (New York: McGraw-Hill, Inc., 1994), 383–89.

33. Office of Education, U.S. Department of Health, Education, and Welfare, *Special Report: Summer Projects* (Washington: Government Printing Office, 1967), 1–4. Title I has continued to fund summer learning. In 1991–92, summer school remained the most popular of Title I add-on programs, and in 1997–98, Title I monies supported 15,736 summer schools nationwide. Gary Burnett, Erwin Flaxman, and Carol Ascher, *The Unfulfilled Mission of Title I/Chapter 1 Programs*, (New York: ERIC Clearinghouse on Urban Education, 1994), 26; U.S. Department of Education, Office of the Under Secretary, Planning and Evaluation Service, *State ESEA Title I Participation for 1997–98: Summary Report* (Washington D.C.: 2000), 10.

34. Barbara Beatty, *Preschool Education in America: The Culture of Young Children from the Colonial Era to the Present* (New Haven: Yale University Press, 1995), 192–200; Maris A. Vinovskis, *History and Educational Policymaking* (New Haven: Yale University Press, 1999), 72–79; Spring, *The American School*, 387.

35. Clara M. D. Riley and Frances M. J. Epps, *Head Start in Action* (West Nyack, New York: Parker Publishing Company, Inc., 1967), xiii, 15.

36. Betty De Ramas, *The Constant Search: The Story of Federal Aid to Detroit Schools* (Detroit: Detroit Board of Education, 1968), 38.

37. U.S. Department of Health, Education, and Welfare, "The 1963 Dropout Campaign: Summary and Analysis of the Special Summer Program to Combat School Dropout Financed from the President's Emergency Fund," *1964 Office of Education Bulletin, No 26* (Washington: U.S. Government Printing Office, 1964), 28–31.

38. Detroit Board of Education *Proceedings*, (1967–68), 14–15, 26.

39. R. S. Meyer, "Why Only Part-Time Education?" *American School Board Journal* 141 (August 1960): 9. See also Nancy E. Adelman, Karen Panton Walking Eagle, and Andy Hargreaves, *Racing with the Clock: Making Time for Teaching and Learning in School Reform* (New York: Teachers College Press, 1997), 83; Morris A. Shepard and Keith Baker, *Year-Round Schools* (Lexington, Massachusetts: D.C. Heath and Company, 1977), 2; *New York Times*, January 10, 2001; William C. Symonds, "How to Fix America's Schools," *Business Week*, March 19, 2001, 76.

40. J. M. Greenwood, a critic of vacation schools, asked in 1902, "How far shall the State interfere and regulate these matters? Does it violate parent-child relations and home if the State supervised summer activity for children?" Nevertheless, Greenwood shared the same fears of the urban environments with proponents of vacation schools but simply advocated for vacation playgrounds. J. M. Greenwood, "Vacation Schools," *Education* 22 (June 1902): 626.

41. Catherine Gewertz, "More Districts Add Summer Coursework," *Education Week*, June 7, 2000, 1, 12.

42. Mary Lee Smith and Lorrie A. Shepard, "What Doesn't Work: Explaining Policies of Retention in the Early Grades," *Phi Delta Kappan* 69 (October 1987): 134; Monica Overman, "Student Promotion and Retention," *Phi Delta Kappan* 67 (April 1986): 612; Gerald W. Bracey, "A Promotion for Social Promotion," *Phi Delta Kappan* 66 (January 1985): 376.

43. Former President Clinton used the phrase in his 1999 State of the Union Address. *New York Times*, January 21, 1999. In New York, former Mayor Rudy Giuliani was a fierce advocate of a similar approach. *New York Times*, January 14, 1999.

44. *New York Times*, September 2, 1999. 228,000 K–12 students attended summer school in total. *New York Times*, July 5, 2000.

45. *New York Times*, December 8, 1999; December 20, 2000. Teachers have also reported being pressured by principals in June to pass students in order to avoid summer school assignments for them. *New York Times*, July 5, 2000.

46. *New York Times*, September 8, 1999; September 16, 1999.

47. *New York Times*, July 5, 2000; July 19, 2000; August 11, 2000; August 25, 2000.

48. *New York Times*, August 26, 2000. See also *New York Times*, July 12, 2000.

49. *New York Times*, August 25, 2000.

50. *New York Times*, June 13, 2001; July 3, 2001; July 14, 2001; August 21, 2001; August 23, 2001.

51. For a case study that depicts the challenges in changing summer habits, the conditions for doing so, and the limits of success, see Judy Fish, "Time: A Barrier to and Impetus for Reform. One District's Journey," in *The Dimensions of Time and the Challenge of School Reform*, ed. Patricia Gandara (Albany: State University of New York Press, 2000), 103–31.

52. Arthur G. Powell, Eleanor Farrar, and David K. Cohen,*The Shopping Mall High School: Winners and Losers in the Educational Marketplace* (Boston: Houghton Mifflin, 1985).

53. *San Francisco Chronicle*, April 29, 2001; *Pittsburgh Post-Gazette*, August 18, 2000; *New York Times*, April 13, 2000; December 6, 1999. These reports were challenged in the findings of survey conducted by the non-profit organization Public Agenda, *Survey Finds Little Sign of Backlash against Academic Standards or Standardized Tests* (New York, 2000), 7. http://www.publicagenda.org/aboutpa/pdf/standards-backlash.pdf.

54. U.S. Commissioner of Education, *Annual Report, 1891–1892* (Washington: Government Printing Office, 1894), 664–65; "Lengthening the School Year," *Elementary School Teacher* 14 (May 1914): 408–10; "The Waning School Term of the Cities," *Los Angeles School Journal* 7 (5 November 1923): 15; Francis H. Oldham, "Length of the School Day and the School Year," *National Association of Secondary School Principals Bulletin* 46 (April 1962): 72–81.

55. This gap between the United States and other nations has existed for much of this century, and it is particularly acute in comparisons of academic time. National Commission on Excellence in Education, *A Nation at Risk: The Imperatives for Educational Reform* (Washington D.C.: U.S Department of Education, 1983); UNESCO, *The Organization of the School Year: A Comparative Study*, 1959, 5.

56. The report argued that "the six-hour, 180-day school year should be relegated to museums, an exhibit from our educational past." National Education Commission on Time and Learning, *Prisoners of Time* (Washington, D.C.: U.S. Government Printing Office, 1994), 10.

57. Nancy Karweit, "Should We Lengthen the School Term?" *Educational Researcher* 14 (June/July 1985): 9–15; Jo Ann Mazzarella, "Longer Day Longer Year: Will They Make a Difference?" 63 *Principal* (May 1984): 14–20.

58. Morton Inger, *Year-Round Education: A Strategy for Overcrowded Schools*, (New York: ERIC Clearinghouse on Urban Education, no. 103 (1994)), 1.

59. Barbara Heyns, "Schooling and Cognitive Development: Is There a Season for Learning," *Child Development*, 58 (October 1987): 1151.

60. See Barbara Heyns, *Summer Learning and the Effects of Schooling* (New York: Academic Press, 1978), 139; Launor F. Carter, "The Sustaining Effects Study of Compensatory and Elementary Education," *Educational Researcher* 13 (1984): 4–13; Gary Walker and Frances Vilella-Velez, "Anatomy of a Demonstration: The Summer Training and Education Program [STEP] from Pilot through Replication and Postprogram Impact," *Public/Private Ventures* (1992), i; U.S. Department of Education, Office of Program Evaluation, *Report No. 8: Summer Growth and the Effectiveness of Summer School*, by Leonard. S. Klibanoff and S. A. Haggart (Washington D.C., 1983).

61. Harris Cooper, Kelly Charlton, Jeff C. Valentine, and Laura Muhlenbruck, *Making the Most of Summer School: A Meta-Analytic and Narrative Review*, Monographs of the Society for Research in Child Development, vol. 65, no. 1, 2000. For research findings that support year-round schools, see Carolyn Kneese, "Increasing Achievement for Elementary Students, Including Those At-Risk, Through the Manipulation of Time and the School Calendar," in *The Dimensions of Time*, ed. Gandara, 89–102; Morris A. Shepard and Keith Baker, *Year-Round Schools* (Lexington, Massachusetts: D.C. Heath and Company, 1977); John D. McLain, *Year-Round Education* (Berkeley, California: McCutcheon Publishing Corporation, 1973).

62. See, Heyns, "Schooling and Cognitive Development," 1151–60; Karl L. Alexander, and Doris R. Entwisle, "Summer Setback: Race, Poverty, School Composition, and Mathematics Achievement in the First Two Years of School," *American Sociological Review* 57 (February 1992): 72–84; Harris Cooper, Barbara Nye, Kelly Charlton, James Lindsay, and Scott Greathouse, "The Effects of Summer Vacation on Achievement Test Scores: A Narrative and Meta-Analytic Review," *Review of Educational Research* 66 (Fall, 1996): 227–68. Heyns demonstrated that most children made real cognitive gains during the school year, that most students learned less during the summer, that some did not learn at all, and that class and racial backgrounds highly correlated to the rate of cognitive development during the summer. Alexander and Entwisle identified additional variables such as level of segregation. The study by Cooper *et al.* reviewed nearly forty studies on this question and uncovered an average summer loss of about one month on a grade level scale, with the result dependent on the subject tested (math and spelling were more susceptible) and the background of the students (class was more significant than race or gender). Two early and influential studies on this issue include M. A. Garfinkle, "The Effects of Summer Vacation on Ability in the Fundamentals of Arithmetic," *Journal of Educational Psychology* 10 (1919): 44–48 and H. E. Elder, "The Effect of Summer Vacation on Silent Reading Ability in the Intermediate Grades," *Elementary School Journal* 27 (1927): 541–46.

63. A number of studies have articulated this point, most recently in Kneese, "Increasing Achievement for Elementary Students," 89–102.

64. Kerry A. White and Robert C. Johnston, "Summer School: Amid Successes, Concerns Persist," *Education Week*, 7 June 2000, 1. http://www.edweek.org/ew/wstory.cfm?slug=39summer.h19.

65. Catherine T. Dancer, *Los Angeles* 38 (June 1993), 34–36; Lisa G. Casinger, "Crossing a New Road: Summer School for Science, not Grades," *Omni* 17 (November 1994), 32; *New York Times*, August 12, 1998; James P. Comer, "The Joys of Summer School," *Parents* 64 (June 1989): 217.

BIBLIOGRAPHY

Addams, Jane. *Twenty Years at Hull-House*, ed. with an intro. by Victoria Bissell Brown. Boston and New York: Bedford/St. Martin's, 1999.

Adelman, Nancy E., Karen Panton Walking Eagle, and Andy Hargreaves. *Racing with the Clock: Making Time for Teaching and Learning in School Reform*. New York: Teachers College Press, 1997.

Alexander, Karl L., and Doris R. Entwisle. "Summer Setback: Race, Poverty, School Composition, and Mathematics Achievement in the First Two Years of School." *American Sociological Review* 57 (February 1992): 72–84.

Alexander, Thorton S. *Vacation Schools*. Cambridge: The Cooperative Press, 1901.

"The All-Year School." *Elementary School Journal 24* (February 1924): 409–11.

"All-Year Schools." *Elementary School Journal 21* (September 1920): 10–12.

American Annals of Education 1–8 (1831–1838).

American Association for the Advancement of Education. *Proceedings* 1–5 (1851–55).

American Educational Monthly 1–13 (1864–1876).

American Journal of Education 1–4 (1826–1829).

American, Sadie. "Vacation Schools and Their Function." *Kindergarten Magazine* 8 (June 1896): 701–4.

American, Sadie. "The Movement for Vacation Schools." *American Journal of Sociology* 4 (November 1898): 309–25.

Angus, David L., Jeffrey E. Mirel, and Maris A. Vinovskis. "Historical Development of Age Stratification in Schooling." in Maris A. Vinovskis, *Education, Society, and Economic Opportunity: A Historical Perspective on Persistent Issues.* New Haven: Yale University Press, 1995, 171–93.

Aron, Cindy S. *Working at Play: A History of Vacations in the United States.* New York: Oxford University Press, 1999.

Association for Improving the Condition of the Poor. *Annual Report.* 49–63 (1892–1906).

Aveni, Anthony. *Empires of Time: Calendars, Clocks, and Cultures.* New York: Basic Books, 1989.

Bailey, T. P. "Vacation Schools." *Journal of Education* 71 (May 12, 1910): 522.

Baltimore Board of School Commissioners. *Annual Report to the Mayor and City Council of Baltimore 70–83* (1898–1912).

Barford, J. G. "Over-pressure in Schools." *The Lancet* 2 (27 September 1884): 570.

Barth, Gunther P. *City People: The Rise of Modern City Culture in Nineteenth-Century America.* New York: Oxford University Press, 1980.

Beatty, Barbara. *Preschool Education in America: The Culture of Young Children from the Colonial Era to the Present.* New Haven: Yale University Press, 1995.

Bedford N.Y. *Document No. 29, School District No. 2, Minutes,* 1826–1913.

Bedford, N.Y. *Bedford School Report* (1828–1874 inc.).

Bedford, N.Y. *Bedford Historical Records.* vol. v: Minutes of Town Meetings, 1784–1841 (1976).

Bedford School Commissioners. *Annual Report* (1830–1874 inc.).

Berrol, Selma Cantor. *Immigrants at School: New York City, 1898–1914.* New York: Arno Press, 1978.

Beveridge, J. H. "Vacation-Club Work." *Addresses and Proceedings of the National Education Association* 54 (1916): 1061–64.

Blackwelder, Gertrude. "Chicago Vacation Schools." *Elementary School Teacher* 6 (December 1905): 211–14.

Blackwelder, I. S. "Report of the Chicago Vacation School." *Elementary School Teacher* 5 (March 1905): 432–38.

Board of Education of Louisville, Kentucky. *Annual Report.* 2 (1911–12).

Board of Education of the Toledo City School District. *Annual Report.* (1908–09, 1910–11).

Boese, Thomas. *Public Education in the City of New York.* New York: Harpers Brothers, 1869.

Boston, Massachusetts. Massachusetts Historical Society. Horace Mann Papers.

Boston School Committee. *Proceedings.* (1877–78).

Boston Schools Superintendent. *Annual Report* 20–30 (1900–1910).

Boyer, Paul. *Urban Masses and Moral Order in America, 1820–1929.* Cambridge, Massachusetts: Harvard University Press, 1978.

Bracey, Gerald W. "A Promotion for Social Promotion." *Phi Delta Kappan* 66 January 1985: 376.

Brody, David. "Time and Work During Early American Industrialism." *Labor History* 30 (Winter 1989): 5–46.

Brown, Laurence A. *Innovation Diffusion: A New Perspective.* New York: Methuen & Co., 1981.

Buenker, John D. "The Progressive Era: A Search for a Synthesis." *Mid-America* 51 (1969): 175–93.

Buenker, John D., John C. Burnham, and Robert M. Crunden. *Progressivism.* Cambridge, Massachusetts: Schenkman Pub. Co., 1977.

Buffalo Superintendent of Education. *Annual Report.* (1898–1912).

Burger, Christine. "Summer Program for Talented Children." *Instructor* 70 (June 1961): 22.

Burnett, Gary, Erwin Flaxman, and Carol Ascher. *The Unfulfilled Mission of Title I/Chapter 1 Programs.* New York: ERIC Clearinghouse on Urban Education, 1994.

Burrows, Edwin G., and Mike Wallace. *Gotham: A History of New York City to 1898.* New York: Oxford University Press, 1999.

Bush, R. H. "Current Practices in Summer School." *School Review* 32 (February 1924), 142–46.

California Superintendent of Public Instruction. *Biennial Report for the School Years 1876 and 1877.*

Cambridge School Committee. *Annual Report* (1901–10).

Campbell, Jack K. *Colonel Francis W. Parker: The Children's Crusader.* New York: Teachers College Press, 1967.

Cardozo Jr., Francis L. "Vacation Schools." *Education* 22 (November 1901): 141–50.

Carson, Barbara G. "Early American Tourists and the Commercialization of Leisure" in *Of Consuming Interests: The Style of Life in the Eighteenth Century*, eds. Cary Carson, Ronald Hoffman, and Peter J. Albert. Charlottesville: University Press of Virginia, 1994.

Carter, Launor F. "The Sustaining Effects Study of Compensatory and Elementary Education." *Educational Researcher* 13 (1984): 4–13.

Carter, Steven. "On American Time: Mythopoesis and Marketplace." *Journal of American Culture* 17 (Summer 1994): 35–39.

Chancellor, W. E. "Forty-eight Week's School Year. *Journal of Education* 73 (12 January 1911): 35–36.

Chicago Board of Education. *Proceedings.* (1895–1916).

Chicago Board of Education. *Annual Report* 43–85 (1896–1941).

Chicago Woman's Club. *The Twenty-First Annual Announcement, 1897–1898.* Chicago: Wm. C. Hollister & Bro., 1898.

Chicago Woman's Club. "Report of the Chicago Permanent Vacation School and Playground Committee." (1899–1908).

Chudacoff, Howard P. and Judith E. Smith. *The Evolution of American Urban Society,* 5th ed. Upper Saddle River, NJ: Prentice-Hall, 2000.

Church, Robert L. *Education in the United States: An Interpretive History.* New York: The Free Press, 1976.

Cincinnati Public Schools. *Annual Report.* 72–82 (1900–1911).

City of Fall River. *Annual School Report.* (1910–1911).

Clark, Daniel. "Education in Relation to Health." *American Journal of Insanity* 43 (1886), 42–54.

Clarke, Edward. H. *The Building of a Brain.* Boston: James Osgood & Co., 1874.

Clarke, Edward H., Henry J. Bigelow, Samuel D. Gross, T. Gaillard Thomas, and J. S. Billings. *A Century of American Medicine, 1776–1876.* New York: Burt Franklin, 1876.

Clark, G. *Innovation Diffusion: Contemporary Geographical Approaches.* Concepts and Techniques in Modern Geography, no. 40. Norwich: Geo Books, 1984.

Cleveland Board of Education. *Annual Report of the Public Schools* 67–73 (1902–09).

Clifford, Geraldine. "'Daughters into Teachers': Educational and Demographic Influences on the Transformation of Teaching into 'Women's Work' in America." in *Women Who Taught: Perspectives on the History of Women and Teaching,* eds. Prentice, Alison and Marjorie R. Theobald. Toronto: University of Toronto Press, 1991, 115–35.

"Closing of Summer Schools." *School and Society* 35 (23 April 1932): 556–57.

Clouse, Barbara Barksdale. *Brainpower for the Cold War: The Sputnik Crisis and the National Education Defense Act of 1958.* Westport, Connecticut: Greenwood Press, 1981.

Cody, Frank. "A Representative City School System." *School Life* 8 (February 1923): 123–24.

Cohen, Ronald D. *Children of the Mill: Schooling and Society in Gary, Indiana, 1906–1960.* Bloomington, Indiana: Indiana University Press, 1990.

Coleman, James, Elihu Katz, and Herbert Menzel. *Medical Innovation: A Diffusion Study.* Indianapolis and New York: Bobbs-Merrill Company, Ind., 1966.

Columbus Board of Education. *Annual Report of the Public Schools.* 1901–23.

Commissioners of Common Schools in Connecticut. *Second Annual Report of the Secretary to the Board* (1840).

Common School Journal 1-2 (1839-40).

Connecticut Superintendent of Common Schools. *Second Annual Report* (1840).

Cooper, Harris, Kelly Charlton, Jeff C. Valentine, and Laura Muhlenbruck. *Making the Most of Summer School: A Meta-Analytic and Narrative Review* Monographs of the Society for Research in Child Development, vol. 65, no. 1, 2000.

Cooper, Harris, Barbara Nye, Kelly Charlton, James Lindsay, and Scott Greathouse. "The Effects of Summer Vacation on Achievement Test Scores: A Narrative and Meta-Analytic Review." *Review of Educational Research* 66 (Fall 1996): 227–68.

Cott, Nancy F. *The Bonds of Womanhood: "Woman's Sphere" in New England, 1780–1835.* New Haven: Yale University Press, 1977.

Couvares, Francis G. *The Remaking of Pittsburgh: Class and Culture in an Industrializing City, 1877–1919.* Albany: State University of New York Press, 1984.

Cremin, Lawrence A. The *Transformation of the School: Progressivism in American Education, 1876–1957.* New York: Alfred A. Knopf, 1961; Vintage Books, 1964.

Cremin, Lawrence A. *American Education: The National Experience, 1783–1876.* New York: Harper & Row, Publishers, 1980.

Cuban, Larry. *How Teachers Taught: Constancy and Change in American Classrooms 1890–1990,* 2d ed. New York: Teachers College Press, 1993.

Cubberley, Elwood P. *Public Education in the United States: A Study and Interpretation of American Educational History,* 2d ed. Boston: Houghton Mifflin Company, 1934.

Curtis, Henry S. "Vacation Schools, Playgrounds, and Settlements." *Report of the US. Commissioner of Education of 1903.* Washington: Government Printing Office, 1905, vol. I, 3–27.

Dain, Norman. *Concepts of Insanity in the United States, 1789–1865.* New Brunswick, N.J., 1964.

Davis, David Brion *et al.* "Forum on Capitalism, Hegemony, and Humanitarianism." *American Historical Review* 92 (1987): 797–878.

Davis, Hugh Graham. The *Uncertain Triumph: Federal Education Policy in the Kennedy and Johnson Years.* Chapel Hill: University of North Carolina Press, 1984.

De Galan, Frederick S. "Summer School Pupils' Progress Study." Detroit Board of Education, *Educational Bulletin* 15, no. 5 (April-June 1932): 1–6.

De Galan, Frederick S. "Some Thoughts on Summer Schools." *Clearing House* 6 (May 1932): 524–28.

De Ramas, Betty. *The Constant Search: The Story of Federal Aid to Detroit Schools.* Detroit Board of Education, 1968.

Deffenbaugh, W. S. "Summer Sessions of City Schools." *U. S. Bureau of Education Bulletin of 1917*, no. 45 Washington: Government Printing Office, 1918, 30–45.

Deffenbaugh, W. S. "Significant Movements in City School Systems." *U. S. Bureau of Education Bulletin of 1929*, no. 16 Washington: Government Printing Office.

Denny, R. I. *et al.* "Accepting the Challenge." *Childhood Education* 8 (May 1932): 484–87.

Denver Board of Education. *Annual Report of School District One*, o.s. 28 (1901–02); n.s. 1–24; (1903–26).

Denver Public Schools, Department of Research. "Study Relating to Curriculum Organization, and to Elimination and Curtailment of Departments, Evening Schools, and Summer Schools in Cities of Population 100,000 and over." Denver: Board of Education, 1932.

Department of Education, City of New York, Manhattan and the Bronx. *Report on Vacation Schools and Playgrounds.* 1898–1900.

Detroit Board of Education. *Annual Report* 2–44, 61–97 (1844–86, 1903–40).

Detroit Board of Education. *Education in Detroit, 1916* National Education Association, 1916.

Detroit Board of Education. *Proceedings* (1917–26, 1965–67).

Detroit Board of Education. *Educational Bulletin* 1–16 (1918–33).

Detroit Board of Education. Detroit *Journal of Education* 1–2 (1920–22).

Detroit Board of Education. *One Hundred Years: The Story of the Detroit Public Schools, 1842–1942.* Detroit: Detroit Board of Education, 1942.

Detroit Public Schools Superintendent. *Monthly Letter* 1 (1921–22).

Dewey, John. *The School and Society,* rev. ed. Chicago: University of Chicago Press, 1915.

District of Columbia Board of Education. *Annual Report.* (1899–1909, 1913–16, 1920–25).

District School Journal for the State of New York 1–12 (1840–52).

Dougherty, John W. *Summer School: A New Look.* Bloomington, Indiana: Phi Delta Kappa Educational Foundation, 1981.

Downs Jr., George W. *Bureaucracy, Innovation, and Public Policy.* Lexington, Mass.: Lexington Books, DC Heath, 1976.

Duffy, John. "School Buildings and the Health of American School Children in the Nineteenth Century." In *Healing and History: Essays for George Rosen,* ed. Charles Rosenberg, 161–78. New York: Dawson, Science History Publications, 1979.

Dukes, Clement. *Health at School Considered in its Mental, Moral, and Physical Aspects,* 4th ed. London: Rivingtons, 1905.

Durham, V. "English Enrichment: Challenging the Talented before Junior High." *Clearing House* 34 (February 1960): 333–36.

Dutton, Samuel T. and David Snedden. *Administration of Public Education in the United States,* 3d ed. New York: Charles Macmillan Company, 1924.

Earle, Alice Morse. *Colonial Days in Old New York.* New York: Charles Scribner's Sons, 1896.

Edes, Robert T. "High-pressure Education; Its Effects." *The Boston Medical & Surgical Journal* 106 (1882): 220–23.

"Editorial." *Education.* (1891–1903 inc.).

Education for Victory 1–3 (1942–44).

Elder, H. E. "The Effect of Summer Vacation on Silent Reading Ability in the Intermediate Grades." *Elementary School Journal* 27 (1927): 541–46.

Elson, W. H. "All-year School Plan in Cleveland." *Journal of Education* 73 (5 January 1911): 11–12.

Farnham, Wallace D. "'The Weakened Spring of Government': A Study in Nineteenth Century American History." *American Historical Review* 68 (1963): 662–680.

Filene, Peter. "An Obituary for the 'Progressive Movement'." *American Quarterly* 22 (Spring 1970): 20–34.

Frank, Henriette Greenebaum, and Amalie Hofer Jerome, comps. *Annals of the Chicago Woman's Club for the First Forty Years of Its Organization.* Chicago: The Libby Company, Printers, 1916.

Fuller, W. *The Old Country School: The Story of Rural Education in the Middle West.* Chicago: The University of Chicago Press, 1982.

Gandara, Patricia, ed. *The Dimensions of Time and the Challenge of School Reform.* Albany: State University of New York Press, 2000.

Gardner, D. E. "History of Public Education in Henrico County." In Virginia Superintendent of Public Instruction, *Annual Report* 16 (1885), 198–99.

Garfinkle, M. A. "The Effects of Summer Vacation on Ability in the Fundamentals of Arithmetic." *Journal of Educational Psychology* 10 (1919): 44–48.

Gewertz, Catherine. "More Districts Add Summer Coursework." *Education Week*, 7 June 2000, 1, 12.

Gill, Brian, and Steven Schlossman. "'A Sin Against Childhood': Progressive Education and the Crusade to Abolish Homework, 1897–1941." *American Journal of Education* 105 (November 1996).

Gold, Kenneth M. "'Mitigating Mental and Moral Stagnation': Summer Education and American Public Schools, 1840–1990." Ph.D. diss., University of Michigan, 1997.

Gold, Kenneth M. "From Vacation to Summer School: The Transformation of Summer Education in New York City, 1894–1915." *History of Education Quarterly* 42 (Spring 2002): 18–49.

Goldfeld, David R., and Blaine A. Brownell. *Urban America: A History,* 2d ed. Boston: Houghton Mifflin, 1990.

Gould, Elizabeth Porter. "Vacation." *Education* 17 (October 1896).

Granucci, Frank E., and Robert J. Griffin. "Enrichment Program for an Elementary Summer School." *Peabody Journal of Education* 38 (May 1961): 353–58.

Greenwood, J. M. "Vacation Schools." *Independent* 54 (1902): 1792–93.

Greenwood, J. M. "Vacation Schools." *Education* 22 (June 1902): 626–30.

Grossman, James R. *Land of Hope: Chicago, Black Southerners, and the Great Migration.* Chicago: The University of Chicago Press, 1989.

Hagerstrand, Torsten. *The Propagation of Innovation Waves.* Royal University of Lund: Department of Geography, 1952.

Haller, Jr., John S. *American Medicine in Transition, 1840–1910.* Urbana: University of Illinois Press, 1981.

Harris, J. H. "Vacation Schools." *Journal of Education* 78 (21 August 1913): 148–49.

Hartford Board of Education. *Annual Report.* (1900–1907).

Haskell, Thomas. "Capitalism and the Origins of Humanitarian Sensibility." *American Historical Review* 90 (1985): 339–61, 547–66.

Heatwole, Cornelius J. *History of Education in Virginia.* New York: The Macmillan Company, 1916.

Hebb, B. Y. "All-Year Schools Have Many Advantages." *School Life* 8 (May 1923): 198.

Henley, Paul B. "Time, Work, and Social Context in New England." *The New England Quarterly* 65 (December 1992): 531–59.

Hernes, Gudmund. "Structural Change in Social Processes." *American Journal of Sociology* 82 (November 1976): 513–47.

Herrick, Mary J. *The Chicago Schools: A Social and Political History.* Beverly Hills, CA: Sage Publications, 1971.

Heyns, Barbara. *Summer Learning and the Effects of Schooling.* New York: Academic Press, 1978.

Heyns, Barbara. "Schooling and Cognitive Development: Is There a Season for Learning." *Child Development* 58 (October 1987): 1151–60.

Hill, C. M. "Extension of the Vacation School Idea." *Elementary School Teacher* 5 (January 1905): 298–301.

Hill, C. M. "Plans for a Farm School at Wheeling, Illinois." *Elementary School Teacher* 5 (March 1905): 428–31.

Hill, C. M. "Prairie View Farm School" *Elementary School Teacher* 8 (September 1907): 24–28.

Hobson, Elsie Garland. "Educational Legislation and Administration in the State of New York, 1777–1850." Ph.D. dissertation: University of Chicago, 1918.

Hogan, David. *Class and Reform: School and Society in Chicago, 1880–1930.* Philadelphia: University of Pennsylvania Press, 1985.

Hough, Charles O., and R. Clyde Ford. *John D. Pierce, Founder of the Michigan School System: A Study of Education in the Northwest.* Ypsilanti, Michigan: Scharf Tag, Label & Box Company, 1905.

Hudson, J. C. "Diffusion in a Central Place System." *Geographical Analysis* 1 (January 1969): 45–58.

"Idea of Vacation Schools." *Charities* 9 (6 September 1902): 220–24.

Indianapolis Public Schools. *Annual Report.* (1916).

Inger, Morton. *Year-Round Education: A Strategy for Overcrowded Schools*, New York: ERIC Clearinghouse on Urban Education, no. 103 (1994).

Jersey City Board of Education. *Annual Report* 44 (1912).

Johnson, Clifton. *Old-Time Schools and School-Books*, Boston: The Macmillan Company, 1904.

Jones, K. A. "Vacation Schools in the United States." *The American Monthly Review of Reviews* 17 (June 1898): 700–716.

Kaestle, Carl F. *The Evolution of an Urban School System*. Cambridge, Massachusetts: Harvard University Press, 1973.

Kaestle, Carl. F. *Pillars of the Republic: Common Schools and American Society, 1780–1860*. New York: Hill and Wang, 1983.

Kaestle, Carl F., and Maris A. Vinovskis. *Education and Social Change in Nineteenth-century Massachusetts*. Cambridge: Cambridge University Press, 1980.

Kansas City Board of Education. *Annual Report* 40–43 (1911–1914).

Karier, Clarence J. *The Individual, Society, and Education: A History of American Educational Ideas*, 2d ed. Urbana, IL: University of Illinois Press, 1986.

Karier, Clarence J. *Scientists of the Mind: Intellectual Founders of Modern Psychology*. Urbana, IL: University of Illinois Press, 1986.

Karweit, Nancy. "Should We Lengthen the School Term?" *Educational Researcher* 14 (June/July 1985): 9–15.

Katz, Michael B. *The Irony of Urban School Reform: Educational Innovation in Mid-Nineteenth Century Massachusetts*. Cambridge, Massachusetts: Harvard University Press, 1968.

Katznelson, Ira. "Was the Great Society a Lost Opportunity?" in *The Rise and Fall of the New Deal Order, 1930–1980*, eds. Steve Fraser and Gary Gerstle, 185–211. Princeton: Princeton University Press, 1989.

Katznelson, Ira, and Margaret Weir. *Schooling for All: Class, Race, and the Decline of the Democratic Ideal*. Berkeley: University of California Press, 1985.

Keller, Morton. *Affairs of State: Public Life in Late Nineteenth Century America*. Cambridge, Massachusetts: The Belknap Press of Harvard University Press, 1977.

Kennedy, J. W. "The All-Year School." *Addresses and Proceedings of the National Education Association*. Washington: National Education Association, 1917, 795–801.

Kilpatrick, William. "Summer Vacation Activities of the School Child." *Report of the Subcommittee on Summer Vacation Activities of the School Child*. White House Conference on Child Health and Protection, Section III: Education and Training, Committee C: The School Child. New York: The Century Company, 1933.

Kirk, John R. "Against Long Vacations." *Journal of Education* 74 (28 September 1911): 314–15.

Kliebard, Herbert. *The Struggle for the American Curriculum, 1893–1958*. Boston: Routledge & Kegan Paul, 1986.

Kliebard, Herbert. *Forging the American Curriculum: Essays in Curriculum History and Theory.* New York: Routledge, Chapman and Hall, Inc., 1992.

Knight, Edgar W., ed. *A Documentary History of Education in the South Before 1860.* Chapel Hill: The University of North Carolina Press, 1949.

Kopan, Andrew T. *Education and Greek Immigrants in Chicago, 1892–1973.* New York: Garland Publishing, Inc., 1990.

Krause, Carl A. and Alfred L. Hoffman. *The Organization and Administration of a City Vacation High School.* New York City Board of Education, 1923.

Labaree, David. *How to Succeed in School Without Really Learning: The Credentials Race in American Education.* New Haven: Yale University Press, 1997.

Lancet (1884).

Landes, David S. *Revolution in Time: Clocks and the Making of the Modern World.* Cambridge, Massachusetts: The Belknap Press of Harvard University Press, 1983.

Lee, Joseph. "Preventive Work." *Charities Review* 10 (February 1901): 587–93.

Lemen, Robert F. "Summer School for the Gifted: Mark Twain Summer Institute, Clayton, Missouri." *School and Society* 89 (Summer 1961): 270–71.

"Lengthening the School Year." *Elementary School Teacher* 14 (May 1914): 408–10.

Leuchtenburg, William. *Franklin D. Roosevelt and the New Deal, 1932–1940.* New York: Harper & Row Publishers, Inc., 1963.

Link, Arthur S., and Richard L. McCormick. *Progressivism.* Arlington Heights, IL: Harlan Davidson, Inc., 1983.

Los Angeles Board of Education. *Annual Report.* (1904–14).

Lynn Department of Schools. *Annual Report* (1899–1907, 1914).

MacCabe, Frederick. "On Mental Strain and Overwork." *The Journal of Mental Science* 21 (1875): 388–402.

Mahajan, Vijay, and Robert A. Peterson. *Models for Innovation Diffusion,* Quantitative Applications in the Social Sciences, eds. John L Sullivan and Richard G. Nieme. Beverly Hills and London: Sage Publications, 1985.

Marshall, Donald W. *Bedford Tricentennial: 1680–1980.* Katonah, N.Y.: Katonah Publishing Corp., 1980.

Massachusetts Board of Education. *Annual Report.* (1837–48).

Massachusetts Teacher 1–27 (1848–1874).

Mattingly, Paul. *The Classless Profession: American Schoolmen in the Nineteenth Century.* New York: New York University Press, 1975.

Matusow, Allen. *The Unraveling of America: A History of Liberalism in the 1960s,* New York: Harper & Row, 1984.

Mayhew, Katherine Camp, and Anna Camp Edwards. *The Dewey School: The Laboratory School of the University of Chicago, 1896–1903.* New York: D. Appleton-Century Company, 1936.

Mazzarella, Jo Ann. "Longer Day Longer Year: Will They Make a Difference?" *Principal* 63 (May 1984): 14–20.

McCormick, Richard L. *From Realignment to Reform: Political Change in New York State, 1893–1910.* Ithaca: Cornell University Press, 1981.

McCormick, Richard L. *The Party Period and Public Policy: American Politics from the Age of Jackson to the Progressive Era.* Oxford: Oxford University Press, 1986.

McLain, John D. *Year-Round Education.* Berkeley, CA: McCutcheon Publishing Corporation, 1973.

McManis, John T. *Ella Flagg Young: and a Half-Century of the Chicago Public Schools.* Chicago: A. C. McClurg & Co., 1916.

Memphis Board of Education. *Annual Report.* (1910–14).

Messerli, Jonathan. *Horace Mann: A Biography.* New York: Alfred A. Knopf, 1972.

Meyer, R. S. "Why Only Part-Time Education?" *American School Board Journal* 141 (August 1960): 9–10.

Michigan Superintendent of Public Instruction. *Annual Report* 1–99 (1837–1948).

Miller, Marvin. "Scholars in Shirt Sleeves: Summer School Comes of Age." *American School Board Journal* 150 (April 1965): 21-22.

Miller, Zane L., and Patricia McLain. *The Urbanization of Modern America,* 2d ed. San Diego: Harcourt Brace Jovanovich, 1987.

Milwaukee Board of Education. *Annual Report* 48–56 (1907–15).

Minneapolis Board of Education. *Annual Report* 28–37 (1905–14).

Mirel, Jeffrey. "Progressive School Reform in Comparative Perspective." in *Southern Cities, Southern Schools: Public Education in the Urban South,* eds. David Plank and Rick Ginsburg, 151–74. New York: Greenwood Press, 1990.

Mirel, Jeffrey. *The Rise and Fall of an Urban School System: Detroit, 1907–1981.* Ann Arbor: University of Michigan Press, 1993.

Moehlman, Arthur B. *Public Education in Detroit,* Bloomington, Indiana: Public School Publishing Company, 1925.

Monkkonen, Eric H. *Police in Urban America: 1860–1920.* Cambridge: Cambridge University Press, 1981.

Monkkonen, Eric H. *Walking to Work: Tramps in America, 1790–1935.* Lincoln: University of Nebraska Press, 1984.

Morrill, Richard, Gary L. Gaile, and Grant Ian Thrall. *Spatial Diffusion.* Scientific Geography, ed. Grant Ian Thrall, no. 10. Beverly Hills and London: Sage Publications, 1988.

Morrison, A. J. The *Beginnings of Public Education in Virginia, 1776–1860.* Richmond: David Bottom, Superintendent of Public Printing, 1917.

Mount Vernon Department of Public Instruction. *Annual Report.* (1910–26).

Murphy, C. R. "How One City Conducts a Summer School Without Public Expense." *American School Board Journal* 84 (1932): 51.

Murphy, Marjorie. *Blackboard Unions: The AFT & the NEA, 1900–1980.* Ithaca: Cornell University Press, 1990.

Muth, Frank M. "Quiet! Scientists at Work. *Industrial Arts and Vocational Education* 51 (January 1962): 23.

Nancarrow, Rolland J., and Claude L. Nemzek. "Influence of Summer-school Attendance upon the Achievement of Intermediate-School Pupils." *School and Society* 52 (12 October 1940): 340–44.

Nasaw, David. *Schooled to Order: A Social History of Public Schooling in the United States,* New York: Oxford University Press, 1979.

National Center for Education Statistics. *The Condition of Education 1998.* Washington: Government Printing Office, 1998.

National Center for Education Statistics. *Digest of Educational Statistics, 1998.* Washington: Government Printing Office, 1998.

National Commission on Excellence in Education. *A Nation at Risk: The Imperatives for Educational Reform.* Washington: U.S. Department of Education, 1983.

National Education Commission on Time and Learning. *Prisoners of Time.* Washington: U.S. Government Printing Office, 1994.

National Education Association. *Addresses and Proceedings* 19 (1880).

Nelson, A. H. "The Little Red Schoolhouse." *Educational Review* 23 (May 1902): 304–15.

Nelson, F. Howard. *How and How Much the U.S. Spends on K-12 Education: An International Comparison.* Washington: American Federation of Teachers, 1996.

Newark Board of Education. *Annual Report* 29–59 (1885–1915).

New Haven Board of Education. *Annual Report.* (1911–23).

New Orleans Board of Directors and of the Superintendent of the Public Schools. *Annual Report.* (1906–11).

New York Board of Education. *Annual Report* 1-12 (1842–53).

New York Board of Education. *Report of the Free Academy.* (1850–51).

New York Board of Education. *Journal.* (1855–1909).

New York Board of Education. "Document No. 1: Inaugural Address of Andrew H. Green, President." New York Public Library Documents (1857).

New York Board of Education. *By-Laws and General Rules and Regulations, 1858.* New York: Pudney & Russell, Printers, 1859.

New York City Department of Education. *Annual Report of the City Superintendent of Schools* 1–23 (1899–1921).

New York City Department of Education for Manhattan and the Bronx. *Report on Vacation Schools and Playgrounds* (1898–1900).

New York City Superintendent of Schools. *Annual Report to the Board of Education* (1866–87).

New York Herald.

New York State Education Department. *Annual Report 1*–35 (series: 1904–Current).

New York Superintendent of the Common School. *Annual Report.* 1835–53 (series: 1821–54).

New York Superintendent of Public Instruction. *Annual Report* 1–50 (series: 1854–1903).

New York Times.

New York Tribune.

Odell, Charles W. "Summer Work in Public Schools." *University of Illinois Bulletin no. 49* (April 22 1930).

Oldham, Francis H. "Length of the School Day and the School Year." *National Association of Secondary School Principals Bulletin* 46 (April 1962): 72–81.

Omaha Board of Education. *Annual Report.* (1913).

Overman, Monica. "Student Promotion and Retention." *Phi Delta Kappan* 67 (April 1986): 609–13.

"Overstrain in Female Education." *The Lancet* 2 (12 July 1884), 73.

Packard, Francis F. *History of Medicine in the United States.* New York: Paul B. Hoeber, 1931.

Pacyga, Dominic A. *Polish Immigrants and Industrial Chicago: Workers on the South Side, 1880–1922.* Columbus: Ohio State University Press, 1991.

Palmer, A. Emerson. *The New York Public School.* New York: Macmillan, 1905.

Parry, O. Meredith. "Use Summer School to Broaden Your Curriculum" *High School Journal* 42 (January 1959): 116–20.

Paterson Public Schools. *Annual Report.* (1908–14).

Pennsylvania School Journal 1–38 (1851–90).

Perry, Clarence Arthur. *Wider Use of the School Plant.* New York: Russell Sage Foundation, 1910.

Perry, Clarence Arthur. *American Vacation Schools of 1912,* pamphlet no. R133. New York: Russell Sage Foundation, 1913.

Peterson, Paul. *The Politics of School Reform, 1870–1940.* Chicago: University of Chicago Press, 1985.

Pfeiffer, Carl. J. *The Art and Practice of Western Medicine in the Early Nineteenth Century.* Jefferson, North Carolina: McFarland & Company, Inc., Publishers, 1985.

Philadelphia Superintendent of Public Schools. *Annual Report* 20–27 (1921–28).

Pittsburgh Board of Public Education. *Annual Report.* o.s. 37–42 (1905–10), n.s. 1–4 (1912–15).

Pittsburgh Playground Association. *Annual Report* 12–17 (1907–12).

Powell, Arthur G., Eleanor Farrar, and David K. Cohen. *The Shopping Mall High School: Winners and Losers in the Educational Marketplace.* Boston: Houghton Mifflin, 1985.

Providence School Committee. *Annual Report* (1870–79, 1895–1918).

Public School Society. *Annual Report* (1818–52 inc.).

Public School Society. "Report of the Committee Appointed to Make the Necessary Arrangements for Terminating its Existence: Dissolution of the Public School Society," 1853.

Putnam, Helen. C. "Vacation Schools and Playgrounds in Providence, R.I." *Report of the U.S. Commissioner of Education of 1899–1900,* vol. 1. Washington: Government Printing Office, 1900, 898–904.

Pyle, G. F. "The Diffusion of Cholera in the United States in the Nineteenth Century." *Geographical Analysis* 1 (January 1969): 59–75.

Randall, Samuel S. *The Common School System of the State of New York.* Troy, N.Y.: Johnson and Davis, Steam Press Printers, 1851.

Randall, Samuel S. *History of the Common School System of the State of New York.* New York: Ivison, Blakeman, Taylor and Co., 1871.

Ravitch, Diane. *The Great School Wars: New York City, 1805–1973: A History of the Public Schools as Battlefield of Social Change.* New York: Basic Books, Inc., 1974.

Ravitch, Diane. *The Troubled Crusade: American Education: 1945–1980.* New York: Basic Books, 1983.

"Recreation Plus Education: Vacation Schools in New York." *Municipal Affairs* 2 (September 1898): 433–38.

Reese, William J. *Power and the Promise of School Reform: Grassroots Movements During the Progressive Era.* Boston: Routledge & Kegan Paul, 1986.

Reese, William J. *The Origins of the American High School.* New Haven: Yale University Press, 1995.

Retting, Lucy. "Summer Vacation, a Problem and a Privilege." *Progressive Education* 8 (May 1931): 379–87.

Rhode Island Board of Education and Committee of Public Schools. *Annual Report* 26–35 (1870–79).

Richmond School Board. *Minutes* (1911–33).

Richmond School Board. *Minutes of the Committee on Teachers and Schools.* (11 July 1911).

Richmond Superintendent of the Public Schools. *Annual Report* 43–63 (1911–32).

Riley, Clara M. D., and Frances M. J. Epps. *Head Start in Action.* West Nyack, New York: Parker Publishing Company, Inc., 1967.

Robinson, Charles Mulford. "Vacation Schools." *Educational Review* 17 (March 1899): 250–60.

Rochester Board of Education. *Report for the Years 1908, 1909, 1910.*

Rodgers, Daniel T. "In Search of Progressivism." *Reviews in American History* 10 (December 1982): 113–32.

Rogers, Everett M. *Diffusion of Innovations,* 3d ed. New York: The Free Press, 1983.

Rosalita, Mary. *Education in Detroit Prior to 1850.* Lansing: Michigan Historical Commission, 1928.

Rosenberg, Charles E. *The Cholera Years: The United States in 1832, 1849, and 1866.* Chicago: University of Chicago Press, 1987.

Rosenzweig, Roy, and Elizabeth Blackmar. *The Park and the People: A History of Central Park.* Ithaca: Cornell University Press, 1992.

Rury, John L. "The Variable School Year: Measuring Differences in the Length of American School Terms in 1900." *Journal of Research and Development in Education* 21 (Spring 1988): 29–36.

Ryan, Mary. *Cradle of the Middle Class: The Family in Oneonta County, New York, 1790–1865.* Cambridge: Cambridge University Press, 1981.

St. Joseph Board of Education. *Annual Report.* (1900–1914).

St. Louis Board of Education. *Annual Report* 52–57 (1904–10).

St. Paul Board of School Inspectors. *Biennial Report* 51–52 (1910–12).

San Francisco Superintendent of Schools and Board of Education. *Annual Report* (1897, 1899–1901, 1907–12, 1924–29).

Schneider, Henry G. "The Summer School and the Teacher." *Education* 17 (December 1896): 227–32.

Schultz, Stanley K. *The Culture Factory: Boston Public Schools, 1789–1860.* New York: Oxford University Press, 1973.

Schultz, Stanley K. *Constructing Urban Culture: American Cities and City Planning, 1800–1920.* Philadelphia: Temple University Press, 1988.

Schuyler, David. *Creating Central Park, 1857–1861.* Baltimore: Johns Hopkins University Press, 1982.

Schuyler, David. *The New Urban Landscape: The Redefinition of City Form in Nineteenth Century America.* Baltimore: Johns Hopkins University Press, 1986.

Scobey, David. "Empire City: Politics, Culture, and Urbanism in Gilded-Age New York City." Ph.D. diss., Yale, 1989.

Scranton Board of Education. *Survey of the Scranton Public Schools.* (1918–20).

Seattle Public Schools. *Annual Report 34* (1916–21).

Seybolt, Robert Francis. *The Act of 1795 for the Encouragement of Schools and the Practice in Westchester County.* Albany: The University of the State of New York, 1919.

Shepard, Morris A., and Keith Baker. *Year-Round Schools.* Lexington, Massachusetts: D.C. Heath and Company, 1977.

Shryock, Richard Harrison. *Medicine and Society in America: 1660–1860.* New York: New York University Press, 1960.

Sklar, Martin. *Corporate Reconstruction of American Capitalism, 1890–1916: The Market, the Law, and Politics.* Cambridge: Cambridge University Press, 1988.

Smith, Mark M. "Old South Time in Comparative Perspective." *American Historical Review* 101 (December, 1996): 1432–69.

Smith, Mary Lee, and Lorrie A. Shepard. "What Doesn't Work: Explaining Policies of Retention in the Early Grades." *Phi Delta Kappan* 69 (October 1987): 129–34.

Soltow, Lee, and Edward Stevens. *The Rise of Literacy and the Common School in the United States: A Socioeconomic Analysis to 1870.* Chicago: University of Chicago Press, 1981.

"Some Wartime Summer Sessions in Independent Schools Will Continue." *School and Society* 62 (20 October 1945): 246.

Special Committee of the New York Board of Education. *Report on the System of Popular Education in the City of New York.* New York: William C. Bryant & Co., 1851.

Spring, Joel. *The American School: 1642–1993,* 3d ed. New York: McGraw-Hill, 1994.

Springman, John C. *The Growth of Public Education in Michigan.* Ypsilanti, Michigan: Michigan State Normal College, Division of Field Services, 1952.

Stone, Edward Martin. *A Century of Education: Being a Concise History of the Rise and Progress of the Public Schools of the City of Providence.* Providence: Providence Press Co., 1876.

Storr, Richard J. *Harper's University, The Beginnings: A History of the University of Chicago.* Chicago: University of Chicago Press, 1966.

"Summer Play Schools." *School and Society* 31 (21 June 1930): 833–34.

"Summer Play Schools in New York City." *School and Society* 32 (6 September 1930): 316.

"Summer Schools = Opportunity." *National Education Association Research Bulletin* 38 (February 1960): 23–24.

"Summer Schools of New York City." *School and Society* 32 (26 July 1930): 122.

Superintendent of Public Instruction for Cambridge, Massachusetts. *School Committee Report.* (1872).

Superintendent of Public Schools in the City of Brooklyn. *Annual Report.* o.s. (1853–83).

Superintendent of the City of Lynn, Massachusetts. *Annual Report.* (1899–1907, 1914).

Syracuse Board of Education. *Annual Report.* (1905–1916).

Tarde, Gabrielle. *Laws of Imitation.* New York: Holt, 1903.

Teaford, Jon. The *Twentieth-Century American City: Problem, Promise, and Reality.* Baltimore: Johns Hopkins University Press, 1986.

Thompson, Edward P. "Time, Work-Discipline, and Industrial Capitalism." *Past and Present,* no. 38 (December 1967): 56–97.

Thompson, J. Leroy. "Is This Education?" *American School Board Journal* 98 (June 1939): 43–45.

Trachtenberg, Alan. *The Incorporation of America: Culture and Society in the Gilded Age.* New York: Hill and Wang, 1982.

Troen, Selwyn. *The Public and the Schools: Shaping the St. Louis System, 1838–1920.* Columbia, MO: University of Missouri Press, 1975.

Tyack, David. *The One Best System: A History of American Urban Education.* Cambridge, Massachusetts: Harvard University Press, 1974.

Tyack, David. "Pilgrims Progress: Toward a Social History of the School Superintendency 1860–1960." in *The Social History of American Education* eds. Edward McClellan and William Reese. Urbana, Ill.: University of Illinois Press, 1988.

Tyack, David, and Larry Cuban. *Tinkering Toward Utopia: A Century of Public School Reform.* Cambridge, MA: Harvard University Press, 1995.

Tyack, David, Thomas Hames, and Aaron Benavot. *Law and the Shaping of Public Education, 1785–1954.* Madison, WI: University of Wisconsin Press, 1987.

Tyack, David, and Elisabeth Hansot. *Managers of Virtue: Public School Leadership in America, 1820–1980.* New York: Basic Books, 1982.

Tyack, David, Robert Lowe, and Elizabeth Hansot. *Public Schools in Hard Times: The Great Depression and Recent Years.* Cambridge, MA: Harvard University Press, 1984.

UNESCO. *The Organization of the School Year: A Comparative Study.* 1959.

University of the State of New York. *Education in New York State, 1784–1954.* comp. and ed. by Harlan Hoyt Horner. Albany, New York: State Education Department, 1954.

U.S. Bureau of the Census. *Abstract of the Twelfth Census of the United States, 1900,* 3d ed. Washington: Government Printing Office, 1904.

U.S. Bureau of the Census. *Abstract of the Thirteenth Census of the United States, 1910.* Washington: Government Printing Office, 1913.

U.S. Bureau of the Census. *Abstract of the Fifteenth Census of the United States, 1930.* Washington: Government Printing Office, 1933.

U. S. Bureau of Education. *Bulletin of 1919,* no. 91. Washington: Government Printing Office, 1920.

U.S. Bureau of Education. *Biennial Survey of Education, 1916–1918.* Washington: Government Printing Office, 1921.

U.S. Bureau of Education. *Biennial Survey of Education, 1920–1922.* Washington: Government Printing Office, 1923.

U.S. Bureau of Education. *Biennial Survey of Education, 1926–1928.* Washington: Government Printing Office, 1930.

U.S. Bureau of Education. *Biennial Survey of Education, 1932–1934.* Washington: Government Printing Office, 1935.

U.S. Bureau of Education. *Biennial Survey of Education, 1938–1940, 1940–1942.* Washington: Government Printing Office, 1944.

U.S. Bureau of Education. *Biennial Survey of Education, 1954–1956.* Washington: Government Printing Office, 1959.

U.S. Commissioner of Education. *Annual Report.* (1867–1940).

U.S. Department of Commerce, Bureau of the Census. *Historical Statistics of the United States: Colonial Times to 1970.* Washington: Government Printing Office, 1975.

U.S. Department of Education, Office of Program Evaluation. *Report No. 8: Summer Growth and the Effectiveness of Summer School,* by Leonard S. Klibanoff and S. A. Haggart. Washington: Government Printing Office, 1983.

U.S. Department of Education, Office of the Under Secretary, Planning and Evaluation Service. *State ESEA Title I Participation for 1997–98: Summary Report.* Washington: 2000.

U.S. Department of Health, Education, and Welfare. *The 1963 Dropout Campaign: Summary and Analysis of the Special Summer Program to Combat School Dropout Financed from the President's Emergency Fund.* Office of Education Bulletin 1964, no 26. Washington: Government Printing Office, 1964.

U.S. Department of Health, Education, and Welfare, Office of Education. *Special Report: Summer Projects,* Washington: Government Printing Office, 1967, 1–4.

"Vacation School in Los Angeles." *Journal of Education* 77 (3 April 1913) 373.

"Vacation Viewed as an Interruption." *Elementary School Teacher* 11 (September 1910) 36–38.

Vandewalker, Nina C. "The Social Settlement Vacation School." *Kindergarten Magazine* 10 (1897–98): 74–85.

Venn, Grant. "A Remedy for Ghetto Unrest." in *American Education.* U.S. Department of Health, Education and Welfare, Office of Education. Washington: May, 1968.

Vinovskis, Maris A. *Education, Society, and Economic Opportunity: A Historical Perspective on Persistent Issues.* New Haven: Yale University Press, 1995.

Vinovskis, Maris A. *History and Educational Policymaking.* New Haven: Yale University Press, 1999.

Virginia Superintendent of Public Instruction. *Annual Report* 1–21 (1871–91).

Walker, Gary, and Frances Vilella-Velez. "Anatomy of a Demonstration: The Summer Training and Education Program (STEP) from Pilot through Replication and Postprogram Impact." Public/Private Ventures, 1992.

Walter, C. J. "Continuation Classes." *Journal of Education* 78 (28 August 1913): 177–79.

"The Waning School Term of the Cities." *Los Angeles School Journal* 7 (5 November 1923): 15.

Warner, John Harley. *The Therapeutic Perspective: Medical Practice, Knowledge, and Identity in America, 1820–1885.* Cambridge, MA: Harvard University Press, 1986; reprint, Princeton: Princeton University Press, 1997.

Warner, John Harley. *Against the Spirit of System: The French Impulse in Nineteenth-Century American Medicine.* Princeton: Princeton University Press, 1997.

Warren, Donald, ed. *American Teachers: History of a Profession at Work.* New York: Macmillan, 1989.

Warren, John C. *Physical Education and the Preservation of Health,* 2d ed. Boston: William D. Ticknor & Company, 1846.

Waterman Jr., Richard. "Vacation Schools." *Addresses and Proceedings of the National Education Association* 37 (1898): 404.

White, Kerry A., and Robert C. Johnston. "Summer School: Amid Successes, Concerns Persist." *Education Week,* 7 June 2000.

Whitney, Evangeline. "Vacation Schools, Playgrounds, and Recreation Centers." *Addresses and Proceedings of the National Education Association* 43 (1904): 298.

Wiebe, Robert. The *Search for Order, 1877–1920.* New York: Hill and Wang, 1967.

Winterer, Caroline. "Avoiding a 'Hothouse System of Education': Nineteenth-Century Early Childhood Education from the Infant Schools to the Kindergartens." *History of Education Quarterly* 32 (Fall 1992): 289–314.

Wirth, Louis. *The Ghetto.* Chicago: University of Chicago Press, 1928.

Wishy, Bernard. *The Child and the Republic: The Dawn of Modern American Child Nurture.* Philadelphia: University of Pennsylvania Press, 1968.

Wood, Horatio Charles. *Brain-work and Overwork.* Philadelphia: Presley Blakiston, 1880.

Worcester Board of Education. *The Annual Report of the Public Schools.* (1896–1909).

Wrigley, Julia. *Class Politics and Public Schools, Chicago, 1900–1950.* New Brunswick: Rutgers University Press, 1982.

"Yale Summer School." *School and Society* 88 (5 November 1960): 408.

Zafforoni, Joe. "Summer Science Activities." *Instructor* 71(June 1962): 64–65, 78.

INDEX

History of Schools and Schooling

THIS SERIES EXPLORES THE HISTORY OF SCHOOLS AND SCHOOLING in the United States and other countries. Books in this series examine the historical development of schools and educational processes, with special emphasis on issues of educational policy, curriculum and pedagogy, as well as issues relating to race, class, gender, and ethnicity. Special emphasis will be placed on the lessons to be learned from the past for contemporary educational reform and policy. Although the series will publish books related to education in the broadest societal and cultural context, it especially seeks books on the history of specific schools and on the lives of educational leaders and school founders.

For additional information about this series or for the submission of manuscripts, please contact the general editors:

Alan R. Sadovnik   Susan F. Semel
Rutgers University-Newark   The City College of New York, CUNY
Education Dept.   138th Street and Convent Avenue
155 Conklin Hall   NAC 5/208
175 University Avenue   New York, NY 10031
Newark, NJ 07102

To order other books in this series, please contact our Customer Service Department:

800-770-LANG (within the U.S.)
212-647-7706 (outside the U.S.)
212-647-7707 FAX

Or browse online by series at:

www.peterlangusa.com